Reticulations

Reticulations

Jean-Luc Nancy and the Networks of the Political

Philip Armstrong

Electronic Mediations, Volume 27

University of Minnesota Press
Minneapolis
London

The University of Minnesota Press gratefully acknowledges the financial assistance provided for the publication of this book from the College of Humanities at The Ohio State University.

Frontispiece: Simon Hantaï, *Collage*, 1953, mixed media on paper, remounted on canvas, 94.5 x 59.5 cm. (37 1/4 x 23 1/3 inches). Courtesy of Galerie Jean Fournier, Paris. Photograph by Jacqueline Hyde.

Portions of chapter 2 were first published as "From Paradox to *Partage*: On Citizenship and Teletechnologies," *TEXT Technology* 5, no. 2 (2008), in the issue "The Digital Humanities and Technologies of Citizenship," edited by Patrick Finn and Alan Galey. An earlier version of chapter 4 first appeared as "Res/Réseau/Reticulation" in the online journal *the anomalist* 1 (2005), edited by Brad Evans and Keir Milburn.

Photographs from the series *Waiting for Tear Gas* courtesy of Allan Sekula.Copyright Allan Sekula.

Published by the University of Minnesota Press
111 Third Avenue South, Suite 290
Minneapolis, MN 55401-2520
http://www.upress.umn.edu

Library of Congress Cataloging-in-Publication Data

Armstrong, Philip, 1962-
    Reticulations : Jean-Luc Nancy and the networks of the political / Philip Armstrong.
        p. cm.—(Electronic mediations ; v. 27)
    Includes bibliographical references and index.
    ISBN 978-0-8166-5489-5 (hc : alk. paper)—ISBN 978-0-8166-5490-1 (pbk. : alk. paper)
    1. Nancy, Jean-Luc—Political and social views. 2. Political science—France—Philosophy.
I. Title.
    JA84.F8A835 2009
    320.092—dc22   2008050301

Printed in the United States of America on acid-free paper

The University of Minnesota is an equal-opportunity educator and employer.

18 17 16 15 14 13 12 11 10 09   10 9 8 7 6 5 4 3 2 1

Undoubtedly, we are still stuttering: philosophy always comes too late, and, as a result, always too soon. But the stuttering itself betrays the form of the problem: we, "we," how are we to say "we"? Or rather, who is it that says "we," and what are we told about ourselves in the technological proliferation of the social spectacle and the social as spectacular, as well as in the proliferation of self-mediatized globalization [*mondialité*] and globalized mediatization? We are incapable of appropriating this proliferation because we do not know how to think this "spectacular" nature, which at best gets reduced to a discourse about the uncertain signs of the "screen" and of "culture." The same applies to "technological" nature, which we regard as an autonomous instrument. We do so without ever asking ourselves if it might not be "our" comprehension of "our-selves" that comes up with these techniques and invents itself in them, and without wondering if technology is in fact essentially in complete agreement with the "with." We are not up to the level of the "we": we constantly refer ourselves back to a "sociology" that is itself only the learned form of the "spectacular-market." We have not even begun to think "ourselves" as "we."

—JEAN-LUC NANCY

Contents

Acknowledgments

This book has benefited from a more or less sustained dialogue with two extraordinary groups of people. The first is my friends and colleagues in the Department of Comparative Studies at The Ohio State University, who, with unusual insistence, continue to open up and reinvent that intellectual space we call the university. The second are my fellow *anomalists*, who offer a permanent reminder—this time at the limits of the university—of what is at stake in the work we do. I trust both groups will understand why in this context I refer to them collectively, why they form part of a larger, critical dialogue to which this book, I hope, contributes.

For invitations to speak and for the intellectual and personal support that has sustained the writing of *Reticulations*, my warm thanks to Mick Finch, Lisa Florman, Paul Ivey, Jan and Ben Maiden (Jan died before the book came to publication, but I hope her rare example lives on in its affirmation of co-existence), Brad Macdonald, Lucien Massaert, Guy Massaux, Steve and Ruthie Melville, Donald Preziosi, Jason Smith, and Chris Thompson. Christian Bonnefoi and Simon Hantaï first taught me to think about things reticulated, and for that I am very grateful, as I am to Allan Sekula for permission to feature several of his photographs in the last chapter, and to Elodie Rahard of Galerie Jean Fournier for permission to reproduce the frontispiece. Finally, I thank Sam Weber, who supported and sustained the writing of this book in innumerable ways, and David Horn, who contributed in equally decisive ways to its completion. I remain deeply indebted to them both.

At the University of Minnesota Press, I would like to thank an anonymous reader for their generous comments and suggestions, as well as Douglas Armato, Daniel Constantino, Susan Doerr, Alicia Sellheim, Davu Seru, and Mike Stoffel for their wonderful help and advice in bringing the manuscript to publication.

Much of the argument that follows turns on thinking an untying and un-binding as constitutive of our ties and bonds, a distancing and detachment as the enabling condition of our attachments to—and with—one another. In order to write this book, Laura, Nikolas, and Keir have come to experience this contorted logic all too often, as have my parents. My heartfelt thanks for their patience.

Introduction

Readers and translators of Aristotle's *Politics* encounter an extreme paradox, even aporia, in the opening sections of the text. Given the ways in which this preliminary reading of the *Politics* informs the central argument of *Reticulations* and the pages that follow, drawing us toward the question of the *essence* of the political that remains the center of the book's own displacement, some initial measure in which this paradox or aporia comes into relief is first necessary.

In the opening lines of the *Politics* (1252a), Aristotle starts from the "general observation" that every *polis* (city, city-state, "historical site") is a *koinonia*, a term variously translated into English as association, community, society, or partnership. Indeed, if every *koinonia* is also "formed with a view to some good purpose," as Aristotle famously proposes, and so oriented toward an "end" that is at once final and perfect (*teleios*), then that association or community that is not only the "most sovereign" among all associations but also includes all the others, that association or community that aims at the highest and most authoritative, supreme, and sovereign of all purposes and the good life (*eu zein*), is the *polis* itself, "the association that is political [*He koinonia politike*]."

Aristotle initially presents the specific rapport between the *koinonia* and *polis* that opens the *Politics* as conforming to a set of logical procedures and epistemic first principles (*archai*). Based on biological classification and its analogies to the political realm, and thus presupposing the analogy between the natural development of living things and the generative life of the *polis*, the logic that Aristotle puts into play seeks to analyze "composite" or "compound" elements till they can be "subdivided no further," a procedure that seeks to reach the "smallest parts of the whole which it constitutes" (1252a, 19–20). Transposed to the political realm, Aristotle thus seeks to examine the composite or component parts of the *polis* (statesmen, monarchs, households, families, citizens, rulers, women, social classes, slaves, etc.) in order to distinguish and gain insight into their differences, not in order to isolate and merely identify individuals or groups within the city but to establish "systematic [*technikos*]" knowledge of the city as a whole, of that self-sufficient whole that exists prior to the parts that constitute or compose it. The entire argument is thus governed from its origins by its ends, a telos that establishes the highest good of the whole based on knowledge of the parts, while the knowledge produced here will furnish the self-generative concept of the *polis* in its self-sufficiency (*autarkeia*), leading us toward a fuller understanding of the sovereign association which is political.

If the analytic procedures and sequential logic Aristotle sets in place from the beginning of the text appear self-evident, or at least constitute a self-evidence that overshadows the opening conceit that Aristotle is working from general observations and opinions (*endoxa*), the concept of the *koinonia* is never in fact subject to the rigorous epistemic first principles that Aristotle claims more generally for his argument. Through the repeated subordination of the association or community to the *polis* itself and its own ends, Aristotle never subjects the *koinonia* as composite or compound part to that point where it *itself* can be subdivided no further. To be sure, we know that *koinonia* as a term implies human relationships having some purpose, whether family relationships, master–slave relationships, friendship, fellowships, business partnerships, and so on. By extension, the *polis* is an association or community whose aim is the best possible life for all those who enter into it. Or again, the *koinonia* is the place of free men united by something in common (*koinon*) and mutual friendship; it is that form of association or partnership where there exists a mutual agreement between partners concerning the just (if not equal) distribution of those benefits generated from their very association. But these descriptions and examples make clear that Aristotle avoids delimiting the *koinonia* as such to its essential principle, since, reduced to its purely undivided element, the association or community is never a single thing or part that exists in, of, or for itself. For as association and community as expressions already suggest, the *koinonia* exists precisely in and as a form of articulation, and an articulation that presupposes a *relation* or relationality between different parts or partners that make up the association or community. The *koinonia* thus implies not only an articulation or relation as its "founding" or "grounding" principle but also the possibility of division, detachment, and separation, as well as an attachment or sharing. In this sense, there exists no purely synecdochic relation between the association and the *polis*, no secure language governing the terms in which to think the association in terms of a genus or "species" (at least as this preformationist metaphorics is elaborated more fully in *The Metaphysics*), no mere positing of the *polis* as an association "of some sort" as numerous translations interject, or no seamless and cohesive communion founding the association—in fact, there is nothing to purely identify here in its absolute singularity—since the association does not constitute an identifiable and fully discernible "part" in the first place. Always in excess or withdrawn and subtracted from the constituent parts that form a whole, the association is strictly com-posite (*sun-theton*), a jointed association or interdependence of parts, but a composite or assemblage of parts whose existence is not reducible to its teleological anticipation as one part of a *pre*given whole, or to preexisting identities that, taken together, go to make up a given totality. The *koinonia* as part is always inscribed by the essential possibility of a partitioning or portioning out, at once beyond, in excess, or subtracted from the totalizing arrangement of parts. Any attempt to delimit its originary place and position is always already exposed to the inherent potential of displacement and disposition, while the framework (*taxis*) or existence of the association or community is always circumscribed, founded or grounded not in a self-identity but in its own exteriority to itself.

To be sure, Aristotle recognizes in his own way that the *koinonia* originates in a relation rather than a unitary thing or stable essence and that a relation can certainly presuppose a whole of which it is a part (in the sense that social relations might presuppose a social totality or organic whole). Turning back to the comparison with biological development, if it is by looking at how things develop naturally from the beginning that one may best study them and see the "process of their growth," as Aristotle argues, then this biological classification attests not to a single thing but to a prior "union," a "pairing" of those who "cannot exist without the other" (1252ª28). It is in this sense that Aristotle recognizes an alterity in and at the origin of all association, community, or partnership. Yet this founding principle is premised for Aristotle not on an epistemic basis but on the "natural impulse" between a given male and female to reproduce the species, a union that then implies for Aristotle not only biological reproduction but also a primary and innately hierarchical distinction within any union between ruler and ruled. The articulation of the originary relation within any association—of the relation *as* relation—is thus effaced or dissimulated in its very transposition to the arche-teleological, self-generative, and autotelic modeling of the reproductive couple, a closure already implied by references to a "union" as an expression. Aristotle's recognition of a relation and alterity at the origin of all

associations not only corresponds to his recognition that things that have relation as one of their essential "properties" not only relegates or marginalizes
them in terms of their ontological consistence or subsistence; it also permanently dissimulates a more originary and essential sense of the association as
koinos or common.[1] The *koinonia* is thus not just public and social, as in the
communal enterprise undertaken by citizens participating as members in a
polis. Nor does it simply conform to the natural impulse, or to relations of
power and hierarchy. For it is common and shared. Or rather, this emphasis
on the common implies not a union or communion that is subordinate to
the ends of the *polis* or the reproduction of the species but a simultaneous
relation and distinction implied by the association as a composite, to a simultaneous articulation and separation, proximity and distance, that opens
out to an originary relation "founding" the association or community that is
not merely common but *in-common* or *shared out*. In fact, less a problem of
epistemology than ontology, it is precisely this sharing out of the common
that becomes the "natural starting point" (1260^{b}36) of the *Politics*.

   In response to this aporetic tension (and we have learned from Pierre
Aubenque's monumental studies that aporia can be read as a constitutive
aspect of Aristotle's thinking), the *Politics* offers a presupposed political
solution to an ontological problematic, at least insofar as the political association that constitutes the *polis* at once presupposes, effaces, and sutures
over the relation or *being-in-relation* that constitutes the very *essence*—the
dis-essentialized essence—of all associations. If Aristotle opens the *Politics*
by recognizing the essential role of the *koinonia* or association in the constitution of the *polis*, it is thus important to recognize that he does not start
from either the individual political subject or a given political identity, an anthropological definition of the human or a form of kinship, a society against
the State or some innate desire to exist together and create communities, all
of which have worked to constitute the mythological origins of the Western
political tradition, even when contesting that tradition. The originary being-
in-relation that "grounds" or "founds" all association or community in the
Politics is even presented in ontological terms prior to the more well-known
definitions of man as the political animal capable of speech, or those expressions of bare or naked life, of the *zoe* and *bios*, definitions that will also undergo
a profound transformation in light of the question of relation at stake here. At
the very moment that Aristotle offers a stable definition of the Greek *polis* in
the opening lines of the book, setting in place one of the founding terms of
the Western political tradition, he reopens that very tradition not just to what

remains *unthought* in that tradition but to a definition of the political that remains, as it were, more political than the political itself, to an originary "sociation" of all association that is not prepolitical or anthropological but withdraws or retreats from the political in the act of presenting it (so that if it remains necessary to posit the *essence* of the political here, as we are arguing, it is an essence that must be thought in and as this withdrawal or retreat).

No doubt it remains symptomatic in this regard that translations of *koinonia* appear more seamless when phrased as a community or society, the more dominant terms framing political discourse, terms that imply a more stable sense of a unified substance, communion, and social cohesion, more a mere aggregate of individuals than the more fragile and contingent articulations suggested by associations, partnerships, and the various assemblages they imply. But the question at stake here is less the conceptual mistranslation that might occur from the Greek into other languages or other political traditions than the possibility that the Greek mistranslates the Greek. It is this mistranslation that inaugurates the possibility that Aristotle's founding definition of the *polis* stems not just from the (im)possibility of defining the *polis* as such but from the very (im)possibility of the *polis* to exist in its self-sufficiency as the most supreme and sovereign association that includes all other associations. (If the Western political tradition is aborted at the very moment it gives birth to itself, then the generative model that Aristotle holds onto can only ever produce bastard offspring and illegitimate heirs.[2]) Nor is it then a question of passing on to another possible ground for the political to establish itself, seeking or creating new concepts of the political that find resonance in their dialectical negation of Aristotle's founding theses. For it is precisely in terms of this very aporia—this sharing out of the in-common that is the "natural starting point"—that Aristotle's text already suggests the necessity of rearticulating this originary being-in-relation of all associations, and rearticulating this relation not in terms of the One and Many, of identites and differences, but according to a different logic, modality, or grammar of being-in-relation. Indeed, such a grammar is understood now not as a question of identities, self-identities, group-identities, or even hybridities but in terms of a relationality informing and subtending any affirmation of pluralities, singularities, and multiplicities. At the same time, the rearticulation of all association in terms of this ontology of relations presupposes a renewed attention to the specific ties, bonds, and connections that constitute the (dis-)junctive basis of all associations, to those relations that are articulated not just in terms of connections but disconnections—at once attachments and detachments, articulation and separation, proximity and distance—opening toward the in-common and sharing out of all being-in-relation. It is in this sense that the origin of the political association is not the foundation that works to construct, through teleological anticipation, an end or purpose—the political *arche*—but opens toward an an-archy of the political *arche*, the an-archy that confounds all beginnings and ruling authority. This is not the mere anarchy that would be the dialectical counterpart of the sovereign *arche*, not that anarchy that would come to determine, through an act of radical negation, the self-sufficiency of the sovereign *arche*. It is not the negation of any foundation and so antifoundational in this sense. Nor again it is the mere irony or ironicizing of the community. For it is this an-archy that opens the possibility of thinking the constitutive or constituent potentiality of all being-in-relation, a being-in-common such that nothing precedes or exceeds it (a politics of means, then, not ends)—in short, an affirmation of being-in-common that does not become subordinate to the most sovereign good or *arche*, subsuming this *arche* and sovereignty seamlessly into one another's terms, but begins (in repetition, incessantly) to make itself sovereign in a new way.

To be sure, we moderns imagine that the component parts of the city can be rearticulated more systematically than Aristotle's relatively crude taxonomies and classifications, refined to a more just measure of what composes the city and its political subjects, whether understood in terms of the social relations or the individual and group identities that populate it (class, ethnic, racial, gendered, sexual, and so on) or in terms of their wider sociocultural intersections and geopolitical exchanges. Aristotle's political categories—the *demos*, the *ethnos*, the masses, the citizen, friendship, the *nomos*, and so on— are thus subject to historical, genealogical, or sociological revision, reconfigured according to those larger transformations that mark the passage from the city-state to the modern nation-state, and from the post-Westphalian decline of nation-state societies to those transnational and cosmopolitan associations, assemblages, and inclusive forms of political organization that clearly remain irreducible to the more circumscribed specificities and exclusionary practices of the Greek *polis*. Or again, our modern systems of communication and information technology find a measure of their radically transformative potential and breadth of global exchange by demonstrating that the space of the *polis* now remains irrelevant, a form of decidedly Western political nostalgia in a world where spatial borders and the walls of the city simply no longer exist in the same way (if they ever did). If we recall the opening sections of the *Politics* in light of this larger critical, historical, and geopolitical context, it is in order to suggest that these modern distinctions and claims count for little, even when opened to comparative analyses with other traditions, and even when reconfigured within the larger terms of postcolonial contexts and conflicts, if they still presuppose the geometrical or dialectical ordering and identification of parts to whole, or if they continue to presuppose a political solution to an ontological problematic. Or again, the critiques leveled at the Aristotelian *polis* remain inconsequential if they do not touch on the logic of identity that governs the sovereignty of the political *arche* and its self-sufficiency, that logic of self-identity that presupposes the self-founding political Subject. For it is this self-founding Subject of the Western political tradition—*zoon politikon*—that at once presupposes and effaces all being-in-relation and the originary and essential an-archy of the in-common.

This argument nowhere suggests a return to Aristotle and political philosophy, a return to some imitable model, or a stable conceptual regime of political signification and social values. It is not a question of seeking an empirical, historical, or archeological reconstruction of the *polis* in order to find the purest expression of democracy and a model of citizenship, against which our modern perversions and tawdry deviations of the political come into further relief. Nor is the difficulty at stake here reducible to the paradox of Aristotle standing outside the *polis* in order to conjure it into being. Nor, by extension, is it a question of taking some measure and studied distance *from* the Greek *polis*, positing and assuming a founding political reference point against which the tendencies defining contemporary globalization and post-foundational politics come into view, a widespread argument and rhetorical strategy that barely disguises its own dialectical and historicist schemas. For as Hannah Arendt understood only too well, there is no *polis* to return to, or no *polis* that has existed beyond the phantasms (shared in different ways by both "left" and "right") of a politics governed by the teleological anticipation of the good life shared by all, those phantasms, including their sociological avatars and political science incarnations, erected over a political abyss, the aporia of those associations and being-in-relation that withdraw and retreat from the political in the act of presenting it.

To be sure, a marked characteristic of much postfoundationalist political thinking is articulated precisely in relation to Aristotle and his seminal role in traditions of political philosophy. Thus, Jacques Rancière's *Disagreement* starts from Aristotle's *Politics* in order to rethink the aporia at the heart of all political philosophy, an aporia that discloses the "supplementary part" of a given or sociologically determinable population, "the part of those who have no part," and thus an aporia in which the question of equality becomes decisive again.[3] When Michel Foucault introduces the concept of the biopolitical in the first volume of *The History of Sexuality*, it is Aristotle's definition of *zoon politikon*—"a living animal with the additional capacity for a political existence"—that provides the initial terms in which Foucault proposes to think modern man as "an animal whose politics places his existence in question."[4] It is then Foucault's reference to Aristotle that becomes the basis of Giorgio Agamben's own rearticulation of the biopolitical in *Homo Sacer* in terms of "bare life," which opens by rethinking the established distinction between simple, natural life, the fact of living, and Aristotle's positing of the good life, of politically qualified life.[5] Rancière and Agamben's respective texts are much indebted to Alain Badiou's radical rearticulation of the State formation in terms of an exception and irreducible excess, an argument explored in the second part of *Being and Event* and immediately prefaced with a long meditation on Aristotle's *Physics*, from which the terms of his argument are also derived.[6] When Jacques Derrida seeks in turn to rethink the founding concepts of the Western political tradition, again it is to Aristotle that he appeals in *Politics of Friendship*.[7] Writing in the wake of Deleuze, it is Aristotle who becomes a foil for Manuel DeLanda's affirmation of assemblages in his proposal for a new philosophy of society, while for John Protevi, the passage through Aristotle becomes the necessary precondition for rethinking the very constitution of the "body politic."[8] In this same context, we might even argue that Judith Butler's book on Antigone finds a measure of its force in displacing both Aristotle and emphasis on the State as the central foci of postfoundational political thinking. In this sense, it is the emphasis on kinship that now rearticulates our founding political categories, at least insofar as it is Antigone who allows us to "confound kinship in a rearticulation of its terms."[9] If we then broaden the references a little, it is always possible to play Marx's Aristotle off against Heidegger's, and both against a more widespread dismissal of Aristotle *tout court*, in which the classical foundation of political philosophy is always potentially reproduced and reinscribed through the negation of its contemporary, critical relevance.

The list of references cited here is neither exhaustive nor fully representative of postfoundational political thinking and so remains partial in many respects—more than a mere declaration of interests but less than a program or school. Nor are the references homogeneous when it comes to rethinking and rearticulating the same founding claims of the Western political tradition; if the relation among these different authors is defined as much by disagreement as dialogue, it is not the same Aristotle that remains at stake, and the weight placed on Aristotle's texts varies according to the different rhythms of reading and interpretation. What these various references share, nevertheless, is a refusal to return to Aristotle or any other classical source in order to resurrect a set of founding political concepts whose self-evidence and contemporary, political relevance might reappear once we brush away centuries of historical distortion, misunderstanding, and mistranslation. Turning to Aristotle and the origins of political philosophy is neither an act of restoration nor of restitution, nor a way of resuscitating or rehabilitating political values that would guarantee a certain *sense* of the political today, an orientation from which a politics might be deduced. If there is a tension that traverses these different readings, commentaries, and interpretations—and it is a tension whose consequences will remain decisive for the very possibility of thinking the history or historicity of the political as postfoundational—it does not stem from any demand to return to Aristotle or other classical sources but from the different ways in which to think the founding political concepts proposed by Aristotle and Western political philosophy *as* founding.

Reticulations argues that it is in the writings of Jean-Luc Nancy that the Aristotelian definition of the political association as self-sufficient is reopened in decisive ways to its an-archic displacement. Remarking that the workings of injustice always presuppose some form of exclusion, Nancy asserts that any community or association always *excludes*, "and on principle."[10] This exclusion can then assume several names—"distinction, exile, banishment, sacrifice, disdain, marginalization, identification, normalization, selection, election, roots, etc." In its very foundation, however, Nancy argues that what the community or association wants to exclude "is that which does not let itself be identified in it," in other words, what we term the "other." From the Greek *polis* on, we have known that this other is the alterity of those barbarians that were a kind of solution, those others that constitute, in their very distinction, the self-consolidating other. In this sense, any political identity can be understood as presupposing an exteriority of relations that it simultaneously effaces in the act of constituting itself with a self-coherent and self-sufficient identity. This schema of exclusion and exceptionalism is well known, and its application to the Greek *polis* or any number of other political identities relatively easy to explore (making its critical exigency no less politically effective or necessary). But Nancy seeks to rearticulate this emphasis on the exclusionary practices of any community or association by rethinking exclusion in terms of an "extreme paradox" in which "the other turns out to be *the other of the with*," in the sense of being one-with-the-others, or in the sense of the relation—the relation *as such—between* "ones" and "others."[11] What we are trying to hold onto in Nancy's argument and the meticulousness of its phrasing is the way in which this "other" or alterity is rewritten and rearticulated as "the *in-* of the 'in-between [*l'en de l'entre*],'" where the emphasis on the relationality that spans—that *is*—this "in-between" opens to what Nancy further terms "the intimate double trait, or sharing out [*partage*], of the association/dissociation where 'sociation' is founded."[12] In consequence, if all community or association is not simply founded on its exclusionary practices but "excludes its own foundation," as Nancy asserts, then such exclusion is necessary because the community or association seeks "to foreclose the stripping away of the ground [*dérobement du fond*] which is its essence." Refusing to situate such thinking as *post*foundational in any chronological or historicist sense, and positing the essence of the political in order to disclose precisely what resists or withdraws from all essentialism, identity, or substance—in short, appealing to an essence that does not immediately fold back into an identification or objectification—it is this essence or "essencing" that must be thought in terms of the an-archy of the political *arche*, that anarchy that is not merely the negation of the foundation but opens toward the very being-in-relation or ontology of relations that "grounds" coexistence and the in-common.[13]

The ontological implications at work here cannot be detached from the larger stakes of the argument. For as Nancy also proposes, "there doubtless remains to be invented an affirmation of separation which is an affirmation of relation," and it is precisely this double affirmation that the State "denies, refuses, represses." In other words, such an affirmative task will not fall under the rubric of a "society against the State," which always risks reducing this problematic to questions of "civil society," and so ignoring the exigency of thinking the separation constitutive of all being-in-relation and the in-common. As Nancy concludes, "the affirmation of relation would have to be a *political* affirmation, in a sense that remains for us to discover."[14]

Nancy's more recent writings and interviews will increasingly question what is implied in thinking this relation as a *political* affirmation, and to do so against a backdrop in which, as is widely claimed, "everything is political." What we want to foreground here is the way in which Nancy's argument concerning the sharing out and simultaneous association/dissociation informing an originary "sociation" not only informs, in turn, our brief reading of Aristotle. It equally informs the chapters that follow, which seek to unpack the seemingly torturous turns of Nancy's argument. The chapters also turn with repeated insistence on rethinking the wider implications of Nancy's argument across a number of more recognizable political contexts, including theories of citizenship within contemporary globalization, questions of political organization, and the "movement of movements." More unusually, though no less decisive to the pages that follow, Nancy's writings demonstrate that this originary "sociation" must be understood as *reticulated*, and that the sharing out and association/dissociation of the in-common be understood as a *network*—in short, drawing from a motif that appears with some frequency throughout Nancy's writings, *Reticulations* argues that it is precisely this *reticulated network* that constitutes the an-archic displacement of the political *arche* and its self-sufficiency.

In the wake of the interior/exterior distinction that governs the space of the Greek *polis*, the question posed here thus remains how to think the space of the political according to this appeal to networks, a space whose topological features, having neither pure interiority nor infinite extension, would be commensurate with this space or spacing of the *in-between* to which Nancy refers. This is not the space of the commons and the subsequent history of its enclosures, not that space that is proper(ty) to the common. Nor again is it a space that is reducible to the tendencies defining contemporary globalization and its networks of communication and information technology. For it is the reticulated spacing of the in-common that concerns and intimates us here, that spacing that is revealed, in and as its withdrawal or retreat, once the ground of the association or community is stripped away to its essence. Nancy further suggests that such a stripping away opens toward that bare space in which we exist, not in our isolated autonomy, self-sufficient identity, or myriad forms of political autism, but in and as our exposure.[15] Articulated less in terms of identity than exteriority (as hyphenating all ex-istence and ex-posure intimates), the task *Reticulations* thus poses is how to think this reticulated spacing as a network, and to do so without presupposing a political solution to the ontological problematic of the in-common. Situated within a broader, critical affirmation of the communist legacy animating much postwar thinking in France, notably in the writings of Maurice Blanchot, Nancy argues that it is precisely this same task that opens the possibility of thinking a "communism to come."

Reticulations is not a book on Aristotle and the foundations of political philosophy or on the reception of Aristotle in contemporary political theory.

Nor is it a book on the writings of Jean-Luc Nancy; it makes no attempt to account for all of Nancy's now voluminous publications or to account for the extensive commentaries and secondary literature devoted to his work (to which, of course, it remains no less indebted). Contrary to appearances, it is not a book that seeks to politicize Nancy's writings either, at least insofar as it is precisely the question of the political and its presuppositions that remains in question in the pages that follow. Nor does it address the larger genealogical implications of this ontology of relations informing and subtending our most resonant and established political concepts. Its ambition is thus more modest and quite circumscribed both in relation to the wider contexts of contemporary political theory and in relation to Nancy's own writings. For the task proposed across the different chapters is to trace out an opening in which we might begin to approach this an-anarchy of the political *arche* and at once weigh and reinvent its political—that is, its inescapably ontological— implications. At the same time, the various chapters approach this questioning of the political *arche* in light of Nancy's frequent appeals to thinking the an-archy of the political *arche* in terms of space. In this sense, *Reticulations* responds to the reticulated spacing that informs all being-in-relation by reopening the question concerning the very space of the political and it poses this question in relation to a widespread discourse of globalization, in which it is precisely the space of the political that has become increasingly difficult to discern.[16]

In *The Sense of the World*, Nancy recalls Carl Schmitt's argument that "the metaphysical image that a definite epoch makes of the world has the same structure as what appears self-evident as the form of its political organization [*hat dieselbe Struktur wie das, was ihr als Form ihrer politischen Organisation ohne weiteres ein-leuchet*]."[17] It is according to such self-evidence or lack of doubt that metaphysics, according to Schmitt, becomes "the most intensive and the clearest expression of an epoch." Nancy immediately qualifies Schmitt's claim by arguing that "he was not in a position to appreciate the extent to which *the metaphysics of our age*, that is, the beginning of the twenty-first century—at least if we actually deal with it rather than replaying 'the thirties'—is what one can call *the metaphysics of the deconstruction of essence, and of existence qua sense*."[18] Written at a time and in a geopolitical context where the implications of replaying or returning to the thirties have become more than a mere rhetorical gesture and framed any number of political imaginaries (imaginaries whose devastating effects much of the world continues to suffer), the task that *Reticulations* sets itself is not just how we might begin to rethink this deconstruction of the "proper" essence of the political proposed by Nancy, and to do so in light of Nancy's related affirmation of the sense of the world. It asks how this task cannot be separated from—indeed opens right onto—an (in)appropriate of (im)proper form of political organization, at least insofar as the question of organization also remains (paradoxically, aporetically, that is to say, collectively) one of our most pressing tasks. As Nancy has taught us, the deconstruction of the proper essence of the political concerns less a discourse of globalization in which the political is newly appropriated than the ways in which it is precisely the world *as* world that is put back (once again) in play.

1

The Deposition of the Political

So it is with the one who believes he meets a companion in the desert of communication: he cannot, without great peril, stop at the moment when what had appeared to him as absolute proximity (as the volatilization of obstacles and the certainty of immediate presence) also reveals itself to be absolute distance—the loss of all relation and the ruin of those partitions by which, up until now, he could still communicate. Would he not, at this point, be justified in once again raising a wall, thus avoiding the mirage and returning to a more stable and clearly defined form of communication? Must he not at a certain moment, and if only in order not to lose it, escape from such an experience? There is perhaps no experience more dangerous, more doubtful, but also, perhaps, more essential; for what it suggests to us is that the proximity and the force of communication depend—to a certain extent, but to what extent?— upon the absence of relation. What it also suggests is that one must be—to a certain extent, but this is precisely an extent without measure—faithful to this absence of relation and faithful also to the risk one runs in rejecting all relation. As though, finally, this fidelity where faithfulness is not possible—this risk, this migration without rest across the space of the desert…could also flourish in the intimacy of a communication.

—Maurice Blanchot

In their opening proposal for a series of lectures and discussions to be held in Paris at the Center for Philosophical Research on the Political, Philippe Lacoue-Labarthe and Jean-Luc Nancy outline the "regulative statement" organizing the Center's work for the 1981–82 year: "Taken as a philosophical question, and from the point of view of what we have provisionally called *the essence of the political*, the question of the political discloses [*fait apparaître*] the necessity of interrogating what makes the social *relation* possible as such; and that is also to say on what does not constitute it as a single or simple relation [*comme simple rapport*] (which is never given), but which

1

implies a 'disconnection' or a 'dissociation' at the origin of the political event itself [*du fait politique lui-même*]."[1]

Lacoue-Labarthe and Nancy's insistence on rethinking the essence of the political (*ta politika*) continues the task they set themselves when the Center was first established in 1980, where the original proposal was also phrased as an interrogation into the essence of the political, indeed "how to question (indeed, can one), today, what must provisionally be called the *essence of the political*?" (*RJ*, 9/*RP*, 105). Such a question, the authors insist, forecloses in advance any attempt to define a "properly predefined program" for the Center's lectures and discussions, including any attempt to create a "systematic representation" of the political as a concept. But the question does create the more modest conditions for opening up "simple tracks cleared [*frayées*] here and there."[2]

In proposing this question, Lacoue-Labarthe and Nancy acknowledge that the interrogation into the essence of the political cannot be detached from the institutional space that not only informs or delimits their address but also makes it possible in the first place. For the question regarding the essence of the political coincides with "delimiting a site" and "circumscribing a domain," one which creates not only a "site, a space of work—and a space of collective work"—in short, a "place of free investigation"—but the "construction of a new object." As the Opening Address to the Center's audience states, the Center was intended to occupy a "marginal or 'withdrawn' [*de 'retrait'*] position" in relation to those "places traditionally assigned in the dialogue (agreement or conflict) between philosophy and politics" (*RJ*, 9/*RP*, 105). The singular space of the Center is thus delimited by only one thing: "the determination to pose the question of the political for itself, and that is to say, at the same time, not to presuppose an answer, and to take it as a question of 'essence'—or as a question of a 'retreat' [*retrait*] of essence" (*RJ*, 28/*RP*, 120–21). If the opening address marks a "position of retreat" or an apparent "return" to the question of essence, then Lacoue-Labarthe and Nancy acknowledge that this withdrawal or retreat does not necessarily exclude "resolutely 'political' intentions" (*RJ*, 10/*RP*, 105). In fact, even though the reference to the political here is bracketed off in scare quotes, it is precisely in and through this retreat of the political and in and through the delimitation of the Center as a space that a number of related political concepts organizing the Center's work come into relief, notably the question of totalitarianism, the latter posed in relation to Marx and Marxism, Heidegger's turn to National Socialism, Jünger's concept of "total mobilization," the seminal writings of

Arendt, and Lyotard's (then recently published) *The Postmodern Condition*. Modifying Sartre's well-known and phenomenologically spatializing claim regarding Marxism, Lacoue-Labarthe and Nancy argue that totalitarianism remains the "unsurpassable horizon of our times." At the same time, and, as we will see, as an *essential* question concerning totalitarianism itself, it is only in and through the same retreat of the political that the question can be posed as to what makes the social relation possible *as such*—not only what constitutes the relation *as* (a) relation but that *there is* relation. This radical re-articulation of relationality not only reposes its potential reduction to the very form of an articulation in the first place; it further takes into account different traditions for thinking social relations as well as different concepts of (social) totality.

If the limits of the political cannot be dissociated from the limits that define the very space of the Center, the delimitation of a space in which to question the essence of the political would appear to enact a radical or transcendental reduction and simultaneous bracketing of the political itself, but only insofar as this reduction and bracketing discloses the *retrait* of the political, at once its withdrawal or retreat and its simultaneous retreating, retracing, and rewriting.[3] It is this retreat of the political in its simultaneous appearance and withdrawal, its "appearing disappearing" or its placement and displacement, that does not mark a *return* to the political, to a concept of the political that exists in its pure, uncontaminated state or given identity, but reopens the "open space" of the Center to a spacing in which the questioning of the political is at once delimited and delimiting. Indeed, the Opening Address or *Ouverture* proposed by the authors contains at once an introductory proposal (a set of questions and themes) as well as this simultaneous openness and opening *toward* the political, as if what constitutes the political here is not a liberal gesture or openness in which "anything goes" but both at the origin and center of this institutional space and yet displaced, without fixed position, exteriorized, on the outside, or as if the political in this scene was waiting in the wings to be addressed while simultaneously remaining center stage.

This disconcerting and disorienting movement between bracketing and opening inaugurated by the delimitation and staging of the Center as a space (a simultaneous framing and exteriority that gestures toward reconfiguring the role of the Greek chorus) is further rephrased in terms of a problematic, a term widely employed by Lacoue-Labarthe and Nancy in their various texts addressed to the Center's audience and pivotal to the earlier writings of Louis

Althusser (writings, it can be argued, that in their own way attempted to re-think the essence of the political by detaching it from its humanistic presup-positions and idealist traditions).[4] In this sense, the question of the political is described by Lacoue-Labarthe and Nancy as belonging to no orthodoxy but as a "genuine problematic, even if it is a problematic in the process of for-mation, a problematic looking for itself" (*RT*, 183/*RP*, 122)—"We are open-ing this space to a problematic collection," the authors state, "to a collection *of* problematics and to a collection which is, *as such*, problematic, multiple, heterogeneous, flexible, without absolute limits and without exclusions" (*RJ*, 28/*RP*, 120). A term that hinges Lacoue-Labarthe and Nancy's own intro-ductory texts in the two volumes published from the Center's lectures, it is precisely this "construction" of a problematic that then makes of the Center itself a "problematic space," one that must put itself, its limits, and position in question, even as it comes to question and delimit the essence of the politi-cal or the position one might hold toward it, and even as the delimitation of any essence is constitutively related to, and indeed inscribed by, that which is excluded. For there is no question of the political here that does not take into account the very space in which that question is posed in the first place, a space, including the positions located or locatable in that space, that can be no more presupposed or assumed in what it delimits than the question and questioner of the political that it seeks to address. In short, it is precisely this language of the problematic that sets in place—or sets in play—an irre-ducible conflict between the "massive, *blinding obviousness*" of the question of the political (an obviousness that translates the French *evidence*) and the "contingent, uncertain, even erratic or fragmentary nature of the procedures which allow it to be tackled" (*RJ*, 19/*RP*, 113).

In their letter circulated to the participants of the Center concerning its clo-sure in 1984, Lacoue-Labarthe and Nancy resume the terms in which the Center was initially established:

> We had said at the time how, with the recession, it became clear that
> the inauguration of the Center in 1980 had coincided with a moment
> when the political question was near enough totally put back in play.
> With the collapse of certainties, with the deterioration of their foun-
> dation and the effacement of their horizons, it became possible—even
> necessary and urgent—to resume the question of what we had then
> called "the essence of the political": to resume it, and that is to say to

open it anew, and to open it prior to or beyond the political positions recently adopted by some people. Not in order to settle in God knows what philosophical no man's land of the political and of politics, but in order to reinterrogate the political and its philosophical 'position' or 'positions' as to its essence (or, indeed, if you prefer, as to its conditions of possibility). To our mind, as to that of many of the other participants or contributors, this type of work presupposed that no certainty, old or new, could hastily seal up the breach opened in what one could call the general mind-set of our time by the de-position of the political. Which, specifically, means this: that nothing of the political is henceforth established, not even and above all its liquidation or its writing off [*son passage aux profits et pertes*] of the West and its metaphysics. (*RP*, 144)[5]

According to the terms of this summary and retrospective overview, Lacoue-Labarthe and Nancy situate the question of the essence of the political not just in relation to the widest metaphysical terms but in relation to their own contemporary situation in the early 1980s, a situation in which the recession, in large part provoked by the oil crises of the late 1970s, coincides with what the authors describe in the same letter as a resurgence or (re) birth of economic neoliberalism and political neoconformism. Although he had not participated in the discussions at the Center, Althusser offers a useful overview of this same contemporary situation. Looking back in October 1982 at the last eighteen months (Althusser had just spent time in various psychiatric institutions), which is roughly the time period in which the Center had been in existence, Althusser notes that "the world had moved on":

It saw the overwhelming victory of the Left in the [presidential] elections of May 10, 1981, and the creation of a socialist government headed by [Prime Minister Pierre] Mauroy, under the "serene" Presidency of François Mitterand. It saw the first "social" measures (should they be called "socialist"?) unsettle the employers, and even make them tremble. (They are, of course, used to trembling—or do they just pretend to be? Still, they witnessed quite a few changes, from the court systems to the minimum legal wage, to mention only those two extremes, the one involving the law, the other wages, the two pillars of our world.) The period also saw the Right attempting to pull itself back together; saw it win a few elections here and there, and play them up in order to convince itself that it still existed; and saw Mitterand traveling around the world in quest of allies for peace and contracts for production. Quite a few other progressive reforms have been announced, reforms that will count as milestones, although, as everyone knows, one has "to wait until the sugar dissolves."[6]

In retrospect, one could presumably make Lacoue-Labarthe and Nancy's own description of the contemporary situation in their closing letter a little thicker than suggested by their own brief contextual gestures, at least when compared to Althusser's commentary, thereby opening the Center's lectures and discussions to different forms of historical, if not historicist, inquiry and interpretation (an inquiry that would no doubt include the overdetermined place of the École Normale Supérieure as an institution in the intricate configuration between philosophy and politics in France). Or one could presumably ask a further question concerning what was specific about the late 1970s and early 1980s as a conjuncture that provoked this collapse of certainties and effacement of horizons, a post-1968 sense of malaise and disarray that included the growing awareness that Mitterand's newly elected socialist government in 1981 had changed little from previous governments (even with Che's former associate, Régis Debray, installed at the Élysée as Mitterand's advisor), or changed little at least as compared to the instituting of the Solidarity movement in the same year and the beginnings of *glasnost* and *perestroika* (references that also appear in the Center's discussions). These references could then be extended to a larger set of analyses—the burgeoning growth of communication and information technologies within the increasingly mediatized political arena and space of spectacle, the unprecedented global expansion of post-Fordist production (Mitterand's search for contracts overseas), and the rise of nationalist and protectionist political discourses and movements on the Right to which Althusser refers—all of which begin to further characterize the early 1980s when the Center was established, and all of which actively shaped the resurgence in economic neoliberalism and political neoconformism in decisive ways. In short, one could (re)politicize or recontextualize the terms of Lacoue-Labarthe and Nancy's own argument, pointing out the ways in which their delimitation of the essence of the political, or their avowed desire to "take some distance" from contemporary events, were motivated less by an initial feeling of "simple political despair"— "the ease or calculation of things" that generated for the authors "every imaginable regression and reduced political debate to almost nothing" (*RJ*, 10/*RP*,

105)—than by a refusal to acknowledge how the Center's very existence was powerless against and perhaps, as Nancy Fraser has suggested, even fundamentally complicit with the very forces of economic neoliberalism and political neoconformism.[7]

However compelling the desire to (re)politicize or historicize the Center's various proposals, lectures, and discussions, and whatever the insights gained from pointing to yet another appropriation of politicophilosophical discourse by the forces of neoliberalism, such an argument nevertheless conflates, reduces, or simply effaces the very questions posed by Lacoue-Labarthe and Nancy in the first place, historicizing the Center in order to conjure it out of existence. Indeed, the attempt to justify the demise of the Center by pointing to the "constitutive dilemma" that organizes Lacoue-Labarthe and Nancy's interrogation into the essence of the political both reduces this questioning to the relatively benign terms of a dilemma (as if the question of the political were reducible to a choice between two equally undesirable alternatives) while effacing the initial determination to question what constitutes, as it were, the very constitution of the political in the first place, where constitution is also understood not just in terms of an essence but what we might provisionally term the composition or grammar of the political. More particularly (and here we begin to sense the inherent risk of any proposal seeking to delimit the *essence* of the political), the argument appears to conflate the question of the essence of the political either with an essentialism, thereby effacing the "logic" of the *re-trait* that radically structures and modifies—indeed, disessentializes—the question of essence, or with some form of transcendental idealism (Lacoue-Labarthe and Nancy's "transcendental safe-house" in Fraser's terms), a conflation that thereby effaces the quite specific re-articulation between transcendence and immanence that structures Lacoue-Labarthe and Nancy's rethinking of totalitarianism in their writings. For we will see that the question of the political is also, indissociably, a question of how totalitarianism is potentially inscribed in our so-called democracies today through the "total domination" of the political, and it is precisely this domination that works to further obscure the question of *relation* that motivates one of Lacoue-Labarthe and Nancy's initial ambitions to establish the Center (a question, it might be noted, that Fraser largely ignores in her lengthy review of the Center's work).[8] In this way, (re)politicizing or historicizing the Center's work will only ever suture over, simultaneously reducing and effacing, the "breach" opened by what Lacoue-Labarthe and Nancy term the "de-position" of the political. In other words, this deposition is understood only as the mere deposing of the political from its formerly elevated position (thus leading Fraser to assume that Lacoue-Labarthe and Nancy simply "cede the terrain of politics" to neoliberals) rather than thinking this deposition in its double movement—as both a questioning and simultaneous displacement of what constitutes a political *position*, including the delimitation of the space or very "terrain" in which such a position might find its place, ground, and political self-orientation, and as a form of political *address*, in which the deposition of the political is not a way of putting the political on trial as in a summary execution but its very presentation, in the sense of its politico-philosophical *Darstellung*, or in the specific sense registered by a deposition, in which a statement is offered and taken down in writing in the place of a spoken testimony. In short, the assumption that Lacoue-Labarthe and Nancy efface the question of politics in their proposal for the Center's existence comes to efface, in turn, the ways in which the deposition of the political opens toward what the authors propose as the "problematic of a *ground* (or of a new ground) of the political" (*RT*, 195–96/*RP*, 131–32). For this deposition also opens toward rearticulating what Lacoue-Labarthe and Nancy affirm as a "new ground" for thinking the question of *relation*, even as this groundless ground opened by all relationality cannot be assimilated to a purely transcendental or metaphysical ground, a *fondement* in which to articulate a political *position*, and specifically a transcendental ground or position that finds its origin or telos—in short, its arche-teleological orientation—in a (political) *subject*.

No less pertinent to the claims that conclude Fraser's review, any attempt to (re)politicize the questions raised by the Center must also begin to take into account Lacoue-Labarthe and Nancy's continual references throughout their various texts to the *closure* or *completion* of the political. Opening onto a quite specific re-articulation between the political and the philosophical, this closure is not subject to an interpretation that is recognizably either political or historical, since it is precisely the assumptions concerning politics and history that are also re-interrogated in the closure of the political, precisely the positions informing and subtending the presup-positions of political or historical discourse that are put back in play in the retreat of the political. In other words, what is put back in play here are those metaphysical presuppositions that presuppose the Subject and so efface the question of relation that begins to emerge here. Following on from Derrida's seminal early claim to rethink all closure as "the circular limit within which repetition of difference infinitely repeats itself,"[9] it is in light of this closure or completion that any attempt to (re)politicize the Center must thus confront two questions that shape Lacoue-Labarthe and Nancy's initial motivation to establish the Center in the first place, two questions that are thrown into relief by the very closure or completion of the political. First, they ask, how are we to think the political in the "modern age," that is, in relation to an age that delimits itself as modern? Or again, how are we to think the political in the modern age as the "actualization or installation of the philosophical *as* the political, the generalization (the globalization) of the philosophical *as* the political—and, by the same token, the absolute reign or 'total domination' of the political"? (*RJ*, 15/*RP*, 110). Secondly, and indissociably, Lacoue-Labarthe and Nancy ask whether the political, as it appears and dominates today, is the effect of a certain "retreat" of the philosophical or a certain "completion" (*affectuation*) of the philosophical (*RT*, 187/*RP*, 125). In posing these two questions, Lacoue-Labarthe and Nancy work to demonstrate that thinking the closure or completion of the political in terms of its retreat simultaneously reopens the very *space* of the political. Indeed, as Derrida notes in his appeal to rethinking any form of closure in terms of a repetition of difference infinitely repeating itself, it is precisely this question of space that is now set "in play."[10]

Situated in light of one another, it is only in and through these two initial questions that we can begin to rearticulate the question of the essence of the political dominating the Center's opening presentation and ensuing discussions. At the same time, it would be necessary to recognize that these two questions at once extend and displace a number of problematics set out in texts and discussions that preexist the Center's own creation in 1980. In the first place, these include Derrida's rearticulation of the *co-appartenance* or "co-belonging" of the philosophical and the political in his widely discussed essay from May 1968, "The Ends of Man," which opens by referring to what has "always linked the essence of the philosophical to the essence of the political," and seeks to rethink what "burdens" and simultaneously reexposes the "*a priori* link" between philosophy and politics.[11] Also preexisting the Center's creation in 1980, the second important reference here is the organization of the Political Seminar by Christopher Fynsk and Lacoue-Labarthe at Cérisy earlier that same year, a colloquium that took its own title, *Les fins de l'homme*, from Derrida's earlier essay.[12] Conceived by the organizers more in terms of a "punctuation" in or of Derrida's writings than an "elaboration," Christopher Fynsk opened the seminar by referring to a *retrait* in or of Derrida's text in relation to politics or to political questions, a retreat that thereby exposes us again to the political as a "limit-question" for philosophy

(*FH*, 487/*RP*, 87). It was in the context of this same seminar at Cérisy that Lacoue-Labarthe had already proposed to think the "de-position" of the political by refusing from the outset any simple return or retreat to a political "safe haven" [*lieu sûr*], arguing that retreating the political must also be thought as active rather than merely reactive, especially in the ways in which this retreat works to rethink what constitutes totalitarianism today as our contemporary problem and unsurpassable horizon. It is against the background of these various texts and seminar discussions that the Center's existence as a space in which to rearticulate the essence of the political comes into further relief, sharing with the organizers at Cérisy the need to "breach the inscription of a *wholly other* politics" (*FH*, 21). And it is against this larger background that Lacoue-Labarthe and Nancy's questions concerning the total domination of the political and the completion of the philosophical become bound together in such a way as to demonstrate not only how the *retrait* of the political finds a measure of its disruptive and immeasurable force but also how the question of *relation* finds an originary measure of its *essentially* political—that is, inescapably philosophical—(self-)transformation and simultaneous affirmation.

The interrogation into the essence of the political reveals that the philosophical questioning *of* the political and the questioning of the philosophical *as to* the political both turn on an acknowledgment of the closure or completion of the political—its *affectuation* or *accomplissement*. As Lacoue-Labarthe and Nancy insist, this questioning nowhere gives way to either resignation or vexation. As a "totalitarian phenomenon," this closure or completion is an initial measure of the "obviousness (the blinding obviousness)" of the political, the "everything is political" which is used to qualify our "enclosure in the closure of the political" (*RJ*, 18/*RP*, 112). Following on from the writings of Hannah Arendt, specifically her demand to exclude every other domain of reference, "the 'everything is political' which near enough universally dominates today," the closure of the political is a response to what Lacoue-Labarthe and Nancy define as the "absolute reign" or "total domination" of the political, a domination that paradoxically conceals an effacement of the specificity of the political in its very saturation and global domination.[13] It is this global domination that defines the "total completion" (*accomplissement sans reste*) or the "undivided reign" (*la règne sans partage*) of the political, in other words, a concept of the political that saturates or exhausts the space of the political because its closure is without remainder or without *partage*, without division or sharing out. In this sense, the closure of the political is structurally inscribed in and as a totalitarian phenomenon that Lacoue-Labarthe and Nancy seek to address, including the political consequences of thinking the passage beyond this phenomenon: "In the epoch where the political is completed to the point of excluding every other area of reference (and such is, it seems to us, the *totalitarian phenomenon* itself), we can no longer decently ask ourselves what theory would still be in a position to promise a political solution to inhumanity (which is still not finished), because we know what the desire for social transparency promises—the utopia of the homogenization of the 'social body,' the hope attached to management or to enlightened direction" (*RJ*, 16–17/*RP*, 111).

Tracing out the terms in which to think this totalitarian phenomenon, the closure of the political thus points toward rethinking the more recognizable forms of historical totalitarianism characterizing political regimes in the twentieth century, including the political instances of totalitarianism (Nazism, fascism, Stalinism, Soviet-style societies) that are said to constitute the various responses to the "crisis of democracy." But the closure of the political also points toward rethinking what constitutes the contemporary forms of totalitarianism characteristic of, or internal to, our so-called democracies today. Elaborating on their initial analysis of this totalitarian phenomenon in the seminar at Cérisy (*FH*, 494/*RP*, 95–96), the question thus remains for Lacoue-Labarthe and Nancy whether a more "insidious" and (as one says of technologies) "softer" form of totalitarianism has not since been installed, more or less without our knowledge, in or even *as* our contemporary democracies. Presented in these terms, the argument finds resonance for Lacoue-Labarthe and Nancy in Lyotard's recently published *The Postmodern Condition*, in which the "social system" is conceived by the "decision-makers" as a "totality in search of its most performative possible unity," leading Lyotard to suggest that such a system is capable of imposing a new sort of "terror."[14] Situated under the general domination of "technical and productivity criteria," Lacoue-Labarthe and Nancy then ask whether this possible "unity" in its totalizing and potentially totalitarian imposition is coterminous with a number of features characterizing contemporary democracies, including "surreptitious reincarnations of the body politic, a relatively constant and 'unbroken' occupation of the places of power, a certain homogeneity of the 'people of suffrage' (albeit only because of the spectacularizing techniques of electoral and political games), frenzied fabrications of consensus (albeit only on the level of economico-political consumption), a diffuse (but powerful) psychologizing ideology? In short, a way of responding to 'democratic crisis' which would be internal to democracy or what we still describe as such,...a totalitarianism of crisis, whose fragility would appear to be the most formidable force" (*RT*, 190–91/*RP*, 128).

The paradox between fragility and force that closes this description of contemporary democracies echoes the fundamental paradox that preoccupies Arendt in her writings, a paradox worked through in texts such as *Between Past and Future* and *The Human Condition* as well as the writings on totalitarianism. Intimating from such references that Arendt's *The Origins of Totalitarianism* should be read in close dialogue with her other writings rather than separate foci of research, as Arendt herself and her commentators sometimes seem to imply, Lacoue-Labarthe and Nancy argue that this paradox turns around "the fact of the disappearance of all 'political specificity' in the very domination of the political." In other words,

> The fact of the political ceaselessly merging with all sorts of authoritative discourses (in the first place, socio-economic, but also technological, cultural, psychological, etc.), and, despite the 'media' circus or the 'spectacularization' of an absent public space, everywhere converting itself into a form of banal management or organization. In the totalitarian phenomena thus understood, nowhere do even the least of specifically political questions come to be asked, do new political questions (corresponding to transformations of the world) have the chance to emerge, if not from inside an accepted ideological phraseology, whether this ideology (in Arendt's sense of the term [i.e., as "the logic of an idea through which 'the movement of history is explained as one consistent process'"]) be that of class, the nation, the meaning of history, the rights of man, the State, etc. (*RT*, 189/*RP*, 126–27)

No doubt such a paradox in no way prevents politics from being done, as Lacoue-Labarthe and Nancy are quick to observe. But the paradox still remains of a politics in its "becoming *unapparent*" (in the sense of "it goes without saying"), and this "unapparence is proportionate to its all-powerfulness. And *vice versa*" (*RT*, 188/*RP*, 126). It is, no doubt, this same paradox— the disappearance of all political specificity in the very domination of the political, the fact of the political ceaselessly merging with all sorts of authoritative discourses—that also opens the task of finding a new language, new concepts, or a new phraseology for rearticulating the terms in which to think the relation between totalitarianism and democracy today, and to do so beyond assumed or accepted ideological phraseologies.[15] It is this same task (to cite some of the most well-known commentaries) that also appears in a number of related proposals to reconfigure this very relation between democracy and totalitarianism, from the post-Arendtian concepts of the biopolitical in the writings of Foucault and Agamben to a post-Enlightenment critique of bureaucratic rationality, administration, or governmentality, or from rethinking established concepts of ideology, power, and totalitarian languages to writings on the society of the spectacle or the society of control. If Lacoue-Labarthe and Nancy's description of the democratic crisis posits the question whether our contemporary democracies are not in the process of "secreting" a new form of totalitarianism, then the claim takes its point of departure from a widely shared observation that a certain "ready-made and much circulated opposition" between totalitarianism and democracy is too simple ("even if it is true and if the differences between these forms is glaring"; (*RT*, 191/*RP*, 128). Extending the ways in which Arendt renders the totalitarian phenomenon irreducible to the various critiques of "classical" or historical forms of totalitarianism, this "new" totalitarianism would also find its resources in a number of well-known theses established by Arendt across all her writings (and not just those directly addressing totalitarianism), theses that include the dominance of *animal laborans*, the thesis outlined in *The Human Condition* where man is defined as worker or producer; the recoding of public space by the social, by society as such (*Gesellschaft*, as distinct from *Gemeinschaft*), in other words, by a "common-life or an interdependence regulated according to life or subsistence, and not according to a public or political end in itself"; and finally, the loss of authority as the distinct condition of power, a loss that, relating itself to the "transcendence of a foundation," goes hand in hand for Arendt with the loss of freedom (*RT*, 192/*RP*, 129). It is these well-known Arendtian theses that then supplement an already established set of political analyses, including Arendt's own writings on totalitarianism as well as those of Claude Lefort, in which totalitarianism is thought in more recognizable if circumscribed terms, which Lacoue-Labarthe and Nancy characterize as a "frenzied resubstantialization," or a "re-incorporation or re-incarnation, a *re-organization* in the strongest and most differentiated sense—of the 'social body.'"[16] Totalitarianism understood in this more restricted sense constitutes either a response to or an attempt to get out of the "impasse" presented by a democratic crisis—of democracy *as* crisis—a crisis whose most notable features include "the disappearance of the authority-tradition-religion triptych, the disembodiment of power, the collapse of ground or the loss of transcendence (mythico-religious or philosophical: reason, nature, etc.), the disruption of hierarchies and the customs of social differentiation, the de-localization of the political (the 'empty space' of power, as Lefort has it) and the rule of political changeover, the desubstantialization of the body politic which no longer is one except in the pure dissipation of suffrage, politics eventually given over to the play of vested interests, etc." (*RT*, 189–90/*RP*, 127). Phrasing totalitarianism in this way, the more established theses on "classical" totalitarianism, at least when presented as an historical phenomenon, thus already gesture toward Lacoue-Labarthe and Nancy's reelaboration and redescription of this phenomenon as it also takes hold of our contemporary democracies.

Extending the analysis beyond Arendt as well as Lefort's own principle theses and analyses, totalitarianism is further rearticulated by Lacoue-Labarthe and Nancy in quite specific terms that remain at once political *and* philosophical, terms that clearly distinguish their argument from the more widely known responses cited above to the totalitarian implications current in our contemporary democracies. Totalitarianism is now thought according to the ways in which it proceeds not just from a re-incorporation, re-incarnation, or re-organization of the social body but from what Lacoue-Labarthe and Nancy term the "incorporation and the presentation of transcendence." In this sense, the new totalitarian phenomenon would itself stem from the "dissolution" of transcendence, and thus from totalitarianism's ability to "penetrate all spheres of life now devoid of alterity" (*RT*, 192/ *RP*, 129; and as Lacoue-Labarthe and Nancy point out, it is no coincidence that this definition of totalitarianism echoes Marx's definition of democracy in his "Critique of Hegel's Doctrine of the State"). Resonating with Lyotard's own argument following Lefort's talk at the Center concerning the incorporation and the presentation of transcendence as the work of art in Nazism and as the reason of history in Stalinism (*RT*, 88), Lacoue-Labarthe and Nancy argue that rethinking totalitarianism's philosophical presuppositions and rearticulation as a question of transcendence not only resists its closure in accepted ideological phraseologies; the transcendence that is subject to dissolution and leads to the effacement of alterity is not a transcendence that governs over and gives meaning to the foundation or ground either. Nor again is it a question here of appealing to a transcendence that founds itself in God, Man, or History: "The question of the retreat [of the political] is not one of 'regaining' a remote or withdrawn transcendence ['*récupérer*' *une transcendance retirée*], but of wondering how the retreat compels us to displace, re-elaborate and replay the concept of 'political transcendence.' And in view of a transformation of the very idea of transcendence (or, if it is less ambiguous to put it like this, the idea of alterity), for us it is indeed a question, in the name of the 'essence' of the political, of a transcendence and an alterity" (*RT*, 192–93/*RP*, 129–30).[17]

The appeal to transcendence here is not to that transcendence that has "installed" totalitarianism or a transcendence that totalitarianism has installed itself, converting such transcendence into the "total immanence of life-in-common." Lacoue-Labarthe and Nancy seek instead to reconfigure the specific relation between immanence and transcendence as this relation opens toward an alterity of any preconstituted, enclosed, or "immanentist" political field. At the same time, it is this appeal to rethinking transcendence in relation to an alterity that cannot be simply conflated with historical or social analyses of totalitarianism, whether posited in the more sociological terms of society or as a social totality, at least insofar as the reduction of totalitarianism to an historical or social phenomenon tends to efface precisely what remains at stake in a politico-philosophical reading—namely, the preinscription of relation or the question of alterity as such. The transcendence that opens toward an alterity thereby extends and simultaneously refocuses Lacoue-Labarthe and Nancy's claim that the totalitarian phenomenon is articulated as a closure of the political that remains without "remainder" or *partage*, without division or sharing out, where these terms also register the effacement of both relation and alterity in the totalizing claim that "everything is political." In this sense, Lacoue-Labarthe and Nancy's appeal to transcendence and alterity is not just a defining measure of their politico-philosophical rearticulation of totalitarianism as it inscribes itself in our contemporary democracies. Nor is it merely an attempt to efface the political implications and consequences of the totalitarian phenomena by imposing on it a philosophical interpretation. For it is the enabling condition in which to think the very retreat of the political, to that *retrait* that reopens the question of *relation* and alterity at the origin of the political event.[18]

Before turning to this question of relation and alterity at further length, a number of consequences follow from Lacoue-Labarthe and Nancy's argument concerning the political today as a totalitarian phenomenon. First, the closure or completion of the political turns on the acknowledgment that the "revolutionary passage to humanity" has ended as a narrative. The closure of the political is thus intimately tied to the argument proposed by Lyotard in *The Postmodern Condition*, where what completes itself (in Lacoue-Labarthe and Nancy's paraphrase) is "the great 'enlightened,' progressivist discourse of secular or profane eschatology," or the "discourse of the re-appropriation of man in his humanity, the discourse of the actualization of the genre of the human—in short, the discourse of revolution" (*RJ*, 16/*RP*, 111). In light of this closure, and a closure that has echoes in Derrida's "Ends of Man" essay cited earlier, Lacoue-Labarthe and Nancy refuse the argument that the unhinging of this narrative and teleological passage leads to a form of tragico-mystical discourse, a "beyond" of the human, or a return to a form of ancient transcendence. As to the possibilities of revolt—and luckily, Lacoue-Labarthe and Nancy suggest, "everything leads us to believe that there are still a few possibilities here and there, but rather more there than here"—the end of the narrative charting the revolutionary passage to humanity is also situated in terms of a radical transformation of the discourse of revolution from any eschatological or teleological passage, a question to which we will have occasion to return in later chapters.[19] But above all, the end of this eschatological or teleological narrative is the end of any "political solutions" to inhumanity, in the sense here of both *political* solutions and political *solutions*, and specifically solutions framed in terms of a desire for total social transparency or the hope attached to "management" or to "enlightened direction"—in short, the very terms in which the homogenization or immanentism of the social body becomes synonymous with totalitarianism. Or rather, the end of this revolutionary narrative rethinks any claim for a political solution proposed in the face of the *crisis* of democracy or the "democratic crisis," this crisis against which totalitarianism also finds a measure of a response.

Second, rethinking the total domination of the political in terms of the closure of the political reopens the question of a political position. The question thus remains how to seek an "engagement" with the political that does not devolve into a mere *gage* or "pledge" given to one politics or another, as if politics were a relatively interchangeable game of pawns in which different positions are staked out and negotiated, at least that type of negotiation of political positions that invariably leads toward reinscribing a certain "homogeneity of the 'people of suffrage'" or "frenzied fabrications of consensus." The question of the political that Lacoue-Labarthe and Nancy seek to address is not closed off in this form of political discourse or into this "form" of politics, in which a political position is established within a range of potential positions (from "left" to "right"), positions in this sense (or as a question of the self-sufficient *sense* of a political "orientation") that do not foreclose the taking of positions, but that cannot be dissociated from the metaphysical presuppositions of the Subject, including the discourse of subject positions. In this way, the total completion or domination of the political coincides with the completion of the political and of the philosophical primarily in its "modern figure," the figure that is outlined for Lacoue-Labarthe and Nancy in the philosophical presupposition or metaphysical speculation of the Subject, or in those philosophical and political positions that imply the figure of the subject in their reciprocal determination: "We do not accept that [the Center's] point of departure need be subjected to a philosophical and/or political figure," the authors claim, "since it is the philosophico-political figure *as such*, or the figure *of* the philosophico-political that we are intending to question" (*RJ*, 28/*RP*, 120).[20] The retreat of the political addressed by Lacoue-Labarthe and Nancy thus reopens and simultaneously displaces any presupposition regarding the political subject and its modulation or figuration of the *anthropos logikos*, a presupposition that includes the very institution of the West as a "political institution," the founding institution from which the West's political concepts are inherited:

> The questioning about the political or about the essence of the political is…what for us must ultimately take stock of the political presupposition itself of philosophy (or, if one prefers, of metaphysics), that is to say, of a political determination of essence. But this determination does not itself produce a political position; it is the very position of the political, from the Greek *polis* to what is deployed in the modern age as the qualification of the political by the subject (and of the subject by the political). What remains to be thought by us, in other words, is not a new institution (or instruction) of politics by thought, but the political institution of so-called Western thought. (*RJ*, 15/*RP*, 110)

In other words—and again we will return to this observation in further detail—if it is precisely this "institution" of Western thought and its corollary in the Subject that is closed or completed, then rethinking the political as an institution is understood less as the establishment of a purely new site or ground in which to assume a position and mark out a new territory or domain; it is the rearticulation or deterritorialization of the exclusionary, delimiting, or instituting conditions that make the political institution of Western thought possible or hegemonic in the first place.[21] It is in light of this deconstruction of the instituting conditions of the political in Western thought that the closure of the political cannot be interpreted as a (nostalgic) return to the Greek *polis*, anymore than Arendt's writings suggest a mourning for the loss of the *polis*. Nor can it be interpreted as a return to some pure origin of the political prior to its assumed corruption or perversion, whether in its totalitarian or purportedly democratic forms. Indeed, it is not even configured in terms of a return at all. For this questioning of the reciprocal involvement and joint closure of the philosophical and the political, this taking stock of the political presupposition of philosophy, leads us, in reality, not to any return to the political, or the past, but to "our situation" or "our state," which Lacoue-Labarthe and Nancy interpret in quite specific terms as the "mimetic or memorial after-effect or *après-coup* of the Greek 'sending' [*envoi*] which defines the modern age" (*RJ*, 15/*RP*, 110). It is this same "after-effect" that opens onto the specific rearticulation of totalitarianism proposed by Lacoue-Labarthe and Nancy, that after-effect defined as the actualization or installation of the philosophical *as* the political in the modern age, or the "total domination" of the political. No doubt Lacoue-Labarthe and Nancy's larger claims for rethinking totalitarianism hinge on how to read the reference here to this Greek *envoi* or "sending," just as these "after-effects" cannot be detached from the closure of the political.[22] Suffice it to remark that the closure of the political does not return us to the Greek origin, and thus to the reinscription of a political position that finds its metaphysical presuppositions in the founding discourse of the West and the political determination of essence. For the *après-coup* of the Greek *envoi releases* or, more strictly, *re*-releases this "sending," a re-release in the sense that the origin is always already a reproduction, or always already a mimesis of repetition, reproducibility, and simulacra. Repetition (un)founds the inauguration of the political, displacing any sense that retreating the political is merely a *return* to the political, to an ideal order of meaning of the political that guarantees its values and norms of signification, both in the past and, by extension, for today.[23] As we will suggest, it is this argument that will have decisive consequences for rethinking the question of political position at stake in Lacoue-Labarthe and Nancy's demand to rethink the political in terms of its de-position, closure, and retreat.

Third, the closure of the political to which Lacoue-Labarthe and Nancy refer cannot be separated from the extensive references to the writings of Heidegger in their various individual and coauthored texts, not only the

Heidegger who thought the "end of metaphysics" but also the Heidegger who attempted to think, in "Overcoming Metaphysics" and other essays from the 1930s, how metaphysics was completed or fulfilled in modern technology. When Lacoue-Labarthe and Nancy thus ask whether the political is today the effect of a certain retreat of the philosophical, their question takes into account the ways in which this retreat is situated in relation to a certain completion of the philosophical, in the sense in which Heidegger thinks the completion of metaphysics. In other words, as Lacoue-Labarthe has argued, it is through Heidegger that we can begin to approach the very "root" of the political, in the sense of its essence or possibility, but only on the condition that, again following Heidegger, "the contours of the political trace and retrace themselves only on the basis of the retreat [*à la mesure du retrait*], in and of the political, of its essence."[24] More pointedly, the reference to Heidegger here is clearly one of the most contentious aspects of Lacoue-Labarthe and Nancy's more general claims concerning rethinking the political, in part because it is not simply Heidegger's own rethinking of the concept of the political in Western thought that remains at stake, nor is it his voluminous writings on how to re-articulate the question of essence, but it is the specificity of Heidegger's own "politics" that is implicated in Lacoue-Labarthe and Nancy's attempt to rethink the political as the *retrait* of the political.[25] And yet, it is this same insistence on the retreat of the political that becomes the mark of an irreducible distance *from* Heidegger. For if Lacoue-Labarthe and Nancy insist on thinking "the philosophical" in distinction from both philosophy and metaphysics in their delimitation of the essence of the political, the distinction itself is established in the wake of Heidegger's furthering or prolonging the discourse of metaphysics in order to "obstinately" preserve philosophy, an obstinacy that serves to obstruct a passage in which to rearticulate *Dasein*'s finitude and radical alterity as a question now of relation. It is this obstinacy that thus shields philosophy from the very "thinking" Heidegger claims as fundamental (the Heidegger, in other words, who claims in the 1930s to receive or redirect via Hegel the Greek *envoi* as the founding gesture of the spiritual destiny of the German people).[26]

If Lacoue-Labarthe and Nancy's rethinking of the closure of the political demands a rereading of Heidegger's texts on the end or *Destruktion* of metaphysics or its *Vollendung*, it is important to recognize that the determining conditions informing this closure or delimitation simultaneously open toward a continual and interminable movement of repetition

(*Wiederholung*) and displacement, a discrepant and discontinuous movement in which the Greek *envoi* is now subject, as it were, to the possibilities
of permanent errancy and incessant detour. More specifically, this closure or
completion, like the word "end," indicates for Lacoue-Labarthe and Nancy
not just an exhaustion that is complete but the "completion of a program *and*
the constraint of a programming," implying at once an "unsurpassable" (*in-
franchissable*) condition and a "delimitation." Or rather, what completes itself
in and as the retreat of the political *does not cease to complete itself*, a logic
of rupture and doubling, of repetition and displacement, that is inscribed in
Lacoue-Labarthe and Nancy's shared insistence on thinking what remains
infinitely *fini*, at once infinitely finished or finite. This end, closure, or perfection is therefore not only situated in a quite specific sense.[27] It is this same
"logic"—in which what completes itself does not cease to complete or perfect
itself—that also opens the *retrait* of the political, a re-treating inscribed by
the force of repetition that informs and sets in play—in short, re-releases—
the rewriting and rearticulation of the political from its closure.

Presented in this schematic form, these three preconditions for rethinking totalitarianism today—the end of the revolutionary passage to humanity,
the questioning of position in terms of the political institution of Western
thought, and the thought of the political in relation to its completion—these
preconditions traverse all of Lacoue-Labarthe and Nancy's writings from the
Center (and of course, beyond as well). But if the retreat of the political is re-
released by its closure, as Lacoue-Labarthe and Nancy claim, then the essential question still remains: "On the basis of what, against what, or along what,
does this closure trace itself?" When this question is posed in terms that are
as much topological and ontological as political, when this question is posed
in which the concept of the political cannot be dissociated from an ontopology that inscribes it, and when some measure or sense of what orients
the space of political thinking today is demanded, it should be clear that the
closure of the political does not simply trace itself against the nonpolitical
(the economic, the technological, the cultural, etc.), which simply presupposes and reinscribes what constitutes the political through its determinate
negation. On the contrary, Lacoue-Labarthe and Nancy argue that the closure opens onto "something," something that would be "the political" or the
"essence" of the political "drawn back or withdrawn [*retiré*] from the total
completion of the political in the techno-social" (*RT*, 196/*RP*, 132). It is this
withdrawal or drawing back that redraws, retraces, or reoutlines the political
from its (spatial) closure, enclosed contours, or conceptual frameworks. This

"something" is not the place in which Lacoue-Labarthe and Nancy merely "cede the terrain" of politics in the name of the political, as if reinscribing the very distinction and spatial closure they seek to rearticulate, or as if effacing their attempt to circumscribe, rewrite, and displace the assumed "passage" that leads from the political (as in a theory of the political) to an identifiable politics. For it is precisely this withdrawal, drawing out, or *retrait* that does not seek to reestablish a stable terrain or horizon (the term that remains central to the phenomenological tradition) but opens onto a radically different space or topology, one (if it is *one*) in which the question of orientation becomes at once decisive and problematic, if not also (given the stakes at play here, in other words, the very "political institution" of Western thought) dis-orienting. It is through the retreat of the political that Lacoue-Labarthe and Nancy seek to outline and circumscribe the "contours" of a (new) political "space" or "ground," a space that is not delimited and framed with recognizable contours, constituting an interiority divided from an exteriority, nor exactly a "wholly other" politics that would arise from the determinate negation of the political. Nor again would it exist suspended over a void or empty space. For the retreat of the political traces out an opening—a spacing, the topology of a "something" that is not nothing—in which the closure of the political not only retraces itself but exposes the question of *relation* that animates Lacoue-Labarthe and Nancy's initial desire to interrogate what makes the social relation possible as such.

The question of space in play here cannot be thought as separate from Heidegger's positing of the overcoming or completion of metaphysics, its *Vollendung*. In his introduction to *Retreating the Political*, Simon Sparks recalls the passage in "The End of Philosophy and the Task of Thinking," in which Heidegger rearticulates this *Vollendung* precisely in terms of its spatial implications: "The old meaning of the word 'end' [*Ende*]," Heidegger recalls, "means the same as place: 'from one end to the other' means from one place to the other. The end of philosophy is the place, that place in which the whole of philosophy's history is gathered in its uttermost possibility. End as completion means this gathering" (cited in *RP*, xi–xii). If Lacoue-Labarthe and Nancy rearticulate this "end" in terms of a *retrait*, one of the decisive spatial or topological implications of their reading of Heidegger is to open up a corresponding and equally decisive displacement of the motif of "gathering" in Heidegger's thought, a displacement whose consequences we will come to explore in later chapters. Suffice it to remark that what we are referring to as a question of topology responds to the spatial paradox Lacoue-Labarthe further articulates in his reading of Heidegger in his own presentation at Cérisy: "The 'there,' a pure 'there'—like Heidegger says, the pure *Da* of pure *Da-sein* as it transcends beings or as it is 'outside' of beings, another way of saying ek-sistence—is the place without a space of its own [*le lieu sans espace propre*], non-localisable as such (and which nevertheless remains a place [*lieu*]), which being needs in order 'to be itself,' that is to say, not to be or to be nothing [*(n)ĕtre rien)*]" (*FH*, 426/*RP*, 66).[28] Before turning more directly to this question of space and the seemingly paradoxical, if not aporetic condition in which to think a place without space of its own, such an exposure to the question of relation as ek-sistence cannot be made prior to repeating— and so displacing—the argument in which Lacoue-Labarthe and Nancy define the closure of the political as the originary condition for thinking the *retrait* of the political.

The "reciprocal implication" of the philosophical and the political that governs Lacoue-Labarthe and Nancy's argument entails that "the political is no more outside or prior to the philosophical than the philosophical, in general, is independent of the political" (*RJ*, 14/*RP*, 109–10). This reciprocal implication does not lead to a vicious circle. It does not lead to a form of tautology, or some common essence and shared provenance that binds the political and the philosophical into a seamless whole (a whole registered in one or another political philosophy). For this reciprocal implication leads us back to a quite specific delimitation of the field in question, to the questioning of the essence of the political as a question informed by a sense of its completion or closure.

As an initial response to the terms of this argument, Lacoue-Labarthe and Nancy's opening address to the Center is organized around a "double exigency," one that turns on the interiority and exteriority of the political and the philosophical to themselves. For the delimitation and simultaneous inauguration of the Center as a space also folds across the delimitation of the very field in question, one in which the political and the philosophical are characterized less by two separate discourses occupying the same space than by their folded and "reciprocal involvement." On the one hand, the Center thus proposes to rethink the *philosophical* questioning of the political. On the other hand, such questioning also presupposes the questioning of the philosophical itself as to the political, or *about* the political, or, more pertinently, *as* the political (and as Lacoue-Labarthe and Nancy insist, these different approaches to the question should not be collapsed into each other but held open in their irreducible difference). In this sense, the philosophical questioning of the political is also the philosophical question of the political, opening toward the "essential (and not accidental or simply historical) *co-appartenance* or co-belonging" of the philosophical and the political (*RJ*, 14/*RP*, 109).[29] It is this co-belonging that therefore begins to take into account the political as a philosophical deter- mination, and vice versa. The reciprocal implication and co-belonging of the philosophical and the political further entails that "the political is no more outside or prior to the philosophical than the philosophical, in general, is in- dependent of the political" (*RJ*, 14/*RP*, 109–10). In this sense, it is not solely a question of critique that is explored here, whether this includes the various forms of political critique or the critique *of* philosophy, in which philosophy's political presuppositions are exposed, for the questioning of the essence of the political cannot be reduced to critique. As Lacoue-Labarthe and Nancy argue, "There is, today, a 'banal commonplace' that exposes in philosophy the gesture of political foundation which organizes it or which it organizes. But this exposure falls short, firstly if it does not distinguish very carefully these two doubtless very different gestures (to organize is not to be organized), and then insofar as it remains a critique—itself political (and that is to say itself philosophical)—of philosophy, instead of troubling itself with questioning the philosophical essence of the political" (*RJ*, 17/*RP*, 111).

In the refusal to close off the question of the political into a critique, it is precisely the proposed "double aim" or "double exigency"—which Lacoue-Labarthe and Nancy come to determine as "recognition of the closure of the political and practical deprivation of philosophy as regards itself and its own authority"—that determines the question of the essence of the political as a question of the retreat of the political. Indeed, it is precisely this double exi- gency of thinking the political and the philosophical together that marks the simultaneous union and disjunction, the attachment and detachment, regis- tered by the very hyphen, the *trait d'union*, that traverses—and so divides— the *re-trait du politique* from itself.

In the first gesture motivating this double exigency, the field in question is created through the radical exclusion of everything that does not directly pertain to the philosophical questioning of the political. Lacoue-Labarthe and Nancy thus mark a distinction between this question of the political and the discourse of political science, political studies, politiology, or (ap- pearances notwithstanding) political philosophy. As they insist, there is no pretension here to anything that could constitute a political theory. More polemically, the authors refuse any empirical approaches to the question of the political, an approach that does not interest them not only because the authors claim that they no longer believe such an approach still to be possible but also because they believe even less that it can still be "decisive" as concerns rethinking totalitarianism (an argument first proposed by Lefort in his lecture on totalitarianism for the Center). This refusal regarding empirical approaches to the political is part of a larger "vigilance" against every so-called positive discourse, or any discourse formed by a pretension to grasp social and political phenomenon on the basis of a "simple positivity," whether this is ascribed to "history or to discourse itself, to force or desire, to work or affect, etc.," terms and concepts in which, as Lacoue-Labarthe and Nancy suggest, "anything, or nearly anything, is possible" (*RJ*, 14/*RP*, 109). This radical exclusion of every discourse that does not pertain to the philosophical questioning of the political, especially any project that seeks to promote a theory or a science of the political, is initially proposed in order to disclose and foreground the inescapably *philosophical presuppositions* that inform and subtend all the socio-anthropological or "direct" approaches to the political. Thus Lacoue-Labarthe and Nancy also refuse all political discourses that "feign independence" from the philosophical, even if, as they acknowledge, this gesture of exclusion does not mean that other approaches to the political are not only possible but even desirable.

Clearing a space in order to rethink the question of the political does not offer a new concept or figure of the political either, one that might be invented in the wake of the end of Marxism, the end of ideologies, the end of the cold war, or in terms of contemporary globalization, at least insofar as rethinking the *essence* of the political is not synonymous with proposing a new concept or figure of the political. Any new concept of the political or anything that presents itself as such invariably derives from an already determined philosophical field, one that Lacoue-Labarthe and Nancy deem "ancient, past, closed" (*RJ*, 13/*RP*, 109): "If the concepts or quasi-concepts of civilization, of culture, of ideology, of mentality, of representation or of symbolism were not so heavily marked (philosophically) and had not served in discourses or contexts so foreign or so barely attentive (when not outright hostile) to philosophical phenomena or to the specificity of the West, they would perhaps be usable or susceptible to reelaboration, providing new means to rethink what constitutes the political today" (*RT*, 186/*RP*, 124). Clearly, Lacoue-Labarthe and Nancy argue, this is simply not the case.

If the first motivation of Lacoue-Labarthe and Nancy's "double exigency" is to exclude everything that does not pertain to "the political," then the argument is further sustained by the irreducibility of "the political" to "politics," the difference registered in French by the distinction between *le politique* and *la politique* respectively, between the concept of the political as such—"the site where what it means to *be* in common is open to definition"—and politics as it is usually understood, including the day-to-day decisions that constitute our political discourse, in other words, "the play of forces and interests engaged in conflict over the representation and governance of social existence."[30] This distinction between the political and politics is not only decisive in terms of the larger argument in which the domination of the political today is an effect of the retreat of the philosophical. For in spite of the "'anything goes' mentality of supposed novelties" that Lacoue-Labarthe and Nancy discern in much contemporary, political discourse—a mentality that more often than not simply reveals the "barely disguised repetition of old positions" from within an already-determined philosophical field—the distinction between the political and politics at once sets in place and sets in play the question Lacoue-Labarthe and Nancy pose in the first place, namely, whether there has ever been a questioning of the political "rigorously, absolutely." Taking its point of departure from this heuristic distinction between the political and politics, it is only in terms of the closure of the political that this ("philosophical") questioning and its ("political") implications begin to emerge.

If the double exigency proposed by Lacoue-Labarthe and Nancy thus turns, through a radical act of exclusion and bracketing, on the philosophical questioning of the political, this nowhere suggests withdrawing to a position defined as philosophical, as if such a position were still tenable today. As the authors insist, any questioning of the essence of the political is neither the "lofty claim of some philosophical privilege (or the privilege of philosophy)," nor, even less, the "pure and simple renewal of the classical appropriation of the political by philosophy" (*RJ*, 13/*RP*, 108). In other words, the political distinguishes itself from any philosophical discourse that aims at founding the essence of politics or a political essence and thus at "instituting or programming an existence of which it would be the correlate" (*RJ*, 17/*RP*, 111). More forcefully, "Philosophy immediately finds itself implicated as a political practice relieved of its own authority: not simply of its possible social or political power, but relieved of the authority of the theoretical or the philosophical as such (however one determines such a practice: critique, back to basics, thinking and distorting re-appropriation (*Verwindung*), step backwards, deconstruction, etc.)" (*RJ*, 17/*RP*, 111–12). In other words, the questioning of the essence of the political would correspond to those gestures of deprivation that also mark philosophy's own closure or completion, a deprivation that does not privilege philosophy but, on the contrary, relieves it of its own theoretical and philosophical authority, as well as its social and political power. The closure of the political outlined by Lacoue-Labarthe and Nancy thus does not lead to a valorization or uncritical assumption of the philosophical but opens instead toward a more radical delimitation of the political and philosophy's reciprocal involvement: "It is as if philosophy, in the movement of its own destitution had not dared touch the political, or as if the political—under whatever form—had not ceased to intimidate it. It is, in other words, as if a part of philosophy (if not its very essence) had, to all intents and purposes, remained off limits to philosophy in the movement of its own destitution…and as if the political remained, paradoxically, the *blind spot* of the philosophical" (*RJ*, 17–18/*RP*, 112). In short, if philosophy also finds itself called into question in questioning the essence of the political, this nowhere presupposes that one can substitute for philosophy a "positive" (i.e., sociological, economic, technological) or "normative" (i.e., ethical, aesthetic—or "political") discourse (*RJ*, 9–10/*RP*, 105). Any "foray" or "exit" outside of the political is thus also excluded, for this *sortie*, whether it takes an ethical, juridical, sociological, aesthetic, or religious form, is always poised to confirm or reinscribe the domination of the political. These turns of argument may constitute an "old schema," Lacoue-Labarthe and Nancy remind us, concluding their opening *Ouverture*, but it is a schema that is "still operative." There is no escaping the question of presuppositions and limits that remain in play here.

Given the exacting delimitation of the philosophical and the political at stake in the retreat of the political, or given the ways in which this retreat reopens the limit that at once attaches and separates the political and philosophical from one another, a conspicuous aspect of Lacoue-Labarthe and Nancy's writings for the Center is the extension of this problematic to Marx and Marxism, as if it were precisely in relation to Marx and Marxism that the politico-philosophical conditions informing the double exigency of Lacoue-Labarthe and Nancy's larger argument were exposed again to one of their constitutive limits. Certainly the importance of addressing Marxism was already proposed in many of the papers and seminar discussions in the earlier *Les fins de l'homme* conference at Cérisy, notably in the papers by Jacob Rogozinski and Gayatri Spivak, as well as in Fynsk and Lacoue-Labarthe's own contributions to the Political Seminar.[31] Marxism is also conceived in the Center's initial program as an inescapable dimension of retreating the political, which Lacoue-Labarthe and Nancy phrase as the "sheer obviousness" of having to address Marxism. Indeed, the very first question concerning the retreat of the political is addressed in their opening remarks to Marxism. At the same time, it is also the reference to Marxism that figures largely in the Center's closure and Lacoue-Labarthe and Nancy's concluding letter to the participants. Since the terms in which Marxism is addressed pertain closely to the question of social relations that defines Lacoue-Labarthe and Nancy's initial ambitions for the Center's lectures and discussions, a preliminary outline of their argument and its essential traits is necessary here. No doubt these references to Marx and Marxism nowhere constitute a close reading of Marx or the Marxist legacy, as Lacoue-Labarthe and Nancy acknowledge. But the authors note that the larger stakes of their references to Marx still turn on the "hope of a critique" as well as a "revolutionary radicalization" of established Marxism (*RJ*, 16/*RP*, 111; a phrase that echoes Lacoue-Labarthe's earlier presentation at the Political Seminar), even if that hope must nevertheless recognize the ways in which, for Marx himself, the political is continually reduced to mere bourgeois illusion.

The initial response to Marxism can be situated in relation to what Lefort has termed the "lacuna of the political" in Marxism, and leads Lacoue-Labarthe and Nancy to a quite specific set of texts in Marx's writings in which the place of the political is addressed. For it is precisely in this "lacuna" that we are said to encounter the "*obvious presence* of the very problematic of the political," which is rephrased, according to the terms by which Marx characterizes authentic democracy in his "Critique of Hegel's Doctrine of the State," as the encounter with the "form of the negation of the *separated* State" (i.e., the purely formal or abstract State) in favor of what Marx defines as the "material impregnation by the State of the content of all the non-political spheres" (*RJ*, 21/*RP*, 114). Echoing the fundamental paradox that haunts Arendt's writings concerning the disappearance of the political in its very domination (and here we should also recall the largely negative role played by Marx's writings in the principle theses of Arendt's *The Human Condition*), Lacoue-Labarthe and Nancy reconfigure this specific problematic beyond the writings of Marx himself:

> It seemed to us that all the Marxist problematics, whatever they may
> have been and whatever analyses they have adopted as regards the
> history and the displacements of Marx's thought, were tributaries of
> this lacuna *and* of this presence—in short, tributaries of this presence

in and through the lacuna of the political—whether they have simply recorded this heritage or whether they have come up against the necessity of posing to it the supplementary, exhaustive question of a specificity of the political. In theoretical and practical contexts as varied as those of, for example, Councilism, Gramscism, Althusserism or Maoism, it is indeed the general form of such a question that has imposed itself. Not only as a question of a *transitory* political form necessary to the movement of revolution (as Marx had raised the problem after the Commune, and as the problem seems to prolong and bury itself in the practices of socialist countries) [Lacoue-Labarthe and Nancy are writing this in the early 1980s] but, more radically, as the question of the singular term which one finds in the "Critique of the Gotha Program" when Marx evokes or invokes the "future *Staatswesen* of communist society," the being-state, the mode of being or state essence which will be or which would be that of communism, or even the space of the state which will be its own: a term which does not furnish the concept, but which opens a pure problem, the problem of the responsibility of limiting the separated State, the separated State-form, to the bourgeois State, or else, and systematically (if the *Staatswesen* designates the being of a non-separated-State), the problem of the implications of a thinking of the total immanence or the total immanentisation of the political in the social. (*RJ*, 21/*RP*, 114–15)

If Lacoue-Labarthe and Nancy's reference to Marx's writings in terms of the "lacuna" of the political closes by referring to the "total immanentisation" of the political in the social, and so folds the argument back to the descriptions of totalitarianism, transcendence, and alterity explored earlier, the argument continues by situating Marx's writings not only in terms of the State but also within a reconfigured conceptual understanding of what constitutes the political as such, from which the question of the State and its limits then come into relief. According to this larger conceptual context, Marx's writings are said to relate to those of Heidegger as well as Georges Bataille, both of whom also addressed this question of the "total immanentisation" of the political in the social by thinking, as does Marx, beyond or at the limit of the political, or by thinking at the "extreme (and for this reason, decisive) boundary of the political" (*RJ*, 22/*RP*, 115). Or rather, what Marx shares with Heidegger and Bataille is a return of the question of the political, and specifically a question of the political that, at least for Heidegger and Bataille, accompanied ("in every sense of the term") Nazism. In this sense, their respective writings thus gesture toward what constitutes a reappropriation of this beyond or limit of the political, a reappropriation that is posited in terms of different schemas of subjectivity (as the people in Heidegger and the artist in Bataille). If Marx thus finds himself situated within a wider set of references and conceptual parameters than usually suggested in readings of his work, or if Marx's ambivalence concerning the *Staatswesen* is rephrased in terms of the relation between immanence and transcendence as that relation plays out across a rethinking of the State's *limits*, suffice it to remark that the problematics raised by Lacoue-Labarthe and Nancy in their discussion of Marx still remain a decisive reference for rethinking democracy and the *Staatswesen* within the contexts of contemporary globalization, as well as in transformations in state sovereignty. This is a question to which we will return when addressing the relation between the "separation" of the State-form and the constitutive rearticulation of an extremity implied by this very separation, an argument in which it is precisely the limits or boundary of the political that also remain at stake.[32]

The closing of the Center returns us to the question of Marxism addressed at its opening. In their "Letter on the Closure of the Political," written and circulated in November 1984, Lacoue-Labarthe and Nancy point to the ways in which the Center, in spite of constituting a "unique site of encounter," no longer fulfilled its original task: "insofar as a 'Research Center' must ensure something other than the successive reception of speakers whose propositions are linked or stimulated by nothing, or nearly nothing, within a common space and in accordance with common concerns, it seems to us that, for some time, the Center has not exactly fulfilled its remit" (*RP*, 144). In part, the closure coincides with the reference discussed earlier concerning the recession in the early 1980s, to this moment when the question of the political was put back in play. But this reference to their contemporary moment, notably the effects of the recession, cannot be detached from the question of Marxism or, more pertinently, the purported "end of Marxism," and it is this specific conjuncture that dominates the presentation of the Center's closure:

> As we also said in 1983, it appeared more and more justifiable to ask
> if any such questioning [of the political] actually remained open
> within the Center, or whether a sort of easily accepted consensus of
> opinion had not been established in its place. This consensus was

not proper to the Center. It was then, and remains so today, what, in eagerness and haste, occurred as the after-effect or the counter-effect of what has been called the "end of Marxism." (This event, quickly enough taken to be unique, simple and identical everywhere and in every respect, would be, moreover, an event already remote in our history—in short, outdated—and already covered over, it seems, by the event of a (re)birth: that of an economic neo-liberalism and a political neo-conformism). *(RP*, 145)

The consensus is only fully established, then, when totalitarianism is understood as merely specific to the regimes of Marxist origin, thus leading toward proclamations concerning the end of Marxism that, for Lacoue-Labarthe and Nancy at least, simply fail or refuse to rethink the question of totalitarianism as a contemporary problem inscribed in our present democracies. These various rhetorical appeals to the end of Marxism signal an equally pernicious refusal or repression, which Lacoue-Labarthe and Nancy characterize as a consensus, defining such a consensus as the "end of questioning as to either the always incomplete and problematic character of the philosophical analysis and determination of so-called totalitarianism, or the distance and the proximity between its Fascist, National Socialist and Communist models, or the relevance of the concept (if it is one) of totalitarianism for grasping the actual realities of regimes or societies (and what problems, already, in the alternative!) that it serves to designate. So many neglected questions, and yet so many questions which might well risk returning one day, in the classic function of something repressed" (*RP*, 145).[33] In the end, the consensus that Lacoue-Labarthe and Nancy discern in the Center's activities turns on the *political* itself, of which Marxism would be the "completed form" and the "total permeation"—"as the absolute danger or as the definitive impasse of thought and praxis." The authors conclude that "an intellectual attitude (for this does not amount to a thinking) which privileges the ethical or the aesthetic, even the religious (and sometimes the social) over the political, has been allowed, little by little, to gain ground" (*RP*, 146), and it is precisely this intellectual attitude that installs itself in the wake of Marxism.

If we recall the ways in which Marx and Marxism figure in the Center's closure, it is not simply to suggest how the references to Marx and Marxism relate to the retreat of the political or Lacoue-Labarthe and Nancy's larger ambition to rethink the essence of the political. For the closing letter also argues that the widespread appeal to the end of Marxism or the end of ideologies becomes "insidiously transformed into the end of every consideration and every operation which has in view the identity of the collectivity, its destination, the nature and exercise of its sovereignty" (*RP*, 146). In one sense, the reference to collectivities that concludes their reference to Marx and Marxism in the letter extends Lacoue-Labarthe's discussion of Councilism in the Political Seminar at Cérisy, to which we will have occasion to return. It equally recalls Heidegger's own references to collectivism in the "Letter on Humanism," as if Lacoue-Labarthe and Nancy's persistent references to Marx and Marxism across their texts for the Center cannot be dissociated from rearticulating Heidegger's claim that sees in all forms of collectivity "the subjectivity of man in totality," or as that which "completes subjectivity's unconditional self-assertion."[34] However strange this confluence of texts and references might seem, we want to note that the question at stake here remains essentially faithful to the "Theses on Feuerbach," in which Marx seeks to fissure any clear sense that all forms of collectivity are predicated on the subject's *self*-assertion, and so turns to the ontico-political question that animates the Center's own inaugural address, namely—the "*ensemble* of social relations."

In *The Philosophy of Marx*, Étienne Balibar sets out to defend a paradoxical thesis. On the one hand, he claims, "there is no Marxist philosophy and there never will be." And yet, "Marx is more important to philosophy than ever before," in the sense that after Marx, "philosophy is no longer as it was before":

> The anti-philosophy which Marx's thought at one point intended to be, this non-philosophy which it certainly was by comparison with existing practice, thus produced a *converse* effect to the one at which it was aiming. Not only did it not put an end to philosophy, but gave rise within its very being to a question which is now permanently open, a question from which philosophy has since been able to draw sustenance and which has contributed to its renewal. There is no such thing as an "eternal philosophy," always identical to itself: in philosophy, there are turning points, thresholds beyond which there is no turning back. What happened with Marx was precisely a displacement of the site and the questions and objectives of philosophy.[35]

Nowhere is this threshold and sense of displacement more evident than in Marx's analysis of social relations. Drawing from Althusser's seminal argument concerning a rupture within Marx's thinking, Balibar argues that the specific rupture in Marx's writings in 1845 was contemporaneous with the emergence of the newly articulated concept of social relation, a concept that marked an irreversible break with the "theoretical humanism" of Marx's earlier writings. In this reading of Marx, the "Theses on Feuerbach" from 1845 takes on a certain significance, not only because the theses represent for Althusser *le bord antérieur extrême* of a break with theoretical human-ism—the extremity of the break's front or leading edge—but also because the theses begin to elaborate on a concept of the subject that displaces the estab-lished philosophical traditions of idealism as well as the "old materialism" of philosophies of nature. More potently, the subject that emerges within this rupture is the subject of revolutionary action and activity, the subject that exists "in practice."

Echoing the sense that the *bord antérieur* might also translate here as the "anterior" or preceding edge, Balibar argues that Marx does not necessarily avoid the very idealism from which he seeks to break. No doubt identify-ing the "essence of subjectivity with practice" and the reality of practice with the revolutionary activity of the proletariat ("which is one with its very exis-tence") suggests that Marx transferred the category of the subject from ide-alism to materialism. But as Balibar suggests, it is equally possible to assert that Marx set up the permanent possibility of "representing the proletariat to itself as a 'subject'" in the idealist sense of the term (26/26).

If this dialectical turn of argument comes into continual tension with any claim that Marx's writings are constituted through a radical rupture with forms of theoretical humanism, Balibar suggests that such dialectical turns are not just closely linked to the history of revolutionary thinking but demonstrate how the philosophical and political are intimately bound in a reciprocal exchange of terms. For the very idea of revolution within moder-nity is inscribed by the "invention of the subject" as the central category of philosophy, to that subject which "relates to all fields of concrete experience (science, morality, law, religion, aesthetics) and makes possible their unifica-tion." This historical invention of the subject is essentially tied to the idea that humanity "moulds or educates itself, to the idea that it gives itself laws and, therefore, finally to the idea that it *liberates itself* from the various forms of oppression, ignorance or superstition, poverty, etc." (26/26). In light of the philosophical tradition of the subject within modernity, Balibar notes that the generic subject of this activity is always double faced: the one theoretical, the other concrete and practical—"in Kant, that subject was *humanity*; in

Fichte it became at a certain point the *people*, the *nation*, and in Hegel, lastly, it was the *historical peoples* as successive embodiments of 'world spirit,' i.e., the progress of civilization" (27/26). If Marx then inherited this tradition by naming the *proletariat* as the "true practical subject"—as the "people of the people" or the "authentically human and communal," or as the subject that "dissolves the existing order" and thus changes itself while at the same time changing the world—and if he simultaneously attempted to transform this same tradition by appealing to ways in which *the subject is practice*, then, as Balibar argues, this transformation or this *Selbsttätigkeit* and *Selbstveränderung* does not necessarily displace the history of idealism from which Marx seeks to escape:

> Without playing with words, one might even go so far as to suggest that this is what makes of Marx and his "materialism of practice" the most accomplished form of the idealist tradition, the form which enables us to understand more than any other the lasting vitality of idealism right up to the present, precisely because that transposition is closely linked to the attempt to prolong the revolutionary experience and embody it in modern society, with its classes and social conflicts.
>
> To do so would be to prepare to understand that adopting the standpoint of the proletarians in a state of "permanent" insurrection resulted not so much in putting an end to idealism, but in installing the materialism/idealism dilemma—the perennial question of their difference—at the very heart of the theory of the proletariat and its privileged historical role. (27/27)

However compelling such a (dialectical) argument, Balibar notes that it is precisely in this theory and privilege that the philosophical *presuppositions* of the subject nevertheless reappear. Indeed, as Balibar further attests, it is precisely in light of this argument that the question of *essence* comes again into focus.

In the "Theses on Feuerbach," Marx writes contra Feuerbach that "the human essence is no abstraction inherent in each single individual. In its reality it is the ensemble of the social relations [*das Ensemble der gesellschaftlichen Verhältnisse*]." In posing the question concerning the "essence" of human beings, the seemingly ontological or anthropological interrogation into this essence is immediately displaced into a question of what human essence is *in seiner Wirklichkeit* or "in its effective reality," in other words, in its effective relation to the "*ensemble* of social relations" in which such an essence is now inscribed. As Balibar points out, the conjunction of French and German in the sixth thesis intimates precisely the kind of unusual displacement at work in Marx's thinking, as if he were seeking to translate the idealist tradition in which the invention of the subject plays a constitutive role into a thought of relation constitutive of that very invention. In this sense, the essence of man is not an "abstraction" inherent in each single individual but constitutes the very grammar or principle of articulation in which to think social relations as always an *ensemble* of relations.

> The point is to reject both of the positions (the *realist* and the *nominalist*) between which philosophers have generally been divided: the one arguing that the genus or essence precedes the existence of individuals; the other that individuals are the primary reality, from which universals are "abstracted." For amazingly, neither of these two positions is capable of thinking precisely what is essential in human existence: the multiple and active *relations* which individuals establish with each other (whether of language, labor, love, reproduction, domination, conflict, etc.), and the fact that it is these relations which define what they have in common, the "genus." They define this because they constitute it at each moment in multiple forms. They thus provide the only "effective" content of the notion of essence applied to the human being (i.e., to human beings). (30/29–30)

In leaving open the question whether this positing of relation is original or specific to Marx, Balibar continues by arguing that such an argument has important consequences, both in the field of philosophical discussion at the level of what is called ontology, as well as in that of politics. In rejecting both the discourse of individualism as well as an organicist or holistic point of view, Balibar suggests that Marx's turn to the French word *ensemble* (a problem prolonged in numerous English translations in which the French *ensemble* is frequently supplemented by adding "aggregate" as a synonym) not only gestures toward thinking the ontological conditions of the relation *as* relation; it further testifies to his refusal to reduce all social relations to a "totality" or "whole" implied by the possible use in this context of the German *das Ganze*. In thinking through the ontological presuppositions that are structurally inscribed in Marx's language of social relations, Balibar further argues that the "constitutive relation" that displaces any unified subject, individual, or human essence opens toward a way of thinking humanity not just in terms of a "transindividual reality" but ultimately to thinking "transindividuality as such." Noting that the term derives from the writings of both Kojève and Lacan, as well as Simondin's seminal and widely influential concept of "transindividuation," Balibar concludes that such a term points not to what exists within each individual (as in a form or substance), nor to what, external to the subject, classifies and orders the subject. Instead, it opens toward "what exists *between individuals* by dint of their multiple interactions" (31/32). Indeed, it is precisely in terms of this transindividuation that Balibar sees an "ontology of relations" emerging in Marx's writings:

> Here, we must admit, an "ontology" is taking shape. However, in place of any discussion of the relations between the individual and the genus, it substitutes a program of enquiry into this multiplicity of relations, which are so many transitions, transferences or passages in which the bond of individuals to the community is formed and dissolved, and which, in its turn, constitutes them. What is striking in such a perspective is that it establishes a complete reciprocity between these two poles, which cannot exist without one another and are therefore in and of themselves mere abstractions, albeit necessary abstractions for thinking the very rapport or relation (*Verhältnisse*). (31/32)[36]

As Balibar continues, these "mere abstractions" of a transindividual ontology are just as much inscribed in the differentiated practices and singular actions that constitute the everyday as they are in such founding texts as the *Declaration of the Rights of Man and the Citizen*. Even more, Balibar suggests that these abstractions are inscribed in revolutionary movements, in the sense that such movements constitute a practice that "never *opposes* the individual's self-realization to the interests of the community and indeed does not even *separate* these, but always seeks to accomplish the one by accomplishing the other," that is, by seeking rights and demands that are necessarily collective. Balibar then concludes his reading of the sixth thesis by acknowledging that this argument does not refer to an "existing state of affairs" or, even less, a "system of institutions," but rather a "process," at least as experienced by those taking part in such a process. But this is exactly what Marx intends; the sixth thesis (which identifies the human essence with the *ensemble* of social relations) and the third, eighth, and eleventh theses (which link all thought to revolutionary practice and change) all turn around the same problematic: that social relations are nothing but an "endless transformation," a "permanent revolution" (32/32–33). In short, speculative as it may seem, Balibar acknowledges that the "ontology of relations" that punctuates Marx's sixth thesis brings us closer than ever to the very question of politics, to the political *as such*.

Extending the brief references to Marx and Marxism in their texts for the Center, and exploring in what ways they have been developed by Balibar, it is a decisive aspect of Lacoue-Labarthe and Nancy's argument concerning the retreat of the political that the question of social relations posed in their opening address cannot be reduced to the State, or an ensemble of social relations or social totality subsumable within a state formation, nor can it be reduced to the concept of power:

> The question of the State, or the more general question of power, appeared to us to be unable to be engaged for itself without passing through the question of the subject. Which also meant that the question of power did not seem by itself to constitute the initial question of the political. But this did not mean that, as far as we were concerned, the question of power lost all proper relevance and that (as many have thought in recent years) the idea of power would conceal a type of effects indissociable from discourse, for example, or the unconscious—effects themselves multiple, diversely localized and dispersed or stratified in mobile configurations. The combinative or aleatory nature of micro-powers dissolves the nonetheless very real actuality of the great powers, whether they be those of class, of State, of monopoly capitalism, or all three at once. Now, the marginalizing or sublimating of either class struggles or political struggles has never been what is at stake for us: these are the givens of the epoch of the domination of the political and technology or of the domination of the political economy. But the stake could be one of no longer subjugating these struggles, in their finality, to this Domination. *(RJ, 23–24/RP, 117)*

If the reference to the "aleatory nature of micro-powers" gestures toward the writings of Michel Foucault (to cite the most prominent reference in this regard), the orientation of Lacoue-Labarthe and Nancy's argument leads toward a question of the subject that does not easily lend itself to the various institutional and disciplinary mechanisms, technologies, subjectifications, forms of governmentality, or biopolitics proposed in Foucault's seminal writings.[37] For the question of relation animating Lacoue-Labarthe and Nancy's appeal to social relations in the retreat of the political is informed less by any historical or genealogical analysis of the subject in its multiple discursive formations and social configurations than by a refusal to subjugate this relation, the relation *as such*, to what they term the "arche-teleological domination of the Subject," and thus to a domination of the subject that mirrors the domination that subjugates class or political struggles. More specifically, if the "political obviousness" of the Subject stems from the "absolute *presupposition* of the *relation of* subjects," then this presupposition guarantees "the ordering of the political as *telos*" and so permits the effacement, in the name of the political, of what constitutes the relation *as* (a) relation. Any questioning of the subject must refuse the enclosure of the subject within the arche-teleological assumption of what constitutes the politics of the subject or the so-called political subject. This refusal pertains as much to the enclosure or appropriation of the subject within the State as it does to the arche-political discourse of the *polis*, that originary space in which the subject is said to exist *as* a political subject, or at least a concept of the *polis* that presupposes the delimitation of a space in which the subject occupies a political position. As Lacoue-Labarthe and Nancy argue, "it is through the ideal or through the idea of the *polis*, more than anything else, that the modern epoch—Romanticism, of course, and all idealism, including socialist idealism—has refastened itself to the Greek origin and finality of the West, that is to say, has tried to reassert itself as the subject of its history, and as the history of the subject" (*RJ*, 23–24/*RP*, 117). And it is precisely this history, specifically, the "mimetic or memorial after-effect or *après-coup* of the Greek *envoi*," that *presupposes* the *relation* of subjects in the act of presenting and promoting the concept of the political subject, the (self-)founding Subject—*zoon politikon*—of the political discourse and history of the West.

Reopening and displacing the metaphysical presupposition that effaces the *relation* of subjects in the name of the political Subject does not imply an effacement of class or political struggles, as Lacoue-Labarthe and Nancy take care to note. But it does imply that those struggles and conflicts must be rethought and rearticulated, not so much in terms of their politics—these are also the givens of the epoch dominated by political economy and technology—but in terms of their own presuppositions concerning the so-called political subject that forms the basis of those struggles in the first place. It is precisely in rethinking these same presuppositions that such struggles are no longer situated as a reactive response to the domnation of the political, a domination *against* which the political subject finds its "own" measure (and this "against" suggests in a Nietzschean vein all the ambiguities inherent in any contestation against the domination or subjugation of the subject). Instead, rethinking these presuppositions in terms of the *relation* of subjects opens toward a radically different composition or ensemble of the political that finds its measure not just in reaction to the subject's domination but in the refusal of, and resistance to, any form of *self*-constitution or *self*-organization, terms that register their founding reference in a subject even as their more ostensible appeal remains to a plurality or collectivity that exists "beyond" the subject. In this sense, the question of relation does not give rise to a politics that is created between distinct and identifiable subjects, each with specific or presupposed identities that then compose an alliance, nor a politics established within relations of power. What emerges instead is a concept of the political whose space is defined by the ("grammar" of the) relation *as such*, in the in-between or in the *between* of subjects, as Balibar suggests, assuming again that it is not precisely the discourse of the subject and its associated discourse of grammars, subject positions, and composition that together close off the question of relation at stake here. At the same time, if such struggles and conflicts remain irreducible to any arche-teleological concept of the political, or any finality that determines in advance their outcome (the "discourse of the re-appropriation of man in his humanity" or the "revolutionary passage to humanity"), then Lacoue-Labarthe and Nancy are retracing a concept of the political that finds its force in-between, and so (for want of a better expression) in permanent revolution, understood here as a nonteleological or eschatological trajectory or nonlinear passage. In short, it is precisely in this sense that Lacoue-Labarthe and Nancy can also acknowledge the necessity of turning to Marx, not only in order to refuse the discourse concerning the purported end of Marxism but also in order to rethink, as a question now of *relation*, the very identity or constituency of the collectivity. Or again, the task remains how to rethink that collectivity when its very self-identity, self-production, and self-affirmation is fissured at its own origins and in its very foundation. In short, the question remains how the constituency of the collective is not reducible to the question of the State, nor that of power, but articulated in and as an *ensemble* of relations.

Lacoue-Labarthe and Nancy's reference to social relations in their introductory overview to the Center's work suggests a departure, displacement, or withdrawal from the more widely accepted terms in which social relations as a concept is proposed. To be sure, the concept has been taken up and set to work within numerous disciplinary and discursive fields (political science, sociology, anthropology, history, cultural studies, and so on), each of which leans on the heuristic importance and explanatory potential of social relations to define the specifically intersubjective relations between members of a given social context or society. We also know the multiple ways in which the concept of social relations has been defined, measured, and quantified, subject to statistical modeling, protocols of sociological investigation, data gathering, case studies, behavioral analysis, policy making, all of which tend to presuppose the relation of individuals to larger, interpersonal contexts and intersubjective dynamics. From theories of social contract outlined by Hobbes and Rousseau to the great sociological and anthropological traditions established by Weber, Durkheim, and Lévi-Strauss, from the acknowledgment of conflicts, agonistics, and dialogics defining social relations in the writings of Marx and Freud to the analyses of group dynamics by Simmel, Bourdieu, and Latour, from philosophies of difference to theories of the other (or the Other), from genealogies of intimacy to redescriptions of love, from the "six degrees of separation" to the analysis of social actors or social movements, from theories of interpellation or agency to the performative subject, not only does the concept of social relations reconfigure the relations or composition of a given group or society; it further extends to different ways of reconceiving theories of kinship and community, family and caste, social bonds or social ties, tribal relations and collective organization, as if the recognition of social relations as a conceptual category coincides with the continued viability of defining not just an identity or group dynamic but a larger social identity, group identity, social totality, a *polis*, the *demos* of a democracy, civil society, a public sphere, or global community. At the same time, these same references turn on ways of reconfiguring the conditions informing social relations themselves, including the relation to questions of economy, psychology, ideology, religion, beliefs, culture, climate, values, and so on. These conditions then allow for a set of more specific categories in which social relations are further redefined and articulated, and so also allow a way of embracing different criteria such as class, race, ethnicity, gender, sexuality, and the potential intersections traced out between these categories, as well as an analysis of the institutional and disciplinary mechanisms (schools, factories, prisons, citizenship, the "society of control," etc.) as well as social technologies and forms of governmentality in which, as the seminal writings of Foucault among others have proposed, social relations are not only created but also reproduced. We also know that what underlies both the description and the analysis of social relations are questions of identity and essence, order and recognition, division and hierarchy, categories that then extend to heuristic distinctions between public and private, the body politic of a nation and international relations, citizenship and cosmopolitan identities, and so on.

In light of this initial overview, there can be no doubt as to the heuristic importance of social relations as a concept, even if there remains an unspoken sense that it never adequately conveys as an analytic category the real complexities and lived experiences through which individuals and groups define their cultural specificities, identities, and relations or perceive the identities and differences of others. But one might also begin to question some of the assumptions informing its conceptual or analytic use, and not only because of the difficulty separating social relations from the onto-political assumptions informing concepts of social totality or society, the ideal of social transparency and open communication, the implicit framework of a nation-state within which social relations are relatively contained, or assumptions concerning the definition of modernity itself, definitions that also include the mythological "origins" of social relations against which modernity sets itself off from its historical past and the progressiveness of its "peoples" from their predecessors. The scientific, sociological, or ethnographic observation and analysis of social relations also tend to presuppose a point of detachment from those observed and analyzed, a condition that informs both the assumed objectivity and scientificity of such an analysis as well as the ability to impose a measure of what constitutes social relations and normative behavior on peoples and geopolitical contexts in which relations are potentially organized according to quite different criteria.

Such questions would also appear to impose themselves given the relatively unproblematized assumptions held in the widespread use of social relations as a concept. They also suggest a more general outline for writing a genealogy of social relations as a concept, notably in response to the presuppositions concerning social relations that inform numerous calls for a politics of the subject or a politics of representation. However, the question to be posed here touches singularly on the retreat of the political to which Lacoue-Labarthe and Nancy are drawing us. For beyond or prior to the assumption that the discourse of power effaces the question of relation in the first place, in what sense does the concept of social relations presuppose a subject that, preexisting the social relationship, is then articulated *into* a social relation, even when the terms are changed to cultural relations, economic relations, race relations, sexual relations, international relations, and so on? Secondly, assuming that the reference to the subject remains pertinent here, to what extent is the specific relation between subjects effaced in the implied reduction of these relations to *social* relations, as if the very term *social* itself obscured precisely what is at stake in thinking the relation *between* subjects, or the relation *as* (a) relation? More problematically, especially given the extensive references to the writings of Arendt in the Center's work, Lacoue-Labarthe and Nancy's own attempt to rethink the essence of the political would appear to be already compromised by their positing of relations as *social* relations, as if, by extension, the question of what constitutes the essence of the political was simply coterminous here with the social. In short, the question still remains open in what sense the reference to *social* relations effaces the very question of *relation* at stake here, of what constitutes the relation *as such*—that "*there is* relation" (as Lacoue-Labarthe will suggest in his presentation at Cérisy).

The obstacles posed by rethinking these questions, coupled with the need to find a language or grammar in order to rearticulate the concept of (social) relations, together suggest what is at stake in Lacoue-Labarthe and Nancy's appeal in their opening address to what makes the social relation or social *rapport* possible as such, a difficulty further emphasized in their italicizing of *rapport* in the text, as well as in their seemingly unavoidable insistence on maintaining all relations as "social" relations. As we will see, Nancy also turns back in later writings to the difficulty of articulating this same question of relation, acknowledging, for example, that the awkwardness of the phrases such as "being-with-one-another" (*être-les-uns-avec-les-autres*)—literally, "being-the-ones-with-the-others"—is an inescapable precondition in which to rethink "the logic of the 'with'" that subtends the relation as relation. The same demand to rearticulate the proximities and differences between a relation and rapport also informs Nancy's reading of Lacan's well-known claim that "there is no sexual rapport."[38] In other words, it no longer suffices to keep repeating phrases such as the "politics of the subject" or the "decentered subject" without working through the question of grammar—of articulation, composition, constitution, relation, disposition, multiplicity, singularity, plurality, becoming, and spacing—through which such concepts and claims find a measure of their own displacement (including the displacement of the very concept of a grammar), or without thinking "who" comes *after* this (decentered) subject, or again without rethinking the ontological presuppositions that guarantee that this "who" is not merely "some-one" but the erasure of a constitutive relationality in its very identity, self-assertion, and self-constitution.[39] As we have come to suggest, it is in light of rethinking these presuppositions that Lacoue-Labarthe and Nancy's reference to collectivity comes into further relief.

In their various proposals for the Center, Lacoue-Labarthe and Nancy draw from a number of earlier essays in which the question of social relations is also explored. These include several coauthored texts responding to the question of the social relations as it is posed with respect to psychoanalysis, in particular the writings of Freud, writings in which Lacoue-Labarthe and Nancy acknowledge how the "multiple and powerful motifs of sociality, of alterity, of relation as such" all work to disturb or displace the specificity of the Freudian subject (*RP*, 118).[40] In this sense, Freud's appeal to the subject invariably presupposes an inescapably philosophical derivation of the subject, notably at those points in Freud's writings where he attempts what Lacoue-Labarthe and Nancy describe as a "reconstruction" or "reaffirmation" of the *zoon politikon,* or when he seeks to outline theories of bisexuality, the prehistory of Oedipus, or an "originary sociality" (*RJ*, 25–26/*RP*, 118). In these early formulations concerning the question of social relations, Lacoue-Labarthe and Nancy's argument concerning psychoanalysis turns on the rapport between the "retreat" of the political and an analogous "retreat" of the *mother* in Freud's writings; in this context, both forms of "retreat" turn on a displacement of identification or an identification "beyond" the identity principle.[41] Taken up in their essay "*La panique politique,*" the argument concludes by suggesting that

> if the "social bond" is a genuine question—and is, by the same
> stroke, a *limit* question—for Freud, it is in that the *given* relation (by
> which we mean: the relation which, in spite of everything, Freud
> *gave himself,* which, like the whole of philosophy, he *presupposed*),
> this relation of a subject to subjectivity itself in the figure of a father,
> implies, in the origin or in the guise of an origin, the birth (or the
> gift, precisely) of this relation. And a similar birth implies the retreat
> of what is neither subject, nor object, nor figure, and which one can,
> provisionally and simplistically, call "the mother." (*RJ*, 26/*RP*, 118–19)

If the father is considered the "founding instance of figurality," then the mother is understood in Freud's writings as the disruption of the figure of identity, or as the "non-figural figure which withdraws identity," and this precisely at the point at which, for the Freud of "Group Psychology and the Analysis of the Ego," the earliest "*Stellungnahme* toward the Other" takes place (*RT*, 197/*RP*, 133): "In originary sociality, it would be, therefore, a matter of an identification not with the mother (this would be, properly speaking, impossible, insofar as the mother is identified with the retreat of (unitary) identity), but with what could be called the beyond-mother [*l'outre-mère*]. That is to say, in accordance with an inaudible, untenable formula, which we must risk nevertheless, an identification with the retreat of identity" (*RP*, 180). This untenable formula does not simply lead toward a complete loss of identification. It is not a question here of identifying all politics with the figure of the Father and then seeking through the Mother some vague appeal against authority and a move toward a reactionary anarchy. Lacoue-Labarthe and Nancy already predict the *Schwärmerei* to which this retreat of identity could open to, but, as they suggest, this situation doubtless only arises for an interpretation already itself subordinate to the political. It is not a question of an all too easy antiauthoritarian acceptance of a swarm or herd mentality in order to find a more "radical" politics, even when posited in the sense of an uncontrollable throng, multitude, or crowd. Nor (prolonging the possible connotations of this *Schwärmerei*) does this retreat fold back into a form of political discourse that, refusing the established forms of political identification, turns toward forms of rapture and ecstasy.[42] In other words, it would be necessary to turn back to Freud's own discussion of the primal horde or masses in this context, as in his own references to "*Massenpsychologie*" (translated not insignificantly into English as "group" psychology), a concept for which Lacoue-Labarthe and Nancy offer an extensive reading in their various essays on Freudian psychoanalysis, notably in terms of the concept of the "mass" in relation to fascism.[43] The relation that is implied in this identification with the "retreat of identity" thus opens onto a number of questions concerning the very subject of the political, including the question of identification as the "social constitution" of identity and as the constitution of "social 'identity.'" In short, foreshadowing their primary argument in the Center's opening problematic concerning a relation that only ever takes place "on the ground of a *non-relation*," the reading of Freud's texts in these earlier essays opens onto a larger series of problematics in which we are asked to think of an originary or "arche-originary" sociality, an "arche-sociality" in which the retreat of the political is repeatedly played out.

While the question of relation constitutes a singular configuration in Freud's writings, it is clearly not specific to Freud alone. As Lacoue-Labarthe and Nancy also argue, in the wake of Hegel and specifically the Hegel who translates *politeuein* as "to lead the universal life in the city"—in other words, as the ability to "conduct relations as the life of the Subject alone"—it is the question of relation that is posited though an identity that constitutes itself only by "being-in-a-negative-relation-to-the-Other" (*RP*, 19), so that it is through Hegel that the question of relation is at once exposed as decisive and simultaneously effaced, dissimulated, or withdrawn. The reference to Hegel here is explored at greater length in Nancy's own lecture at the Center on "The Hegelian Monarch," first published in *Rejouer le politique*, in which the question of relation is rethought through a reading of Hegel's *Philosophy of Right*, specifically as it disarticulates the presuppositions concerning the State in Hegel's writings.[44] In the wake of Hegel, Lacoue-Labarthe and Nancy argue that the question of relation remains the "obsessive fear and stumbling block" for much of contemporary thought, citing the names of Bergson, Heidegger, Lévinas, Freud, Husserl, and Bataille as exemplary in this regard (*RT*, 197/*RP*, 134). Indeed, if it is only in the wake of Hegel and the "completion" of the political that the political becomes an "enigma, lacuna, or limit" for philosophy, then it is in light of this very closure or completion that a proliferation of questions at the end of the nineteenth century and the first half of the twentieth century begin to open up concerning the problem of relation, questions articulated through a number of associated terms—"of the Other, of the *alter ego*, of 'forms of sympathy,' of the agonistic, of the sources of morality and religion, of being as being-with, etc." (*RJ*, 24/*RP*, 117–18). At the same time, the concept of social relations also appears in the increasingly widespread emphasis on rethinking what constitutes "the people" on the one hand and sovereignty on the other, two concepts in which the question of the Subject cannot be dissociated from both the State and civil society. Again, what becomes at once effaced and presupposed here is the constitutive relationality informing these different political concepts, both individually and in their reciprocal determinations.

Before exploring any possible genealogy subtending this larger question of relation, a more modest elaboration of the concept is first necessary. For if rethinking the political cannot be reduced to a state formation or the effects of power, as Lacoue-Labarthe and Nancy argue, in what ways does it become necessary to rethink or rearticulate the question of relation, specifically as the question of relation opens toward a retreat of the essence of the political? Or rather, if behind the self-evidence of the political is dissimulated the self-evidence of the subject, then in what sense is this displacement of the subject's self-evidence a simultaneous opening toward a more radical destruction of the political subject from its metaphysical or onto-theological presuppositions?

In their opening address to the Center, Lacoue-Labarthe and Nancy discuss the necessity of taking up this question of relation, specifically when understood in terms of the "social bond," *lien*, or "tie," not as a presupposition and yet as "impossible to deduce or to derive from an initial subjectivity" (*RJ*, 25/RP, 118). Any initiative to question a politics of self-sufficiency, autonomy, or autocracy thus has no choice but to confront the question of relation, bond, or tie, not as a solution but as a question, one in which we are asked to think in terms of the "impossibility of presupposing the solution of the relation," whether this be in a sovereign subject or in a community. Indeed, it is in this sense that the question of relation cannot be detached from the retreat of the political itself. More specifically, it is precisely in terms of the retreat of the political that the "sharp end" of the question of relation comes into view, one that focuses for Lacoue-Labarthe and Nancy "a problem of *retreat* in relation to and *in* the installation of the political, in the erection of the political": "A problem of the *retreat*, and that is to say the problem of a non-dialectical negativity, the problem of an advent [*avènement*] (of identity and relation) by (the) abstraction [*par soustraction*] (of the 'subject'); or even the problem of that which gives relation *as* relation, insofar as the nature of relation (if it ever had a nature) is the reciprocal retreat of its terms, insofar as relation (but can one ever speak of [*the*] 'relation' [in the singular]?) is given by or proceeds from the division, from the incision, from the non-totality that it 'is'" *(RJ*, 26/RP, 119).

If Lacoue-Labarthe and Nancy insist on the question of relation as a fundamentally immeasurable measure of the retreat of the political, then their reference here to a "division" and "incision" radically displaces any appeal to a politics that *presupposes* the concept of social relations or a politics that derives from the subject. For as we have seen from the opening quotation from the Center's regulative statement, Lacoue-Labarthe and Nancy also point to a "disconnection" (*déliaison*) or a "dissociation" that remains at the very origin of the political event itself, a disconnection or dissociation that displaces any given relation understood as single or simple, or displaces any traditional ordering of ontological exposition, and so opens toward a relation—that which gives relation—that is never given in advance of its multiplicity and potentially plural articulations. Turning us back to the thought of dissociation and disconnection outlined in the earlier regulative statement, Lacoue-Labarthe and Nancy observe that "All the contributions to the Center's work have indeed implied, more or less directly or more or less thematically, a thought of 'relation' (or the 'social tie or bond' [*lien*]) as constituted by a spacing [*écart*] or a 'disconnection' [*déliason*] whose nature or structure has, until now, been formulated only in opposition—let us say—to self-relation [*rapport-à-soi*] (to the Subject as self-present [*présence-à-soi*]). It could be that the retreat is the—theoretical and practical—gesture of relation itself" *(RT*, 203/*RP*, 140).[45]

In other words, *the* political or *ta politika*, what defines human being(s) not just in terms of "social relations" but as *zoon politikon*, opens toward a relation that cannot be thought or articulated without taking into account a constitutive disconnection or dissociation, an untying and severance in and through which relations become possible to articulate in the first place. Or rather, a division, incision, or displacement is the enabling condition in which to think all relations *as* relations. In this sense,

> the question of relation and of the retreat…brought us back to the
> political by bringing us back to the question of a disjunction or a
> disruption more essential to the political than the political itself,
> and which, moreover, seems to us to provide the stake, on several
> different accounts, for more than one contemporary interpretation.
> A stake which, for now, we will sum up in the following way: the
> transcendental of the *polis* is not an organicism, whether that of a
> harmony or of a communion, nor that of a distribution of functions
> and differences. But no more is it an anarchy. It is the an-archy of the
> *arche* itself (assuming that the demonstrative pronoun "it" can still
> apply in the lexicon of the "transcendental." *(RJ*, 27/*RP*, 119–20)

Lacoue-Labarthe and Nancy's decision to situate the Center's work under the title of a question of the retreat of the essence of the political thus opens toward this "an-archy of the *arche* itself," at least when the *arche* is also translated in its Aristotelian definition as an originary or inaugural governing and occupation of public office by a ruling authority. The reopening of this Aristotelian definition to an originary disjunction responds to what Lacoue-Labarthe and Nancy further locate as the exigency of getting away from the metaphysical ground of the political or from any transcendent or transcendental ground that founds and finds itself in a subject. The question of relation, understood in terms of a constitutive disconnection and dissociation, a severing or desertion, not only repeatedly shows up in the Center's lectures and presentations, it remains, as Lacoue-Labarthe and Nancy acknowledge, "*the* central question." Moreover, any opposition to securing a ground for the subject or a ground that presupposes social relations cannot be dissociated from a question of finitude, and it is precisely this motif of finitude that also opens for Lacoue-Labarthe and Nancy onto the question of relation, which now constitutes the "true place" of finitude's determination (*RT*, 196–97/*RP*, 133). Or rather, as they further speculate, with all the precautions and hesitations necessary for any interrogation into or approach toward the question of *essence*, "as such," the question of relation is "even, perhaps, the question of the essence of the political."

Given the ways in which Lacoue-Labarthe and Nancy refer here to the essence of the political in terms of an essential relation, or a relation without relation, gesturing toward a retreat of the political that opens beyond or prior to the political, we can begin to argue that different political traditions, whether liberal, republican, or communitarian, socialist or communist, democratic or totalitarian, as well as more recent political proposals for a politics based on identity, recognition, or communication all tend to affirm social relations by refusing an *originary* disconnection or dissociation as the enabling condition of any given relation. Indeed, it now becomes possible to locate a number of pivotal terms for thinking the political as all more or less posited through the effacement of the relations they nevertheless presuppose, including the seemingly foundational concepts of the people, sovereignty, civil society, cosmopolitanism, and citizenship, but also concepts that appear to embrace a more pluralistic ambition, such as identity politics, the movement of movements, hybridity, radical democracy, the multitude, and so on. In other words, disconnection, dissociation, severance, and desertion are invariably posited as the (determinate) negation of social relations, social bonds, and social ties, and thus posited as the initiating cause of social fragmentation, the loss of social cohesion and group attachments, the dissolution of community, or the breakup of a larger social totality such as the nation—all of which are then overcome through the identification, strengthening, and eventual reunifying of relations, bonds, and ties that were already latently present and unified in their fictional origins. In short, dissociation and disconnection are understood not in terms of an an-archy of the *arche* but as a negation that is dialectically overcome and reappropriated in the always latent but arche-teleological realization of the self-present political subject or community, even when such a subject or community is proposed as plural. If it is then on the basis of these assumptions, presuppositions, and forms of dialectical reappropriation that a politics is then deduced or a position staked out, then it is precisely in rethinking these same assumptions and presuppositions and forms of reappropriation in terms of a retreat of the political that a "wholly other politics" comes into appearance and finds its initial force.

In a recent interview, Nancy refers back to his earlier work with Lacoue-Labarthe at the Center by recalling the question of limits that defines the relation between the political and the philosophical, limits that turn on thinking the political in terms of its retreat:

> Philosophy and politics are twins, contemporaries for the last twenty-six centuries. In the form of metaphysics understood as the thinking of presence (of given-present-being) (which does not exhaust the auto-deconstructive resources of this metaphysics), philosophy entails a politics of foundation and authority (of *arche*), just as politics entails a philosophy of the founding origin (be that in the people or in the sovereign or in both, or else precisely in the philosopher king). To speak of deconstruction is to speak of a relinquishing of the foundation (of the groundwork, the ground, the substrate, the support, and so on) that is situated at the very heart of the construction (What is there beneath the foundations? What ground? What blood? What origin? What is the cornerstone? What holds the stones together? What cement?). It is thus to speak not only of another politics that would change the foundation (common rather than private, equality rather than freedom) but of a complete transformation of politics or else a retracing of the political (what Lacoue-Labarthe and I had once called the retreat of the political in the sense of its *retracing*). That is what Derrida sought in his own way—not one more politics, but another thought *of* politics, or else another thought *than* politics, if politics is inextricably linked to the *arche* in general—the an-archy of the *arche*.[46]

In an "Annexe" first circulated to the participants of the Center during its existence and later published in *Le Retrait du politique*, Lacoue-Labarthe and

Nancy already suggest a renewed need to outline the definition and stakes of what they have termed the "retreat of the political," a necessity that arises not only from its central place in the organization of the Center's work but also from a more general unease in the reception of the term by the other participants. Beyond the positing of the retreat as the *Aufhebung* of the political and the questions this operation might imply for any reading of Hegel, and beyond the role the political plays in Marx, and thus, as we have previously suggested, the possible readings of the political this opens toward, both in Marx's own writings and their legacy, Lacoue-Labarthe and Nancy reconfigure the question of retreat in quite specific relation to Heidegger. For the references to *Entzug* or "withdrawal" and various closely associated terms in Heidegger's writings mark the *retreat* of all presentation, which only takes place in and as the concealment, dissimulation, or disappearance of what presents itself—in other words, the retreat that Heidegger proposes as the structure or movement of truth as *aletheia*. If Lacoue-Labarthe and Nancy refer to Heidegger in this context, then the retreat or withdrawal that marks Heidegger's writings cannot be detached from Derrida's extensive readings of this same structure or movement, notably in his seminal early essay "The Retreat of Metaphor" cited earlier. In light of Derrida's various texts on Heidegger and "The Retreat of Metaphor" in particular, the Heideggerian emphasis on the retreat of what presents itself is now read across and displaced toward a more general problematic of retreating, rewriting, and retracing (all various translations of *retrait*). This reading is not imposed *on* Heidegger's writings but takes up the ways in which Heidegger's various appeals to a *Zug* (as in *Entzug* or *Grundzug*) are also read across and displaced by his own references to a rift or tearing, notably those references to *Riss* as they are developed in the essay "The Origin of the Work of Art." In and as a withdrawal or retreat—the *retreat* or *Entzug* in the Heideggerian sense—or in and as the presentation that *takes place* as the concealment or the disappearance of what is presented, Derrida's reading of Heidegger thus opens toward a problematic of "taking-place," which Lacoue-Labarthe and Nancy describe, combining *Zug* and *Riss*, as a "re-tracing," and a retracing or rewriting that opens a "new" incision or inscription, which then cuts out again that which retreats (*RT*, 202/*RP*, 138–39). Here Lacoue-Labarthe and Nancy's scare quotes around "new" suggest a measure in which Derrida's reading does not *add* anything new to the original text, nor does it content itself with a critique, but it releases or re-releases a transformative potentiality closed off or effaced in Heidegger's own argument or more propositional statements.

In the discussion following one of Lacoue-Labarthe and Nancy's presentations at the Center, Derrida returns to the role that dissociation plays in the ontological structure of *Dasein* in Heidegger's writings, remarking that these writings are punctuated by a series of dissociative terms, such as *Zerstreuung* (a distraction or dispersion) or *Zersplitterung* (a fragmentation or splintering). What imports in these references, Derrida reminds us, is not the negative resonances that *zer* implies as a prefix: distraction, dispersion, fragmentation, and splintering are not to be taken negatively, in the sense of a dialectical negation or even rupture; rather, the prefix *zer* is to be understood in terms of the Latin root that informs the French or English *dis-*. Working through the different definitions of this prefix, we note that *dis-* implies a relation to something that is at least two, "in twain," and so further implies a movement in different directions, or a dispersion in which something comes apart (and so implies a movement away or abroad). *Dis-* also suggests a "between" that separates and distinguishes, a privation that implies removal or a reversal of action (and so a withdrawal in the sense of something dissociated), or an intensification, notably with verbs that already have a sense of division, separation, or undoing. In the terms that Derrida recalls from Heidegger, there is thus an "originary dis-tension" of *Dasein*, and it is precisely in such a distension that, for Heidegger, history and spatiality originate (*RT*, 204/*RP*, 141).

Derrida's brief suggestion raised in the Center's discussions returns us to §75 of *Being and Time*, "The Historicity of *Dasein* and World History," in which Heidegger turns to the ways in which *Dasein* is "dis-persed [*zer-streut*]" in the "multiplicity [*Vielerlei*] of what 'happens' daily."[47] As Heidegger argues, if *Dasein* "wants to come to itself, it must first *pull itself together* [*zusammenholen*] from the *dispersion* [*Zerstreuung*] and the *disconnectedness* [*Unzusammenhang*] of what has just happened, and because of this, it is only then there at last arises from the horizon of understanding of inauthentic historicity the *question* of how one is to establish *Dasein's* 'connectedness [*Zusammenhang*]'." The question that Heidegger asks here is then given two forms, one considered more "authentic" than the other, or one that gives rise to an "in-constancy" to *Dasein's* relation to what happens on an everyday basis and the other a "constancy." In the first, Heidegger suggests that it is not a question of asking "How does *Da-sein* acquire such a unity of connection [*die Einheit des Zusammenhangs*] that it can subsequently create a connection or linking [*Verkettung*] of the succession of 'experiences' that has ensued and is still ensuing?" Rather, it is a question of asking, "In which of its own kinds of being does it lose itself in such a way that it must, as it were, pull itself together only subsequently out of its dispersion, and think up for itself a unity in which this together is embraced? [*in welcher Seinsart seiner selbst verliert es sich so, daß es sich gleichsam erst nachträglich aus der Zerstreuung zusammenholen und für das Zusammen eine umgreifende Einheit sich erdenken muß?*]." It is only in light of this second question that Heidegger claims that "the resoluteness [*Entschlossenheit*] of the self against inconstancy [*Unständigkeit*] of dispersion is in itself *a steadiness that has been stretched along* [*die erstreckte Ständigkeit*]," an argument to which Derrida makes allusion in his emphasis on the originary distension of *Dasein* as the modality in which history and spatiality originate.

We might argue that Lacoue-Labarthe and Nancy's initial program for the Center is nothing more, or nothing less, than a demand to think through this section and argument from Heidegger's *Being and Time*, or at least a demand to reopen the questions Heidegger poses and simultaneously closes here *as* questions. Or rather, the impetus to question finds its initial motivation in demonstrating that Heidegger closes off and effaces the radicality of his own propositions, an argument that is reinforced through a longer reading of Heidegger's refusal to fully engage the question of *Mitsein* and *Mitdasein* in his writings, and a refusal whose "political" implications Lacoue-Labarthe and Nancy have taken up in other texts at some length.[48] In terms of the specific argument proposed in *Being and Time*, the question that remains open is whether Heidegger's demand that *Dasein* "pull itself together" reproduces a more general problematic of "gathering" in his writings and so effaces the originary and constitutive force of dispersion, disconnection, and loss out of which the "constancy" of a unity (*Einheit*) or selfhood is founded. Or rather, when Heidegger appeals to *Dasein* pulling itself together "only subsequently" (*nachträglich*) out of its dispersion, then the chronological implications of this sequence efface the radical *belatedness* of the unity that is produced, a belatedness that (as the discourse of psychoanalysis widely attests) is co-originary with the constitutive dispersion and dissociation of self-present subject or any established connection between subjects. At the same time (and here Stambaugh's translation opens a dimension of Heidegger's text that is more implied than stated) any attempt by *Dasein* to pull itself out of its dispersion and disconnection exposes this constancy to a fictioning force, in the sense that *Dasein* and its "kinds of being" (*Seinsart*) must "think up for itself"— that is, it must invent or create, or must perform—the "unity" in which this together is "embraced" (a fictioning that Heidegger will return to in his

Kantbuch). Any positing of a social relation, social bond, or social tie that acts as if there no constitutive and originary dissociation or disconnection will always expose itself to what is termed a "phantom of unity" (to take up the term employed by Lefort and Derrida in their presentations at the Center), even as this performance or fictioning is now constitutive of all social relations, ties, and bonds. In other words, it is here that we can begin to rearticulate Heidegger's appeal to different *Seinsart* or "kinds of being" as an extension of *Dasein*'s "constitution"—the *Seinsverfessung des Daseins* also outlined in *Being and Time*—which implies at once a political constitution, a disposition, and an articulation, in the sense of a fictional composition or writing. Or rather, any political constitution implies less a political standing, the "constancy" of the self-standing erection of the political, or the marking off of a position, than its distension, its being-with and alongside, at once a disseminating movement in different directions and a coming apart—all of which contribute to understanding the grammar of the "disposition of being" as a spacing, and all of which are inscribed in Lacoue-Labarthe and Nancy's demand to rethink the political in terms of its retreat.

The intricate details of language at work here cannot be detached from the larger stakes at play. In proposing to think the question of retreat, Lacoue-Labarthe and Nancy suggest that the Heideggerian and Derridean inflection of the retreat may be reread back across the writings of both Hegel and Marx. The passage from Heidegger will also have decisive implications for rethinking the question of collectivity and self-affirmation that is also at stake here. But what concentrates their argument is the claim that it is only in terms of Derrida's displacement of Heidegger's appeal to a retreat that the *philosophical* use of the term is justified and that it is precisely in its philosophical use that "the entire singular logic of the retreat demands to be articulated *in terms of the political*" (*RT*, 202/*RP*, 139). More specifically, "the retreat (of the essence, and thus of the 'retreat') of the political" is part of a more general problematic elaborated in the writings of Derrida of the *breach* (*l'entame*) or the trace, of the "trace without propriety" (*RJ*, 27/ *RP*, 120). But this acknowledgment of Derrida's deconstructive readings of Heidegger also implies both a questioning of Derrida's own writings and a simultaneous critique of their reception, an approach that was the very subject of the Political Seminar at Cérisy. For it is precisely the question of the political that reconfigures Derrida's problematic of the "breach," at least insofar as the question of the political for Lacoue-Labarthe and Nancy is said to *disinstall* this problematic from the "textual" field (at least when reduced to the "literary" field) to which it is commonly attributed (*RJ*, 27/*RP*, 120). Or rather, Lacoue-Labarthe and Nancy's texts for the Center can be read here as a way of aggravating the "*a priori* link" and "co-belonging" between the essence of the philosophical and the essence of the political that organizes the opening argument of Derrida's "The Ends of Man" essay, thereby reaggravating this *a priori* link in such a way as to draw out the "political" implications of this co-belonging, and to do so in ways that were (at least at the time) relatively circumscribed in both Derrida's writings themselves and certainly in their reception. In repeating and so displacing Derrida's problematic of the "breach" in rethinking the essence of the political, or in reading the "retreat of metaphor" across the "retreat of the political," Lacoue-Labarthe and Nancy are not suggesting that Derrida's writings begin to constitute a method that might be applied to the political (there is no "deconstructive politics" in this sense). Nor does this retreat imply a "nostalgic lamentation" for what withdraws, as if prescribing some return to the Greek *polis* and the pure, uncontaminated, and self-identical political origins of the West. On the contrary, as the affirmation opened by the "breach" also implies, Lacoue-Labarthe and Nancy argue that the retreat of the political "must allow, or even impose, the tracing anew of the stakes of the political" (*RT*, 194/*RP*, 131), even as it is from the retreat of the political that the political itself—its question or exigency, its disposition—arises. In short, the *retrait* of the political is less a method or a theory than that which, in and through its retreat, "makes something appear" or "sets something free."

In light of this affirmation, and an affirmation that is at once absolute and absolutely contingent, the "logic" of this *retrait* opens toward two general statements, statements that will allow us to circumscribe more clearly what is at stake in this retreat. First, the retreat of the political, in the sense of its withdrawal, is offered in the sense of its being well-known and in the sense of its obviousness, the "blinding obviousness" of the "everything is political," which, to recall, can be used to qualify our "enclosure in the closure of the political" (*RJ*, 18/*RP*, 112). As we have discussed earlier, the retreat of the political is thus the paradoxical condition of its sheer pervasiveness and total domination. But the retreat of the political is also the retracing of the political or its remarking, not in the manner of a *sortie* "outside" of the political or "beyond" the political but always "exceeding something in the political." Or again, if the question of the political turns on the question of its essence, and if this same retreat of the essence of the political renders possible a questioning that "refuses to confine itself to the categories ordinarily grouped under 'the political' and probably, in the long run, to the concept of the political it-self" (*RJ*, 18/*RP*, 112), then such a refusal does not turn on moving *beyond* the political in order to establish a new terrain or concept of the political. For the logic of the retreat is arguably less paradoxical than motivated by a number of different "operations" whose logic, as Lacoue-Labarthe reminds us, is not just incessantly transformative but "abyssal," for in every retreat, that from which one is retreating retraces itself, thus calling for an affirmation of the (retreat of the) political.

If we insist on working through again the terms in which Lacoue-Labarthe and Nancy think this retreat of the political, it is necessary to recognize that a pivotal dimension of their argument is the ways in which this retreat is recast in spatial terms, or in terms whose topographical and topological implications remain to be explored. For the retreat of the political is further delimited by the authors as something that "draws back into (or from) the modern *city*," where the city is understood in Arendtian terms as a "complex (eco-socio-techno-cultural) unity." In other words, within the constitution of that "complex unity" that remains irreducible to the State, it is precisely the city—or rather, the "civility" of the city—that pulls back in the retreat of the political (*RT*, 191/*RP*, 129). It is this withdrawal that simultaneously traces out a space in which "something" begins to emerge, a withdrawal that simultaneously traces out a spacing that, in its very emergence, "makes something appear or sets something free." And it is precisely in this emergence that what appears does so not in terms that give rise to a mere *sortie* outside or beyond the city but in terms that can now be read as topological—as a "'new' incision or inscription" that repeatedly cuts out again that which retreats.

The intrinsic potentiality of relations to disperse, distend, and dispose themselves in their (in)finite multiplicity thus returns us to the very space of the *polis* that we have had occasion to refer to on several occasions. Indeed, we want to argue that it is this founding political concept that also informs the very terms in which Lacoue-Labarthe and Nancy retreat the political. In their opening address at the Center's inauguration in 1980, Lacoue-Labarthe and Nancy argue, "The *polis* presupposes the relation—the *logikos* relation or *logos* as relation—which it nonetheless inaugurates—and perhaps this is what makes of it *the* philosophical ground" (*RJ*, 24/*RP*, 117). The argument echoes Lacoue-Labarthe and Nancy's rearticulation of Aristotle's definition of *zoon politikon*, suggesting that the *logos* that defines the political subject is not what is proper to the subject but itself to be articulated *as* a relation. Nancy has subsequently rephrased this same argument in terms of an appeal to *dialogue*, translated not as speech, discourse, or a conversation that is said to take place between two distinct and separate individuals—a space defined by a sphere of communication regulated by its ideal transparency— but as the rhythmic spacing or interruption of the logos, a rhythmic *spacing* of all *dia-logue, une partage des voix* that is now inscribed in and as the sharing out and division of the *ensemble*, of all being-together.[49] If this conclusion turns us back to Aristotle's seminal definition of *zoon politikon*, and thus to its pivotal place in established traditions of political philosophy, Lacoue-Labarthe and Nancy's presentation of Aristotle's concept of speech also opens a decisive displacement of this very tradition. For the "sharing out" of ethical speech is now subject to an aporia between a *sharing* and a simultaneous *division* of speech, and it is this very aporia that traverses all "being-together" and "living-together" at an oblique angle. Or it is this *partage* that opens any given *ensemble* to a division and dissociation—an incision—that is now the enabling, nonempirical condition and simultaneous affirmation of any *ensemble* as such.

If the *polis presupposes* the relation that it nonetheless inaugurates, Lacoue-Labarthe and Nancy's more general claim is dedicated to returning to the most "archaic constitution" of the political, and thus to exploring the "essence of the political assignation of essence." As they note, such questioning will reopen the very concept and value of the archaic in general. What is at stake here is the (philosophical) desire to find and found some origin, primitiveness, principle, or authority underlying and informing the political, some *principiat*, but only insofar as this origin exists in and through the divisions and dissociations that displace it as an origin, divisions and dissociations in which the question of relation becomes the "grounding" an-archy of the political *arche*, or the rhythmic spacing and relationality of all dialogue and political speech. But in what sense does the *polis* "inaugurate" a relation that it also presupposes? And even if we reintroduce the qualifying "perhaps" omitted in the English translation, in what sense does this presupposed and an-archic relation (perhaps) constitute "*the* philosophical ground" of the political? In short, why grant such a privilege to the *polis* in this inaugural and an-archic moment?

Such questions begin to suggest that the inaugural privilege claimed by Lacoue-Labarthe and Nancy is defined less by some doubt than by a constitutive ambivalence, one that is addressed in the writings of Heidegger as well as Arendt. In the case of Heidegger, Lacoue-Labarthe had already cited Heidegger's discussion of the *polis* in *Introduction to Metaphysics* in his lecture during the political seminar at Cérisy. In this text, Heidegger notes that *polis* is usually translated as city or city-state (*Staat und Stadtstaat*), terms, he suggests, that fail to capture its full sense. For *polis* means "the place [*die Stätte*], the there [*das Da*], wherein and as which *Da-sein* is as historical. The *polis* is the place of history [*die Geschichtsstätte*], the *Da in* which, *out* of which and *for* which history happens."[50] Or again, Heidegger defines the *polis* as "the ground or place of human *Dasein* itself," that is (as one recent translation suggests), it is the "spot" where all the *Bahnen* or "routes" humanity makes for itself "cross"; the *polis*, in essence, is this crossing-place, *die Kreuzungsstelle*. It is this reference to the *polis* that Derrida also recalls in his discussion of an originary "distension" of *Dasein*, as if what remains at stake here is forcing open this "spot" away from any essential gathering spot or single place of gathering, opening it to the site of an encounter with the other, a crossing-point rather than a self-contained spot, a nexus or node in a world of relations and trajectories, a world of comings and goings rather than a fixed, geometrical point or coordinate. What comes into relief here is a *polis* defined by its exteriority rather than any stable identity, groundwork, foundation, substance, or interiorized essence—in short, a *polis* that demands to be thought in and as the movement of the world "as play" rather than the walls of a city.

In response to this same argument from *Introduction to Metaphysics*, Lacoue-Labarthe comments that the essence of the political for Heidegger is, by itself, "nothing political" and that "no philosophical investigation can take measure of its 'retreat.'" In other words, if we are to maintain the word "political" in this context ("which I believe one must, out of a concern for clarity," Lacoue-Labarthe adds), this can only be on the condition, as Heidegger invites, of "completely re-elaborating the concept" (*RP*, 71), a task that suitably defines Lacoue-Labarthe's own writings following the Center's closure. Arendt's definition of the *polis* in *The Human Condition* also offers a forceful reelaboration and rearticulation of Heidegger's earlier commentary, one that comes into close proximity to Lacoue-Labarthe and Nancy's own articulation of the *polis* as presupposing the relation it nonetheless inaugurates. Defined as the "organization of the people as it arises out of acting and speaking together," such that its "true space" lies "between people living together," the *polis* becomes for Arendt the *creation* of a space *between* the participants. In principle, then, the *polis* can find its "proper location almost anytime and anywhere."[51] Or rather, the potential for relations to constitute themselves in their inherent plurality and multiplicity is not just constituted from a space

between but from the permanent displacement of the *polis* as predetermin-
ing enclosure or structure defined by the inclusion of the *ensemble*. On the
one hand, it is precisely this potential displacement of the *polis* from itself
that is closed off in Arendt's appeal to the *polis* as the "proper location" for
this very potential, at once circumscribing the space of the political within
a given contour, without exteriority. This is the argument that lends itself
to the claim that Arendt mourns the lost force of the *polis* in relation to our
contemporary retreat from the political into the social. On the other hand,
Arendt's argument opens the possibility of thinking relations in their (in)
finite plurality and multiplicity, in which it is precisely this emphasis on the
space *between* that opens the *polis* to its constitutive outside, so that it is precisely the *polis* that becomes the inescapable and enabling measure of thinking the very limit of the political in terms of its retreat. In this sense, the
reduction of the constitutive force of possible relations does not stem from
the fact that they are "social" relations but from the refusal to rearticulate
the limits that define the *polis* itself, in the sense that it is not just defined as
the inauguration of what it also presupposes (as Lacoue-Labarthe and Nancy
demonstrate) but as delimited by its own exteriority.[52]

How to rethink this exteriority is as decisive as it is problematic and a
question to which we will return at some length in subsequent chapters.
For the moment, the question remains how to think the relationality that
is constitutive of the *polis* and its (im)possibility without falling back or returning to the very anthropological determinations or inchoate *Schwärmerei*
Lacoue-Labarthe and Nancy seek to avoid. Or rather, as they remark concerning Pierre Clastres's seminal writings, would not the claims of political
anthropology and the positing of a society against the State already close off
and presuppose the question of relation in the very valorization of society,
even when inflected through the most radical appeals to rethink forms of
social and anthropological organization?[53] But the same question can be now
posed to Lacoue-Labarthe and Nancy and their insistence on retreating the
political. For even if the *polis* presupposes the relations that it nonetheless
inaugurates, what justifies or legitimates the *polis* itself as the inaugural, initiating, or "proper" scene of all relations in their (in)finite plurality and multiplicity? And what justifies this inaugural moment not just in relation to
the Greek *envoi* and the institution of Western thought of the political, but
in light of the related attempt to think the "an-archy of the *arche*" of the political, the very terms in which the Center proposes to rethink the essence of the
political in the first place? In short, does the *polis* not simply presuppose the

relations it nonetheless inaugurates but presuppose an exteriority through which it constitutes itself as *polis*, an exteriority that itself comes to delimit and simultaneously rearticulate the (im)possibility of relations in their (in)finite plurality and very multiplicity? In short, if the *polis* presupposes the relation that it nonetheless inaugurates, and if it is precisely this argument that *perhaps* opens onto the question of *the* philosophical ground— and such questions are not situated in terms of simply negating the *polis* but re-elaborating and displacing its spatial presuppositions—how should we begin to rethink the ways in which Lacoue-Labarthe and Nancy turn this hesitation concerning the *polis* into the singularly aporetic condition for thinking how the political today *takes place*?

It is a significant feature of the reception of the Center's work and Lacoue-Labarthe and Nancy's texts in particular that the question of (social) relations appears marginal or even inconsequential when compared to the more predictable question of politics, notably the question as to how to derive a politics from the various proposals concerning an interrogation into the essence of the political understood as the simultaneous retreat of the political. Not that the question of relation has not been taken up by others writing in close proximity to the problematics raised by Lacoue-Labarthe and Nancy.[54] But the question of social relations as articulated in the Center's work is largely effaced in the literature in comparison with the more dominant political themes animating the papers and discussions. If we have presented Lacoue-Labarthe and Nancy's various proposals for the Center in some detail, drawing extensively from the language in which they themselves present the Center's proposal to retreat the political, this is not only to reinforce the larger conditions, contexts, and stakes in which to rethink and rearticulate the question of relation. It is also to argue that the question of relation cannot be detached from the retreat of the political that frames the various proposals for the Center and so cannot be detached from the larger series of concepts and problematics also defining the Center's lectures and discussions. The question of relation is thus articulated in terms that do not simply animate but impose the initial presentation of the Center's work, including the question of the essence of the political, the relation between the political and the philosophical, the rearticulation of the Western tradition informing the political subject, and the reframing of the question of totalitarianism. Indeed, as Lacoue-Labarthe and Nancy intimate, the question of relation not only finds its conceptual force in its proximity to these larger terms, but it also constitutes—"even," "perhaps"—the very essence of the political.

If this argument concerning the question of relation continually turns us back to reciprocal determinations between the political and the philosophical, the argument also opens onto two hypotheses and thus two possible trajectories in which Lacoue-Labarthe and Nancy propose to rethink the retreat of the political proposed in the first place. Indeed, crucial to the chapters that follow, these two hypotheses turn toward two spatial problematics or two topological features that we have seen beginning to emerge in Lacoue-Labarthe and Nancy's argument.

The first hypothesis returns us to the question of totalitarianism and the writings of Arendt discussed earlier. As Lacoue-Labarthe and Nancy claim, "Our 'retreat' accompanies, in reality, a retreat of the political *itself* within and from the epoch of its world domination. And that is to say that the 'everything is political' conceals an effacement of the specificity of the political. This specificity implicates the political as a space (or as an act) separate and distinct (but not in an illusory way) from the other components of the social whole. The retreat would thus retrace the contours of this specificity, whose actual and effective conditions would need to be reinvented (this is, for example, one aspect of Arendt's thinking)."

The second hypothesis suggests an alternative trajectory: "Our retreat operates in relation to the political in general and absolutely, and that is to say in relation to the intrinsic political determination of the onto-theology of *Realpolitik* as it appears through the theoretical face of the Hegelian State or through the empirical face of the calculation of forces. What retraces itself, then, would be a space *other* than political (which was, moreover, Bataille's route and, no doubt, finally Heidegger's). In any case, this 'other' would remain to be named" (*RT*, 202/*RP*, 139).

Acknowledging that these two hypotheses were more or less present throughout the talks and discussions held at the Center and reiterated in Nancy's more recent interview cited earlier, Lacoue-Labarthe and Nancy insist that it is not a question of choosing between the two hypotheses. If the political seminar at Cérisy sought to "breach the inscription of a *wholly other* politics," as its organizers had stated, then these two hypotheses reinforce the ways in which this inscription of an other politics is not simply breached in order to secure another space for the political, a space that might exist *beyond* the political. For this inscription reopens the political to its permanent reinscription, one whose breaching amounts neither to a finite closure nor to a mere conceptual dispersion or evacuation of the political, where the political is said to exist free of all borders and spatial delimitation. Or if there is a "constitutive dilemma" here (to recall Fraser's critique), it is not one that simply gives itself over to neoliberal consensus, at least not without some violence to the stakes involved, and not without retreating into a form of political self-assurance and self-sufficiency that these hypotheses refuse to guarantee or legitimate. The question still remains, in other words, whether the retreat of the political is inscribed in a "retraced politics" or in something "other" than the political. Or the question still remains whether effacing these hypothetical questions, closing them off in the name of a recognizable politics, or seeking a passage from the question of the political to a discernible and fully realizable political practice (what Fraser terms the "step into politics") all simultaneously efface the question of relation that traverses Lacoue-Labarthe and Nancy's two closing hypotheses at an oblique angle.[55]

These two hypotheses can be rephrased in such a way that Lacoue-Labarthe and Nancy do not offer us a *passage* to a recognizable politics, or a dilemma, or a possible dialectical reconciliation of these hypotheses. Rather, they offer us an *aporia*. Indeed, if the two hypotheses open toward two trajectories that are impossible to reconcile, then this aporia now constitutes less the impossibility of politics, or its paradox in Arendt's sense, or a "dialectics of aborted desire," as Fraser suggests, for the elaboration of this aporia is the enabling condition for thinking the retreat of the political in the first place. Moreover, within the terms established by Lacoue-Labarthe and Nancy's two hypotheses, the aporia that closes their proposal is easily effaced in light of a demand for a politics that is based on the more predictable distinction between theory and practice, at least insofar as such a distinction rests on the positing of political discourse in terms of a "coherency" in which the passage from theory to practice is invariably articulated. Responding to this distinction between theory and practice and the assumptions underlying these terms, Lacoue-Labarthe and Nancy argue that the distinction itself is constructed around a "teleology of the realization of theory in practice" and thus upon a "merely 'ideal' or 'regulative' status of this very teleology," one in which the passage to a recognizable politics follows a path that is linear in its quasi-eschatological trajectory. In short, it is this demand for a recognizable politics that effaces the very aporia that organizes Lacoue-Labarthe and Nancy's closing hypotheses concerning the retreat of the political.

Nancy's own writings subsequent to the closure of the Center may be read in part as an incessant rearticulation of this same aporia.[56] The appeal to aporia has also been one of the decisive motifs of Derrida's writings as well. But within the more circumscribed terms proposed in Lacoue-Labarthe and Nancy's texts for the Center, the aporia outlined across the two concluding hypotheses does not lead to the positing of a terrain (however contested and conflictual) but opens to a quite specific articulation or, more strictly, *delimitation* of (a) space, and notably a retracing of the contours that circumscribe (a) space. It is this retracing that then seeks to outline and circumscribe not just the (re)invention of a space but the "contours" of a (new) political "space" or "ground," a space that is not delimited and framed with recognizable contours but traces out an opening or a spacing in which to think the very closure of the political. In this sense, such a space is never autonomous, fully enclosed, or self-contained. Neither is it merely framed nor does it exist without frame. If Lacoue-Labarthe and Nancy point toward the political as a space that is "separate and distinct" from the other components of the social whole, then this separation and distinction does not mark off a self-enclosed or autonomous space designated for politics alone and its specificity (the political as such, the essence of the political) but opens toward a retreat of the political that would incessantly and permanently "*retrace* the contours of this specificity." In other words, according to the logic informing the retreat of the political, in every retreat, that from which one retreats retraces itself. It is precisely in this incessant retracing of the political in its retreat that the political and its contours are incessantly and repeatedly invented and reinvented, if indeed such an invention is still called the political (as in Lefort's appeal to the "invention of democracy") or if such an invention is not in fact the possibility and radical potentiality of thinking and remarking a space "*other* than political."[57]

The rearticulation of this aporia can be rephrased in terms of Lacoue-Labarthe and Nancy's insistence on rethinking the political in terms of its closure. For this closure is not the condition of a passage (from theory to practice, from an interrogation into the essence of the political to politics, from an ethics to a politics, from speculation to the real), a passage in which the closure is simply the enabling condition of its eventual and dialectical self-effacement. Nor is it a question of obstructing this passage (and here the earlier phrasing of Heidegger "obstructing" the passage in which to think *Dasein*'s radical alterity remains crucial and suggests one of the stakes implied in rethinking the terms of this aporia). But nor is the closure a way of securing and enclosing the political in its self-sufficiency, self-regulated identity, or autonomy. For this closure is continually reopened in the retreat of the political, reopened in the sense in which what completes itself does not cease to complete itself. It is this retreat of the political that then forces open again the decisive question posed by Lacoue-Labarthe and Nancy in their introductory texts: "On the basis of what, against what, or along what, does this closure trace itself?"

Pursuing the spatial and topological implications of these initial descriptions and questions, the closing hypotheses suggest that it is precisely the *polis* that constitutes not just the central and decisive emblem of this aporia but its enabling condition, for the *polis* becomes the term in and through which to think the retracing of the contours of the political in its specificity. According to the first hypothesis, it is the contours of the *polis* that do not form a space separate and distinct from the social whole but demand retracing (and here we recall how the argument doubles back across Lacoue-Labarthe and Nancy's reading of Marx's references to the *Staatswesen* in his "Critique of the Gotha Program"). As Lacoue-Labarthe and Nancy note, and as later chapters will explore more fully, Arendt's writings will clearly play a prominent role in this retracing of the political specificity of the *polis*. The second hypothesis would respond to a quite different sense of that founding space of the political subject. For here the space that is other than political would respond to the argument that there is no *polis* that exists prior to the articulation of relations, or prior to the endless circulation, becoming, articulation, relation, and disposition of being—in short, there exists no political space that is instituted prior to the an-archy of the *arche*. A space "other" than political would then respond to the ways in which this an-archy is registered in the constitutive disconnection or dissociation of any given relation, by a relation that is given by or proceeds from an incision—in short, by that an-archy that is more essential to the political than the political itself. If Lacoue-Labarthe and Nancy refuse to choose between these ways of thinking the irreducible specificity of the political—between its permanent reinvention and a space other than political—then the *polis* constitutes the aporetic hinge to their closing hypotheses, one that they refuse to close off or resolve.

More pointedly for our contemporary situation, the *polis* is at once the space in which the political exists within the founding political institution of the West and that space whose limits, today, remain not just open to question but subject to all those acts of deterritorialization that have come to be known through the term "globalization"—in other words, the terms in which the *polis* has become seemingly irrelevant for our contemporary, global politics. If Lacoue-Labarthe and Nancy's closing hypotheses turn on an aporia, then such an aporia might begin to suggest what still remains at stake in thinking this effacement or withdrawal of the *polis* within the contexts of contemporary globalization, or at least a discourse of globalization that refuses to address and engage the question of exteriority that the *polis* simultaneously exposes. Or again, this aporia reopens how we are to think the political in light of a "political sphere" that contemporary forms of neoliberalism seek to efface. As Nancy claims in recent interview concerning the future possibilities of a "(neo)communist" politics, such a politics

> could be a politics of spacing as well as of collecting, a politics of the singular as well as of the common. But these formulas do not yet amount to "politics"—far from it! A philosopher does not have a politics to propose: he has to explicate the conditions under which politics is possible today. And these conditions are perhaps now in the process of becoming very different from those we have known: that is, first of all, that "politics" cannot aspire to the totality of social existence, common or not common. Marx wanted politics to disappear as a separate sphere, "to impregnate all the spheres of social existence": but today it is the proper distinction of the political sphere that requires renewed attention (because it is this distinction that liberalism wants to undermine if not suppress).[58]

If the aporia that closes the Center works to reopen this "proper distinction," it is not simply to concede the terrain of the political to neoliberalism, nor to enclose the assumed propriety of the political off from its contamination by the nonpolitical. The aporia works instead to *unwork* these distinctions, displacing this opposition, thus reopening this "political sphere" to an incessant displacement of its limits (again, it is precisely this question of displacement for Lacoue-Labarthe and Nancy that necessitates their turn to Marx). Or again, such an aporia is articulated in and as what Lacoue-Labarthe had described as a "non-localisable place," "*sans espace propre*," opening toward the barely noticeable parenthetical remark that the retreat of the political "draws back into (or from) the modern city" (*RT*, 191/*RP*, 129). Lacoue-Labarthe and Nancy rephrase what withdraws here as the *civité* of the city, as if the founding measure of this "civility" were not an attribute of the subject, nor the State, nor a way of defining a good citizen, but the immeasurable an-archy of any given *arche*.[59] In is in such an-archy that the relation to the "space" of the *polis* remains at stake and still in play, not because the terms of the argument are subsumed within the discourse of globalization but because it is through this very aporia that the question of the collective and associated forms of political organization—in short, being-in-common as being-in-relation—also begins to reemerge.

In retrospect, we could suggest that this aporia defines the closure of the Center itself as a space, in the sense that it is less a question of finding a passage *beyond* the problematics defining the Center's existence and moving on to a new space, but of re-marking the repetition of these problematics, and so of retracing the contours that define the Center's own specificity and political limits, its own *Staatswesen*. In the terms that Lacoue-Labarthe and Nancy employ in their closing letter to the participants, it is a question of prompting a "rupture" through which there perhaps exists a "chance that something else might reinvent itself," a rupture that itself constitutes a "political exigency" and that demands not just a pause but also the possibilities ("when the time comes, if it comes") of a "new departure" (*RP*, 147). In this sense, the rereading of Lacoue-Labarthe and Nancy's texts for the Center resists any simple passage beyond the problematics at stake in the Center's very inauguration, suggesting that their appeal to a rupture here should be read as a *bord antérieur extrême*, opening toward a more discrepant movement of rupture and doubling, of suspense and suspension, of repetition and displacement, in short, a disconnection and dissociation that constitutes the aporetic conditions for continuing and moving on. It is in this sense that the closing letter to the Center's participants also recalls Lacoue-Labarthe and Nancy's closing presentation at the end of the *Les fins de l'homme* conference at Cérisy. They conclude,

> Something was produced over these last six days. Not one thing but, yes, something—a relative coherence, a certain connection or linking up [*enchaînement*]. In any case, crossings [*croisements*] took place, an interweaving formed and wove itself [*un entrelacement s'est formé, cela s'est tissé*]. One might be led to conclude: there is a text. This does not mean that *a* text is written or is now finished writing itself but that there were, let us say, certain emphases [*insistances*] (after all, what is a text if it is not a certain network of emphases [*réseau d'insistances*]?) That's what seemed to us desirable to collect up and hold on to, at least provisionally. Not in order to conclude, but rather to reserve the possibility of *starting out again*. (*FH*, 689)

As if echoing the various ways of translating the *polis* as a *Kreuzungsstelle* or crossing place, the aporia that concludes the texts for the Center becomes rewritten here and its after-effects disclosed, not as a passage "beyond" but as a chiasmus, crossing, or text, not as a simple or single point to be grasped or critiqued but exposed to an essential dispersion or disposition, to that play and spacing of relation that now takes place in—and as—a network.

2

From Paradox to *Partage*

On Citizenship and Teletechnologies

The coming of all to the public relation—"citizenship"—is what constitutes the political as a sense to come but, consequently, also as a sense that cannot be subsumed under the signification of a "State," at least not without implying at the same time the multiplicity and pluri-locality of relations within "the" relation that is not "one."

—Jean-Luc Nancy

Devoted to the concept of citizenship as its annual theme, the opening protocol to a recent Humanities and Social Science Congress offers a representative overview of the challenges confronting citizenship at the beginning of the twenty-first century, notably as the concept is affected by the various transformations and tendencies defining contemporary globalization. Opening with the claim that citizenship is itself a "paradoxical concept," the protocol then outlines the terms in which citizenship can be thought today:

Underlying [citizenship's] apparent meaning of belonging are the conflicting notions we attach to it—rights versus duties, freedom versus responsibility, local allegiance versus global affiliation—and the tensions that arise from these notions. Not constrained by political or geographical boundaries, the concept of citizenship extends to communities of interest, sexual orientation, disability, gender, ethnicity, and a host of variously defined identities. The paradox of citizenship is further reflected in the differences in citizenship over time—from the historical experience of citizenship as something bestowed upon individuals and reflective of imperialism and colonialism to present perceptions of citizenship as self-defined, self-appointed and democratic.

The way we define citizenship, and our sense of belonging (or exclusion) are influenced by the social, economical, cultural and physical environments we inhabit, while artistic and literary creation often serves to express, examine or resolve the inherent paradoxes we perceive. The multiplicity of definitions is a reality that lends itself to exploration from a multi-disciplinary angle.

The sub-themes [proposed for the Congress]—Environments, Exclusions and Equity—provide further points of reference for academic investigation. As a collective citizenry, we share the responsibility for our natural and social environments. Environmental sustainability has become an increasingly pressing concern for governments at all levels, and individual citizens of all countries. What constitutes the paradox of citizenship is that it is at once inclusive and exclusive—intentional, explicit, covert or unintended, individual and groups' exclusion from the citizenry carries clear implications for the society at large. Finally, questions of equity remain at the centre of most debates surrounding social issues.[1]

The protocol's general proposal reproduces the increasingly widespread argument that citizenship should be expanded as a concept to include a more flexible array of rights and sociopolitical issues, embracing at once "communities of interest, sexual orientation, disability, gender, ethnicity," as well as a "host of variously defined identities." In light of this inherent plurality and constituent diversity of political referents, the concept of citizenship now refracts into a "multiplicity of definitions" and a related survey of "multidisciplinary" angles and "sub-themes," in which the concept can be now approached not just thematically but from different disciplinary perspectives, even including artistic and literary creation. Given the loss of established "political or geographical boundaries," and notably their displacement through the global proliferation of communication and information technologies, the multiplicity of definitions further corresponds to the ways in which citizenship is not determined in any univocal or linear manner but influenced by a constellation or confluence of different factors, including the "social, economical, cultural and physical environments we inhabit."

Taken to be representative of recent debates concerning citizenship within the contexts of contemporary globalization, the protocol's general claims prompt three related questions. First, if the expansiveness of the concept of citizenship tends toward a larger survey of sociopolitical identities and a multiplicity of potential definitions and disciplinary perspectives, in what sense does this transition and its supporting argument amount not just to a potential (re)politicizing of citizenship beyond its traditional limits or categories but to a concept of citizenship that at once presupposes and simultaneously effaces the very question of the political, or the political *as such*? In other words, in what sense does the rethinking of citizenship proposed in the protocol touch not just on the play of interests and forces characterizing contemporary politics and social existence on a global scale but the very concept of the political, *ta politika*—in short, the archi-constitution of the "political animal"? A measure of the difficulty in which to approach this initial question stems in part from the protocol's presupposition that citizenship is synonymous with, or reducible to, "social issues," "society at large," and "variously defined identities," as if the concept of citizenship only finds its contemporary, political significance in terms of its *social* relevance and the sociocultural constitution of these various identities. No doubt one of the intended benefits of transforming the concept into social issues and various sociocultural identities is to enable a wider display of citizenship's social effects (in the wake of Thurgood Marshall's seminal distinction between civic, political, and social rights[2]) as well as a wider determination of its potential social and cultural implications, including how citizenship actually touches the day-to-day experiences of individuals and groups existing either within a given polity (now translated into "society at large") or excluded from it. But the question still remains whether it is precisely in this transition to more social, if not sociological, definitions of citizenship that the question of the political is effaced, and effaced precisely at the point at which the politics of citizenship is reconfigured according to the tendencies informing globalization, the displacement of political and geographical boundaries defining the sovereignty of the nation-state, the creation of new forms of allegiance, affiliation, and assemblage on a global scale, and the related proliferation of communication and information technologies. A further measure by which to assess the displacement of the political into the social is inscribed in the protocol's continual oscillation in ascribing citizenship to individuals, identities, groups, society-at-large, and collective citizenry, as well as in its more expansive survey of related concepts (belonging, allegiance, affiliation, equity, and democracy), as if the concept of citizenship were pluralist enough to merely presuppose the relative inclusivity of each of these terms within its newly discovered purview.

Secondly, the opening protocol organizes the more expansive concept of citizenship under the term "paradoxes," a logic that presumably serves to capture many of the difficulties confronting the concept of citizenship today. These difficulties include a genealogy of the concept's long and conflictual history to the present, its complex relation to the multiple tendencies defining globalization, and its relation to transformations in the sovereignty of nation-states (including the discrepancy between "developed" countries, the role of citizenship in "weak" states, and the myriad forms of existence that fall outside of both). The difficulty of circumscribing the concept of citizenship with any clarity is further related to the difficulty of establishing what constitutes belonging, identity, and affiliation within multicultural societies, or what constitutes rights and norms within new geopolitical arenas and the cosmopolitanism of trans- or postnational institutions, organizations, and exchanges. But in what ways do the myriad difficulties outlined here specifically evolve—or devolve—into paradoxes? And in what ways do the difficulties posed by citizenship in these different contexts open the more vexing question as to the continued viability of citizenship itself as a concept for rethinking the future of democracy, as if the paradox in question becomes the dialectical, historicist, or teleological means through which citizenship either finally exhausts its significance and political signification or opens itself to new conceptual determinations? The question thus posed here is whether the protocol's appeal to paradox (for which the term "global citizenship" constitutes an initial emblem) not only foregrounds but also simultaneously effaces the aporias informing both the genealogies and global contexts for rethinking citizenship today? Or does there exist another logic informing citizenship—another syntax of the political relation, another grammar subtending the "coming of all to the public relation"—that remains irreducible to paradox?[3]

Lastly, it is a conspicuous feature of recent debates concerning citizenship that the question of technology plays a relatively marginal and subordinate role, at least when compared to its political, economic, social, and cultural implications, even if the same technology, notably telecommunications and information technology, figures prominently in any discussion of globalization and its principle tendencies. The question at stake here thus turns on the ways in which contemporary communication and information technologies both touch on as well as transform the very concept of citizenship itself. Indeed, the question at stake turns on the ways in which these same technologies provoke a further displacement between the potential (re)politicizing of citizenship within the contexts of globalization and the necessity of rethinking the political as such.

As the opening protocol intimates in its very structure, the narrative in which rethinking the discourse of citizenship is proposed continually fragments or displaces itself from any linear unfolding, as if the discourse of citizenship folds back within itself a division or discrepancy between the absolute *contingency* of citizenship in a global context and the purported (and yet historically or culturally contingent) *universality* of human rights, a tension from which the discourse of citizenship nevertheless finds much of its conceptual force and contemporary, political pertinence.[4] The narrative also opens itself toward a measure of radical uncertainty not just as to the ends and goals to which citizenship is traditionally oriented—the evolving progression in Marshall's analysis in which civil and political rights culminate with an affirmation of social rights, the possibilities of closing the "citizenship gap," the creation of fully inclusive, participatory democracies, and so on—but also an uncertainty as to the critical relevance and very future of the concept in the twenty-first century, notably under conditions informed by globalization, the plight of refugees and noncitizens, and the global and local migrations of labor in the contexts of contemporary capitalism. Echoing the protocol's opening claim that citizenship is itself a paradoxical concept, Derek Heater concludes a recent history of citizenship by asserting that a "paradox strikes at the very heart" of the concept: "Interest in the subject and status is now greater than it has been for some two hundred years or more; yet at the same time, it might appear to be disintegrating as a coherent concept for the twenty-first century."[5] Responding to the same question of citizenship's uncertain future as a concept, Herman van Gunsteren proposes instead to displace an understanding of citizenship in terms of "destiny" to one that embraces more recognizable if precarious "communities of fate," where community is understood to include both physical environments as well as virtual communities, encompassing at once territories and networks.[6] And in one of the most decisive test-cases for proposing post- or transnational concepts of citizenship—the European Union and its constitution—Étienne Balibar concludes a recent essay with the phrase, "Europe impossible: Europe possible."[7]

And yet, as these different references begin to suggest, the paradoxes underlying these narratives can also be rewritten, for the fragmentation, displacement, and potential disintegration of those linear narratives in which citizenship is historically shaped can also be read as the enabling condition in which to rearticulate the concept and its potentially multiple genealogies. This is notably the case when the discourse of citizenship refuses to devolve into mere fragmentation and eventual dispersion, nor assumes a linear, narrative exposition toward a clear "destiny," but embraces a multiperspectival analysis and a "pluralist ethos."[8] The refusal of a narrative in which citizenship unfolds as a coherent or linearly evolving discourse now coincides with the appeal to a "multiplicity of definitions" and "multi-disciplinary angles" proposed in the opening protocol and widely discussed in the recent debates concerning citizenship's continued viability as a concept. This multiplicity and pluralization of the concept not only finds its critical and rational justification in relation to the multiple tendencies defining globalization. It equally responds to forms of multiculturalism characteristic of numerous contemporary societies; to the differentiated, flexible, and hybrid constitution of different groups, political identities, and subject positions (positions both marked and continually displaced by and beyond the intersection of gender, sex, class, ethnicity, and race); and to the extension of rights to cultural differences that remain irreducible to the traditional categories of civil, political, and social rights (i.e., prison rights, disability rights, sexual rights, children's rights, animal rights, environmental rights, and so on). In Aihwa Ong's succinct terms, the "demands for cultural acceptance, along with affirmative action mechanisms to increase demographic diversity in major institutions and areas of public life," have shifted discussions of citizenship from a focus on political practice based on shared civic rights and responsibilities to an insistence on the protection of "cultural difference."[9] In the context of the opening protocol, this protection and affirmation of cultural difference further extends to citizenship as "self-defined" and "self-appointed," a claim that participates within a more expansive set of discourses concerning identity politics, calls for cultural diversity, feminist interventions in citizenship debates, a politics of recognition, as well as the "right to be different" (itself a simultaneous extension and displacement of the former "right to have rights"). Similarly, the expansiveness of citizenship as a concept corresponds to the pressures and demands imposed by the increasing number of excluded and marginalized peoples (indigenous peoples, undocumented migrant labor, guest workers, refugees), to those living within and between existing sovereign states and their juridical systems, to new articulations of inclusivity and exclusivity, and to the role citizenship might play in the transition from established political and social categories to the biopolitical management of life itself. In this more recent context, the future of citizenship as a constitutively plural and multidisciplinary concept is then secured through its own rearticulation with a number of other concepts, including theories of cosmopolitan democracy, global citizenship, global civil society, diasporic citizenship, embodied and performative citizenship, nomadic citizenship, denizens, flexible citizenship, multicultural citizenship, radical democracy, universal personhood, cyber-citizens, networked citizens—to cite a number of recently proposed terms. The question thus remains whether this rearticulation of the concept marks a rupture with the discourse of citizenship, its dialectical *Aufhebung* into new political concepts and frameworks, or some other modality in which to define citizenship's future transformations or conceptual displacements.

Faced with these transformations and displacements in a global context, a new and potentially more decisive paradox then begins to emerge. For if the constitutive plurality and multidisciplinary perspectives informing the identity of the citizen open to a more flexible array of rights claims, and if the proposal and demand for rights continues to burgeon, then, as Heater also argues, "citizenship, which claims a cohering function, must either shrink to a weaker, because competing, form of allegiance among others, or expand to embrace them all and lose its coherence."[10] For many, it is precisely this paradox and potential evacuating of the concept that is already inherent in such terms as cosmopolitanism, radical democracy, or global citizenship, as if mirroring the related question whether appeals to multiculturism and identity politics prolong a discourse of citizenship in the very act of dismantling or destroying it. For others, notably Michael Walzer, citizenship participates within a larger concept of "critical associationalism," opening alongside a parallel set of allegiances and commitments, even as citizenship remains capable of mediating between them in the constitution of a civil society.[11] For others again, these different paradoxes and the potential incoherence or effacement of citizenship as a pertinent political concept all come into permanent yet equally productive tension with the potential repoliticizing of citizenship and its expansion through multiple forms of allegiance and membership. The question thus remains whether it is the State, civil society, or a more global institution, organization, or assemblage that becomes the primary site for identification and allegiance.[12] In light of these various proposals, the rearticulation of the concept of citizenship thus includes the potential to rethink the ambivalent role of citizenship within the revolutionary tradition, where the bestowal of citizenship is not just the distinguishing mark of "the people" and their national allegiance, nor just reflective of imperialism and colonialism as the protocol suggests, but perceived (and by many in the world, still perceived) as the enabling measure of both personal and collective freedom or the basis for radical social transformation. The same demand to rethink citizenship also raises the potential to reconfigure the very identity of the social and political subject in its (irreducible) relation to the sovereign State, to reconfigure the relation between conditions of belonging and exclusion in a world informed by neoliberalism and globalization, and to offer citizenship as a potent political concept for rethinking the future of democracy beyond the post-Westphalian state, cold war geopolitics, the collapse of the communist bloc, and the virtual disintegration of the welfare state. In short, working through these genealogical as well as contemporary problematics points not to citizenship's lack of coherence but the structural necessity of its flexibility, suppleness, and (re)creation as a constitutively paradoxical concept.

Given the potential ways in which citizenship might be rearticulated today, the choice, then, is not between the coherence and incoherence of citizenship as a concept. Nor is it simply a question of the continued viability of the concept in the face of empirical evidence, including the quantitative changes in global displacement (over twenty-five million refugees in the world at the beginning of the twenty-first century, tens of millions of undocumented migrant workers, including an estimated 100 million people as unregistered domestic migrant workers in China alone).[13] The question is now threefold, reconfiguring the paradoxical status of citizenship in potentially new ways.

First, if one of the most pressing problems posed today is permanent "access" to rather than simply "entitlement" to citizenship, as Balibar argues, then this distinction points to an "active and collective civil *process*" rather than a simple legal status.[14] Or as Balibar further argues, it suggests a "collective political practice" that is always "in the making." In this sense, citizenship becomes a continual site of struggle and conflict, in which the desire for "permanent" access to citizenship is continually exposed to the necessity of engaging in a civil "process" that precludes permanence and juridical legitimation. The question thus remains not only how this set of distinctions relates to recent characterizations of citizenship as paradoxical but also whether this very "process" should remain, in all senses, civil. At the same time, the question remains how this emphasis on the civil both reproduces the biopolitical management of the citizen within a State formation while marking off the other as *un*civil (the immigrant, the refugee, the foreigner, and so on).

Second, and arguably more radical in its implications, the question remains whether the "nexus" between human being and citizen is now broken, and so whether other figures come into existence that replace the concept of the citizen altogether and point to different forms of allegiance or community. Taking up Arendt's earlier writings on the subject, Giorgio Agamben proposes the figure of the refugee to meet this task,

Given the by now unstoppable decline of the nation-state and the general corrosion of traditional political-juridical categories, the refugee is perhaps the only thinkable figure for the people of our time and the only category in which one may see today—at least until the process of the dissolution of the nation-state and its sovereignty has achieved full completion—the forms and limits of a coming political community. It is even possible that, if we want to be equal to the absolutely new tasks ahead, we will have to abandon decidedly, without reservation, the fundamental concepts through which we have so far represented the subjects of the political (Man, the Citizen and its rights, but also the sovereign people, the worker, and so on) and build our political philosophy anew starting from the one and only figure of the refugee.[15]

In light of Agamben's proposal, we might ask what remains of the paradoxes animating contemporary discussions of citizenship when this nexus between being and citizen is broken and the refugee exposes us to this thought of a "coming political community"? Or again, if we need to "abandon decidedly, without reservation," fundamental political concepts such as citizenship in order to be equal to the "absolutely new tasks ahead," what is the rapport between the appeal to paradox in the recent literature on citizenship and the latently dialectical and historicist schemas informing not only much of this literature itself but Agamben's own demand to start *anew* from the figure of the refugee, as if the eventual effacement and negation of citizenship becomes the (dialectical) means through which the figure of the refugee now comes into full relief?

Third, the question remains whether concepts such as "global citizenship" are capable of transforming the empirical realities facing noncitizens today into the thought of a global democracy, the praxis of collective governance, and demands for equality and justice on a global scale, a task that perhaps remains irreducible both to the figuration to which Agamben appeals and to the present existence of our so-called liberal democracies (those democracies and nation-states, as Agamben wryly notes, where the noncitizen is more commonly handed over to humanitarian organizations and the police). Again, what place might the emphasis on paradox hold in this larger context?

Traversing this cluster of questions, the decisive problematic that begins to emerge is whether citizenship exposes itself to its own conceptual displacements, and thus to its own permanent if paradoxical reinvention, or whether citizenship should be replaced by other figures, other subjects of the political, other civil processes, other collective practices, other tasks—in short, another way of rethinking or retreating the political, another way of imagining the world.

It remains a conspicuous feature of recent debates concerning citizenship that the question of technology appears to play a relatively marginal role, even if communication and information technologies hold a distinctive and prominent place within the principle tendencies defining globalization. In light of this feature of recent debates, the question thus remains how reconfiguring the place of technology within the discourse of citizenship not only involves analyzing the various "technologies of citizenship" that remain central to any genealogy of the concept.[16] For the question is how communication and information technologies both inform any attempt to write a genealogy of citizenship while simultaneously transforming and displacing the concept itself. Stated more tendentiously, it is not a question here of situating technology in relation to other multidisciplinary approaches and perspectives on citizenship, as if technology takes its relative place alongside other prominent themes and issues pertaining to citizenship today. Nor is it simply a question of mapping out the role of technologies in the creation of such concepts as netizens, cybercitizens, or virtual communities, or of assessing the decisive impact of technology on the politics of communication, including the Internet (the "network of networks"), the digital divide, or the transformative possibilities of cyberculture and cyberpolitics in globalized economies, all of which have also had decisive implications for citizens, noncitizens, and collective allegiances, and all of which have shaped what constitute politicized identities today. For the question here is at once more structural and essential and concerns the ways in which the question of technology comes to impose and transform not only the concept or grammar of citizenship today but also any proposal seeking to rearticulate the concept of the political as such.

In *Echographies of Television*, the transcript of an improvised film interview between Jacques Derrida and Bernard Stiegler, the discussion turns at one point to the ways in which concepts of democracy, politics, and citizenship are all transformed by contemporary teletechnologies (including television, telephones, and other telecommunication systems), in which the reference to *tele-* as a modifying prefix emphasizes transmission across a spatial distance.[17] As Derrida and Stiegler argue, if the concept of democracy itself has been "governed, controlled, and limited" by boundaries and the borders (physical and conceptual) of the nation-state, and so by acts of "territorialization," and if political discourse is inseparable from citizenship ("acquired or 'natural,' by blood or by soil")—a concept equally defined by "inscription in a place, within a territory or within a nation whose body is rooted in a privileged territory" (76/64–65)—then it is precisely in relation to contemporary teletechnologies that these geopolitical boundaries and territorial markers are subject to possibilities of displacement and permanent dislocation. Indeed, whether demands are made to establish or protect national borders and state sovereignty ("given, lost, or promised," as Derrida nuances), or whether claims are advanced for citizenship and democratic rights, these demands and claims all find a measure of their historical, juridical, and discursive formation inscribed in, and simultaneously delimited by, geopolitical markers and topographical or spatial boundaries. "What the accelerated development of teletechnologies, of cyberspace, of the new topology of 'the virtual' is producing," Derrida argues, is thus a "practical *deconstruction* of the traditional and dominant concepts of the state and citizen (and thus of 'the political') as they are linked to the actuality of a territory" (45/36).

To be sure, there is nothing speculative or merely abstract about Derrida and Stiegler's argument concerning the "decomposition" or "disqualification" of the state as a sovereignty tied to the control of a territory. For "concretely, urgently, every day," these geopolitical limits and the juridical frameworks they presuppose are continually put in play by the most mundane and increasingly pervasive use of telecommunications. Even as we witness a massive resurgence of physical and symbolic barriers and walls defining numerous geopolitical situations, even as we witness widespread appeals to be "at home," to protect our "homelands" and securitize borders, and even when (as Sassen argues) this decomposition or disqualification is played out predominantly within national contexts, the various promotions of state authoritarianism characterizing our contemporary geopolitical space come into continual conflict with what Derrida locates as the "ever-increasing inefficacy" of state authority prompted by teletechnologies (if there is a paradox in play here, it is the state-sanctioned deregulation of telecommunications that creates and reproduces the deterritorialization, decomposition, and disqualification of the state's own sovereignty). Or as Derrida further claims, "this technical transformation—of the telephone, of the fax machine, of television, e-mail and the Internet—will have done more for what is called 'democratization,' even in countries in the East, than all the discourses on behalf of human rights, more than all the presentations of models in whose name this democratization was able to get started" (82/71). When and wherever a television is switched on, when and wherever a phone call is made, when and wherever an Internet connection is established, the question of "critical culture, of democracy, of the political, of deterritorialization erupts" (77/65), whether this situation also implies the relatively simple procedures of using a mobile phone, going online, or analyzing how the techno-artistic production of film and television now possesses the ability, unprecedented in the history of humanity, to find itself almost immediately plugged into a global market. The tele- that informs contemporary communications technology thus not only implies transmission across distance, it "*displaces places.*" This displacement further reopens such concepts as "public space" or the "public sphere" to new spatial delimitations, new topographies and topologies, to what Derrida nuances as what "happens" or "comes into place [*qui arrive au lieu*]" and what "happens to take place" and to "taking-place [*qui arrive à (l')avoir lieu*]" that affects the very experience of place and space (45/36). The opposite of an archive, stock, or deposit of images or information that one might presuppose in terms of its "localization" in a given place—"the sedentariness of a gross ensemble that would be collected in a single site" (79/68)—teletechnologies disclose a more ambivalent situation in which the "border is no longer a border" and images continually bypass customs. It is this ambivalence that provokes an eruption or dislocation of space while transforming the specific delimitation of spaces and places into a more general problematic of "spacing."[18] Rather than a transmission across a space that implies the relatively homogenous extension of that space, a set of coordinates that can be plotted and mapped, teletechnologies presuppose the becoming-space of time and the becoming-time of space, a spacing traced out not only as a play of gaps and intervals, of continuities and discontinuities, of stases and accelerations (or of "plateaus" and "smooth and striated space," in Deleuze and Guattari's seminal terms), but as the very opening to exteriority itself and as such. No doubt as numerous discourses on globalization have suggested, it is in light of these gaps and intervals that the uneven and heterogeneous spacing of the local, national, and global is played out as different strata, scales, and rhythms of conflicts and inequalities. But if the global effects of teletechnologies are structurally implicated within this context, what remains in play in this spacing is not merely the (re)politicizing of technology in relation to the territorial presuppositions of democracy and citizenship within globalization. For what also remains in play are the way in which the conceptual foundations of democracy, politics, and citizenship are reopened to new conceptual genealogies, and so continually reconfigured according to a quite different temporal rhythm and spatial recomposition.[19]

Following Derrida and Stiegler's interview, the question posed here is whether the teletechnologies that displace territorial borders are merely one aspect of a larger display of issues defining our political present—in which case, to recall the opening protocol, citizenship will be discussed from a multiplicity of potential angles and disciplinary perspectives—or whether this political present, including the juridical concept of the state's sovereignty, has a relation, and an "essential relation," as Derrida insists, to the media, telepowers, and teleknowledges that constitute our contemporary, global teletechnologies. As Derrida and Stiegler argue, when delimited by territorial and spatial boundaries, democracy and the politics informing citizenship do not simply stand in a "relation of exteriority" to the teletechnologies one might want to be able to critique in their name. The concepts of democracy, politics, and citizenship do not constitute a "secure ground" on which one might set this technology apart and assess its (political) implications, for these concepts are themselves subject to the very process of critique and deconstruction imposed by this technology in the first place. Indeed, if the very concept of the political is determined spatially or territorially, then teletechnologies suggest how the very "link" that binds the political and the local—what Derrida calls the "topolitical"—is not just displaced in spatial terms but itself necessarily subject to incessant rearticulation and dislocation. Phrased in these terms, it is thus important to acknowledge from the outset that it is not then solely a question of (re)politicizing technology, of putting technology in a political, social, or global context and then determining its political, social, or global effects. Nor is it a question of merely writing another history of technology and so rewriting its political implications according to a different set of genealogical insights. For it is this same technology that transforms the very concept of the political by means of those acts of territorialization and deterritorialization through which the political, democracy, and citizenship constitute and de-constitute themselves in the first place.

Two consequences ensue from this argument. On the one hand, rearticulating the relation between technology and the political points to a corresponding reinvention or reconceptualization of citizenship, coinciding with renewed attention given to the relation between citizenship, language, and telecommunications. Given the intimate rapport between technology and citizenship in the constitution of the civil process and "civilization," including the rapport between the learning of alphabetic writing and the constitution of citizenship itself, and given the increasingly pervasive and unprecedented presence of teletechnologies in the contemporary world, Derrida and Stiegler argue that such a reconceptualization of the terms in which citizenship is articulated should also coincide with extensive programs in education and training in technology. At the same time, teletechnologies today necessitate different forms of critical pedagogy and critical literacy, new definitions of interactivity, a cultural politics of imagery and memory, as well as critical awareness in thinking about the organization of knowledge and archives. As Derrida and Stiegler suggest at some length in their interview, a pressing need remains to invent a critical culture, a kind of education appropriate to the media and contemporary teletechnologies.[20] On the other hand, as Derrida also warns, the lack of education, the relative "incompetence," and together their "incommensurable increase" in understanding the implications of this same technology should be situated in light of the decline and transformations affecting all forms of state sovereignty. Indeed, it is precisely in this critical conjunction between technology and the transformations defining the sovereign nation-state that Derrida locates one of the keys to most of the "unprecedented phenomena that people are trying to assimilate to old monsters in order to conjure them away" (68/57), including the return of the religious fundamentalisms, nationalist archaisms, and the "phantasms of soil and blood, racisms, xenophobias, ethnic wars and ethnic cleansings" (91/79).[21]

In light of the geopolitical configurations defining our contemporary world, Derrida concludes that the effects produced by teletechnologies offer at once a threat and a chance, demanding both critique and deconstruction. More provocatively, Derrida argues that the development of teletechnologies moves us beyond critique by delimiting an obscure "categorical imperative": not just of rethinking democracy "beyond these 'borders' of the political," as numerous discourses on globalization suggest, but of thinking "the political beyond the political" or "the democratic beyond democracy" (76/65). In short, teletechnologies cannot be detached from the wider thought of a "democracy to come."

If the critique of teletechnologies and their effects is necessary, as Derrida argues, it is equally necessary to go beyond critique. And if the deconstruction of the conditions and assumptions informing teletechnologies is always a "practical deconstruction," involving such everyday procedures as making a phone call or going online, the terms in which to rethink these conditions and their political implications cannot de detached from rethinking the concept of the political as such. The necessary "politicization" of technology and a corresponding "sensitivity to the necessary democratization of all these phenomena" cannot be separated out from a larger task to "revive what is generally occulted ('depoliticized') about the political" (76/64). In this sense, if the concept of the political is itself delimited by territorial boundaries and the borders of the nation-state, then the forms of "politicized" critique leveled at contemporary teletechnologies and their "political" effects must respond in turn to the deconstruction or "deterritorialization" of the political itself. Or if the concept of the political cannot be detached from a topology (an argument already decisive in the writings of Carl Schmitt and recalled in Derrida's *Politics of Friendship*), then "perhaps," Derrida argues, "the political must be deterritorialized; no doubt it is deterritorializing itself [*peut-être le politique doit-il se déterritorialiser, sans doute le fait-il aussi*]" (76/65).

Comparing the original French and English translation is instructive here, not least because the English folds back across the original in order to rewrite and displace its grammar (or as if this performative dimension of translation also folds across and deterritorializes all state borders and territorial limits that define themselves in terms of national languages, mother tongues, and monolingualism). First, Derrida takes up the distinction explored in the first chapter, between *le politique*—a term that points to the concept of the political as such, to the political as the site where our very *being-in-common* remains in question—and *la politique*, which implies politics in the context of everyday conflicts over political issues and politicized representations of social existence. Derrida's phrase also captures the sense of imperative and obligation that technology imposes on the political "to deterritorialize itself." But the potential force of the political to deterritorialize itself remains, in the end, insufficient, for Derrida adds immediately that "no doubt that is what it does [*sans doute le fait-il aussi*]," as if the political must deterritorialize itself among other things. The English translation rewrites this clause by suggesting not only that "the political must be deterritorialized"; it continues by suggesting that "no doubt it is deterritorializing itself." According to this translation, the transitions between the active and passive in the French and English versions further aggravate the difficulty of establishing the exact rapport between technology and the political. For if the English translation responds to the French proposal that "the political must deterritorialize itself" (in the reflexive) by arguing that the political must "*be* deterritorialized," then the process of deterritorialization stems in the English from a force *exterior* to the political, a force that is outside or beyond the borders of the political that then intervenes within those borders. In other words, teletechnologies come to deterritorialize the political, implying an exteriority to the political that is effaced in the original French through the use of the reflexive verb, where the political "deterritorializes itself [*se déterritorialiser*]," even if this exterior force is perhaps implied or presupposed in the reflexive verb form. When the English suggests that "the political must be deterritorialized; no doubt it is deterritorializing itself," the relatively marginal clause in the French, which merely suggests that the political deterritorializes itself among other things, is thereby transformed in such a way that the translation captures at once the force of technology to deterritorialize politics from the outside and simultaneously for the political to constitute an act of deterritorializing (itself). A moment of political self-reflexivity is not just inseparable from an external agency, force, or motive; it opens onto a radical undecidability regarding the active and passive conditions for thinking the rapport between technology and the political. Situated within a post-Heideggerian rethinking of *techne* and the "essence of technology" (a reference that Derrida acknowledges elsewhere in the interview), the reading of the English translation across the original suggests how teletechnologies and the political open into a supplementary relation to one another, in such a way that the essence of technology and the essence of the political become coessential—that is, disessentialized—in their reciprocal contamination. It is only in and as the grammar of this supplementary dislocation, displacement, and exteriority of the political from its own conceptual and territorializing borders that rethinking the political always implies an extremity and constitutive spacing, a "beyond" or "outside" of the political, or it always implies that democracy is never present to itself as a self-contained and fully formed concept but "to come." It is in this coming that teletechnologies are not simply implicated in their deterritorializing effects but radically inscribed.

If the political and the technological open onto supplementary relation, the displacement and dislocation of the political posed by teletechnologies also comes to rearticulate Derrida's claim that such technologies pose at once a threat and a chance. Certainly the real and imagined threat posed by teletechnologies to democracy, politics, and citizenship is extensive, especially given the role of such technologies in the marked turn toward various forms of religious fundamentalism, discourses of nationalism, the destruction of established forms of social cohesion, and any number of phantasms of collective identity.

These threats and their technological implications are also widely debated across numerous local, national, and global arenas, giving rise to numerously diverse diagnoses, prognostications, and remedies. However, the "chance" presented by this same technology is considerably more difficult to elaborate, especially since the chance to which Derrida appeals remains irreducible to a simple dialectical counterpart to the threat posed by the same teletechnologies. Coinciding with the displacement from questions of destiny to "communities of fate" (to recall van Gunsteren's distinction), the reference to chance here is not to some form of competition either, "in the strictly economic sense of commercial exploitation," as Derrida insists.[22] Nor is the affirmation of chance to which Derrida appeals fully synonymous with the widespread proposals to rethink the role of technologies in the creation of potentially new forms of identity, community, or social and political representation, even as Derrida acknowledges that teletechnologies open a certain "permeability" that might give rise to debate and diversity, or "a veritable stimulation" and permanent renegotiation that includes a "struggle of exigencies" (85/73). Rather, Derrida's numerous references to "chance" in *Echographies* move us beyond a mere pluralization of such exigencies and work toward rethinking the permeable displacement and deterritorialization of borders as the simultaneous opening or exposure to *alterity*. It is precisely this exposure to alterity that is both presupposed and effaced in any appeal to national identities and the terms (birthplace, language, culture, and so on) in which such identities are defined, the very identity on which the discourse of citizenship is traditionally tied. An initial measure of the difficulty in thinking this question of alterity is evident in Derrida's reference to the "link" that traditionally binds the political to territorial boundaries. For once the link between the political and the local—the "topolitical"—is dislocated or displaced, then the identity of the political subject or citizen defined by sovereign territories is itself subject not just to dislocation and displacement but the opening to alterity, an exposure to the other that always appears (literally or virtually, in person or spectrally) at or beyond the border of the political. Or rather, as Derrida also argues, any schema of identity, subject, or community presupposed by democracy, politics, or citizenship is itself exposed, through the very teletechnologies in *use*, to "disidentification, singularity, rupture with the solidity of identity, de-liaison" (78/67), and it is precisely in these terms that the opening to alterity must be thought.

The "chance" to which Derrida refers frequently in *Echographies* now becomes the enabling and constitutive condition in which to rethink the "*dé-liaison/dé-placement*" of any political identity or citizen-subject. Rearticulating these terms, we could suggest that the "liaison" and "placement" that binds individuals to one another in a (political) community or as citizens within a given territory is offered up to a throw of the "dice [*dé*]" in their radical "*dé-liaison*" and "*dé-placement*" from any secure ground or native soil. This gamble—the crapshoot of the political—suggests that there exists no foundation or guiding political principle from which to measure or legitimate the constitution of a political subject, citizen, or tie that forms a community or polity, no founding reason or orientation that establishes or grounds a sense of belonging once and for all. The "*aléa*" or chance presupposed here does not imply (a return to) chaos, some vague, romanticized appeal to anarchy and rootless nomadism, a nihilistic posturing, a complacent acceptance of total social disintegration and fragmentation, or an indeterminacy that lacks all possibilities for decision and responsibility. Instead, the chance that inaugurates the "*dé-liaison/dé-placement*" of any political identity or citizen-subject creates the precondition in which to think the absolute and always singular opening to alterity, to what we might now term the promise and affirmation opened by the chance encounter. Taking up a post-Althusserian philosophy of the encounter, it is this chance encounter that then constitutes the very opening in which the political is always "beyond the political," at least insofar as it is the chance encounter that also becomes the measure (itself immeasurable) in which to think the very dislocation and deterritorialization of spatial limits and topological boundaries provoked by the teletechnologies in use.[23]

The opening toward alterity evoked throughout the interview with Stiegler is worked through more rigorously in Derrida's other writings, notably as the affirmation of alterity relates to a larger rethinking of foundational political categories and concepts. Tied to the same problematics that pertain to citizenship, this question of alterity thus relates more specifically to Derrida's more extensive reading of the politics of friendship and fraternity, a renewed, genealogical attention to the concepts of cosmopolitanism and hospitality, a deconstruction of the friend-enemy and host-stranger binaries, a rethinking of inherited traditions of law, rights, ethics, justice, responsibility, and violence, a reading of Marx, and a book that centers on transformations in the concept of sovereignty, all of which include references to technology, and all of which participate within Derrida's proposal in his later writings to think a "New International" and a "democracy to come."[24] If these writings are now well known and widely discussed, relatively inconspicuous within this broader rethinking of foundational political concepts is Derrida's affirmation of networks in his interview with Stiegler. Rather than situating the interview with Stiegler alongside Derrida's other writings, then, the more circumscribed reading proposed here turns on how this appeal to networks relates to the widespread assumption that networks enact a dislocation and deterritorialization of all established national boundaries and sovereign or territorial limits. At the same time, the more demanding question also remains how the appeal to networks contributes not just to a rethinking of globalization but to this thought of the "political beyond the political" or a "democracy to come."

In the interview with Stiegler in *Echographies*, Derrida thus proposes to rearticulate the spatial dislocation provoked by teletechnologies precisely in terms of networks.[25] Responding to Stiegler's proposal that this dislocation would itself create a "political community," "something like the thinking of a community of networks, or a technological community" (77/65), Derrida first pries apart the relation between networks and the concepts of community to which networks are repeatedly attached. For if the concept of community invariably presupposes for Derrida a "unity of languages, of cultural, ethnic, or religious horizons," then this concept of community (Agamben's "coming political community" of refugees notwithstanding) tends to reinforce and reproduce the various schemas of identity and belonging intrinsic to the political constitution of a nation or the territorial boundaries of a sovereign state. Even when networks are said to enact the deterritorialization of the boundaries of the nation-state, the concept of "networked communities" still presupposes a *concept* of the political that reinscribes the spatial and topological preconditions of a sovereign territory and thus the spatial assumptions underlying the concept of the political itself. On the other hand, so long as networks are posited "without unity or homogeneity, without coherence," then Derrida proposes that they create and make possible a "new distribution" or "*partage*," including a *partage* of images and information no longer governed by a territorially delimited, national or regional community (77–78/65–66). Networks, in short, displace the very concept of the "horizon" and the points of spatial and thus subject orientation it sets in place (whether linguistic, cultural, ethnic, or religious) by opening up this *partage*.

Drawn from the writings of Jean-Luc Nancy, as Derrida acknowledges, and referring back to Stiegler's earlier reference in the interview to the "sharing" of alphabetic writing and its implications for citizenship in ancient Greece, the *partage* Derrida evokes in French translates at one and the same time as both "sharing" *and* "division," and thus a "sharing out."[26] In this sense, a *partage* in relation to networks takes into account what it is possible to have "in common," what is shared, "the fact that several people or groups can, in places, cities or non-cities...have access to the same programs" (77/66). But Derrida also takes into account a *partage* as division, arguing that networks always imply "dissociations, singularities, diffractions." If networks create what is "common," that commonality is also constitutively inscribed by the possibilities of dissociation, de-liaison, distance, and detachment, and it is precisely in these terms that the schemas of identity presupposed by the concept of a networked community become displaced to the affirmation of singularity implied by Derrida's understanding of networks. Turning us back to the question of relation informing Lacoue-Labarthe and Nancy's proposals for the Center for Philosophical Research on the Political—that is, the disconnection or dissociation at the origin of the political event, the relation without relation—there is no thought of association or connectivity implied by networked telecommunications without dissociation, no liaison without de-liaison, no proximity without distance, no attachment without detachment, and it is precisely this deconstructive logic for Derrida that is effaced in appeals to community or in the widespread affirmations of connectivity between members of a community, whatever the organizational forms such connectivity implies or makes possible. Detached from any proposal to reconfigure the role of teletechnologies in the creation of networked communities, and notably the related insistence on issues of connection and connectivity as politically enabling and progressive, the "logic" of the *partage* created by networks is thus the permanently displaced site of "disidentification, singularity, rupture with the solidity of identity, de-liaison" (78/67), in short, the enabling condition for reaffirming the opening and exposure to alterity, to the other's singularity, to the chance encounter. At the same time, it is precisely in and through this same *partage* in networked telecommunications that the openness and exposure to alterity becomes a constitutive and decisive condition in which to think the political beyond the political and a democracy that is to come. For the *partage* inscribed in networked telecommunications is not reducible to the networks of information technology and telecommunication systems, to what Derrida himself labels the "networks of national or international economic and teletechnoscientific powers" (87/75) or the networks of "techno-tele-media apparatuses" described in *Specters of Marx* in the "tableau of an ageless world," even if Derrida's interventions in the interview and elsewhere often suggest that networks are only that. The network is not essentially technological either, nor only a "system" of telecommunications. For networks become the enabling condition for thinking the limits of the political, or for articulating another "delimitation of the *socius*," in the sense of an orginary "sociation" that exists prior to every organized *socius*, "society-at large," or *politeia*. In short, networks constitute the conditions for creating a potential relation to and with the other—the chance encounter—that preexists the bonds (natal, linguistic, cultural, ethnic, or religious) that define citizenship within a sovereign territory or community.[27]

In light of Derrida's argument concerning networks, three questions come into further relief, three questions that must be posed if we are to begin to think through the future viability of citizenship as a concept when faced with the deterritorializing effects of these same teletechnologies.

First, if the *partage* implied by networked teletechnologies displaces the spatial presuppositions informing the concepts of democracy, the political, and citizenship, and so opens toward what Derrida terms a spacing or "coinscription of space" that no longer corresponds to these same political models inscribed by territorial boundaries and clearly defined spatial limits, how might this spacing or coinscription of space relate to the global tendencies animating the world today, and thus to identifiable, geopolitical conflicts? Second, in what ways has the association between networks, telecommunications, and reconfigured concepts of community and connectivity (widely accepted in the literature on "virtual communities," for example) lent itself to a political *figuration* or *myth*, rather than to the necessity of parsing out the grammar—of a simultaneous attachment and detachment, proximity and distance—in which to rethink the ties, webs of relations, and social bonds that articulate an exposure to alterity, an exposure that includes the chance encounters that take place both at and beyond the borders of the nation-state? In other words, if we are to accept that the relation between technology and citizenship remains political, or needs (re)politicizing, in what sense does this relation also demand that we rethink the political relation as such, beyond or prior to the phantasms of identity, nationalistic and religious fundamentalisms, and political autism characterizing much of the world today, but also beyond or prior to the widespread call to politicize identities by articulating them within a flexible plurality of associations, connections, and allegiances, or beyond or prior to their subsumption in a figure (in Arendt and Agamben's terms)? Lastly, and indissociably, is there a concept of citizenship that answers to the specific logic of the *partage* presented by Derrida and Nancy in their writings, and is this logic essentially different from the *ontological* situation outlined by Balibar in rethinking the concept of the border itself—"you can be a citizen or you can be stateless, but it is difficult to imagine *being* a border"?[28] Or in what sense does this *partage* begin to mark a displacement from the discourse of paradox animating so many contemporary discussions of citizenship to rethinking this same ontological question proposed by Balibar, to rethinking the border space or spacing that, no longer ontological in any accepted or presupposed sense, divides and shares us out from—and with—one another?

In his essay "Beyond Human Rights," Giorgio Agamben argues that nation-states need to address the political presuppositions concerning the "inscription of nativity" as well as the state-nation-territory trinity that is founded on that principle.[29] As he cautions, "it is not easy to indicate right now the ways in which all this may concretely happen." Referring to the problem of contemporary Jerusalem, to take a prominent example, Agamben takes up one of the options that the city become, "simultaneously and without any territorial partition," the capital of two different states, concluding that "the paradoxical condition of reciprocal extraterritoriality (or, better yet, aterritoriality)" implied by this option could become a model of new international relations: "Instead of two national states separated by uncertain and threatening boundaries, it might be possible to imagine two political communities insisting on the same region and in a condition of exodus from each other—communities that would articulate each other via a series of reciprocal extraterritorialities in which the guiding concept would no longer be the *ius* (right) of the citizen but rather the *refugium* (refuge) of the singular" (24).

By extension, the future of Europe would not be a Europe of different nations but an "aterritorial or extraterritorial space" in which all the residents of the European states, both citizens and noncitizens, would be in a position of "exodus" or "refuge." This seemingly paradoxical and aterritorial space is then marked by the irreducible difference between birth and nation, a difference that contributes for Agamben toward recreating the concept of (a) "people," a political concept that remains hostile to any national identification or that sense of belonging that constitutes a nation's given peoples and their rights. Being European would now signify the "being-in-exodus" of the citizen, a condition that could obviously be one of immobility (or that nomadism of "true nomads," in Deleuze and Guattari's terms, "of those who no longer even move or imitate anything").[30] According to the paradoxical condition of "reciprocal extraterritoriality," Agamben further specifies, "This space would coincide neither with any of the homogeneous national territories nor with their *topographical* sum, but would rather act on them by articulating and perforating them *topologically* as in the Klein bottle or in the Möbius strip, where exterior and interior in-determine each other. In this new space, European cities would rediscover their ancient vocation of cities of the world by entering into a relation of reciprocal extraterritoriality" (25).

Agamben's proposal does not return us to Europe's earlier vocation of colonial mastery of the world. If Europe becomes a space of "reciprocal extraterritoriality," then Europe is no longer defined as a political entity separated by borders from other political entities (other nations, other regions) that it can dominate territorially. For Europe is now inscribed in the "reciprocal extraterritoriality" with other political spaces in the world (also defined by their extraterritoriality), and in such a way that the world is not so much defined by globalization or the presence or absence of borders than this perforated indeterminacy of any given interiority and exteriority, and thus the global spacing of political spaces that constitutes the world as world.[31] Since there exists no "autonomous space" in the political order of the nation-state for something like a "pure human," as Agamben further argues, being-in-exodus is thus commensurate with a corresponding spatial displacement on a global scale. Agamben concludes his essay by stating, "Only in a world in which the spaces of states have been...perforated and topologically deformed and in which the citizen has been able to recognize the refugee that he or she is—only in such a world is the political survival of mankind today thinkable" (26).

Agamben does not refer in the essay to networks, but it should be clear that the language in which networks are commonly articulated shares many of the same features of Agamben's turn to the topological language of the Klein bottle and Möbius strip. More pertinently, Agamben's proposal to think the "paradoxical condition of reciprocal extraterritoriality" appears to approximate Derrida's reference to networked telecommunications as defined by the "coinscription of space," a coinscription whose *partage*—whose simultaneous sharing and division, whose sharing out—is nowhere reducible to the territorial preconditions of the sovereign nation-state, and so no longer corresponds to models of democracy, politics, and citizenship based on the marked inscriptions of spatial boundaries. No doubt we could question whether the radical potentiality of "being-in-exodus" or the positing of the refugee as "limit-concept" are closed off in their very force by Agamben's frequent references to political *communities*, as well as in his appeal to the refugee as *figure* (a question to which we will also return in later chapters). As Derrida also proposes in rethinking the politics of friendship (itself readable as a calculated conceptual deviation from the concept of community), any "relationship with the other" presupposed and inscribed in "being-in-exodus" implies a "heteronomic and dissymmetrical curving of social space—more precisely, a curving of the relation to the other," and it is this heteronomy and dissymmetry that precludes affirmations of community by opening a spacing that is "prior to all organized *socius*, all *politeia*, all determined 'government,' *before* all 'law.'"[32] At the same time, Agamben nowhere thinks this being-in-exodus in terms of a constitutive distancing and dissociation that are also the enabling condition of all sharing out. Or rather, the logic in which the *partage* opens toward a sharing that is also a division or sharing out is not strictly commensurate with the mere "in-determinacy" of any interiority and exteriority, nor an "aterritoriality" that Agamben labels "paradoxical," nor an extraterritoriality that is merely "reciprocal" within present conditions of global exchange. For the *partage* of networked telecommunications opens toward a chiasmatic structuring or spacing in which the interior and exterior are continually displaced from their potential reduction to an *a*-territorial space. In short, we might argue that Agamben's own references to the Klein bottle and Möbius strip need to be read back across any sense that this prefix constitutes a mere privation or negation as the dialectical precondition of exodus rather than a spacing inscribed in and as all being-in-exodus.

In their introduction to *Cities without Citizens*, Eduardo Cadava and Aaron Levy also propose to rethink the question of citizenship by situating the concept in relation to the various transformations defining the contemporary city. The authors argue that the contemporary city, situated in relation to the expanding forces of capital, globalization, and information technologies, can no longer be said to name "the geographical unity of a habitat, or an insulated network of communication, commerce, sociality, or even politics."[33] Not that the forces of capital, globalization, and information technologies have simply removed all limits and borders, as much contemporary rhetoric concerning globalization might suggest. Indeed, as the authors argue (quoting Balibar), and as any number of contemporary events including "economic wars, civil wars, ethnic conflicts, wars of culture and religion, and the unleashing of racisms and xenophobias" forcefully remind us, less than ever is the contemporary world a "world without borders." And yet, situated in relation to the tendencies informing contemporary globalization, the conditions in which to think the established rapport between citizenship and cities necessarily remain open to question and rearticulation, and it is this task that is proposed for their exhibition and accompanying catalogue.

In light of these initial claims, Cadava and Levy introduce the essays in the catalogue by taking their point of departure from an acknowledged "risk," outlining two general propositions, "each of which appears impossible in relation to the other." First, the authors argue, "there have never been cities without citizens." Second, "there have always only been cities without citizens." Recalling the principle terms in which citizenship is comprised, they then explain and justify this "impossible" relation and its seemingly paradoxical logic:

> To claim that there have never been cities without citizens is simply to recall that, by definition, cities can exist only if they are inhabited by citizens who, inscribed in a network of affiliations that constitute the very structure of the city, or granted rights such as those of the right to political participation or the right to suffrage or education, can claim that the space in which they live is a city that guarantees these affiliations and rights. This also means that citizenship can exist only where we understand a city to exist—where citizens and foreigners are distinguished in terms of rights and obligations in a given space. To say that there have never been cities without citizens, then, is simply to indicate that there is a relation between the identity of the city and that of its citizens. If cities always have citizens—and this is true even if we know that these citizens have been understood and defined according to several different historical models of citizenship—it is because they announce themselves as principles of articulation between birth, language, culture, nationality, belonging, rights and citizenship.

On the other hand,

> To claim that there have always only been cities without citizens... is to recognize that any assertion of citizenship can only take place by simultaneously defining the limits and conditions of citizenship— by defining, that is, the non-citizen, the foreigner, the alien, the stranger, the immigrant, the refugee, the criminal, the prisoner, or the outsider—and similarly, that any delineation of the borders of the city must mark what remains within the city but also what is excluded from it. This means, among so many other things, that there can be no

cities or citizens without laws of segregation and exclusion—without borders, barriers, interdictions, displacements, censorships, racisms, and the marginalization and eviction of languages and peoples. In other words, "cities without citizens" also evokes the violence, the laws of denaturalization and denationalization, the deprivations of civil rights, the strategies of depopulation, forced deportation, enforced immigration, the refusal of the rights of asylum, the murderous persecutions, massacres, colonizations, exterminations, exiles, and pogroms that so often have punctuated and defined the history of cities.

If the argument proposed here opens onto a wider possibility of writing a genealogy of citizenship, notably in terms of the constitutive forms of exclusion that punctuate all discourses of inclusivity and participatory membership in a *polis*, then the language in which the authors propose to rearticulate this "impossible" relation appears to find many of its conceptual resources in Derrida's proposal for a "democracy to come" or Agamben's proposal for "coming political communities." As Cadava and Levy argue, if their exhibition proposal opens a way to rearticulate the relation between cities and citizenship, then this reconceptualization raises the possibility for "new experiences of communities, frontiers, and identities, without models and perhaps even without citizens as we generally have understood them." Indeed, it now becomes possible to "imagine a democracy that in fact would exist beyond citizenship and citizenry," allowing us to further imagine cities that, "coming without citizens, would open the spaces for new forms of democratic communities." In this sense, the "impossible" or paradoxical relation that animates the rapport between citizenship and cities in their opening argument now constitutes the enabling condition in which to imagine the invention of a city that is open to the future not only because it is "open to its own alterity" but because it would enable a "sociality that is not determined in advance by the fact of belonging to a community, a state, a nation, or even just a language." These new communities would thus involve "alliances that go beyond the 'political' as a domain as it has been commonly defined (since this designation usually has been reserved for the citizen in a nation linked to a particular territory), and therefore would define the cities of tomorrow in relation to a democracy that is still yet to come and yet to be imagined."

Cadava and Levy's argument prompts several observations, notably as it brings back into relief the place of citizenship in rethinking the political beyond the political or a democracy to come.

The "impossible" relation between cities and citizenship proposed by the authors does not necessarily lend itself to our initial presentation of their argument in terms of paradox. As Engin Isin has argued in rethinking different genealogies of citizenship from a more Foucauldian perspective, the rapport between inclusivity and exclusivity can be rethought and rearticulated by contrasting the discourse of citizenship as voiced by citizens themselves with the claims of those excluded from citizenship. In other words, any genealogical investigation into citizenship would need to "problematize the margins or points of contact where the inside and outside encounter, confront, destabilize, and contest each other," and to do so, Isin argues, from the perspective of alterity itself:

> The focus on otherness as a condition of citizenship assumes that in fact citizenship and its alterity always emerged simultaneously in a dialogical manner and constituted each other. Women were not simply excluded from ancient Greek citizenship, but were constituted as its other as an immanent group by citizens. Similarly, slaves were not simply excluded from citizenship, but made citizenship possible by their very formation. The alterity of citizenship, therefore, does not preexist, but is constituted by it. The closure theories that define citizenship as a space of privilege for the few that excludes others neglects a subtle but important aspect of citizenship; that it requires the constitution of these others to become possible.[34]

The problem with the logics of exclusion and enclosure is that they assume that such identities as "woman" and "immigrant" *preceded* citizenship and were excluded from it, rather than arguing that citizenship is itself *constituted* though these so-called self-consolidating others. The impossible and seemingly paradoxical relation between cities both "with" and "without" citizenship is thus more suitably understood in terms of the constitutive if irreducible coimplication of citizens and noncitizens within a space of conflict, a "complex terrain of contested identities," as Isin states. As *Being Political* amply demonstrates, it is this "dialogic" relation that remains irreducible to paradox while making at once possible and necessary a genealogical investigation into the discourse of citizenship itself.[35]

And yet, it is precisely this genealogical investigation that still leaves open the question of citizenship's future possibility as a concept, at least insofar as the question remains whether "being political" is still to be articulated in terms of citizenship or opens up other ways of thinking different forms of relation (or identities in Isin's terms), other articulations of plurality, allegiance, and affiliation beyond citizenship. The question also remains whether Derrida's references to the "logic" of networked telecommunications in terms of a *partage* or Agamben's appeal to the topological characteristics of extraterritorialities remain compatible with Isin's genealogical investigation into the "dialogic" relation between citizen and noncitizen, and thus whether Isin's investigations into citizenship still assume a strict spatial difference between an interiority to the city and its exteriority, a difference deconstructed or at least set in play by Derrida's and Agamben's respective arguments.[36] What remains at stake, however, at least beyond the potential readings of Isin's text intimated here, is that the seemingly paradoxical and "impossible" relation between citizen and noncitizen reconfigured by Isin and proposed by Cadava and Levy does not close off the possibility of imaging "new communities," "cities of tomorrow," and a "democracy to come." Indeed, this initial impossibility enables us to think these very possibilities and imaginings in the first place.

The terms in which Cadava and Levy's argument is proposed nevertheless conclude with the virtual or implied effacement of citizenship within this very future, or at least motions toward forms of democratic communities and alliances in which the concepts of citizenship and citizenry framing the initial discussion now potentially play no role. The concept of citizenship within this argument thus acts not simply as a catalyst for imagining new communities and a democracy to come. Nor does it simply divide out into an irreducible and impossible relation between citizen and noncitizen. Rather, citizenship becomes an integral part of an argument in which the concept is at once posited and negated in its own self-transformation and eventual self-effacement. The implicitly dialectical, historicist, and teleological schema informing the argument is registered above all in the ways in which Cadava and Levy's appeal to communities to come is parsed out as a community or democracy that exists "beyond citizenship" or in alliances that "go beyond the 'political,'" as if this "beyond" constituted the historical or dialectical dividing line in which citizenship is then surpassed and sublated. This simultaneous positing and negation of citizenship is then the condition for opening a future democracy that is not strictly "to come" but, in Cadava and Levy's words, "still yet to come and yet to be imagined." As if echoing the difficulty of disentangling the "coming" of a political community in Agamben's writings from a rupture premised on a dialectical or historicist teleology, the schema implied here comes into further tension with the ways in which the reader is continually asked to "imagine" the future, as well as by the future (if conditional) tenses in which the various proposals for thinking "cities of tomorrow" are presented as offering something "new."

No doubt it remains of strategic (and perhaps even utopian) necessity to "imagine" this possibility of new communities and democratic alliances. Cadava and Levy's argument is also hedged in with numerous precautions and clauses that close off any possibility of establishing a "destiny" for the city based on some transcendental, historicist, or theological premise. The argument also forecloses the possibility of imagining this future in terms of a single or singular figure, at least in the terms suggested by Agamben's references to the refugee. But the argument nevertheless posits the potential effacement of citizenship as the means through which this future is opened as a future and new communities become imaginable, and "cities *without* citizens" constitutes both the point of departure in the exhibition catalogue's title and the introduction's conclusion. Even if the "impossible" relation between cities and citizenship is not reducible to paradox, the entire argument sustains itself at a critical limit, folding back within itself a latently teleological passage in which the impossibility of citizenship is the negative dialectic of democracy's future, even if that future is itself nowhere destinal or prescribed in advance of itself but open to its own alterity and "yet to come." At the very least (and here we recall Heidegger's interrogation into the phrase "not yet" in *Being and Time*), the appeal to "still yet" punctuating Cadava and Levy's argument demands to be reinterrogated for the ways in its grammar tends to presuppose a dialectical and historicist schema or linear passage that their more general argument simultaneously negates, displaces, and reopens.

In this sense, it remains hardly surprising why the discourse of citizenship holds a pivotal if fundamentally ambivalent, paradoxical, if not aporetic role in so much contemporary political discourse, and Cadava and Levy's various proposals are no doubt indicative of a more widespread unease concerning the future possibilities of citizenship as a viable and (still) potentially transformative political concept when confronted by the forces of capital and globalization as well as the coming communities and assemblages that work to resist these very forces. At the very least, Cadava and Levy's argument foregrounds the apparent necessity of having to rethink the concept of citizenship in order to question its contemporary, political validity as a concept and its relation to new forms of political community. Indeed, it could be argued that the fundamental ambivalence that results from such arguments may be interpreted as stemming, at least in part, from an uncertainty whether the revolutionary tradition in which citizenship finds one of its most resonant resources is still relevant. This is a question that may be said to divide out according to numerous factors, including the continued pertinence of citizenship to the articulation of class and other sociocultural conflicts, the role citizenship plays in the emancipatory struggles against colonization and imperialism, and the demand for human rights and global citizenship voiced by millions in the face of the extreme precarity of "bare life" and the present global conditions of human existence. Phrased somewhat differently—and this suite of negations already attests to the difficulties at stake here, or already sets off the force and affirmation of the "to come"—the question remains what nondialectical, nonhistoricist, or nonteleological concept of "political" transformation might now come to the fore if the revolutionary tradition informing citizenship discourse and its destiny is considered closed.[37]

Such ambivalence in citizenship's continued (ir)relevance cannot be separated from the continual push and pull of paradoxical, historicist, dialogical, and dialectical schemas orienting both the substance and form of numerous recent discourses on citizenship, a push and pull from which any discussion of citizenship is hardly exempt.[38] This ambivalence is nowhere more apparent than in the frequently cited appeal to the concept of the "global citizen," a seemingly paradoxical term that becomes all the more difficult to circumscribe given the ways in which multinational corporations in their newsletters and publicity relations rhetoric valorize the same appeal to "global citizenship" as Marxist autonomists such as Hardt and Negri, notably in their list of celebrated proposals for the multitude's alternative to global capitalism and Empire's imperial form. More pertinent in this immediate context, the latently dialectical schema that we have suggested plays a vestigial role in Cadava and Levy's proposal turns us back to Derrida's own proposition to think the political beyond the political and the democratic beyond democracy, as if this "beyond" determined in advance that a democracy "to come" is less an opening to alterity and chance than a prescribed dialectical passage (or as if the "messianicity" or "messianic space" to which Derrida widely appeals in his more recent writings could never be fully separated from a certain messianism). Indeed, when compared to Cadava and Levy's proposals for citizenship in *Cities without Citizens*, it remains surely significant that Derrida's references to citizenship are divided, suggesting on occasions that citizenship has no decisive role to play in rethinking foundational political categories, and then at other times insisting on its central importance, as when his own proposal for a New International (with which Cadava and Levy's argument shares much in common) is described in part as not a way of associating citizens belonging to given nation-states but as opening toward "a new concept of citizenship, of hospitality, a new concept of the state, of democracy."[39] But it is also just as significant that Derrida subjects this "beyond" and "to come" to a logic that holds itself as irreducible to any dialectical, historicist, or teleological schema, to a coming "community," as well as to the *creation* of a new concept. For, as he argues, it is not a *new* concept of democracy that remains to be thought but "a new determination of the given concept of democracy, in the tradition of the concept of democracy." In other words, the thought (or imagining) of the "new" and the "possible"—the democracy "still yet to come and yet to be imagined"—cannot be dissociated from a more unsettling temporal and conceptual displacement of given determinations, opening toward an absolute imminence, to what comes, occurs, arises [*vient, advient, survient*], that not only makes possible a genealogy of different concepts but simultaneously deconstructs the *inherited* concepts of the political, citizenship, and democracy, including their genealogical as well as spatial affiliations.[40]

It is in this sense that democracy is not so much "still yet to come" but, more succinctly, "to come." Derrida's injunction gestures less toward an imagined future than toward a coming of democracy that is nowhere present in any given or existing democracies but exists (still yet?) in its very coming.[41] This "to come" thus points to an aporia punctuating, suspending, or unhinging the present, where democracy as an equality between everyone, as justice and equity (the "given concept of democracy" or the "tradition of the concept of democracy") does not exist as a preexisting or pregiven political concept when faced, in the present and future, with a "new determination" of democracy as unconditional affirmation of and absolute respect for the singularity of others in their radical and irreducible heterogeneity, including those others, those chance encounters, that exist beyond or at the borders of those common territorial spaces that define the political constitution of a "democracy." A democracy to come is not then a future form of democracy, a new political regime or community, or a collection of political subjects that we are asked to imagine and that could be realizable one day, given the right conditions. Indeed, a "democracy to come" is not even a political concept or something we might imagine in the future. Nor is it a regulative idea in the Kantian sense, as Derrida has repeatedly argued. Rather, the "to come" must be thought in terms of an aporia, as the mark of an impossibility, but an aporia and impossibility that become the enabling condition in which to rethink and re-mark democracy as a promise whose determinations demand permanent and unconditional reinvention, rearticulation, and affirmation in the present—new risks and tasks that hold no juridical guarantee or political legitimation—even as such a promise gives us the means to critique existing democracies.[42]

The question nevertheless remains open whether the concept of citizenship might still play a role within this affirmation of a democracy to come. At the same time, if rethinking the relation between cities and citizenship remains central to any democracy to come, as Cadava and Levy persuasively argue, the question still remains whether all these various proposals return us once again to the argument outlined earlier by Heater, in which citizenship, which usually claims a "cohering function," must now either "shrink to a weaker, because competing, form of allegiance among others, or expand to embrace them all and lose its coherence." No doubt the different genealogical readings of citizenship could demonstrate that this alternative is inscribed in the discourse of citizenship from its very origins and so already offers a displacement and reconceptualization of citizenship from the choice Heater offers us. But the fundamental ambivalence concerning the future (re)invention or (re)creation of citizenship as a concept persists, and the role citizenship might play in a democracy to come still remains open to question. Indeed, this question becomes all the more decisive given Nancy's claim (cited in our opening epigraph) that "the coming of all to the public relation"—which Nancy sets off from the rest of the text though hyphenation and paraphrases in scare quotes under "citizenship"—is what constitutes the political "as a sense to come," even if this "sense to come" cannot be subsumed "under the signification of a 'State,'" at least not without implying at the same time "the multiplicity and pluri-locality of relations within 'the' relation that is not 'one.'"[43] But in what sense is this very "multiplicity and pluri-locality of relations" still reducible to, or synonymous with, citizenship, given that citizenship (still) constitutes for Nancy the political as a sense to come? Or in what ways does this displacement of the problematic to a question of *sense* transform the very terms of the argument?

In *The Sense of the World*, Nancy argues that the Western political tradition is constituted from two mutually informing models of political organization, two models that define the political in its "self-sufficiency" (*autosuffisance*):

the model of citizenship and the model of the political subject. It is these two terms that "propose nothing other, together or separately, than an absolute emergence or constitution of sense," a "double polarity of our entire political space" that Nancy characterizes as the "space of self-sufficient *sense*" (*SM*, 163/*SW*, 103). Arguing that the subject and citizen "represent two postures of the claim to sovereignty and the institution of community," Nancy then argues that the different combinations of these four terms, including their single and singular combination together, not only all "gravitate around the index or ideal of self-sufficiency, to the point where *the political* as such seems to have therein its very Idea" (*SM*, 172/*SW*, 110); it is the combinations and modalizations of these four terms that "organizes, saturates, and exhausts the political space closing itself today." It is precisely in and through this closure or in and through the exhaustion of this Idea that the terms and stakes are reopened in which to discern and rearticulate the "political exigencies of today."

In rethinking this saturation and exhaustion of political sense in terms of its spatial closure, Nancy first turns to the distinction between the citizen and the subject by insisting on their "formal" differences. For even if there has never been a "pure example" of either the politics of the citizen or the politics of the subject, it is according to this initial heuristic distinction that the citizen is not the same as the subject, at least if the subject is understood according to the philosophical or metaphysical concept of the subject:

> The citizen is, first of all, *one, some*-one, or *every-one* [*un, quelque un, ou tout un chacun*], while the subject is, first of all, *self* [*soi*], that is, the circling back through which a *one* raises its unicity to the power of unity. The citizen comprises numerous unicities, the subject comprises an identificatory unity. This is why the city (which, as it is necessary to emphasize, doubtless has never taken place as such but figures the projection of one of our two poles) is represented, first of all, as a public space, or the public qua space, and as a space of citizens, that is, neither as a territory nor as a domain nor as a *no-man's-land* but as a circulation, a reticulation, an exchange, a sharing out [*partage*], a localization that is at once multiple, overdetermined, and mobile. In this space, the citizen takes (its) place and circulates. (*SM*, 164/*SW*, 104)

Coterminous with this distinction between a shared out unicity and the identificatory unity of a self-contained and self-absorbed "self," Nancy's presentation of citizenship (which he acknowledges derives primarily from Aristotle and the Stoics) negotiates from the outset a seemingly paradoxical tension between different spatial descriptions, suggesting, on the one hand, that citizenship (the "public qua space") "takes place" in the "space" of the city, even if this (public) space is not a strictly delimited "territory," "domain," or a "no-man's-land" but the space—the spacing or taking-place—of circulation, reticulation, exchange, *partage*. If the citizen is thus defined in terms of a "localization," the term does not imply a strictly spatial circumscription in which the citizen is situated within a pregiven space but opens toward a "pluri-locality of relations." It is the spacing and taking-place of "*one, some-one, or every-one*," a multiplicity that is at once mobile, overdetermined, and shared out. In short, the city has never "taken place" as such because the place or localization of the citizen (with)in the city is rearticulated precisely in terms of this mobile circulation and reticulated spacing:

> The citizen is, above all, the one who occupies and traverses this space, the one who is defined by it, by the sharing out [*partage*] of its exteriority. To be a citizen is one or more roles, one or more ways of proceeding [*une démarche*], a way of comporting oneself, a gait [*pas*]. In this way, the citizen is a mobile complex of rights, obligations, dignities, and virtues. These do not relate to the realization of any foundation or end other than the mere institution of the city. In a sense, the citizen does nothing other than share out [*partager*] with his/her fellow citizens the functions and signs of citizenship, and in this "sharing out" his/her being is entirely expressed. It is thus that the "Greek" city (and to a certain extent also the "Roman" city) appears to us to be perfectly *autoteleological*, where the *autos* would be utterly deprived of all interiority, without relation either to what we designate as the "private sphere" or to what we call "the nation." In this regard, the city has no deeper *sense*: it is related to no signified other than its own institution, the minimal signified of the city's mere contour or cutting out [*la découpe de la cité*], without other "identity," "mission," or "destiny" to conquer or expand. The in-common of the city has no identity other than the space in which the citizens cross each other's paths, and it has no unity other than the exteriority of their relations. In a certain sense, citizenship in accordance with its pure concept is always virtually citizenship of the "world." *(SM,* 165/*SW,* 104)

If Nancy's description of citizenship offers an evocative sense of citizenship's performative role, in which the citizen's very "being" does not exist prior to the city but is expressed in its civic performativity and a "mobile complex" of rights and obligations, the argument also suggests why citizenship is the most superficial of political concepts, having no deeper sense or foundation other than that which creates the city's autoteleological and formal institution, its mere contour or cutting out of a space, its spreading out, as it were, across the surface of the world. Here the city as "mere institution" is an instituting of citizenship without essence, interiority, or pure immanence, and an instituting that cannot be governed over or signified by a source that remains transcendent to such an instituting or that determines the teleology of its destiny. As Nancy will argue, it becomes the "empty truth of democracy." For the city only exists as the space in which citizens relate to one another, having no identity or unity other than (in) the "exteriority of their relations." Or rather, if we refuse to outline a space that preexists the citizens, a pregiven space in which the citizens then find themselves situated and identified by being born into the city, the city at once constitutes and simultaneously effaces its spatial limits when the relations among citizens open toward an exteriority that cannot be contained by the city as such. Citizenship in this sense always implies a relation to the world beyond the mere contour of the city, or a world that is not simply beyond the city in spatial terms, outside its walls and boundaries, but already inscribed in the city's exteriority to itself as a strictly circumscribed or delimited space.

In terms of this definition of citizenship as a "pure concept," global citizenship or cosmopolitanism is thus not opposed to citizenship as it is traditionally understood within the confines of a nation-state but already presupposed as one of citizenship's most essential or structural possibilities. If this argument has echoes in Agamben's dream of returning to the original vocation of Europe's cities and their "reciprocal extraterritoriality" in the world, it also effectively retranscribes the appeals to global citizenship in the contexts of contemporary globalization, or at least a discourse of globalization that effaces the question of exteriority at stake here. But Nancy significantly locates this turn to global citizenship less in its more general global or European context than in its revolutionary tradition. For if the spatial rearticulation of the city's interiority and exteriority is coterminous with thinking the citizen's relation *toward* the world rather than assigned place in the world, it is the citizens of the French Revolution for Nancy who think of themselves as having an "international, European, that is cosmopolitan dimension."

Nancy's turn to the revolutionary tradition is evident throughout his writings, notably in his larger rethinking of the founding revolutionary concepts of freedom, equality, and fraternity. Within the more strictly circumscribed context of citizenship, however, the turn to the revolutionary tradition becomes more focused, passing by way of three prominent references: Hegel, Schmitt's rethinking of the political as the secularization of theological concepts, and Rousseau's "contract."

The reference to Hegel takes us back to the other pole that organizes Nancy's rethinking of the political in terms of its self-sufficiency, and notably to the place where the play of exteriority opened by citizenship—becoming, relation, spacing—is closed off, incorporated (into the "body politic"), and appropriated. In this appropriation of the citizen's relation of exteriority, the citizen becomes subject "at the point of sense, at the point of the (re)presentation of sense" (*SM*, 167/*SW*, 106). For the city is also subject to what Nancy terms the "demand for a subjective appropriation of sense" in order to *found* itself as a city:

> The Subject, in general, in accordance with its structural and generic law as stated by Hegel, retains within itself its own negativity. It is this self-same appropriation and incorporation of negativity (for example, a becoming, a relation, a spacing) that constitutes a "self" and a "being-self" as such. Thus, the political subject—or politics in accordance with the Subject—consists in the appropriation of the constitutive exteriority of the city (just as, doubtless, reciprocally the city consists in the projection, *partes extra partes* of the interiority of the subject). For the space of the city an identity and substantiality are pre- or postsupposed as its principle or end—as the organic configuration of a "people," or the "nation," or as property and production. And this pre-supposition of the self (one ought to say: this presupposition that *constitutes* the *self*) comes to crystallize identity in a figure, name, or myth. Politics becomes the conduct of the history of this subject, its destiny, and its mission. It becomes the revelation or the proclamation of a sense and of an absolute sense. *(SW, 167/SW, 105–6)*

The claims of a people and a nation in terms of a shared destiny are thus teleologically grounded in the presupposed subject, the self-contained subject that becomes the decisive measure in which to appropriate citizenship's exteriority to itself and so to figuring the city's origins and future. Recipro-cally, the subject makes itself into a citizen "at the point where the expressed essence tends to express itself in and as a civic space and, if one can put it like this, to 'display' [*étaler*] subjective essentiality" (*SM*, 167–68/*SW*, 106).[44] No doubt this "display" will come to play an increasingly conspicuous role in the staging of the nation and its peoples as historical spectacle or the spectacle of its founding and self-legitimizing origins, transforming the performative role associated with citizenship into the mediatized and commercialized pageants of patriotism and the flag-waving rehearsals of civic community and history that have come today to pass for democracies and the spiritual bonds and destiny of a people and their nation. But as Nancy notes, the subjective ap-propriation of sense rearticulates citizenship's exteriority and worldliness by also making possible the form of Empire and imperial expansion, in the sense that Empire here is defined as the "most manifest state of the combination of two heterogeneous determinations: a 'citizenship' and a 'subjectivity'—or 'subjectivities'—each of which buttresses the other" in a form of political self-constitution (*SM*, 168/*SW*, 106–7). In this way, the people of a nation do not merely distinguish themselves from others who exist, as it were, outside the city and in other parts of the world. They distinguish themselves precisely through a self-consolidating other, grounding and identifying a self-consti-tution that posits itself—its being in and for itself—as universal. Again, it is Hegel who points us toward this extreme tension. Recalling Hegel's argument from the *Logic*—"the I is in essence and act the universal: and such communi-ty or partnership [*Gemeinschaftlichkeit*] is a form, although an external form, of universality"—Nancy comments that dialectical logic always requires the passage through exteriority as essential to interiority itself. Nevertheless, he continues, within this same logic, "it is the 'interior' and subjective form of the 'Me' that is needed in order to finish the project of finding itself and pos-ing itself as the *truth* of the universal and its community."[45] No doubt we have not finished elaborating on the implications of Hegel's truth and projections for the histories and genealogies of our Empires and various practices of im-perialism. Nor should we exclude the difficulty, registered in the passage from Marx's proletariat to the "Internationals" to our contemporary NGOs in the North, of fully distinguishing this claim for universality founded on a pre-supposition that constitutes a self-identity from the revolutionary claim to be international, European, and cosmopolitan.

When politics becomes the conduct of the history of this subject, its desti-ny, and its mission, or when for Nancy such a politics becomes "the revelation

or the proclamation of a sense and of an absolute sense," then politics becomes entangled in religion. Or as Nancy argues, when the presupposition of
the self in the self-constitution of the political subject comes to determine the
organic configuration of a people or the destiny of a nation, it is not merely
the crystallization of an identity in a "figure, name, or myth" that comes into
existence; it is a "revelation" of sense and thus religion that also remains at
stake. A politics of the subject is always for Nancy a religious politics. Again,
the terms of Nancy's argument turn us back to the revolutionary tradition:
"The city as such pushes religion in principle away to the infra- or supra-civic
spheres, at the risk of proposing a substitute, a 'civic religion,' which regularly
fails, from Pericles to Robespierre, to take charge of the religious demand,
that is to say, of the demand for a subjective appropriation of sense" (*SM*,
166/*SW*, 105). Or rather, when citizenship is constituted as a model of political self-sufficiency, this religious demand suggests that the city remains,
in principle, "untenable and abstract," without foundation or destiny, without
anything that grounds or identifies it as a source of self-legitimacy. Intimating that any political "proclamation" cannot be detached from a theological
"revelation," and so further intimating that it remains difficult to disentangle
revolutionary proclamations from spiritual missions—in short, politics governed by the Cause or the conditions of sacrifice—Nancy's argument gestures
here toward Carl Schmitt's seminal discussion of the "theologicopolitical," of
the political as the secularization of religious concepts.[46] And yet, however
decisive this reference to Schmitt, the question of sense informing Nancy's
demand to rethink different models of political organization in terms of their
self-sufficiency cannot be reduced to this linear narrative of secularization.
As Nancy argues (and here again we recall the two hypotheses that closed
the previous chapter), the purported rupture with the "theologicopolitical"
that 1789 is meant to represent historically is now displaced into two breaks—
one that leads to "the city (to democracy) as to a space that would no longer
be theological at all," and one that gestures toward a politics of the modern
subject (to the nation-state), "where a laicized theology or, if one prefers, a
romanticized theology—of the 'people,' 'history,' and 'humanity'—substitutes
itself for 'sacred' theology" (*SM*, 166/*SW*, 105).

As we will see, this distinction not only recalls the aporia closing the previous chapter. It remains strictly untenable. But as in the initial distinction between politics according to the subject and politics according to the citizen, this
distinction has heuristic value. For the two paths outlined here lead toward a
"crossroads" or, as Nancy nuances, a "cross" of all Western politics, specifically

representing what is at stake in the West with regard to sense—that is, between an "inappropriable exteriority" and an "appropriative interiority." According to this initial opposition, Nancy's reconfiguring of the citizen and the subject further points toward a conflict between two ways of conceiving community and sovereignty haunting the Western tradition. On the one hand—and here Nancy condenses his most well-known writings on the subject—community can be thought as the "sharing out [*partage*] of the very spacing in accordance with which there are singularities," a sharing out that remains, as such, inappropriable. On the other hand, following the metaphysical presupposition of the subject, community is "the interiority in which sharing out appropriates its negativity, becomes the subject that founds and subsumes within itself this sharing out," and so endows itself with a substance of its own. Or again, the citizen's transformation into the subject—which constitutes the appropriative sense of political self-sufficiency or political sense—is the point where community "gives itself (as) interiority," opening to an immanence or immanentism of community that now founds itself on the effacement of citizenship's worldliness or its "sharing of exteriority." Reciprocally, the citizen becomes subject at the point where sovereignty no longer simply becomes the "formal autoteleology of a 'contract'" between citizens, an "autojurisdiction" that mirrors the city's autoteleological and formal institution but expresses also a substance or essence. And such a substance or essence can figure as a people, a leader, the fatherland, a class, and so on. As Nancy states, "Sovereignty can either be nothing more than the empiricotranscendental (or aleatory-necessary) circumscription that determines the law of such and such a city as the *ne plus ultra* of the 'civity' of this city, the first and last point of its institution and decision, or else this *ne plus ultra* can appropriate to itself the negativity that constitutes it, and can thus present itself as the self-engendered substance of the supremacy it states" (*SM*, 168–69/*SW*, 107).

The reference to supremacy here appears to point at once to the question of totalitarianism elaborated in Lacoue-Labarthe and Nancy's writings for the Center, as well as to Schmitt's understanding of the theologicopolitical. But contrary to any claim that seeks to outline the inexorable dissolution of the nation-state as the enabling condition for resisting all forms of sovereignty—a claim resonant, for example, in Agamben's appeal to a coming political community cited earlier—Nancy further seeks to distinguish a form of sovereignty constituted out of a "self-engendered substance" from a radically different sense of the concept, notably a concept of sovereignty (assuming that it is indeed a "form" or "concept" of sovereignty still in play here) that might begin to respond to what Nancy phrases as "a being-in-action of being-together such that nothing precedes or exceeds it." "Sovereignty has no doubt lost the sense it had," Nancy claims, "reducing itself to a kind of 'black hole' of the political. But this does not mean that the sense of being-in-common, inasmuch as sense is in common, does not have to make itself sovereign in a new way" (*SM*, 143/*SW*, 91).[47] Echoing his discussion of community above, sovereignty can either become the "mere outline of an area of a shared out jurisdiction" (*le simple tracé d'une aire de juridiction partagée*), in which it remains precisely the question of space that remains implicated and its areality open to retracing, or it can identify itself as the "subject of a founding legitimacy" and a founding that remains self-enclosed, interiorized, embodied, and self-contained, at once identified and identifiable in a given (mythical, symbolic) figure or site that must, in its very supremacy, "present itself." Or to redescribe such a tension in terms of Hegel again, if dialectical logic always requires the passage through exteriority as essential to interiority itself, then Nancy concludes that "what is left for us to hold onto is the moment of 'exteriority' as being of almost essential value, so essential that it would no longer be a matter of relating this exteriority to any individual or collective 'we' without also unfailingly [*indéfectiblement*] holding onto [*maintenir*—attaining to] *exteriority itself and as such*."[48] In this sense, it is precisely the question of space as well as collectivity that remains to be rethought.

It is in relation to this same set of problematics concerning forms of political self-sufficiency that Nancy turns to Rousseau. For if Rousseau holds an exemplary place not just within the revolutionary tradition but within this genealogical displacement of forms of political self-sufficiency, then it is because Rousseau exemplifies the moment for Nancy when the word *people* "signals the turning point where the citizen, despite everything, transforms itself into a subject or enters into relation with the pole of the subject" (*SM.* 167/*SW*, 105). In this sense, Rousseau's appeal to the "general will" cannot be fully separated either from a politics of self-sufficiency or (as Schmitt will attest to in his references to Rousseau in *Political Theology*) from the "politicization of theological concepts." But the tradition of contract that informs Rousseau's argument also opens toward a quite distinct reading, one in which Rousseau cannot be quite so easily assimilated to Schmitt's theses:

> The model of the contract remains insufficient or impoverished [*indigent*] in this respect, in that it presupposes subject-parties who

enter into the contract. And yet, its only sense is to constitute these "parties" themselves. Its only sense is to think the tie *to be tied*, and not already tied. In other words, to think the sense of the *in-common* neither as the truth of a common subject nor as a "general" sense superimposed on "particular" senses, but, to the contrary, as the absence of any "general" sense outside of the internally numerous singularity of each of the "subjects of sense" [*la singularité nombreuse d'autant de "sujets de sens"*]. As much as Rousseau "secularizes" Sovereignty, he demultiplies its truth by deferring its sense, by opening up for it an unheard-of history that is still our own. This is no longer "becoming secular" but "becoming-worldly [*mondialisation*]" that is to say, placing sovereignty back within existence, naked existence. (*SM*, 147/*SW*, 93)

As Nancy further argues, echoing his earlier description of citizenship, beyond all the different theories of the contract, one must see in this tradition "the thought of the *res publica* as of a *res* whose entire *realitas* (or substantiality) resides in the formal institution itself," and not in a self-engendered substance or founding legitimacy that the general will appears to presuppose (*SM*, 166/*SW*, 105). Here Rousseau points not toward "principles" of the political, principles he is repeatedly assumed to offer traditions of political philosophy, but toward the political "*in statu nascendi*," which Nancy rewrites as "the tying of the social knot" or "the knotting of the social tie [*le nouage du lien social*]." As Nancy will claim of Rousseau's contract in *The Inoperative Community*, Rousseau was the first to conceive of a communication or *partage* of singular beings, of singularities "exposed to the outside." In Rousseau's thinking, that is, "Society comes about as the bond *and* as the separation between those who, in 'the state of nature,' being without any bond, are nonetheless not separated or isolated. The 'societal' state exposes them to separation, but this is how it exposes 'man,' and how it exposes him to the judgment of his fellows. Rousseau is indeed in every sense the thinker par excellence of compearance [*comparution*]."[49]

The seemingly paradoxical grammar of this *partage* or compearance is rearticulated by Nancy in terms of a "disjunctive conjunction," one that the motif of the contract at once alludes to and dissimulates. As Nancy concludes, "The whole question is whether or not we can finally manage to think the 'contract'—the tying of the tie—according to a model other than the juridicocommercial model (which in fact supposes the bond to have been already established, *already presupposed as its own subject*: this is the founding abyss or decisive aporia of the *Social Contract*). To think the social bond according to another model or perhaps without a model. To think its act, establishment, binding" *(SM, 174/SW, 111).*

In this sense—that is, the sense that works to displace the space of self-sufficient sense or the space of political self-sufficiency—it is the tying of the social tie, the tie that remains to be tied without presupposing the tie as already given, it is this motif of a tie that reopens not just traditions of contract but the political as such, the political "qua archi-constitution of the 'political animal'" *(SM, 147/SW, 93).*

If we have quoted from *The Sense of the World* at some length here, drawing close to Nancy's language and turns of argument, it is not only in order to remeasure what is at stake in contemporary discussions of citizenship within the contexts of globalization. Nor is it only in order to give Nancy's rethinking of the politics of self-sufficiency an inescapably philosophical as well as genealogical revision to widespread proposals to resituate citizenship in terms of global citizenship, cosmopolitanism, and the flexible articulation of pluralized political identities and allegiances. Clearly, the political stakes implied here cannot be detached from their philosophical presuppositions. Indeed, rethinking these philosophical presuppositions does not reduce the political to the philosophical but creates the preliminary conditions for rethinking the stakes of citizenship today, of asking not only "who comes after the subject?" but who, as it were, comes after citizenship.[50]

While these distinctions and exchanges between political concepts also bring into play different ways of parsing out the single and singular combination(s) between citizen, subject, community, and sovereignty within the Western political tradition and so reveal the conditions in which political space has constituted itself as a "space of self-sufficient sense," the question further remains how to move beyond or prior to these distinctions or how to respond to what this closure simultaneously opens up. Indeed, if these two poles of the subject and citizen in the Western political tradition have in fact continually informed each other—to such a degree, Nancy suggests, that they perhaps remain in an "intimate solidarity or connivance" rather than in distinction—should the opposition as such be called into question, beyond its heuristic value? Or rather, in what sense should we rethink this presumed "crossroads" of the Western political tradition? Should this crossroads lead toward the task of inventing *new* political concepts, assuming that it is possible to create a new concept of the political without reinscribing these differences dialectically in the very act of moving beyond them? But then perhaps this crossroads is less an invitation to pass beyond these concepts in order to create a new concept of the political and more of a cross or crossing, in the sense of a chiasmus, in which these conceptual distinctions and their self-sufficient sense should be configured differently, subject to both critique and deconstruction. In short, in what ways does this chiasmus displace the opposition between the "abstract spatiality" of citizenship and the "appropriative violence" of the subject, or in what ways is this chiasmus entangled and folded into Nancy's affirmation of the tie to be tied?

Closer to the terms in which we opened our earlier discussion of citizenship, the question also remains whether Nancy's rearticulation of citizenship in these passages from *The Sense of the World* opens toward a paradox or whether some other logic is in play. We have seen how citizenship enters into a dialectical relationship with the subject in order for both to found their own self-sufficiency or autonomy, and an autonomy whose political consequences and implications can be traced out as stemming directly from this very dialectic. But does the analysis of this genealogical exchange between foundational political concepts pass beyond a dialectical model to the constitution of a paradox? And would the appeal to paradox only ever reinscribe the double polarities of the Western political tradition, becoming nothing more than a symptom of the distinction between the "abstract spatiality" of citizenship and the "appropriative violence" of the subject and not then knowing how to go beyond (or prior to) the opposition or not knowing how to think this opposition differently and undialectically, even as the reference to paradox appears to acknowledge the real conceptual difficulties at stake here? Conversely, does Nancy's insistence on reconceiving the appropriable and inappropriative *partage* of community also open toward a paradox? Or again, in what sense does this insistence on a *partage* remain irreducible to both dialectical and paradoxical logics, even when this *partage* is itself described (perhaps inescapably) as an "extreme paradox" or simply "paradoxical"?[51] In short, in what ways does Nancy's repeated references to a *partage* open onto an affirmation of the political that remains irreducible to the established models of political self-sufficiency, even as such an affirmation takes these conceptual exchanges and genealogical displacements into account as the enabling condition of such an affirmation?

The interrogative mode that continually shapes and punctuates the question of citizenship does not foreclose the possibility of specific affirmations of (political) existence, as later chapters will come to explore. Before we turn to this sense of affirmation, however, it is first necessary to give some measure of the difficulties, if not aporias, that remain in play in any attempt to rethink the terms of citizenship today. Turning back to Nancy's analysis of citizenship at the point at which our commentary just concluded, Nancy poses for us a number of critical questions that must be addressed if we are to move beyond citizenship or reconfigure it from established models of political self-sufficiency. More concretely, Nancy asks whether it is ever possible to avoid "identifying the 'pure' outline of the city," thus closing off the exteriority, spacing, becoming, and relationality that (dis-)articulates the concept of citizenship itself. Consequently, can we avoid turning the citizen into a subject, even if "insubstantial and nonfigured," or even if (as theorists of cosmopolitan democracy such as David Held argue), "the artificial person" at the center if the modern State should be reconceived in terms of cosmopolitan public law and the international "community" becomes "sovereign."[52] Or again, can we avoid making the *res publica* into the "identificatory substance of a community"? Nancy responds, "Our entire history seems to answer that it is not possible— or that to attempt to maintain in its purity either one demand or the other is immediately to precipitate oneself into the inverse purity: the totalitarian subject turns out to be suicidal, but democracy without identification turns out also to be without any *demos* or *kratein* of its own" (SM, 169–70/SW, 108).

More provocatively, this historical response cannot be separated from our contemporary geopolitical situation: "At this very moment, when political subjectivity is doubtless to a great degree coming undone, and when substantial sovereignty is splitting up, are we not in the process of learning that the virtual advent, or in any case the almost universally desired advent, of a world citizenship (beginning with that of Europe) nonetheless risks corresponding to the triumph (itself without sharing out [*partage*]) of what has been called 'market democracy'?" (SM, 170/SW, 108).

When the future of citizenship is thus faced with this triumph of market democracy, and when any alternative to the reduction of citizenship to the global condition of advanced capitalism must simultaneously entail overturning or displacing the models of political self-sufficiency in which both citizenship and a politics of the subject are constituted, then how are we to proceed? Is it a question of choosing between these two models, or is it now a question of noting that they remain fundamentally and essentially complicit with one other, demanding that we move on to other political concepts that would resist more effectively this subordination of the global citizen to the mechanisms of market democracy, mechanisms that are perhaps reproduced by this very figure of the global citizen? But then, would one of the consequences of maintaining citizenship be to reveal that the exteriority of relations that governs citizenship's more formal constitution subject it to what Nancy envisages as the possibilities of "extreme inequality and injustice"? In other words, in light of the essential emptiness of its autoteleology, the citizen is permanently exposed to the "infinite appropriation or devouring of (a) 'capital,'" which may be read here as at once a principle figure of the State and capitalism. And as Nancy's section on "labor" in *The Sense of the World* attests, the contemporary transformations in work and the global migration of labor are profoundly implicated in this very problematic. Furthermore,

> Is democracy—as the "nothing" of the subject, as pure citizenship—condemned to exhaust itself in the dream of a "politics-without-or-against-the-State" (assuming that the State is simply assimilable to subjectivity, which is no doubt not possible without further ado), on the one hand, while on the other, identification (State, nation, people, figure in general) would be unilaterally given over to the devouring of totalitarian and religious appropriation? Or will we pass on, more subtly, into the unraveling of this antinomy, the nothing-of-the-subject becoming absolute subject of an appropriation as powerful as it is empty, an appropriation whose logic and global figure [*figure mondiale*] would be (a) capital itself? (*SM*, 170–1/*SW*, 109)

In posing these questions—questions again that at once echo and simultaneously transform the closing hypotheses that conclude Lacoue-Labarthe and Nancy's texts for the Center in Paris—it is significant that Nancy not only phrases the question of citizenship *as* a question, thereby suggesting that the future of citizenship remains subject to continual rearticulation if we are to move beyond the various models of political self-sufficiency. This interrogative mode also brings into relief the different logics of analysis that have defined our argument since the beginning of the chapter, whether such logics turn on the positing of multiple identities, celebrations of plurality, the spatial relation between interiority and exteriority, the dialectical reciprocity between two distinct models, the unraveling of an antinomy, or the seemingly infinitesimal displacements between citizenship understood as a paradox within our contemporary global situation and citizenship exposed as *partage*. The difficulty is exacerbated when the exteriority of relations that define citizenship in its "pure" form opens the possibility of citizenship's (nondialectical, nonparadoxical) (self-)transformation and simultaneous (self-)effacement when faced with the appropriating "logic" of (a) capital as "global figure." But such an attention to the underlying logics and presuppositions in which to rearticulate citizenship makes little or no sense unless it is situated in light of Nancy's larger question of the "sense of the world" (the title of the book in which these references to citizenship are largely elaborated). For if (a) capital has indeed become a global figure, and a figure against which we might begin to measure both the antinomy between the dream of a "politics-without-or-against-the State" and "the devouring of totalitarian and religious appropriation," as well as the unraveling of this antinomy, Nancy points less to globalization as constituting an explanatory discourse in this context than to the more essential question facing us today, the very question invariably effaced or presupposed in the numerous discourses of globalization: "Can the world cut a *figure* [*faire figure*]? Can it be fashioned and presented in *its own* identity?"

We will return at some length in later chapters to this question of the figure and its relation to a politics of the tie, to the configuration of the space of the in-common that for Nancy "forms the contour, if not the aporia, at least of the paradox of political sense today" (*SM*, 142/*SW*, 90). What remains decisive for the moment is Nancy's emphasis on the presentation of the world *as* world. For is not the world, Nancy asks, precisely "an in-finity of presentation"? But then how does one distinguish "presence from pres-ence," where the latter implies "the *praes-entia* of being-present," an *e-venire* or the infinity of a coming into presence that is never fully present, finished, and self-sufficient? More pertinently (and here we recall our earlier references to Derrida's "democracy to come" and Agamben's "coming political communities"), instead of reducing the world to a question of *identity* (and again, is this not the presupposition and guiding premise behind all the discourses of globalization or the unspoken horizon of capitalist expansion?), the question still remains "how *to hold onto* the *coming of what is coming* [*comment se tenir à la venue*]" (*SM*, 171/*SW*, 109). As concerns this aporia or aporetic positioning—how to hold oneself exposed to this coming, for which there remains no horizon of expectation in advance of the taking-place of this event—Nancy does not merely leave the question hanging endlessly open, not knowing how to go beyond what Derrida once termed "the ahistorical lure of logico-formal paradoxes."[53] For Nancy rethinks this aporia both in its relation to founding political categories as well as in relation to its revolutionary implications:

This tension constitutes the extreme tension between citizen and subject, between the community of one and the community of the other,
between sovereignty and itself. It extends across all of the *Social Contract* and all of our Revolutions, as well as across all of our attempts
to put an end to these things. It extends across the entire political
apparatus of sense in the West: but sense in the West cannot not be at
least *also* political. It makes up the very dialectics or distension of this
sense—the dialectics in the course of coming unraveled [*se dénouer*]
into distension, that is to say, into an extreme tension that resolves
itself as well into an extreme relaxation. No longer any subject, but
no citizen either. No longer any infinite return into oneself, but no
shared out finitude either. Nothing but bad infinitude or bad finitude:
it is the same thing, the simultaneous absence of ties and spacing.
(*SM*, 171/*SW*, 109)

The reference to paradox in the recent literature on citizenship becomes
a way of warding off the unraveling of this dialectic and so manages to hold
at bay the ways in which this unraveling either resolves itself (the exteriority
of relations and ties between citizens now effaced through the potential of
totalitarian and religious appropriation) or distends to such a degree that the
complete absence of ties exposes the citizen to atomization and the "infinite
appropriation" of capital. But such a warding off of this tension also effaces
precisely what is at stake in rethinking the models of political self-sufficiency
and political sense that constitute the Western political tradition: how to attest to this *venue* and the ineluctable force of this "to come." Or rather, in
order to transform this aporia from a form of negation to one of affirmation,
how does holding onto what is coming open onto a politics of the tie, of ties in
their irreducible and worldly spacing? Or how are we to think an "atheologi-
cal" politics of *non*-self-sufficiency, where the negation implied here becomes
the immeasurable measure of the tie *to be tied* and not already tied? Such a
politics is not indebted to a discourse of crisis in order to claim its initiative.
It is not subject to the dialectical (and fundamentally theological) symmetry
between the "permanence of the old" and the "pure innovation" of the new.
Or again, the negation implicated in a politics of non-self-sufficiency is not a
determinate negation that would take us *beyond* what Nancy phrases as the
quadruple instance subject-citizen-sovereignty-community in order to found
a *new* (unfounded) concept of the political. Indeed, we could argue that it
matters little whether we name this politics of non-self-sufficiency in terms

of citizenship or not, for it is the conditions in which to think the *partage* of the citizen's exteriority that counts (or as if the concept of citizen were placed permanently under erasure, crossed out in its very appearance). The refusal of forms of political self-sufficiency is not determined by negation but by this *sharing out*, which Nancy also rephrases as a *supplementary* condition of the tie to be tied, a supplementary tie that displaces the play between these founding political concepts "by making apparent another determination" of the political. Thinking the tie as supplement does not suppress the tensions between these political concepts but changes the stakes, above all "to those we have become accustomed to designating with the opposition between 'right' and 'left'" (*SM*, 175/*SW*, 112). More specifically,

> this supplementary determination does not arise [*rèleverait*] from a demand for sense or from the postulation of a signification. It does not make of sense a political production, as does, in contrast, the polarity subject/citizen. Consequently, it does not institute the political as another world charged with the task of presenting—now sense itself, now a pure space. It is merely, along the very surface of the world [*à même ce monde*]—along the surface of our world that it is no longer a matter of either interpreting or transforming, if to transform still means to interpret, to engender a sense and an end—the specific determination of the tie, the in-common *through which there is sense* that circulates and that ties and connects or links itself [*s'enchaîne*], *perhaps without having any global or final signification* (not knowing, moreover, any global or final state), and without having any "sense" other than tying itself, which is not a signification. (*SM*, 176/*SW*, 112)

Here the connection is not between two established and presupposed parties, in which subjects communicate or connect with one another; as in Rousseau's contract, the only sense of this connection is to constitute these parties themselves. Or again, such a constitution is less structured and erect than the reticulated circulation of tying-up with and alongside, at once attached and detached, in proximity and simultaneously spaced and separated (out)—in short, *partagé*. The supplementary determination of the tie to be tied is not a *new* sense of the political, nor simply paradoxical, but an acknowledgment and affirmation of something more modest though no less demanding, at once radical and quite banal—that "the political is the place of the in-common as such" (*SM*, 139/*SW*, 88). In order to think this place of the in-common, Nancy insists that the "space of sense" does not take place for "one alone" but is common space (less a "pure space," in other words, than the topology of surface effects). Or again, sense is the "tensor of multiplicity," and a multiplicity whose grammar (if indeed it remains a question of grammar) is parsed out in terms of the multiple connections, circulations, and links inaugurated here, of ties to be tied. "Sense is the fact that sense begins and begins again with each singularity and completes itself neither in any singularity nor in the totality, which is nothing but the linking of renewed beginnings" (*SM*, 139/*SW*, 88). It is this supplementary determination of the tie to be tied in its endless reticulation that reopens the "archi-constitution" of the political animal to its essential an-archy, to the chance encounters that constitute another measure in which to think existence as exposed, shared out. And it is in this sense—the sense that reopens the closed space of self-sufficient sense—that "the coming of all to the public relation," of a citizenship to come and the political as a sense to come, remains to be thought.

3

The Disposition of Being

Exteriority, taken as the essence of being, signifies the resistance of the social multiplicity to the logic that totalizes the multiple.... The I's form no totality; there exists no privileged plane where these I's could be grasped [se saisir] in their principle. There is anarchy essential to multiplicity. In the absence of a plane common to the totality (which one persists in seeking, so as to relate the multiplicity to it) one will never know which will, in the free play of the wills, pulls the strings of the game; one will never know who is playing with whom.

—Emmanuel Lévinas

In a passage from *Being Singular Plural*, Nancy detaches the concept of networks both from its various technological determinations as well as from the histories and theories of communication in which networks today find much of their contemporary relevance:

If "communication" is for us, today, such an affair—in every sense of the word...—if its theories are flourishing, if its technologies are being proliferated, if the "mediatization" of the "media" brings along with it an auto-communicational vertigo, if one plays around with the theme of the indistinctness between the "message" and the "medium" out of either a disenchanted or jubilant fascination, then it is because something is exposed or laid bare—the bare and "content"-less web [*trame*] of "communication." One could say it is the bare web of the *com*- (of the *telecom*-, said with an acknowledgment of its independence); that is, it is *our* web or "us" as web or network, an *us* that is reticulated and spread out, with its extension for an essence and its spacing [*espacement*] for a structure. We are "ourselves" too inclined [*disposés*] to see in this the overwhelming destiny of modernity. Contrary to such meager evidence, it might be that we have understood nothing about the situation, and rightly so, and that we

have to start again to understand ourselves—our existence and that
of the world, our being disposed in this way [*notre être ainsi disposé*].¹

Nancy's argument—which does not constitute a thesis, for there is no
thesis or position to be held on "being dis-posed"—suggests less a return to
some mythical origin of communication than a way of thinking inscribed
and structured by *repetition*. It is the through the force of this repetition that
we "start again" to understand at once "our existence and that of the world."
Or once again, Nancy's argument draws us not to an interiority or an enclosed space, in which we turn away from the world and back into ourselves,
but opens us toward a disposition, in the sense of a mood, an inclination,
an attunement or *Stimmung*, in which we acknowledge neither the origin of
communication nor some transcendent source that legitimates all communication and governs its rules, but a "disposition of Being." It is precisely this
disposition that defines our very existence as existence *in the world* rather
than returning us to an interiorized essence, a self-contained subjectivity,
a behaviorism or psychologism—in short, a discourse of the autonomous
subject. If the existence of our being in the world is also inseparable from
a certain materiality (at least if the *trame* or "web" that binds us is understood in the materiality of its structural distribution and reticulation), it is
an existence in which the *trame* or "fabric of being" is at once dis-posed and
simultaneously ex-posed, not only in the world but in the exteriority and
extension of what ex-ists, in "an *us* that is reticulated and spread out."² The
question Nancy thus poses from the outset is how to think the "disposition
of Being," this disposition that marks our finite existence in the world, as essentially reticulated.

In order to pursue this initial question, the world here is not understood
as a space, context, or environment extraneous or external to existence, as
the phrase being "in" the world might suggest, and as if our natality or existence preceded the world in which we subsequently find ourselves, for the
"bare web of the *com-*" toward which Nancy draws us is simultaneously
the "laying bare" of the world itself, the world *mise à nu*. The question, in
other words, turns on the ways in which the affirmation of existence and our
"being disposed" is inseparable from the "network of the world,"³ a world in
which the "reticulation of contiguities and tangential contacts" that comes
to articulate our shared coexistence with others becomes the measure, itself
immeasurable, of our "being-in-common" or our "being-with-one-another."
In this sense—and for Nancy, as we have seen, it is precisely a question of

sense—the "sharing of being" suggested by an "*us* that is reticulated and spread out" *is* the "sharing of the world," where what is "shared" or *partagé* is not a common humanity or a common world but also translates as what is divided or shared out—*in-common* and not merely common. Rather than the passage from the "closed world" to the "infinite universe" (to recall the title of Alexandre Koyré's celebrated book cited in *The Sense of the World*), the world is now reconfigured as a "web" in which the world becomes world or worldwide in its "reticulated multiplicity," and it does so not as a passage from one weltanschauung or worldview to another, nor as a discourse of globalization, but from the "singular multiplicity" of the world's "origins" (*ESP*, 27/*BSP*, 9). Neither interiorized nor self-contained, neither self-sufficient nor presupposed in its self-propriety, the reticulated "us" in which existence is shared out in its exposure or radical exteriority does not refer back to an originary essence, determining structure, or transcendence beyond or prior to the world; it grounds itself in nothing that gives orientation or stability to the web or network in its infinite extension, or its infinite extensibility and communicability. In short, the path that Nancy opens up here, the path that leads us toward a "bare and 'content'-less web," is not a return to the origin or essence of communication hidden behind the contemporary flourishing of technologies and its accompanying theories. For this web or network of communication is the enabling condition in which to think the very disposition and exposure of Being, where what is exposed or what exists is the "bare web of the *com-*," the "with" or *cum* which—and in which—we "ourselves" communicate in and *as* a network.

Before elaborating further on Nancy's references to networks in *Being Singular Plural* and their decisive role in rethinking existence in terms of the "disposition of Being"—the initial task proposed in the pages that follow—it becomes immediately clear that the language and concepts marking Nancy's argument are far removed from the usual contexts in which the discourse of networks finds much of its contemporary purchase and critical relevance. Given the proliferation of new technologies of networked communication characterizing our more recent modernity, the exponential interest in systems of information technology, the dominance of media networks and globalized mediatization, the post-McLuhanesque and Baudrillard-inspired fascination with mediums, messages, and screens, and the widespread acknowledgment that the discourse of networks constitutes the basis of numerous fields of contemporary research and application—in short, given our contemporary "affair" with networked communication—Nancy's passage from *Being*

Singular Plural, and notably the language that informs it, also challenges a number of widely held assumptions concerning the role of networks within the discourse of modernity. Indeed, to suggest that networks play no role in modernity's "destiny," or no role in narrating the passage from modernity to postmodernity, would seem to empty networks of their increasingly widespread role in both understanding and transforming the world in which we live, depriving us at the same time of one of the heuristically most effective means by which we might imagine a future. To suggest that networks play no role in understanding our modernity or postmodernity would also appear to remove networks from the discourse of globalization, a discourse in which networks figure extensively. Given this background, then, it becomes necessary before returning to Nancy's text to first outline the ways in which he detaches the concept of networks from these well-known arguments.

In refusing to situate the proliferating discourses of communication in terms of modernity's "destiny," Nancy withdraws networks from any prescribed historical schema, or from any discourse in which the appeal to communication is synonymous with some measure of progress or development within modernity, whether this is understood in terms that are historicist, teleological, linear, evolutionary, or dialectical. Contrary to much of the literature on the history of networks and their increasingly pervasive role in shaping the world we inhabit, there is no attempt at historical periodization, no cycles or trends, no watershed years or symbolic events. In short, networks do not constitute for Nancy the privileged emblems of our (post-)modernity or the determining and instrumental representation of our contemporaneity.

As part of this refusal to situate networks in terms of modernity's destiny, the passage we cited from *Being Singular Plural* does not situate networks in terms of systems of telecommunication and information technology, whether these systems and their associated technology are situated historically or in light of more contemporary innovations (cybernetics, digitalization, cyberculture, virtual reality, the Internet as "network of networks," and so on). The *trame* to which Nancy refers in the passage might well translate into the "web of communication," but Nancy does not refer in the original to *le web*, the more common expression in French for Internet communication and the World Wide Web. Nor does Nancy consider networks in terms of globalization and its various tendencies—not just telecommunications, global media, and information technologies but the increasingly dominant role of networks in geopolitics and global relations, in global economies and global capitalism, in post-Fordist management, manufacturing and marketing, as well as in the various tendencies defined by biopolitics, global viruses, war and surveillance, social movements and NGOs, and so on—a discourse of globalization in which these various tendencies are often considered synonymous with forms of networked organization, connection, and distribution.

In light of the more usual contexts informing contemporary research and application, Nancy's references to networks in terms of the "disposition of Being" or "existence" suggest a marked transition in vocabulary from preoccupations with society and the "social," and so nowhere turn to the increasingly abundant literature in sociology (including the available software programs) in which the discourse of networks has largely figured. This includes studies of the "network society," of new forms of community and group affiliation, of the rise of virtual communities, blogs, and chat rooms, as well as the more specialized fields of social network analysis, actor-network-theory, and so on.

More generally, Nancy's appeal to networks in *Being Singular Plural* finds no support in the growing awareness of their epistemological as well as social and political implications, nor in the wide display of disciplinary and interdisciplinary contexts in which the discourse of networks plays an increasingly prominent role, including the highly specialized knowledges derived from neural science, crystallography, electrical engineering, theories of evolutionary biology and self-adaptive systems, algebra and mathematical modeling, graphology, marketing, digital capital, and so on, specialized knowledges that are always more varied than the customary overviews of networks usually suggest. Nor again does Nancy draw from the mutation and translation of these specialized knowledges into more expansive systems of thinking the complexity of the world in its multiple articulations or signification. From the gurus of the "new science" of networks to recent proposals to rearticulate global "assemblages," from Niklas Luhmann's "systems theory" to Gilles Deleuze and Félix Guattari's rhizomatic "lines of flight," from Annelise Riles's demand to think networks "inside out" to Manuel Castells on the "internet galaxy," from theories of complexity to Manuel de Landa's "meshworks"—to name only some of the most well-known references—the discourse of networks has clearly constituted one of the most decisive challenges to both disciplinary and epistemological thinking.[4] Such writings transform the epistemological implications of networks from their more specialized fields of origin to new assemblages of social or anthropological research, new materialist historiographies, new forms of "nomadic" and deterritorialized thinking, new posthuman bodies, new sites of conflict and relations of power, all ways in which the world is now characterized by flows, connections, and becomings whose functioning "logic" is more reticulated than structural, more complex than linear, more recursive than dialectical, more emergent than totalizing. Beyond the usual rhetorical appeals to interdisciplinarity, such work opens out toward new conceptual and materialist genealogies, the invention of new languages, and the creation of new concepts—in short, new affirmations, inventions, or creations of the world in the multiplicity of its potential articulations or virtual reticulations.

If Nancy shares this sense of affirmation, and if his own writings have incessantly worked toward rearticulating this invention and creation of the world *as* world, the reference to networks in *Being Singular Plural* corresponds little to this heterogeneous array of new knowledges, languages, and concepts. Such reticence does not stem from Nancy's disinterest in questions posed by communication, language, or technology, which he reframes in terms of "eco-technics" and defines (via the writings of Braudel) as "the global structuration of the world as the reticulated space of an essentially capitalist, globalist, and monopolist organization that is monopolizing the world" (*SM*, 159–60/*SW*, 101). Nor does such reticence stem from Nancy's disinterest in the discourse of globalization, itself a problematic translation of Nancy's own insistence on thinking the *mondialisation* of the world, of the world in its becoming world-wide, of the world as it "worlds"—all of which he rearticulates through a question of *sense*.[5] Nancy's voluminous writings have also turned with marked insistence toward many of the most difficult challenges facing our contemporary world. But it is precisely not in *these* terms that he poses for us the question of networks. Estranging or distancing us from the increasingly predictable ways in which the multiple discourses of networks are situated and discussed, or re-opening as yet unexplored genealogies of the concept, the passage from *Being Singular Plural* with which we opened the chapter appears to enact instead a radical "reduction" to a—or *the*—question of Being.[6] This bracketing is less phenomenological in its method and orientation than a "laying bare," a *mise à nu*, also translated as an "exposure," in which what is laid bare or exposed is reducible not to an origin, substance, or identifiable essence but that which gives itself over to relation, articulation, or reticulation—the "bare and 'content'-less web of communication." In this sense, Nancy's reference to networks does not stem from any desire to create a *new* language or a *new* concept but to disclose, in and as a repetition of what constitutes "existence" and "the question of Being," the conditions of being-*with* inscribed in all communication. It is precisely these conditions that are largely effaced in the proliferation of discourses that accompany the myriad forms of contemporary communication technologies, even when articulated in terms of new forms of identity, connectivity, subjectivity, or community.[7] Or rather, Nancy is clearing away a space in which networks come again into appearance, but the space that is exposed or created is not a clearly delineated, autonomous, or self-contained space, one in which a position is locatable and a subject finds its (self-)orientation or representation. For the space exposed here is less a space that exists in and of itself than an *espacement* or "spacing," a reticulated spacing touched on in the previous chapter that is at once spatial *and* temporal, delimited and delimiting. Following Nancy's proposal to think this spacing in terms of an "areality," we might also term such a space a post-phenomenological and post-Mallarméan spacing, in which the very "heart" of Being is laid bare in its "disposition." The space that is thereby disclosed, or the spacing that subverts all attempts at phenomenological disclosure, is the space of "naked" or "bare" existence—a "desert," to use Nancy's favored motif from Nietzsche, or a barren or abandoned space—but an existence that exists in its own exteriority to itself, and so in "the bare web of the *com-*," the *with* that marks the reticulated spacing of coexistence rather than solipsistic or autistic isolation.[8]

It is this spacing whose topological folds we will need to discern again in the pages that follow. For the task that Nancy also poses for us is how to delineate, circumscribe, and retrace the contours of a space in which the reticulated spacing of networks is fully commensurate with Being in its disposition, or with Being laid bare and abandoned. This same task comes into further relief when we also ask how the reticulated spacing of Being in its disposition relates to the more familiar observation posed by the discourse of globalization concerning the political transformations of space and the spatial transformations of the political, including the displacement of territorial markers and the deterritorialization of borders. Taking up again the role of teletechnologies explored in the previous chapter, the question thus remains in what sense Nancy's affirmation of the reticulated spacing of Being transforms the more widely known argument proposed in numerous discourses of globalization, in which networks are said to enact the deterritorialization and global rearticulation of state sovereignty, or the displacement of all territorial inscriptions of space and movement. And in what sense does this same proposal to think Being in its disposition touch again on the archi-constitution of the "political animal" also raised in previous chapters?

As an initial response to this task, Nancy's references to the disposition of Being in *Being Singular Plural* clearly suggest an open engagement with the question of ontology. Or rather, we might claim that Nancy situates his understanding of the disposition of Being at the *level* of ontology, were it not precisely the spatial or topological presuppositions implied by levels that networks displace in their reticulated spacing, thus opening toward different, non-Cartesian topologies that characterize networks and their reticulated organization and distribution. If the reticulated displacement of Being provoked or solicited by its disposition nevertheless opens onto a question of ontology, Nancy's argument in *Being Singular Plural* refuses to situate the ontological as a regional ontology but seeks instead to enact a radical displacement of the traditional order of ontological exposition. In this sense, the disposition of Being is not reducible to an identity, individual subject, or ego that is then given a social dimension, articulated within a group formation or social relation. It is not a question of simply adding a communitarian dimension onto a "primitive individual given," even if it were to occur as an essential and determining addition. As Nancy recalls, "Just think of the numerous circumstances of ordinary discourse in which this order is imposed on us: first the individual, then the group; first the one, then the others; first the rights-bearing subject, then real relationships; first 'individual psychology,' then 'collective psychology'; and above all, first a 'subject,' then 'intersubjectivity'—as they astonishingly persist in saying" (*ESP*, 64/*BSP*, 44).

In addition to the most banal uses in everyday language, it would be difficult to under-estimate the innumerable discourses—political, social, juridical, scientific, religious, economic, anthropological, cultural, historical—that *presuppose* this sequencing, even when offered as a critique of the subject or its so-called decentering. As Nancy argues in *The Sense of the World*, such presuppositions not only govern the traditional order of ontological exposition but inform and reproduce the metaphysical *position* of the Subject, where it is precisely this metaphysical position that is presupposed in one or another of its forms—"as a supposed substantial support for determination and qualities, as point of presence supposed to be the source of representations, as a negation that supposes itself to be the power if its own suspension and overcoming, as a relation to the self (where the *to* is supposed to be the very presence of the *self*), as a power of realization supposed to engender reality, or as the supposed being of the existent" (*SM*, 112/*SW*, 69)—and where the *absolute* presupposition for the synthesis for all these forms is God.[9] From the outset, Nancy's insistence on the *dis-* inscribed in the disposition of Being is precisely the refusal of this metaphysical presupposition and positioning of the Subject and so initiates the contortion and convolution of these priorities, sequences, and hierarchies of ontological ordering and exposition: "It is not a matter of adding to a postulation of individuality or autonomy a certain number of relations and interdependencies, no matter what importance one may accord to such an agenda. The 'someone' does not enter into relation with other 'someones,' nor is there a 'community' that precedes interrelated individuals [*les uns et les autres*]: the singular is not the particular, not *part* of a group (species, gender, class, order). The relation is contemporaneous with the singularities. 'One' means: the ones *and* the others, the ones *with* the others" (*SM*, 116–17/*SW*, 71).

If the subject is more a belated consequence than a prior condition of all "intersubjectivity" and "interrelated individuals," or if the disposition of Being at once determines yet remains irreducible to a discourse of the subject, even when the subject's (decentered) identity is constituted through the intersections of race, ethnicity, gender, sexuality, and class, then "being disposed" is inscribed by this relation that is strictly contemporaneous with the exposition or spacing of singularities.[10]

The ontology in question here is thus an ontology that seeks to rethink the relation between the foundational philosophical concepts of the 'One' and the 'Many,' articulated now not as a question of identity, subjectivity, multiple individualities, or intersubjectivities, but in terms of pluralities, singularities, and multiplicities. Or, as the title of Nancy's book proposes, the disposition of Being opens toward the "singular plurality" or "plural singularity" of Being (both possible translations of *être singulier pluriel*), where the singular does not preexist the plural but itself remains always plural, always opening onto "singularities" and "multiplicities" and not the singular or the multiple as substantial, countable, or isolated forms. If there is still an ontology at stake here, it is one that points toward a renewed grammar or syntax of Being, a re-articulation of being-in-relation that is no longer ontological in any measurable sense within the tradition of philosophy, but that cannot be detached from that very tradition.[11] In "The Forgetting of Philosophy," Nancy rephrases this being-in-relation as the "being of the 'we'" that comes before all anthropology, all humanism, and all antihumanism, or again as "an ontology that is yet to come [*encore à venir*]," which does not mean that it *will* come, as Nancy insists, but that it is ordered "according to a dimension of a 'coming' or a 'coming to pass' [*d'un 'venir' ou d'un 'survenir'*]"[12] As an ontology to come, being-in-relation is the mark of displacement, itself asyntactical, agrammatical, and immeasurable, that is also registered in Nancy's insistence on a series of modifying prepositions and hyphens punctuating the text of *Being Singular Plural*, the dis- and ex- that repeatedly modifies all

position and stance, all ontological stature and erection. It is these prepositions and hyphens that inaugurate the *com-* or "being with" by permanently
remarking the radical exteriority and desedimentation of all ontological and
metaphysical presuppositions, by permanently recomposing Being in terms
of its singular plurality and plural singularity:

> Being singular plural: in a single *trait*, without punctuation, without
> a mark of equivalence, implication, or sequence. A single continu-
> ous-discontinuous mark tracing out the entirety [*ensemble*] of the
> ontological domain, being-with designated as the "with" of being, of
> the singular and plural, and dealing a blow to ontology—not only an-
> other signification but also another syntax. The "meaning of Being":
> not only as the "meaning of Being" but also, above all, as the "with" of
> meaning. Because none of these three terms precedes or grounds the
> other, each designates the co-essence of the others. This co-essence
> hyphenates essence itself [*La co-essence met l'essence elle-même dans
> le trait*]—"being singular plural"—which is a mark of union [*trait
> d'union*] and also a mark of division [*trait de division*], a mark of
> sharing out [*trait de partage*] that effaces itself, leaving each term to
> its isolation *and* its being-with-the others. *(ESP, 57–58/BSP, 37)*

At once recalling and reconfiguring the central motif of the *re-trait* of the
political in Lacoue-Labarthe and Nancy's writings for the Center in Paris,
the prepositions and hyphens that repeatedly punctuate the text of *Being
Singular Plural* work to displace the metaphysical presuppositions that serve
to ground and secure the subject's position in the world and so remove all
possibility of establishing the "meaning of Being" in terms of a self-positing
identity, the "I" or "One" as a self-contained unity, including the singular
affirmation of *das Man*. Or such prepositions and hyphens open toward the
discretion of Being in its disposition rather than an ontology that seeks to locate a substance, common essence, or the subject's self-propriety and seamless coherence. In consequence, the implied identity or totality suggested by
the phrase "entirety of the ontological domain" is permanently displaced by
these same prepositions and hyphens to the plural singularity and singular
plurality of the *ensemble* whose "domain" implies less a strictly circumscribed
spatial dimension than a reticulated spacing coextensive with this *ensemble*.
At the same time, the grammar, syntax, and punctuation informing Nancy's
text and its affirmation of being disposed cannot be detached from the related

acknowledgment that "the logic of 'with' often requires heavy-handed syntax in order to say 'being-with-one-another' [*être-les-uns-avec-les-autres*, literally, being-the-ones-with-the-others]."[13] As Nancy cautions, it is perhaps not an accident that "language does not easily lend itself to showing the 'with' as such" (*ESP*, 14/*BSP*, xvi). Nancy's very writing of *Being Singular Plural* is then the enacting and performance of this acknowledgment, as if the act of writing were permanently inscribed in rethinking the metaphysical presuppositions of the Subject and the displacement of these presuppositions toward the disposition of Being in its simultaneous articulation and reticulation. Elaborating further on this question of writing in *The Sense of the World*, and as if presaging its reelaboration in *Being Singular Plural*, Nancy argues,

> The world is sense or "origin" in a mode that precisely no longer can be indicated in the style of a categorization of "modes" in general, that is, of a punctuation of concepts, but that produces itself, that produces its sense, only *as* the serial articulation and drawing out [*l'enchaînement et l'entraînement*], indeed, the transport [*l'emportment*], of another style, writing, and exscription of philosophy....The *world* invites us to think no longer on the level of phenomenon, however it may be understood (as surging forth, appearing, becoming visible, brilliance, occurrence, event), but on the level—let us say, for the moment—of the dis-position (spacing, touching, contact, crossing). (*SM*, 34/*SW*, 176)

Given the preliminary difficulty in which language does not easily lend itself to showing the "with" as such, *Being Singular Plural* can be read as a continual rearticulation and rephrasing of this one question, this question of the "disposition of Being."[14] The disposition of Being also haunts the metaphysical as well as phenomenological tradition of the Subject that Nancy's writings traverse at an oblique angle, even as the prepositions and hyphenation displace the pre- and post- that lend themselves to the historicization of these same traditions or the positing, narration, or dialectical overcoming of their shared modernity and destiny. In this sense, the disposition of Being finds itself rephrased in different ways, whether as Descartes's "*ego sum*" or Rousseau's "contract," Hegel's "Absolute" or Bataille's "community," Marx's "proletariat" or Freud's "Oedipus," Lacan's "Other" or Hardt and Negri's "multitude," as if each of these terms were now reexposed to its ontological and metaphysical presuppositions. In turn, Nancy's appeal to the disposition of Being cannot be detached from rethinking what constitutes the political *as such*, or the very "essence" of the political already explored in Nancy's earlier writings with Lacoue-Labarthe, a proximity to the political to which we will also have occasion to return. But it is from Heidegger's *Being and Time* that Nancy's reference to the disposition of Being clearly finds its terminological and conceptual resources. For it is in light of Heidegger's *Being and Time* that we can begin to measure the displacement between the *Seinsfrage* or "question of Being" that marks the guiding premise of Heidegger's text and Nancy's insistence on rethinking *Dasein*'s existential constitution in terms of its "disposition," as if Heidegger at once posits the possibility of thinking Being in its disposition and yet withdraws it from its most radical implications or force. Indeed, "disposition" also translates Heidegger's *Befindlichkeit*, which is often translated as "state of mind" but suggests not an inner state but a "fundamental existential" (as Heidegger phrases it in §29 of *Being and Time*). In this sense, the disposition of Being is not a passive mood internal to a subject so much as a primordial mode of *Dasein*'s disclosedness in the world, a mode that is not strictly demarcated by an interior and exterior distinction but reopens the *spatial* dimension that characterizes for Heidegger the ec-stasy of *Dasein*'s being-*there*. In this regard, it is symptomatic of the larger stakes of Nancy's argument that he introduces *Being Singular Plural* by pointing to the ways in which his affirmation of the plural singularity and singular plurality of Being is first and foremost a response to Heidegger's rewriting of all "first philosophy" as "fundamental ontology," arguing that it is necessary "to redo fundamental ontology (as well as the existential analytic, the history of Being, and the thinking of *Ereignis* that goes along with it) with a thorough resolve that *starts from the plural singular of origins*, from *being-with*" (*ESP*, 45/*BSP*, 26). "The question of Being" and the "question of the meaning of Being" that govern *Being and Time* are now both rewritten as an affirmation of "being-with" and "being-with-one-another." Or again, "being-with" becomes for Nancy the "most proper problem of Being," while the essential "plurality" of beings is at the very "foundation [*fondement*]" of Being (*ESP*, 30/*BSP*, 12), phrases in which it is precisely the force of Being in its disposition that suspends or interrupts all plurality or foundation understood in terms of an identity, closure, or self-sufficiency.

Neither a critique of Heidegger, nor a form of "Heideggerianism," Nancy's argument takes its point of departure from a certain slippage, reservation, subordination, or reserve within Heidegger's *Being and Time*, at least in the sense in which Heidegger's existential analytic is said to still harbor some "principle" by which "what [this analytic] opens up is immediately closed off ":

> Heidegger clearly states that being-with (*Mitsein, Miteinandersein, Mitdasein*) is essential to the constitution of *Dasein* itself. On this basis, it needs to made absolutely clear that *Dasein*, far from being either "man" or "subject," is not even an isolated and unique "one," but is instead always the one, each one, with one another [*l'un avec l'autre*]. If this determination is essential, then it needs to attain to the co-originary dimension and expose it without reservation. Despite Heidegger's affirmation, it has often been remarked that the assertion of co-originarity gives way to the consideration of *Dasein* itself. It is appropriate, then, to examine the possibility of an explicit and endless exposition of co-originarity and the possibility of taking into account of what is at stake in the togetherness of the ontological enterprise (and, in this way, taking account of what is at stake in its political consequences). *(ESP, 46/BSP, 26)*[15]

When Nancy gestures toward the stakes of a political rewriting of Heidegger's texts, such rewriting cannot be dissociated from the exposition of co-originarity that also remains at stake here. Or rather, as Nancy also insists, it will become necessary to "forcibly reopen a passage" beyond or prior to the ways in which Heidegger poses an "obstruction" to this very passage, and an obstruction that works by "deciding the terms of being-with's fulfillment and return [*remplissement et le repliement*]" (*ESP*, 117/*BSP*, 93). It is this decision that effaces or folds back the exposition of co-originarity that Heidegger simultaneously discloses as essential to *Dasein*'s constitution, and it is this same decision, culminating in an affirmation of a "people" and their "spiritual destiny," that shapes Heidegger's political allegiance in the 1930s to National Socialism.

If Nancy's argument turns us back to the role Heidegger's writings play in Lacoue-Labarthe and Nancy's writings for the Center in Paris, what counts for the moment is the way in which "being-with" is not a *subsequent* modification of Being but contaminates it in its very essence and origins and so remains absolutely contemporaneous with Being in its temporal emergence and finite transcendence. "Being-with" is Being's "equiprimordial ontological condition" and so remains essential to *Dasein*'s "constitution" (a term that nevertheless tends to close off the distension, spacing, or reticulated extensibility of "being-with" toward which Nancy is also drawing us, even as the *con-* of this constitution recomposes, at best bends and contorts, the implied standing of ontology's erect stature). "Being-with" as a "being-many" is not at all accidental or arbitrary—"it is in no way the secondary and random dispersion of a primordial essence"—for it forms "the proper and necessary status and consistency of original alterity as such" (*ESP*, 30/ *BSP*, 12). The existential analytic of *Being and Time*—the analytic that re-foregrounds being as ecstatic but whose exteriority remains precisely in play here—is now reopened to the coprimordiality of the "with" inscribed in *Dasein*'s alterity from itself, and in such a way that there remains no ontological ground or foundation, or no fundamental ontology, that preexists existence, nothing that obstructs the exposition of co-originarity by folding being-with or all being-in-relation back to a self-identity: "Being does not preexist its singular plural. To be more precise, Being absolutely does not *preexist*; nothing preexists; only what exists exists. Ever since Parmenides, one of philosophy's peculiarities has been that it has been unfolding this unique proposition, in all of its senses. This proposition proposes nothing but the position and disposition of existence" (*ESP*, 48/*BSP*, 29).

It is this proposition concerning the simultaneous position and disposition of existence that displaces the metaphysical presupposition of the Subject, opening toward an interminable displacement in which the syntax and grammar of Being in its singular plurality and plural singularity is rewritten and rearticulated.

In light of Nancy's continual rearticulation of this unique proposition, both in *Being Singular Plural* and in other writings, we can begin to further elaborate on the conditions informing this proposition concerning the position and disposition of existence and its larger implications. But any attempt at elaboration must confront two cautionary notes. First, in parsing out the logic in which Being is at once posed and disposed, Nancy warns us that the "strict conceptual rigor" of being-with inscribed in and as this disposition "exasperates the discourse of its concept" (*ESP*, 54/*BSP*, 34). The disposition of Being does not create a coherent concept or thesis and so remains resistant to conceptual or thematic explanation, at least an explanation that points toward an axiomatic principle or ontological foundation that comes prior to the disposition of existence, comes prior to the disposition that becomes a measure, itself immeasurable and incommensurable, of all existence. Secondly and indissociably, any elaboration of Nancy's affirmation of existence in terms of the disposition of Being inevitably closes off the textual presentation in which this disposition itself comes into being in his writings—the pauses, the punctuation, the repetitions, the fragmentation of argument, the rephrasings, the citations, the ruptures—in short, these traits that are not just the signature of Nancy's thinking and argument but characterize the discrete movement of Nancy's text.

Given these necessary cautions, the argument we are pursuing here turns on the way in which it is precisely Nancy's appeal to *networks* that at once informs and inflects this unique proposition concerning the position and disposition of existence, and so it is this same appeal to networks that opens toward a reticulation of Being that this same philosophical tradition since Parmenides at once proposes and simultaneously withdraws from view. The argument thus focuses on the ways in which Nancy's ontological appeal to networks attests to what is violently effaced in ontology, namely, coexistence, relation, articulation, circulation, becoming, disposition, spacing, reticulation, or what Nancy has also termed a *défaillance* of all essence, in the sense of its waning, decay, swooning, defaulting, or refusal to appear (as in a court appearance). Or rather, it is this violence that emerges when Heidegger continually subordinates *Mitsein* or "being-with" to the existential constitution of *Dasein* and then effaces *Dasein*'s radical alterity from itself by deciding the terms of being-with's fulfillment and return into itself, or by recuperating this alterity in the name of a people's destiny or a gathering. It is the same violence that Hannah Arendt begins to address when she appeals instead to the basic "human condition" in terms of "human plurality," a reference acknowledged by Nancy in the opening pages of *Being Singular Plural*. More generally, the networks that now govern the singular plurality and plural singularity of Being, as well as Nancy's reconfiguring of the position and disposition of existence as essentially reticulated, places his writings singularly within a larger community of thinkers in which this same philosophical and metaphysical tradition is rethought in terms of the relation between singularities, pluralities, and multiplicities. In short, it is this appeal to networks and their reticulated spacing that parses out, at once repeating and rearticulating, the grammar and syntax governing the foundational philosophical concepts of the One and the Many.[16]

Two further consequences follow from this reading of Nancy. First, Nancy's rethinking of existence in terms of the disposition of Being further reopens the question of existence to the place of the common or the "in-common," terms that haunt the margins of this same philosophical tradition. As the writings of Deleuze, Badiou, Agamben, and Hardt and Negri amply suggest, the problematic of the common has also emerged as increasingly central within recent affirmations of the political force of singularities and multiplicities. Nancy's affirmation of coexistence is thus a simultaneous affirmation not of "the common" as such but the "in-common" or "being-in-common" (and again, the modifying preposition removes all possibility of reducing the common to a self-identity or of establishing a common or communal essence). All being is thus being-in-common and not a common Being or a celebration of a common humanity. It is precisely being-in-common, we will argue, that Nancy also proposes to rethink in terms of networks, where all being-in-common is essentially reticulated.

Second, the disposition of Being is rearticulated by Nancy as the space *between* the One and the Many. Or it reopens the delineation of a circumscribed space in which to think the being-*there* of *Dasein* to a spacing that has no fixed geometrical or spatial coordinates, no beginning or end, but *is* (the) "between." It is this spacing that also remains at once proposed and repeatedly effaced within this same philosophical tradition since Parmenides. The reticulated spacing that we have come to characterize as essential to Being in its disposition and the spacing of singularities is now rephrased as the articulation of this "between." Recalling a key philosophical reference for any discussion of space, Kant's *Critique of Pure Reason*, Nancy argues, "'Being' is neither a state nor a quality, but rather the action/passion according to which what Kant calls 'the [mere] positing of a thing' takes place ('is'). The very simplicity of 'position' implies no more, although no less, than its being discrete, in the mathematical sense, or its distinction *from*, in the sense of *with*, other (at least possible) positions, or its distinction *among*, in the sense of *between*, other positions. In other words, every position is also disposition" (*ESP*, 30/*BSP*, 12).

Being thus has no other meaning except as the "dis-position of this 'between,'" as the "stretching out" or *distension* opened by the singular as such. At once extending and reconfiguring Heidegger's emphasis in *Being and Time* on *Dasein*'s own "spatiality" or *Räumlichkeit*, on the *Da* of *Dasein*'s "being-*there*," this spacing is then defined in and as the very between of the "in-between," in the sense of its interval, its partitioning, its between-two or *entre-deux*.[17] If being in this sense becomes the focal point of our interest, in the sense of our being *inter-esse*, then this primordial interest opens toward the permanent displacement of an identifiable and self-contained site, focal point, or horizon in and from which to measure such an interest or provide us the perspectival distance to objectify that interest. If "Being is put into play between us," as Nancy argues, then the "between" also now becomes the most "minimal ontological premise" and the "with" of being-with becomes "the punctual and discreet spacing between us" (*ESP*, 47/*BSP*, 27). Indeed, if everything "passes *between us*," as Nancy insists, then this between possesses neither a consistency nor continuity of its own (*ESP*, 23/*BSP*, 5). Rather (as the English translators of *Being Singular Plural* propose), while the French verb *se passer* is more commonly translated as "to happen," what happens "between us" is now rearticulated in and *as* a "relation" (*BSP*, 195).[18] What "takes place" between us, in the sense of what happens between us or what comes to pass, is no longer defined as a taking *place* but as the spatiotemporal spacing of the relation, of the relation *as* relation, *between* us, where emphasis is placed on the relation as such—the between—rather than the elements or previously separate identities that enter *into* relation. Being is thus articulated by neither its subsistence nor consistence but by its transitivity, in which we attest to the transitive nature of Being in its disposition or being-in-relation: "'Being-there' (*Dasein*)—which Nancy translates into French as *Être-le-là*, thus reinforcing "the-being-there" of *Dasein*—"is thus *to be* according to this transitive verbal value of the dis-position." In short, "being-there is [the] dis-posing [of] being itself as spacing/proximity" (*être-le-là, c'est dis-poser l'être lui-même, comme écartement/proximité*; *ESP*, 120–21/*BSP*, 96). Again, it is this transitive spacing/proximity of Being in-between—an "agrammatical or exscribed transitivity" that also discloses the aporia of Being as the condition of being disposed—that we are proposing to rethink in terms of the reticulated spacing implied by networks.[19]

This initial elaboration of the unique proposition concerning the position and disposition of existence gives some initial measure or orientation to Nancy's way of thinking Being in its disposition, at least insofar as it is the force of this disposition or its *frayage*—its clearing, marking, and tracing out, to use one of Nancy's favored terms—that also works to displace all given sense of measure and orientation in which to think existence. But just as decisive to the larger argument proposed here, Nancy's *Being Singular Plural* is not just framed in terms of a rethinking of Heidegger's *Being and Time*, as our initial commentary and its terminology might suggest and as the secondary literature on Nancy's writings has explored at some length. For the disposition of Being that finds one of its initial resources in Nancy's reading of Heidegger in *Being Singular Plural* is also rearticulated in relation to

Husserl, as well as in light of a number of other problematics quite distant from either Husserl's or Heidegger's thinking.[20] Such problematics include Nancy's engagement in *Being Singular Plural* with the "becoming global" of the West, a becoming worldly of the world that is conterminous with the history of capitalism and not just Being, or with a world in which both the history of capitalism and the history of Being must be thought in terms of their simultaneous proximity and distance from one another. This becoming global or worldly further coincides with those sections of *Being Singular Plural* in which Nancy turns to rethink the writings of Marx as well as the traditions of Marxism and communism, sections that include a reappraisal of Guy Debord and the Situationist's concept of the spectacle, in addition to references to a range of writings that are also situated in terms of an engagement with these same Marxist and communist traditions.[21] If the reception of Nancy's writings in general has turned with some insistence around his seminal and influential rereading of Heidegger, including the inescapable engagement with Heidegger's politics, then Nancy's references to Marx and Marxism not only constitute a sustained rather than marginal problematic traversing his ontological argument. They resituate *Being Singular Plural* in light of a much longer engagement with Marx, Marxism, and communism in Nancy's other writings. Indeed, if a quotation from Marx appears alongside a quotation from Hölderlin in the epigraphs to the opening essay—a quotation in which Marx thinks through the conflictual relation, at once ontological and political, between "human nature," "human community," the "being of each individual," and "social being"—the quotation not only shapes and colors our subsequent reading of *Being Singular Plural* but constitutes a hinge to Nancy's own previous commentaries on Marx and Marxism. These commentaries extend from one of his first published texts (a review of Althusser's *For Marx* and *Reading Capital*) to numerous later texts that engage the Marxist and communist traditions, including Nancy's coauthored texts with Philippe Lacoue-Labarthe for the Center in Paris, *La Comparution*, *The Inoperative Community*, *The Sense of the World*, and the more recent book on globalization or *mondialisation*.[22] As Nancy's argues in *La Comparution*, it may not be a question of rereading Marx (this privilege is apparently still reserved for Heidegger and others), but the question still remains "of what Marx must now make us write,"[23] as if it is in Marx that we might find some obscure ethical or categorical imperative, or as if it is in response to Marx that the exigency of writing finds its renewed measure and larger stakes. "It is no longer necessary to be a member of the Party," Nancy argues, "in order to share, despite oneself, certain truths that come from Marx" (*ESP*, 136/*BSP*, 110). Or again, Nancy claims, "It makes sense to me to want to retain from Marx (I would say Marx here rather than Marxism) a certain force or vehemence, a demand for truth and justice, for the truth of justice."[24] Unlike Derrida's *Specters of Marx*, then, Nancy's engagement with the Marxist tradition is not the belated outcome of continual demands to engage philosophy or deconstruction's more political dimensions but already registered in Nancy's earliest publications.[25] Marx is already inscribed in a way of thinking structured by repetition, so it is also through Marx that we "start again" to understand at once "our existence and that of the world." In short, if Heidegger's fundamental ontology frames the opening argument posed in *Being Singular Plural*, and if the existential analytic of *Being and Time* is considered "the project from which all subsequent thinking flows, whether this is Heidegger's own later thinking or our various ways of thinking against or beyond Heidegger himself" (*ESP*, 117/*BSP*, 93)—an assertion that appears quite characteristic of Nancy's writings and certainly their larger reception—then any reading that seeks to do justice to *Being Singular Plural* must also begin to address Nancy's related provocation in the same text that "the truth of our time can only be expressed in Marxist or post-Marxist terms" (*ESP*, 86/*BSP*, 64).

Equally pertinent to this reading of *Being Singular Plural*, the role that Marx plays in Nancy's writings cannot be separated from Nancy's more pervasive references to Communism (as an historical and geopolitical reference) and communism (understood as a limit concept, or an onticopolitical problematic). For if it is not possible to think of "our time" unless one thinks of it as that of the "communist question," as Nancy states, or if it remains no accident that "communism and socialism of all sorts are responsible for an essential set of expectations that belong to the modern world" (*ESP*, 61/*BSP*, 41), the question also remains how the exigency to rethink the question of communism is inseparable in Nancy's writings from rearticulating the disposition of Being in terms of being-with and coexistence. It is this exigency that comes into focus at least from *The Inoperative Community* onward, but it finds echoes in Nancy's earlier writings as well. As we will also propose, the disposition of Being is thus not only a radical revision of Heidegger's existential analytic but an intimate—indeed, coessential—aspect of Nancy's assertion that "thought cannot move forward an inch if this question [of communism] is not taken up again, rearticulated, itself questioned, and deconstructed."[26]

No doubt Nancy's generous affirmation concerning the Marxist and communist traditions is not offered without critical reservations. As he argues in *Being Singular Plural*, in order to fully take into account capitalism and its effects, it becomes necessary to withdraw capitalism from its own representation in "linear and cumulative history, *as well as* from the presentation of a teleological history of its overcoming or rejection," and to do so in ways that are far more radical than Marx ever indicated himself (*ESP*, 41/*BSP*, 22). Moreover, Nancy claims that this task cannot be undertaken unless we first understand "what is most at stake in our history, that is, what is most at stake in philosophy," one of the tasks that Nancy addresses in his early review of Althusser. To rephrase this same reservation in terms closer to our earlier analyses of Heidegger, although Marx is considered radical in his demand for the "dissolution" of politics in all "spheres of existence" (to recall Marx's argument in the "Critique of Hegel's Doctrine of the State" that Nancy's cites frequently), Marx nevertheless ignores that the "separation between singularities overcome and suppressed" in this dissolution is not, in fact, an accidental separation imposed by "political" authority, but rather, as Nancy argues, "the constitutive separation of dis-position" (*ESP*, 43/*BSP*, 24). In this sense, reading Marx not only folds across Lacoue-Labarthe and Nancy's earlier proposals to rethink the "disposition of the political" but shares the same problem characteristic of all communism: that however powerful they both remain for thinking the "real relation" and true nature of the social individual (as the opening epigraph in *Being Singular Plural* from Marx attests), neither are able to think "being-in-common" as distinct from community. Nor does Marxism or communism fully unfold the distinction between human beings understood in terms of production or self-production, and the self-creation of free labor, an argument that Nancy has explored in several texts, and again related to how a community is said to produce itself rather than become "inoperative" or "unworking" (as translations of *la communauté désœuvrée* might suggest).[27] In this sense, the disposition of Being finds its decisive force in its displacement of the Marxist problematic—this problematic that extends from Marx back to Aristotle and from Marx forward to Hardt and Negri—concerning the *production* of being or the simultaneous self-production and self-affirmation of the subject.

Whatever Nancy's reservations regarding Marx and Marxism, these nowhere negate his more general insistence on rethinking the disposition of Being in such a way that its ontological implications cannot be separated from what Marx "must now make us write," nor from an engagement with thinking the world as world in its very globality:

To say that [the disposition of Being] is an ontological question—or even that it is *the* ontological question, absolutely—does not mean we have to leave the realm of economics and sickness, any more than we have to abandon the order of *praxis*. On the contrary, as I have said, this question is simply that of what is called "capital," and even the question of "history" and "politics." "Ontology" does not occur at the level reserved for principles, a level that is withdrawn, speculative, and altogether abstract. Its name means the thinking of existence. And today, the situation of ontology signifies the following: to think existence at the height of this challenge to thinking that is globalness [*mondialité*] as such (which is designated as "capital," "(de-)Western-ization," "technology," "historical rupture," and so forth). (*ESP*, 67/ *BSP*, 46–47)

In light of this challenge, the demand to rethink both the Marxist and communist traditions rearticulates Nancy's affirmation of the disposition of Being from its seemingly exclusive rapport with Heidegger's thinking, or at least parses out its grammar in ways that cannot be reduced to a sole preoc-cupation with Heidegger's fundamental ontology, however decisive Nancy's reading of Heidegger remains in this regard. This shift in emphasis does not suggest a strict opposition between the two critical traditions that neverthe-less both remain at stake here, whatever Heidegger's own antipathy or am-bivalence in relation to Marxism, or whatever excoriation of Heidegger's writ-ings by Marxists. It is not a question of a choice, or of staking out a set of priorities or strict hierarchies. But the acknowledgment of the full range of Nancy's references in *Being Singular Plural* does foreground a more circum-scribed question that also motivates and structures the larger argument pro-posed in the pages that follow—namely, whether it is precisely Nancy's appeal to the reticulated spacing of being-in-relation in *Being Singular Plural* that not only is inscribed in rethinking being-with and being-in-common but informs this displacement from an exclusively Heideggerian questioning to Nancy's insistence on expressing the "truth of our time" in Marxist and post-Marxist terms. The appeal to networks is not then a way of mediating these different traditions or of bringing them to some harmonious collusion. Nor especially is it a question here of effacing Heidegger's political commitments by overlay-ing a form of political engagement onto an otherwise purely philosophical, speculative, or ontological foundation. Rather, this insistence on acknowledg-ing the full scope of Nancy's references in *Being Singular Plural* exposes us to a question that also begins to emerge here: How does the reticulated spacing of Being in its disposition find its renewed measure or grammatical rearticulation in light of Nancy's simultaneous appeal in his writings to an "ontology to come" and a "communism to come"?

Before turning to this question at further length, it should be stressed that such a refocusing of Nancy's *Being Singular Plural* makes of Nancy neither a Heideggerian nor a Marxist. Even less does it suggest a politicizing of Nancy's writings, as if there were a political dimension originally lacking in his rethinking of the disposition of Being that would now be finally fulfilled and fully realized. In a recognizably political sense, Nancy's writings already engage the most political events of our time, an engagement that is a marked characteristic of numerous of his texts and clearly evident in *Being Singular Plural* itself, which opens with an horrific litany of bloody conflicts animating the world in 1987 (when Nancy was writing the book) and closes with several chapters that also explore a number of contemporary political events, including the use of technology in the first Iraq war, the rape of Bosnian women in the former Yugoslavia, the role of U.S. imperialism, and the rise of religious fundamentalism. Whatever the real political import of these references, however, they do not simply constitute a more immediate political context for rethinking the ontological tenor of our being in the world and its disposition, as if these references might finally give some political thickness to an otherwise purely abstract, speculative, or philosophical preoccupation with our finite existence in the world. What marks Nancy's argument, both in *Being Singular Plural* and elsewhere, is precisely its way of rendering problematic any assumption concerning the potential politicizing of the ontological and thus the ability to render problematic the assumptions informing any ambition to (re)contextualize philosophy in a wider political dimension.

These more general concerns give way to a more specific set of observations. As we have begun to explore, the preoccupation with the disposition of Being cannot be separated from a number of related problematics, in which rethinking the political as such cannot be detached from both its philosophical and ontological presuppositions. The problematics at stake open toward a number of related arguments, including the distinction between "politics" and the "political" outlined in the first chapter, the exigency to rethink this distinction itself in order to question what constitutes the political in its *essence*, a rethinking of the concept of the *polis* in terms that are at once political *and* philosophical, a decisive rearticulation of the nature of political speech or the political *logos*, and a reelaboration of the concepts of sovereignty and citizenship and their relation to contemporary globalization. In this sense, the disposition of Being not only relates to but also simultaneously reopens a number of foundational political categories and concepts within a longer tradition that must be thought in terms that remain at once political *and* philosophical. It also points toward Nancy's demand to rethink the very syntax or grammar of the political as such, not in terms that might be considered metapolitical, extrapolitical, or infrapolitical, and even less apolitical, but *archepolitical*. Or rather, to repeat Nancy's earlier proposal with Lacoue-Labarthe, the disposition of Being opens toward rethinking the archi-constitution of the "political animal," where it is precisely this disposition that sets in play the an-archy of the political *arche*. The disposition of Being is thus not just implicated in this larger framework of political problematics but must be thought in terms of networks and the reticulated spacing of coexistence, and it is this spacing that is now commensurate with the an-archy of any given *arche*.

Given the specific range of questions and affirmations of existence at stake in rethinking the political in terms of its ontological presuppositions, and as others have frequently pointed out, Nancy's writings do not easily lend themselves to a recognizable politics, as if presupposing that a demonstrable politics should be the goal of some prior philosophical speculation, or as if a concrete political intervention were the potential outcome of a passage that passes through some prior, theoretical abstraction. As Nancy has repeatedly made clear, the questioning and displacement of such a dialectical and ultimately teleological argument nowhere forecloses the necessity of recognizably political commitments, nor does it negate the conflicts and struggles animating politics in all of its day-to-day complexities. But nor does this refusal of what constitutes the political as *telos* foreclose Nancy's equal insistence that we reconfigure the widespread claim that "everything is political," or the claim to politicize everything (the economy, culture, society, discourse, the subject, and so on).[28] In reconfiguring the argument concerning the self-sufficiency of the political across the various texts composed for the Center in Paris, what remains at stake here is Nancy's demand to rethink the political *and* the philosophical in terms of their respective closure, and a closure that would create the conditions for thinking their shared *retrait*. Irreducible to the teleological expectations and anticipations of a fully realizable politics, we again recall that Nancy offers a provisional definition of this retreat by claiming that the retreat of the political does not signify the disappearance of the political; "it only signifies the disappearance of the philosophical presupposition of the politico-philosophical order, which is always an ontological presupposition" (*ESP*, 57/*BSP*, 37). The retreat of the political is not a complete effacement of the political. But it does work here to expose the ontological presuppositions in which to think Being in terms of the reticulated spacing of its disposition.

If we recall the terms and arguments animating Nancy's earlier texts on the retreat of the political, suffice it to argue that Nancy's reengagement with the question of ontology in light of both Heidegger *and* Marx does not lead us to a discourse of political philosophy, nor, contrary to appearances, to a political ontology, epithets that Nancy has repeatedly repudiated. Nancy's rethinking of the politico-philosophical conditions informing the disposition of Being participates in rearticulating a number of fundamental political concepts and foundational political categories, but it cannot be reduced to an ontological position either, nor to a political or social theory. Nor again does this politico-philosophical investigation produce a concept of the social or social totality subsumable within the State or a state formation. Nor again does Nancy's appeal to the disposition of Being find its political rationale or orientation in a discourse of power or hegemony, in rights or norms, in a friend-enemy distinction or a politics of the Other, in practices of exclusion or social inclusivity, in a politics of recognition or redistribution, in the discourse of the body or desire, in a politics of identity or technologies of the self, even as Nancy's writings have addressed such alternatives and their political and ontological implications, and even as such widely discussed proposals to rethink what constitutes an effective range of political interventions might also be potentially rearticulated in light of the disposition of Being that focuses our attention here. Situated within this wider context of political categories and proposals, Nancy's writings and interviews have also sought to engage some of the most prominent attempts to rethink the political in relation to the ontological, from the most established thinkers within the Western political and philosophical tradition (Aristotle, Plato, Rousseau, Hegel, Marx, Nietzsche, Freud, Heidegger, Benjamin, Bataille) to more recent texts by a number of contemporary thinkers. The references are clearly partial in many respects but name those whom Nancy also refers with varying frequency in his own writings. At the same time, the appeal to ontology in rethinking the political also situates Nancy's writings in light of a number of other prominent proposals, as when Foucault appeals to biopolitics as the "historical ontology of ourselves," or Laclau and Mouffe define the political not as a superstructure but as having the status of an "ontology of the social," or Agamben argues that the "protracted eclipse" of politics today stems from "losing sight of its ontological status," or Judith Butler seeks to locate a "liminal social existence" that "emerges in the condition of suspended ontology."[29] The question now remains how Nancy's appeal to the disposition of Being and the singular plurality of being-in-relation both relates to these well-known and widely discussed proposals as well as rethinks this otherwise shared rearticulation of the politico-philosophical tradition. More pertinently, the question remains how Nancy's reconfiguring of the disposition of Being in terms of a reticulated spacing of networks also suggests at once a proximity to, as well as a simultaneous distance from, this same set of proposals. But what marks the following argument is even more circumscribed. For if networks become a decisive measure of Nancy's own proposal to rethink the *retrait* of the political or its ontological presuppositions, as we are arguing, then the question also posed here is how Nancy's affirmation of being-with and coexistence in its reticulated spacing returns us to the very heart of the Marxist and communist problematic, which, we recall, Nancy had described with Lacoue-Labarthe as "the identity of the collectivity, its destination, the nature and exercise of its sovereignty." Or rather, given this relatively early claim from their writings from the Center in Paris, it is not a question of returning us to the problematic of collectivities and finding in them the "overwhelming destiny of our modernity" (and here Marxism and communism cannot be fully separated from Heidegger's own appeals to a people's "spiritual destiny"). For the question now is of remarking the ways in which the question of the collective refuses its self-identity and self-production by opening itself to an ontology or communism to come. Or again, it is a question now of *repeating* this problematic of the collective, of placing each of these terms in scare quotes—"identity," "collectivity," "destination," "sovereignty"—of assessing how these terms at once open toward and displace the quadruple instance of subject-citizen-community-sovereignty at an oblique angle, and then of demonstrating, within the closure and simultaneous retreat of the political, how it is in light of this problematic of the collective that we start again "to understand ourselves—our existence and that of the world, our being disposed in this way."

Before turning more directly to this rethinking of collectivities in light of a reticulated spacing, we note that the language and conceptual orientation of Nancy's writings clearly suggest a marked distance from the larger discourse of networks, in which the political implications posed by networks also play a prominent and often central role. Indeed, it is clear from this literature and the rhetorical claims that frequently accompany it that networks have decisive political implications, from their ability to reconfigure the very sovereignty of nation-states to the sociopolitical effects produced by global media, and from the organization that subtends the "movement of movements" to increasingly widespread discussions around cyber-politics. Networks open up numerous possibilities for rethinking political practices, in particular those new forms of cyber-democracy that embrace at once the Zapatistas, "hactivists," and smart mobs; in other words, those groups that might also be read as presupposing a radical rethinking of former emphases on collective organization. From the global linkages between minoritarian or indigenous groups to NGOs, from "cyber-marx" to the "cybertariat," networks and the new "modes of information" and communication also create new potentials for political transformation, new forms of civic networking and online participation, new definitions of the public sphere, new border politics, and so new sites of social conflict and antagonism, new relations of power, or new global arenas of postnational and postcolonial contestation. But the widespread celebration of networked organization, collaboration, and experimentation also finds itself confronting an increasingly pernicious display of transformations in the very forms of exploitation, domination, and exclusion characterizing our contemporary global situation—and thus radically new configurations of power—all of which also find their "logic" in networks. The "left" holds no monopoly on networked politics (assuming that the appeal to networks allows us to prolong such distinctions as a measure of political contestation), and global capitalism, war, militarized neoimperialism, media consolidation, and religious and nationalist fundamentalism have all clearly found one of their most decisive resources in networked practices. At the very least, this conflict of interests and engagements suggests how networks have become one of the most pivotal sites in which the political and global present is being played out and the future is at stake.

A permanent tension and fundamental ambivalence thus governs any appeal to the politics of networks, confronting us with a number of disorientating conflicts and tensions. To take one conspicuous example, networks are called upon to create the conditions for reaffirming communism within post-Fordist economies, while for others, the post-1989 collapse of the communist bloc creates a space in which networks are synonymous with the defense of Western liberal democracies, global capitalism, and the NASDAQ. Or networked organization is said to subtend both the mobilization of global justice movements as well as global flows of capital, which operate from the same logic of networked communication in which military surveillance is also conducted, and so on. Such ambivalence in the political implications of networks finds one of its most sobering if symptomatic moments when John Arquilla and David Ronfeldt simply equate al-Qaeda, drug smuggling cartels, anti-WTO anarchists in Seattle, and civil society activists "fighting for democracy and human rights," not only arguing that they all share the same forms of networked organization but even suggesting that they are "*all* proving very hard to beat"![30] But no less ambivalent in political terms is the widespread argument that whatever networks touch is immediately politicized, and so the political implications of networks—an appeal to "everything is political"—makes it increasingly difficult to discern the political fault lines, or the actual sites of contemporary struggle and conflict, as if networks had also come to obscure the more secure and established arenas of social and political contestation, or as if the relation between networks and the discourse of power also demanded rethinking.[31] For many, of course, this situation inaugurates a myriad display of opportunities and new spaces for transformative political practices. For others, it simply closes politics off, making the turn to networked forms of political organization not just complicitous with capitalist spectacle and mediatized consensus but synonymous with the end of effective political alternatives to capitalism and the most repressive aspects of contemporary globalization.

This overview is clearly schematic, and a more nuanced survey of networked practices would more clearly demonstrate the precise range and irresolvable conflicts animating the so-called politics of networks. But the overview suffices to demonstrate how Nancy's appeal to networks engages their political implications in a quite different sense. Such an engagement does not stem from any suggestion that the multiple ways in which networks are politicized remain inconsequential or without effective potential for political transformation. The question instead becomes at once more modest and immodest, exposing us to an argument in which networks cannot be detached from rethinking ontology. More specifically, if the question of ontology touches on the very *retreat* of the political, we want to argue that it is this same retreat that then constitutes the conditions of possibility for rethinking the very "identity" of the collectivity, including its "destination" and the nature and exercise of its "sovereignty."

The reticulated spacing of Being works to reopen the philosophical presuppositions of the politico-philosophical order and so exposes the ontological presuppositions of this order. In this sense, the disposition of Being that comes to light is not simply marked by a question of position or displacement, or the subject or community's deterritorialization, as if this pointed to a mere dispersion of positions, or as if this disposition simply concentrated itself in the "decentered subject." The *dis-* that informs and inflects the displacement of any identifiable position must also be thought in terms of an originary dissociation and disconnection of any given relation, or any given tie or bond. As we have seen, there is no social tie or no reticulated spacing defining our shared coexistence that is not established from a constitutive and enabling dissociation and disconnection, a fact already implied in the translation of a *partage* as a division as well as a sharing out, as well as in Nancy's critique of Marx's demand for the dissolution of politics in all spheres of existence and its refusal to engage the constitutive separation and detachment inscribed in the disposition of Being. The link that binds any community together must always be thought in relation to what remains unbound, its ties untied, and so the relation that informs these bonds and ties presupposes a nonrelation, a spacing inherent to relation itself, and the rupture of all proximity. The politics of the tie toward which Nancy draws us is thus a rethinking of the political that finds one of its logics of articulation in the disposition of Being, and so a disposition inscribed by a severing and distancing that is more (in)essential to the political than the political itself.

Unfolding and refolding the syntax and grammar of the political in terms of the disposition of Being not only exposes us to a rethinking of the radical ontological constitution or composition of the political in and as its articulation of (social) relations; it exposes us to what ties and binds the disposition of being-with in the reticulated spacing or network of singular pluralities and plural singularities. As we have seen at the end of the previous chapter, Nancy will extend this reference to networks in *The Sense of the World* by insisting on its etymological connections to nets, proposing a "politics of the knot [*nouage*]" or a "politics of the tie [*lien*]," a language that finds one of its most significant sources in the platonic comparison between the art of politics and the art of weaving and already implied in Nancy's references cited earlier to the "web" or *trame* of communication. In other words, the language Nancy proposes for rethinking and rearticulating the concept of the political not only binds the language of (social) relations and the articulation of knots or ties to networks but also opens networks to a genealogy of the concept of networks itself.[32] But such a rearticulation of the political through the language of knots, ties, and networks also opens toward a rethinking of the fundamental political concepts that invariably *presuppose* these same ties and relations, concepts that do not merely include the subject, the citizen, sovereignty, and community, but extend to the concept of organization and collectivity that also remains at stake here. As Nancy argues, it is not a question of abandoning these concepts in favor of an alternative set of political concepts but displacing their internal tensions and relations by foregrounding a politics of ties or knots they simultaneously efface. "What we are seeking," Nancy argues, is thus, "a politics of the tie as such, rather than its *dénouement*, its untying or realization in a space or substance," a politics where it becomes "less the tie that binds than the tie that reties, less that tie that encloses than the tie that makes up a network" (*SM*, 177/*SW*, 114). It is this appeal to networks that constitutes a refusal of any absolute "untying" of ties, a *dénouement* of ties that also translates as a refusal of anything that culminates in an autonomous or isolated space, a gathering, or substance—in short, a politics of *autosuffisance* or self-sufficiency. In this sense, what we call politics would not become a form or a substance but a gesture, "the very gesture of the tying and linking of each to each, tying each time unicities (individuals, groups, nations, or peoples) that have no unity other than the unity of the knot, unity linking to the other, the linking always worldwide and the world having no unity other than that of its linkages" (*SM*, 175/*SW*, 112).[33] If this is a politics that requires "an entire ontology of being as tying," as Nancy proposes, it does so only insofar as this tying refers us in its very gesture to an originary and essential spacing of all relations, to a spacing that then rearticulates the ontological presuppositions of the politico-philosophical order.[34]

In light of the constitutive dissociation and disconnection informing all relations and ties, Nancy's appeal to networks clearly transforms the widespread emphasis on *connection* that dominates numerous discussions of networks.[35] Dissociation and disconnection now parses out a way of thinking in which the displacements constitutive of *dis-* (of dis-position, dis-placement, dis-sociation) or of *ex-* (of ex-posure, ex-position, ex-istence, ex-tension) are inscribed in the connections that define shared coexistence or the *com-* of "being-with," but only insofar as this connection finds its originary ontological presuppositions permanently exposed to the possibility of a nonrelation or dis-connection, and thus to the possibility and potentialities of the anarchy of any ontological origin or political *arche*. The *dis-* that governs the disposition of being is not a negation of Being or its historicization, nor simply a loss of community from its former existence, but defines the separation and detachment that is the condition of all connection and communication, a term that now more closely responds to the German *Mit-teilung*. In this sense, com-munication may be said to *with-part* itself, implying at once a division, separation and partitioning, as well as a sharing, distribution, or bifurcation of what with-parts or "communicates" itself.[36]

What comes into focus here is then not so much a politics of communication or a new mode of information, in which emphasis is placed on the relay of a message or lines of contact and connection made possible by the new communication and information technologies. Or again, if this "with-parting" of communication is still a communication, it is one that relates little to what passes for the various theories and ideologies of communication informing the discourse of networks today. As Nancy writes in *The Sense of the World*, extending the argument concerning the politics of the tie, "What we are looking for is a consideration of the tie that takes it to be incommensurable with the ligature of the fasces....And if it is necessary to use this word at least once: yes, it is a politics of communication, but taken in the opposite sense of all our communicative ideologies, where 'each communication is, above all, communication not of something held in *common* but of a *communicability*,' according to the formula of Giorgio Agamben. Where, consequently, sense is not what is communicated but *that* there is communication" (*SM*, 177–78/*SW*, 114).[37]

Networked communication is thus rewritten and rearticulated here as a politics of the tie or knot, a politics that cannot be fully knotted into the ties that bind the fasces, the bundle of wood that was carried by Roman magistrates as an emblem of their power, and so a politics that remains irreducible to the ontopolitical presuppositions in which fascism finds its form of self-enclosure and self-sufficiency in a common essence, the fusion of the people as a seamless whole subsumable under the *arche*. Commensurate with the reticulated spacing of networks, of an "'us' as web or network," and so of the "between" that scans coexistence, the politics of the tie finds its measure of articulation not just in a renewed articulation of communication but in and as *language*, "at once within language and beyond (or just short of) language, but always responding to something inherent in language," in that language itself is, as Nancy argues, "the insubstantial tie" (*SM*, 180/*SW*, 115). Language is here articulated in its post-Saussurian definition as the "tracing out [*frayage*] of the essencelessness of relation" (*SM*, 184/*SW*, 119), at least insofar as language is the condition for thinking the "insubstantial tie" that makes the communicability of all communication possible *as* communication. If

Nancy's appeal to language refers us back to Aristotle's definition of man as political animal capable of speech, then the "tracing out of the essenceless-ness of relation" that defines language in its most minimal articulation points us toward what Nancy proposes as a "concatenation of acts of speech," where this concatenation in its essential plurality and multiplicity "is not complet-able, is infinitely reticulated, infinitely interrupted and retied." Indeed, it is these "acts of speech" that tend toward the most "naked function" of lan-guage or its *phatic* function, in other words, that language which is shared, that enables sociability and presupposes relation, which Nancy paraphrases as "the maintenance of relation that communicates no sense other than the relation itself" (*SM*, 182/*SW*, 117). It is precisely the essencelessness and in-substantiality of all relation (which is not a lack, nor suspended over a void) that determines the tying and permanent retying of any given tie or bond, thus foreclosing in advance the possibility of a fully autonomous subject, a self-contained space, a gathering, or a politics of self-sufficiency. If the net-work of communication is thus the enabling condition in which to think the very disposition and exposure of being, and if what or who is exposed is "the bare web of the *com-*," the "with" or *cum* which—and in which—we "our-selves" communicate in and *as* a network, then this bare web and exposure must also be thought from out of an originary and essential dissociation and disconnection of all relations. In short, taking its point of departure from the question of the "essence" of language, Nancy asks us to think how the "trac-ing out of the essencelessness of relation" is the condition of all communica-bility and connectivity.[38]

The withdrawal of communication from channels, systems, and medi-ums of telecommunication and connection, or the withdrawal from the relay or transport of information and the technologies with which they are ac-companied, simultaneously returns us to the question of space explored in previous chapters. For it is the disposition of being as a reticulated spacing that reconfigures the very space of the political, or those places and spaces in which we might imagine that our politics finds some circumscribed measure of visibility, orientation, and legitimation. If this emphasis on space cannot be detached from the question of communication, including contempo-rary telecommunication systems, the question of space at stake in Nancy's affirmation of the reticulated spacing of Being should also be situated in light of a wider series of problematics. Stated schematically, these include rethinking the politicizing of space and the spatializing of politics that de-fines much of the discourse concerning globalization and geopolitics. It also includes rearticulating the established conventions inherent in different traditions of political discourse, conventions in which references to topography and topology become a condition of that very discourse. From the institutional spaces in which politics exists in its more circumscribed and representative forms to the assumptions concerning public "spheres," "public space," or social and political "terrains," a quite specific vocabulary dominates a heterogeneous and often quite conflicting display of both philosophical and political discourses.

Situated within this larger spatial problematic, Nancy's refusal to subordinate the disposition of Being and its reticulated spacing to the "overwhelming destiny" of modernity now finds much of its critical resonance when related to different attempts to rethink space and spatial relations and their role in rethinking modernity and postmodernity. Such epochal or paradigmatic claims registered in the writings of Henri Lefebvre, David Harvey, Edward Soja, Saskia Sassen, and Fredric Jameson—to name only some of the most well known—are also inflected by a more pervasive sense that transformations of the political coincide with related spatial transformations, from Arendt's concept of the "space of appearance" to Althusser's or Laclau and Mouffe's appeal to political topologies, from Foucault or de Certeau's respective spatializing of power relations to Deleuze and Guattari's concepts of deterritorialization or "smooth" and "striated" space, from Gayatri Spivak's appeal to the "virtualization of frontiers" as the opening of demographic rather than territorial frontiers to Arjun Appadurai's concept of the "production of locality" within global relations, from Hardt and Negri's articulation of a "topology" of different figures of exploited labor and a "topography" of their global distribution to Giorgio Agamben's concept of "aterritoriality" as the site in which to resituate the figure of the refugee. These more specific arguments then lend themselves to the numerous ways of rethinking political ecologies, the global deterritorialization of state sovereignties, or the transition from established models of geographical discourse into virtual and political geographies. It is against this larger background of references that Nancy's appeal to a reticulated *spacing* of Being begins to find a measure of its critical pertinence and force.

If a long tradition of articulating the political to the geographical and the topographical lies behind these different spatial references, or indeed if the tradition of metaphysics can be reread in light of its spatial or geometrical references, Nancy's appeal to a reticulated spacing of Being is not reducible to a post-phenomenological rethinking of the "horizon" within the phenomenological and hermeneutic traditions, however decisive Nancy's reformulation of such traditions and their presuppositions.[39] For Nancy's engagement with rethinking the rapport between the spatial and the political also leads to a fundamental rearticulation of a number of well-known political discourses and their spatial assumptions. These include the assumptions that inform the claim that society is a contested space, whether phrased as a "sphere" (as in the writings of Habermas or to use Marx's favored term in his "Critique of Hegel's Philosophy of Right"), a "topology" (as in Laclau and Mouffe's definition of the social), or a "terrain" (the term through which Nancy Fraser and Simon Critchley contest Lacoue-Labarthe and Nancy's own rethinking of the political). As we have previously recalled, this same tradition finds one of its most resonant revisions in Carl Schmitt's rethinking of the concept of the political in terms of topology, an argument that is equally decisive for Derrida's rereading of Schmitt in *Politics of Friendship* and elsewhere. Given his way of rethinking the political in relation to the ontological, Nancy's interest in situating the disposition of Being in terms of the reticulated spacing of networks cannot be detached from what Derrida has also termed both a "topolitics" and its "ontopological" presuppositions, where *ontopology* is defined as "an axiomatics linking indissociably the ontological value of present-being [*on*] to its *situation*, to the stable and presentable determination of a locality, the *topos* of territory, native soil, city, body in general."[40] Contesting this link between "present-being" and its *topos*, Nancy will also take into account Lévinas and Blanchot's respective ways of thinking "being in relation" as this relation is articulated in a "curvature of space," references that inform both Derrida's reading of friendship as an archi-political concept as well as Nancy's own appeal to the disposition of Being as a reticulated spacing.[41]

If we recall all these references in their most abbreviated form, what counts here are the larger stakes in rethinking the spatial assumptions informing political discourse in general, and Nancy's articulation of Being as a reticulated spacing in particular. For Nancy's rethinking of the disposition of Being and its reticulated spacing not only demands to be situated within this diverse background of references and discourses. What also remains at stake here is the very possibility of rearticulating the spatial assumptions and "ontopological" presuppositions informing the foundational political concept of the *polis*, an argument we raised at the end of the first chapter. If this remains a project that Nancy shares in decisive ways with the writings of Arendt, rethinking the ontological presuppositions of the *polis* finds one of its initial challenges in light of the widespread assumption that the tendencies informing contemporary globalization, whether thematized as the spatial concentration of capital in a new distribution of financial centers, networked telecommunications, or calls for global citizenship, all render the concept of the *polis* simply irrelevant, at best a form of political (and decidedly Western) nostalgia in the face of the radical possibilities opened up by the general tendencies defining global displacements, by the burgeoning number of global institutions and movements, by the World Wide Web and the Internet as "network of networks," and so on. This rearticulation of the *polis* and the related concept of a polity, which should be read as commensurate with Nancy's rethinking of Being in terms of its disposition, not only accompanies Nancy's rethinking of the founding political concepts and canons informing the Western tradition of political discourse or political philosophy, at least insofar as this tradition is now reopened in terms of the discourse of political self-sufficiency. As Jason Smith has argued, Nancy's return to a certain "archaic, matrical structure of being-in-common" also touches on what is most urgent in our contemporary, global space. Indeed, Smith argues that Nancy's theorization of the political is not the "representation of an ontological substructure of political forms" but attempts to rethink what constitutes the political today in ways in which the global and the spatial are inseparable. As Smith extends the argument,

> The ferocious deterritorizations of capital, the installation of mediatic networks of an unheard-of density, and the promotion of international law and its reference to "humanity" all conspire in the effective (and not simply theoretical or methodological) dismantling of our system of standard political referents. This eclipse of the state-from and all of its classical determinations—the person of the sovereign, the adherence of this figure to a border and a territory, the concept of citizenship and mythical references to a "people"—is well under way, and it is precisely this shredding of obsolete forms that Nancy characterizes as a laying bare, a denuding, or an emptying. This historical decomposition of the political exposes its essential structure: it assumes the form of an exposed surface, an empty space.[42]

We will come to question whether this "exposed surface" or "empty space" has a "form" rather than a spacing whose topological conditions remain to be defined, and so whether, as Smith later acknowledges, such a topology "refers not to a form, but to *an opening* or *a space*." Or rather, Nancy's appeal to a "deserted space that is the condition of all being-with"—a place "resisting all appropriation: a space *left* free, abandoned or deserted"—this space must also be thought as the condition of the reticulated spacing that motivates Being in its disposition rather than lending itself to a political *form* (as in Claude Lefort's typologies of political forms) or a "form-of-life" (to use Giorgio Agamben's seminal phrase borrowed from Wittgenstein).[43] What remains pivotal here is the way in which Nancy's argument exposes us to an "originary sociality" characterized in terms of the "merest opening of space," a "minimal opening of a space" whose folds, Smith reminds us, are not yet invested with recognizable contours. It is then this question of space that remains to be thought in terms of a politics to come, a politics composed virtually of the reticulated spacing of ties to be tied.

This question of space equally cannot be detached from Nancy's argument concerning the question of communication and communicability. For if such an "originary sociality" of being-with is not just an exposure but finds its condition in an originary dis-sociation, then the dissociation that informs this spacing and its possibilities not only finds one of its measures in light of the "shredding of obsolete forms" defining our contemporary, global space. It opens the possibility of thinking the reticulated spacing that now governs the (in)finite possibilities of being-in-common, being-with, and coexistence— in short, an entire ontology of Being as tying that informs a communism or ontology to come. The originary and essentially finite dissociation and disconnection of all relations cannot be detached from a simultaneous spacing of these relations in their infinite opening—a space left *free*—exposing us to a differential or folded space without center, totality, or recognizable contours, and thus to a radical displacement of any given spatial model that presupposes a framework that clearly demarcates an interiority from its exteriority (as the walls of the city or the borders of a territory might suggest). To be sure, and as we have already seen, such an argument is already widely discussed in the discourse of both networks and globalization, notably as the space of the political is increasingly transformed by networked telecommunications and information technologies. But Nancy's argument demands that the spatial implications registered by the reticulated spacing of networks do not merely lend themselves to re-politicizing politics in terms of space, or to finding new political geographies and cartographies commensurate with new information and communication technologies, however suggestive and politically appropriate such gestures might be. The argument demands also that we rethink the philosophical presuppositions of the politico-philosophical order, and thus rearticulate the ontological and ontopological presuppositions of this very order in terms of Being in its reticulated disposition and spacing. Again, the an-archy of the *arche* must be thought here in terms of an originary *spacing* of all relations, of topologies that, indiscernible, remain open, a space left free.

We have argued that Nancy's appeal to networks in terms of the plural singularity or disposition of Being reopens the founding concepts of political discourse, the very concepts that inform, and are simultaneously informed by, the politico-philosophical order. In appealing to networks and the disposition of Being as a way to rethink these foundational concepts, including the quadruple instance of subject, citizen, sovereignty, and community, the displacement of these concepts through the appeal to networks simultaneously implies a rethinking of the syntax or grammar that subtends a number of social, political, and anthropological traditions, in which it is precisely the reticulated spacing of Being that reopens these traditions to questions of relation, spacing, circulation, becoming, articulation, and disposition. In this sense, Nancy's argument also works to reconfigure established definitions of kinship and social relations, contract and group affiliation, social ties and conditions of belonging, as well as a number of closely related concepts that also imply questions of relation, such as love, friendship, hospitality, and religious bonds.[44] In addition to the established tenets and canons of political discourse, this wider array of related concepts points to the intricate rapport between philosophical, political, anthropological, as well as religious traditions, demanding that we begin again to take into account how rethinking the relation between these different traditions is repeatedly collapsed back into questions of history, the social, or culture, the very fields, to be sure, in which the discourse of networks today finds its most resonant, and ostensibly political, resources, but the very fields in which the question of relation is at once presupposed and simultaneously effaced.

Situated within a larger genealogical schema of politico-philosophical concepts, we have also argued that Nancy's writings begin to suggest how such concepts become reconfigured in relation to an insistent problematic of singularities and multiplicities. The disposition of Being also reopens this genealogical schema to its ontological presuppositions. The question therefore remains whether the disposition of Being is still subsumable within, or reducible to, a *polis* or the *demos*, a theory of the subject or the State, a polity or society, a *Gemeinschaft* or *Gesellschaft*, or whether this same disposition points beyond—or prior—to these dominant political concepts. At the same time, the question at stake here is also how any rearticulation of this genealogical schema relates to a number of more recent proposals that all claim to move *beyond* such traditional or established political *topoi*, proposals that seek, whether through historical rupture, dialectical sublation, or both, to transform established political concepts into the creation of new concepts. Whether phrased as the multitude, biopolitical assemblages, the movement of movements, or global cosmopolitanism, this range of recent proposals is further supplemented by new exemplary figures that do not fit easily within a more established and territorially inscribed tradition of political discourse (the refugee, the militant, the *sans-papiers*, the global citizen, and so forth). It is in this larger context that Nancy's affirmation of the disposition of Being also demands to be read.

More modestly, though no less pertinent to the question of networks foregrounded here, Nancy's appeal to the reticulated spacing of Being and a politics of tie also demands to be situated in light of a broader rethinking of political organization, where organization is understood in relation to a number of related terms, including collectivities, coalitions, affiliations, associations, alliances, differential solidarity, collaborations, cooperatives, councils, unions, movements, and so on—all ways of conceptualizing political organization that, not insignificantly, networks are said to radically transform, at least when networks are understood in the more usual sense of communication and information technologies, and all forms of organization that are capable of remaining exogenous to a state formation in their heterogeneity and potentially global reach. No doubt these different ways of conceptualizing political organization lend themselves to the same potential charge that Nancy levels at communism—that they remain unable to distinguish being-in-common from community, and so devolve or coalesce into celebrations of the bonds and ties that define a common essence, a fusion of peoples, and a self-contained or self-produced identity. In other words, such terms tend to presuppose forms of *self*-organization, *self*-affirmation, and *self*-sufficiency that are defined more by substance than exteriority, and which presuppose, as their arche-organizational principle, the metaphysical position of the Subject, even if that Subject is considered collective. These contingent forms of political organization and coalition continually fold into a self-identity registered in their very existence as a *given* affiliation, *a* council, a *named* collectivity, and so on. Or as Nancy recalls, such givens suggest how the question of both *form* and *organization* remains at once a transitory form and a strategic and contingent necessity, as Marx himself argues and as the Marxist legacy and revolutionary tradition has repeatedly insisted. But it is also the case that the ontological and ontopological presuppositions of this *ensemble* of contingent political organizations is open to permanent rearticulaton in terms of the ties that no longer enclose such organizational forms into a seamless or autonomous whole, where the tie that binds fuses into a common essence, but become incessantly retied into the possibility of thinking being-in-common, being-with, and coexistence in their absolute contingency, singular spacing, and extreme precarity. As Nancy has argued in a related vein, if the concepts of society, community, and assemblage all bare the mark of a certain closure or self-sufficiency, the question still becomes how to think the "with," of "singulars singularly together," where this togetherness "is neither the sum, nor the incorporation [*englobant*], nor the 'society,' nor the 'community' (where these words only give rise to problems)." Rather, Nancy attests, the "togetherness of singulars" is "singularity 'itself'": "it 'assembles' then insofar as it spaces them; they are 'linked' insofar as they are not unified" (*ESP*, 53/*BSP*, 33). The same ambivalence registered in Nancy's placement of so many key terms in scare quotes could also be said of the term collectivity itself, which tends to presuppose an essentially closed order but which Nancy has also described in terms of its necessarily "unstable and taut equilibrium."[45] But such ambivalence is also the necessary prerequisite for thinking the spacing of different assemblages or the spacing of singularities inaugurated by a politics of the tie, by a linking that constitutes no unity. In this sense, the appeal to networks does not link the different and disparate organizations together, even in terms of their differentiated solidarity, in which the link forms the bonds of a communication, or as if each particular organization was *part* of a group (species, gender, class, order, global movement, and so on). For Nancy's appeal to networks insists on reconceptualizing this problematic of political organization in terms of the relation that is contemporaneous with the singular plurality and plural singularity of Being. Or to recall the terms in which he rethinks the self-sufficiency of the political, he reconceptualizes it in terms of *sense*.

In this way, if we touch that point where any commentary on Nancy continually runs the risk of reduction and appropriation, we also find ourselves exposed to what remains perhaps most enigmatic, most provocative, and most transformative in Nancy's thinking. Pursuing the thought that sense today resists all signifying finality and enclosure, Nancy argues that sense "opens directly onto *us*":

It designates us as its element and as the place of its event or advent. But we are not a signification: neither a "humanity," nor a *polis*, nor a "project." We are the plural that does not multiply a singular—as if we were the collective figure of a sole reality (all the materialist critiques of idealism went no further than this)—but that, on the contrary, singularizes a common dispersion, this time irreducibly material *and* absolutely spiritual. We are the community of sense, and this community has no signification; it does not subsume under a Meaning the exteriority of its parts, nor the succession of its moments, since, it is the element of meaning only insofar as it is exposed by and to this exteriority and succession.[46]

Nancy's argument recalls the reading of Hegel in our earlier discussion of citizenship, notably the claim that what is left for us to hold onto is "the moment of 'exteriority' as being of almost essential value, so essential that it would no longer be a matter of relating this exteriority to any individual or collective 'we' without also unfailingly holding onto *exteriority itself and as such*" (*ESP*, 50/*BSP*, 30). But questioning the appeal to collectivity in terms of either a "collective figure" or a "collective we" does not foreclose the possibility or necessity of rethinking questions of collectivity or organization in which it is precisely the play of exteriority that becomes constitutive of these very terms and their decisive political implications. The play of exteriority informing the reticulated openings and spacings that articulate the collective as an *ensemble* is not just a way of reopening the most established tenets of political discourse and its related institutional structures. Nor is it simply bound or caught within a closed sense of the idealist/materialist divide. Nor again does Nancy's affirmation of existence in terms of a reticulated spacing only open toward a genealogy of the politico-philosophical order by situating this disposition as irreducible to the political and philosophical presuppositions of different forms of political self-sufficiency or "immanentism," including the ontological presuppositions of totalitarianism itself. For what remains at stake here is the way in which Nancy's affirmation of sense also reopens a genealogy of the "left," and a genealogy in which it is precisely this play of exteriority that also remains implicated.

In *The Sense of the World*, Nancy proposes that the politics of the tie and its infinite retying has "sought itself obscurely, from Rousseau to Marx and from the barricades to the councils, in the diverse figures of the 'left,'" even though this same politics has always been "obscurely mixed up with the schema of self-sufficiency," and so never "sufficiently disengaged from the expectations and demands of the theologicopolitical" (*SM*, 177/*SW*, 113). We will have occasion to return to the coincidence between the left's residual basis in the theologicopolitical and its initial presentation here in terms of "figures." Nonetheless, Nancy insists, the "left" has always disengaged itself from this schema of self-sufficiency "insofar as the 'leftist' exigency has been that exigency that arises neither out of a foundation (or archi-subjectivity) nor out of a legitimacy (or archi-citizenship) but, rather, without foundation and without right, incommensurable, unassignable, as the exigency to grant its 'rightful place' [*de faire 'droit' et 'place'*] in the in-common, to every singular tying, to the singularity of all ties" (*SM*, 177/*SW*, 113–14).

It is precisely within this same proposed genealogy of the "left" that Nancy's frequent references to the concept of fraternity also find a renewed measure of their importance, an emblem here of rethinking finite coexistence and a politics of the tie within the revolutionary tradition characterized by the epithets "liberty, equality, fraternity." In this sense, the various appeals to fraternity in Nancy's writings might be termed a paleonymic strategy in which the revolutionary potential of collective political organization is played off against the continual closure and self-sufficiency implied by fraternity and brotherhood in terms of their religious, humanist, communitarian, and patriarchal traditions—in other words, Nancy outlines a concept of fraternity that might be possible if elaborated (as Lacan intimates) "without father or mother, anterior rather than posterior to all law and common substance" (*SM*, 178/*SW*, 115).[47] At a time when the discourses of freedom and liberty have been evacuated and their political force devolved into slogans and advertising campaigns for marketing imperialism and the expansion of market democracy, it remains a significant feature of Nancy's writings that he works to rethink the revolutionary concepts of freedom and equality by turning to one of the most neglected and impoverished aspects of the revolutionary tradition, to what remains possible of collective organization and resistance, to the bonds and ties that fraternity is said to enact and simultaneously presuppose, in spite of the obstacles, ambivalences, and compromises necessarily implied in any use of the term (obstacles, ambivalences, and compromises that Nancy also extends to such related terms as the people or the multitude). At the very least, the appeal to fraternity and the being-with or disposition of being-in-relation that punctuates its implied grammar and spacing offers an initial measure of distinguishing an affirmation of plural singularities and singular pluralities from the "autistic multiplicity" that Nancy describes in the opening pages of *Being Singular Plural,* this autism that constitutes our contemporary "theater of bloody conflicts among identities."[48]

In arguing that Nancy's writings open toward rethinking this genealogy of the politico-philosophical order, including the related proposal for a genealogy of the left, the argument now centers on the ways in which the disposition of Being and its reticulated spacing reopens the ontological presuppositions of an ensemble of contingent political organizations. But such a project comes into relief only on the condition that no one political subject comes into existence as an identifiable figure, and no one form of political organization becomes an adequate response to a given political conjuncture. In other words, Nancy's emphasis on singularities, pluralities, and multiplicities places less emphasis on creating new models, new concepts, or new figures of political organization, however necessary and contingent they may be, than on thinking though how to take into account the ontological presuppositions informing the singularity of a given organization's politico-philosophical order, presuppositions in which it is precisely the play of exteriority that defines the "togetherness of singulars" as constitutive of its very singularity.[49]

An initial measure of this argument is also found in the proposal briefly outlined by Lacoue-Labarthe in one his texts for the Political Seminar at Cérisy, when he argues that it becomes necessary to prolong a revolutionary critique of Marxism by taking into account the various Councilist currents, citing the Socialisme or Barbarisme group and Situationist International in France. No doubt Lacoue-Labarthe's references could be extended beyond this limited set of references. But what resonates here is his insistence that, however such currents potentially devolve into forms of *self*-organization, thus reinforcing a Marxist metaphysics in which the "proletariat as Subject" is presupposed, such Councilist currents both represented and still represent the only "provisional politics" when faced with what Lacoue-Labarthe further describes as the disastrous consequences of the "bureaucratic counter-revolution" as well as the preservation or consolidation of bourgeois power.[50] Again, the references might seem a little dated today from the moment in which they were initially uttered, and the question of imperialism at stake in Lacoue-Labarthe's description arguably quite different in our contemporary geopolitical contexts. But it is in these same terms that that Nancy's genealogy of the "left" should also be understood, with the proviso that the metaphysical presuppositions informing the self-organization of such Councilist currents are now also subject to ontological displacement, opened to the reticulated spacing of singularities that are linked without any unity.

In light of this larger argument, the question of community or "community of sense" that has come to largely dominate the reception of Nancy's writings (at least in English) not only finds a measure of its force in light of a distinction from different forms of communitarianism. It now recedes from its position of relative prominence in Nancy's writings and their reception. Or rather, the continual rearticulation of being-*with* and coexistence throughout Nancy's writings also extends to what binds and unbinds, extends and refracts, the "bare web of the *com-*." Community, the common, communication, communion, and communes are thus rethought not only in their internal proximities to, and distances from, one another but in terms of a larger ensemble of potential political alliances and contingent affiliations.[51] The concept of community becomes one aspect of a larger politico-philosophical and ontological problematic, even as Nancy's extensive writings on community clearly remain decisive for rethinking both the founding concepts of political discourse as well as different forms of political organization to which we are appealing here. Similarly, Nancy's relatively circumscribed list cited earlier concerning "individuals, groups, nations, peoples" now finds itself subject to a certain closure, saturation, or exhaustion of political signification, and so expands to a multiplicity of potential terms implying relations, groupings, and ties that are not reducible to an exclusively Marxist appeal to collectivities or councils either but which find their originary decision in light of this very closure and exhaustion of political signification.

If the proposal to rethink the politico-philosophical order is now considered central to Nancy's writings, and if Nancy's rearticulation of the ontological presuppositions informing the founding tenets of political discourse is also considered constitutive of Being in its disposition and to coexistence in its reticulated spacing, such a proposal is still governed by a number of initial premises. In other words, if Nancy seeks to rearticulate the ontological presuppositions of a contingent *ensemble* of political organization, as we are arguing here, or if he rethinks this *ensemble* in terms of its reticulated spacing, such a proposal is predicated on thinking an originary sociality from out of an essential laying bare or the "bare web of the *com-*," and so from a politics of the tie that emerges out of a dissociation and disconnection of all given relations. At the same time, the conditions for rethinking this same *ensemble* finds one of its initial orientations in light of a distinction between being-in-common or being-with and politics, where the valorization of the former over the latter suggests a measure of rethinking the political as such, or the retreat of the political (which, to recall, is not the disappearance of the political but the withdrawal of the philosophical and ontological presuppositions of the politico-philosophical order). Thinking the political here *in statu nascendi* thus suggests that this *ensemble* is not to be considered as an institution per se, however fragile and precarious its institutional nature, but as a nascent *instituting* of potential relations, in the sense of their coming into being and coexistence, or their "birth to presence," to redeploy another of Nancy's terms. The transitive movement or spacing implied here suggests that such organizational formations are marked by their contingency and incommensurability rather than representational or institutional function. Or rather, the instituting of relations is marked by what Nancy has described as a "tendentially indistinct anonymity" whose "grouping is given, while its tie properly so-called is not" (*SM*, 140/*SW*, 89), a phrase that now glosses any attempt to rearticulate the ontological presuppositions of any given political ensemble or organization. In short, this multiplicity of a potential *ensemble* of political organizations finds and founds its conditions of (im)possibility in the an-archy of any given *arche*, in the transitive relationality implied by the disposition of Being and its reticulated spacing, and so in "an entire ontology of Being as tying" (*SM*, 175/*SW*, 112).

It is precisely in *these* terms that Nancy's appeal to networks demands to be read. And it is precisely in relation to networks and the reticulated spacing of all being-in-relation that we can now begin to outline the related proposal, which Nancy receives through Blanchot, to think an ontology to come as a communism to come, to that communism "which excludes (and is itself excluded from) any already constituted community."[52]

4

Being Communist

I would like to pose a question to Toni Negri: Can the multitudes say "us"? And if that is the case, what "us" is this?

—Jean-Luc Nancy

One no longer exists outside of language...language has become the foundation of life.

—Antonio Negri

The closing lines of Hardt and Negri's *Empire* are marked by a transition from the "joy of being" to the "joy of being communist."[1] The authors do not comment on this shift in emphasis, simply allowing the passage, exchange, or modulation from "being" to "being communist" frame their refusal of the "misery of power" and their affirmation of "biopower and communism, cooperation and revolution" (*E*, 413). The reference to "joy" shared by both "being" and "being communist" is clearly recognizable as part of a politico-philosophical lineage that passes through Spinoza and Nietzsche to Deleuze and Guattari, and so gives us a sense in which both "being" and "being communist" are also affirmations and celebrations of immanent existence and autonomous creation. The specific articulation closing Hardt and Negri's text between "being" and "being communist" nevertheless invites a number of other readings, readings that would need to parse out the singular logic that binds being and communism or the ontological and the political, for which the epithets political ontology or political philosophy frame or even efface the problem rather than constitute a solution.

If Hardt and Negri's concept of the multitude constitutes an "assemblage" in which "being" and "being communist" appear seamless, and a seamlessness echoed in their insistence throughout their writings on the "common," then the concept of the biopolitical becomes the key term in which an ontology ("being") and a politics ("communism") coexist. It is well known that

Hardt and Negri redraw the concept of biopolitics from the later writings of Foucault (who refers to biopolitics as the "critical" and "historical ontology of ourselves") as well as the writings of Agamben, with the proviso that Hardt and Negri's concept of the biopolitical enacts a displacement of Foucault and Agamben's respective writings by taking its point of departure from "below."[2] Their reading of the biopolitical thus does not start from "constituted power" but from the multitude's "constituent power," specifically those forms of immaterial labor characterizing post-Fordist production. Pivotal to Hardt and Negri's larger argument is the way in which all these concepts are phrased in terms of the multitude's "alternative ontological basis" (*E*, 47) or, as Negri outlines in his exchange with Derrida, a "postdeconstructive ontology."[3] It is precisely an ontological definition of the multitude that creates the "substrate" or "grammar" of the multitude's constituent power.[4] The immanent potentiality or virtuality of such an ontology stems not just from the multitude's constituent power or the "biopolitical production of subjectivity" but through its refusal to close itself off in traditions of political philosophy centered on the "negativity of being." For it is precisely the multitude's "new sense of being" that shapes the alternative to the "properly ontological lack" that characterizes Empire's imperial form. Given the way in which Hardt and Negri establish their argument, the question thus remains whether their appeal to the biopolitical both assumes as well as simultaneously obscures, even effaces, the grammatical rearticulation of "being" and "being communist" that closes their text and frames their argument.

In one sense, the singular articulation between "being" and "being communist" is already obscured and even permanently effaced in Hardt and Negri's own writings through their repeated and quite insistent reference to *figures*, to those multiple figures—"the "figure of the militant," the "figure of the poor," the whole population of figures that closes the book—who together compose the multitude. This transformation of the multitude into figures (including what the authors term "the figure of a concept") reaches a decisive moment in the closing scene of *Empire*, in which the people "dissolves" and the "figure" of the militant, in hand with St. Francis of Assisi, comes onto the screen. It is this figure "who best expresses the life of the multitude" (*E*, 411). Indeed, the entire trajectory of *Empire* could be described as outlining a transformation in which the "virtual conditions" in the "becoming-subject" of the multitude "become real in a concrete figure" (*E*, 407). The authors are quick to note earlier in the text that this figure is not an "ideal form," even if it can be recognized or identified. And yet, throughout *Empire* (and extended in Hardt and Negri's other writings), concepts are more or less considered synonymous with figures, raising the question whether figures can not only do the same work as (the creation of) concepts but also contain within themselves this "becoming" of the subject that is then figured or, as the authors also insist, "incarnated" in the multitude.[5]

In light of this more pervasive transformation marking Hardt and Negri's presentation of the multitude, we can outline three consequences concerning the play of figures in the text. First, in spite of Hardt and Negri's repeated refusal to situate the multitude within a linear or historicist unfolding, the transition from the virtual to the real and concrete is already inscribed in, and predetermined by, the more or less surreptitious slippages marking the text, in which concepts fold into figures. Named and recognizable—the poor, Bartleby, St. Francis, the Zapatistas, and so on—these references are all presented in terms of figures who are identifiable and then held up as exemplary. In this sense, either turning the multitude into a series of figures effaces the hybridity, singularities, or virtualities of "becoming-subject" that together organize the multitude's ontological and singular constitution, or else these slippages between figure and singularity demand a rethinking of the figure capable of containing within itself its virtual displacement, a (dis)figuring whose contours remained to be defined.[6] In other words, in spite of Hardt and Negri's insistence on distinguishing biopower from the biopolitcal production of singularities, the question still remains whether the reduction of the *bios* to figures effaces the very force Hardt and Negri seek within the biopolitical production of subjectivities, the very force that creates and sustains the conditions of "being communist" and its alternative ontological basis.[7]

More pertinent in the context of Hardt and Negri's references to immaterial labor, the turn to figures situates *Empire* in light of Ernst Jünger's *Der Arbeiter* (1932), in which the worker is presented in light of what Jünger terms a "*Gestalt.*" If we cite *Der Arbeiter* in this context, specific to the reading of *Empire* at stake here is Deleuze and Guattari's brief acknowledgment of Jünger in the "Treatise on Nomadology," notably their alternative reading of *Der Arbeiter* that closes with a proposal to think workers as "new figures of a transhistorical assemblage," figures they consider "neither historical nor eternal, but untimely."[8] Indeed, if Deleuze and Guattari also foreground this assemblage in terms of figures, and if their argument in part shapes Hardt and Negri's subsequent affirmation of the multitude, then it becomes important to acknowledge that a determining aspect of Deleuze and Guattari's argument is the rearticulation of the "line" or limit that preoccupies Heidegger in his own references to Jünger in "The Question of Being."[9] As Deleuze and Guattari suggest, for example, Jünger portrays the Rebel as "a transhistorical figure drawing the Worker, on the one hand, and the Soldier, on the other, down a shared [*commune*] line of flight where one says simultaneously 'I seek a weapon' and 'I am looking for a tool.'" In the creation of this Worker-Soldier assemblage and its "lines of flight," what counts for Deleuze and Guattari is to "draw [*tracer*] the line, or what amounts to the same thing, cross [*franchir*] the line, pass over [*passer*] the line, for the line is only drawn by surpassing the line of separation [*la ligne n'est tracée qu'en dépassant celle de séparation*]."[10] Recalling the inscription of a separation as the constitutive condition of all attachment and relations in Lacoue-Labarthe and Nancy's texts for the Center, Deleuze and Guattari's as well as Hardt and Negri's presentations of this transhistorical assemblage in terms of a "line of flight" suggest that their respective reference to the *figure* of the Worker-Soldier continually reinscribes or recircumscribes this line of demarcation through the very appeal to a figure, at the same time as it *mediates* Hardt and Negri's argument that Empire is conceived as an immanent plane *without mediation*, having no outside and existing without limits. For it is this very appeal to the figure that continually interrupts the "immediacy" and "immeasurable" constitution of the multitude in relation to Empire itself, thus reducing its "mixed constitution" to a figurable, mediated, and thus identifiable form of representational (if not electoral) politics— precisely the political option they refuse for the multitude. Phrased slightly differently, Deleuze and Guattari never seek to rethink the ontological presuppositions of this *commune* or "shared" line of flight between the Worker and Soldier, suggesting that this sharing or commonality of the assemblage is achieved dialectically, or at least quasi-dialectically, *en dépassant* or "surpassing" the line of separation, rather than rethinking this separation as constitutive of the sharing or communal as such.

Emphasis on the figure in *Empire* further reopens the text to a larger problematic of appearing, exposure, and presentation, terms that reveal a literary, mimetic, or fictional dimension that is at once discernible and repeatedly (dis)simulated throughout the text. This phenomenological description implies a continual dramaturgy or choreography of curtains rising and falling in the text, of photographic exposures and negatives, of scenes of annunciation and homeric narratives, of figures appearing on screen and fading out, a "new phenomenology of labor" that oscillates between a politics based on the Greek amphitheater and its chorus and another based, at least in the wake of Deleuze, on a cinematic model. If this same phenomenological description is reproduced in the "ontological drama of the *res gestae*," then this dramaturgy also comes into continual conflict with the "spectacle" forms of capitalism cited elsewhere in *Empire*, including the "virtual spaces" and "diffuse apparatuses of images" analyzed in the writings of Guy Debord and the Situationists. No doubt the phenomenological, dramaturgical, and cinematic emphasis in *Empire* on the multitude's various forms of appearance and exposure does not posit itself as merely resistant to the mediation of spectacle. But this emphasis is never fully detached from the play of figures throughout the text, nor can it be separated from the very presentation (understood here as a question of a philosophical *Darstellung*) of Hardt and Negri's own argument. Or rather, the references to figures simultaneously reveal and dissimulate a constitutive tension in the text between questions of mimesis and presentation, on the one hand, and a refusal of a politics of representation, on the other (or the multitude as work of sublime art faced by the monstrosity of Empire). According to this reading, we might even suggest that *Empire* becomes one of the great treatises on mimesis opening the twenty-first century.

Tracing through the repeated transformations of the multitude into figures will also have decisive consequences for Hardt and Negri's larger ambition to write not just a "philosophical book," as they maintain, but "a philosophical fable about the decline of metaphysical mediation and the rise of ontological immanence." For it is never clear whether this fable is made possible by the conversion of the multitude into figures, or whether it is precisely this same conversion that reintroduces or reinscribes the metaphysical and transcendental mediations that Hardt and Negri seek to displace in their appeal to the absolute immanence of the multitude and its constituent power. The emphasis on figures in their writings also constitutes an inescapable dimension of all political discourse intent on disengaging itself from the theologicopolitical (a task suggested elsewhere in Hardt and Negri's reading of Spinoza). Extended back across the writings of Deleuze and Guattari from which they draw, the question becomes more generally how an appeal to the figure remains constitutive of all political discourse still bound by the (nondialectical) opposition between immanence defining the field of political collaboration and transcendental forms of political sovereignty, as if, within the Schmittian analysis of the theologicopolitical, the figures to which Hardt and Negri refer are in fact vestiges of the figures defining the history of political sovereignty. If Hardt and Negri insist that their appeal to the figure is irreducible to an "ideal form," their text nevertheless demonstrates that they never fully efface the figure's platonic, mimetic, and metaphysical origins. In short, Hardt and

Negri never fully separate the multitude's ontological or immanent constitution from its ontotheological—or ontotypological—support.[11]

If *Empire* is marked by a structural tension between the multitude conceived
in terms of its constituent power and its transformation into figures, and if
this tension continually displaces or rewrites the passage marking Empire's
larger trajectory from the "decline of metaphysical mediation" to the "rise of
ontological immanence," then the question remains how this appeal to the
figure also relates to one of the most decisive aspects of Hardt and Negri's
argument, namely, the multitude's networks of communication and biopolitical collaboration.

On the one hand, the numerous references to networks throughout Hardt
and Negri's writings draw from the systems of communication and information technologies characterizing our (post)modernity, systems and technologies that have largely shaped and even overdetermined the reception of
their writings. However, while Hardt and Negri acknowledge that a distributed network such as the Internet creates a "good initial image or model,"
it is more important to register how forms of collaborative and immaterial
labor tend to "create and be embedded in cooperative and communicative
networks," specifically the forms of collaborative and immaterial labor defined by new transformations in communication technologies, at least when
such technologies are further situated in terms of the relations of production
defining post-Fordist economies.[12] Networks thus constitute the means by
which to acknowledge not only the social relationships and encounters that
are created through telecommunications but, more importantly, the specific
conditions informing immaterial and collaborative labor on a global scale:
"Immaterial labor tends to take the social form of networks based on communication, collaboration, and affective relationships. Immaterial labor can
only be conducted in common, and increasingly immaterial labor invents
new, independent networks of cooperation through which it produces. Its
ability to engage and transform all aspects of society and its collaborative
network form are enormously powerful characteristics that immaterial labor
is spreading to other forms of labor" (*M*, 66).

It is these independent networks that then serve to create a "preliminary
sketch" of the multitude's social composition, where the multitude's collaborative network form and social composition both animate the movements
of resistance against Empire while constituting the "postmodern transition of organizational forms" characteristic of immaterial labor, notably

those organizational forms working to create an alternative global society.[13] If Hardt and Negri valorize the specifically networked form of communication and collaboration constitutive of immaterial labor, these networks must then confront the networks that constitute the delocalized biopower of Empire itself, specifically those networks that are inscribed in Empire's own inherently conflicted if imperial constitution: "On the one hand, Empire spreads globally its network of hierarchies and divisions that maintain order through new mechanisms of control and constant conflict. Globalization, however, is also the creation of new circuits of cooperation and collaboration that stretch across nations and continents and allow an unlimited number of encounters" (*M*, xiii).

Confronted with these "two faces" to globalization, Hardt and Negri's appeal to networks sets in play a confrontation between those networks that consolidate and reproduce Empire's forms of biopower, in which nearly all of humanity is now to some degree "absorbed within or subordinated to the networks of capitalist exploitation" (*E*, 43), and the alternative and autonomous networks created through collaborative encounters within immaterial labor itself. Rethinking Deleuze and Guattari's analysis of the Worker–Soldier cited above, if the present military, for example, does not simply *use* networks but must itself "*become* a full matrix, distributed network" (*M*, 59), then immaterial labor also creates the conditions for this becoming-networked of the multitude, for "it takes a network to fight a network." More specifically (and again drawing from the language of Deleuze and Guattari's *A Thousand Plateaus*), Hardt and Negri further outline the terms of this conflict: "The general outlines of today's imperial constitution can be conceived in the form of a rhizomatic and universal communication network in which relations are established to and from all its points and nodes. Such a network seems paradoxically to be at once completely open and completely closed to struggle and intervention. On the one hand, the network formally allows all possible subjects in the web of relations to be present simultaneously, but on the other hand, the network itself is a real and proper non-place" (*E*, 319–20). Hardt and Negri thus conclude that the struggle over this imperial constitution will have to be played out on this "ambiguous and shifting terrain" of networks, a terrain whose topographical or topological features are best described as a paradoxical "real and proper non-place."

Responding to these widely discussed arguments concerning the role of networks in Hardt and Negri's writings, and recalling the ways in which this appeal to a "real and proper non-place" finds a number of echoes in Lacoue-Labarthe and Nancy's reading of Heidegger, the question now remains how the insistent appeal to figures in their writings determines their very attempt to circumscribe the "real and proper non-place" of networks as the singular "terrain" of struggle, as if their own acknowledgment that resistance to Empire is played out on a terrain that is ambiguous and shifting was itself inseparable from the necessary place and play of figures marking the text. For it is precisely in terms of figures that the multitude's forms of resistance become at once discernible and visible within this shifting terrain, a way of turning a "non-place" into something "real and proper." Or rather, the play of figures in the text suggests how this terrain of networks and its real and proper nonplace is ultimately transposed into a rigorously defined orientation and topography. In other words, providing some measure of stability and orientation, the repeated turn to figures further allows for a rigorous geometrical ordering in which the multitude collaborates "immanently" and "horizontally" through networks and yet strikes "vertically" at the "virtual center" of Empire in struggles and forms of resistance defined by their unmediated intensity and "singular emergence" (E, 58).[14]

The question nevertheless remains how to think the relation between the networks informing the multitude's organizational forms, collaboration, and social composition and its ontological constitution. For, given the way networks are instrumental in creating a "social multiplicity" and an open and inclusive democratic global society, what are the ontological conditions that allow for this multiplicity "to communicate and act in common while remaining internally different" (M, xiv)? As Hardt and Negri argue, within the networks of collaboration defining the multitude's constitution, it is not a question here of everyone in the world becoming the same, for networks create the possibility that, while remaining different, "we discover the commonality that enables us to communicate and act together" (M, xiii). In other words, the "internal differences" of the multitude must discover "the common" that allows them to communicate and act together. Considered as a new philosophical concept that responds to our current situation in global economies, the common at stake here is thus something we are said to "share," something less discovered than produced: "Our communication, collaboration, and cooperation are not only based on the common, but they in turn produce the common in an expanding spiral relationship. This production of the common tends today to be central to every form of social production, no matter how locally circumscribed, and it is, in fact, the primary characteristic of the new dominant forms of labor today" (M, xv).

The grammar articulating "the common" is thus quite singular, as is the topological (and implicitly Hegelian) orientation of this "spiral." For if the multitude is an "open and expansive network in which all differences can be expressed freely and equally, a network that can provide the means of encounter so that we can work and live in common" (*M*, xiv), then the multitude's composition is made up of "innumerable internal differences" that remain irreducible to the "unity of a single identity—different cultures, races, ethnicities, genders, and sexual orientations; different forms of labor; different ways of living; different views of the world; and different desires" (*M*, xiv). In short, the multitude is a multiplicity of all these singular differences, and it is precisely this multiplicity that then produces the *common*.

It is a significant feature of Hardt and Negri's argument that the networks informing this grammar are the networks borrowed from theories of "distributed intelligence" or "swarm intelligence," references that will then inform the grammatical rearticulation of the multitude at stake here: "The swarms that we see emerging in the new network political organizations...are composed of a multitude of different creative agents. This adds several more layers of complexity to the model [created by research into distributed intelligence]. The members of the multitude do not have to become the same or renounce their creativity in order to communicate and cooperate with each other. They remain different in terms of race, sex, sexuality, and so forth. What we need to understand, then, is the collective intelligence that can emerge from the communication and cooperation of such a varied multiplicity" (*M*, 92).

In light of these references, a number of questions remain, notably whether Hardt and Negri's appeal to the networks of distributed intelligence and swarm intelligence efface precisely what remains at stake in their positing of the *common*—namely, "being communist," or the multitude's new sense of being and alternative ontological basis. In other words, we might ask whether the ways in which networks actually touch on the social composition or organizational forms of the multitude is effaced or dissimulated in the very act of presenting the multitude's multiplicity as at once distributed and swarming. For how exactly do the ontological claims Hardt and Negri make for the multitude become articulated with the simultaneous affirmation of the "form," "composition," "organization," and "immanence," as well as distribution of immaterial labor? Or how do networks simultaneously re(con)figure the communication *between* subjects situated "*in*" the "web of relations," the multiplication of recognized "differences," as well as the insurgent composition or disposition of the very "being" that discloses the multitude's "ontological substrate" and "joy of being communist"? In short, in what ways does the reference to distributed and swarm intelligence tend to efface or dissimulate the ways in which networks are simply a convenient model but become inscribed in and as the singularly ontological sharing out or being-in-relation of the common? Or in what ways are networks inscribed in and as the disposition that reopens the grammatical articulation of all constituency (as in Hardt and Negri's affirmation of con-stituent power) while simultaneously displacing the very production of the common in terms of its *self*-production and *self*-affirmation?

Addressing the "political necessities of today" in *The Sense of the World*, or discerning the very terms in which we might begin to address these necessities, Nancy seeks to circumscribe the different traditions proposing a politics of "self-sufficiency" while foregrounding a politics of the "tie."[15] It is this "knotting or tying of the tie [*nouage du lien*]" that opens toward a rearticulation of the political that corresponds to what Lacoue-Labarthe and Nancy had earlier phrased in terms of its *retrait*, understood now in terms of "dependence or interdependence, of heteronomy or heterology." Implying a politics without theatrical model, this rearticulation of the political through a politics of the knot opens "an entire ontology of Being as tying," demanding that we touch that limit or "extremity" where "all ontology, as such, gets tied up with something other than itself" (*SM*, 175/*SW*, 112). As long as we do not touch this limit or extremity, Nancy argues, we will never displace the "theological sphere" governing the various schemas of political self-sufficiency.

If Nancy's rearticulation of the political in terms of the ontological is part of a wider attempt to discern the political necessities of today, then the question remains how to articulate this retreat of the political when, for "two-thirds of the planet, it is the very possibility of a tie of whatever sort that has been undone. And if the havoc continues," Nancy suggests, "it is the tie of all that will be in question—indeed, it already is" (*SM*, 181–82/*SW*, 116). The question also remains how to think the political when the hollowing out of democracy appears to create a void filled by capitalism as a "global figure"—"at this very moment, when political subjectivity is doubtless to a great degree coming undone, and when substantial sovereignty is splitting up, are we not in the process of learning," Nancy asks, "that the virtual advent, or in any case the almost universally desired advent, of a world citizenship (beginning with that of Europe) nonetheless risks corresponding to the triumph... of what has been called 'market democracy'?" (*SM*, 170/*SW*, 108). In other words, the question remains how the forces of market democracy work to efface the politics of the tie to which Nancy is drawing us and so further efface a rearticulation of the political in light of the larger questions of democracy, sovereignty, community, and citizenship that comprise the larger context for thinking this politics of the tie in *The Sense of the World*. For this double effacement participates within a wider postponement of thinking the *mondialisation* of the world, translated less immediately by "globalization" than the becoming worldly of the world, the becoming worldwide of the world as the enabling yet irreducible condition in which to think the very concept of the global. As *The Sense of the World* argues, and as Nancy's more recent writings have forcefully suggested, the turn to the discourse of globalization, understood as a term that subsumes a definable number of historical and contemporary tendencies or vectors, tends to efface thinking our being *in* the world as being-*toward* the world, and so *refuses* (in all senses) the very *partage* or sharing out that articulates this politics of the tie in the first place.

In proposing "another approach" to the political, one that would distinguish itself from a more general "laicized theologicopolitics" analyzed by Carl Schmitt, we have already seen how Nancy argues that a politics of self-sufficiency always amounts to failing to tie the tie because it is always supposed to be "*already* tied, given" (*SM*, 163/*SW*, 103). In other words, the question remains how to think political ties as always "still *to be tied*" and so refuse all nostalgia for the desired reintegration of a fragmented society or divided nation, a split subject or a humanity in shreds, a (re)fusion of the (or a) community in which political and social ties either eventually disappear in order to (re)create a cohesive identity or devolve into further atomization. As Nancy writes, "In the different figures of self-sufficiency, sometimes it is the social tie itself that is self-sufficient, sometimes it is the terms or units between which the social tie passes. In both cases, in the end [*pour finir*] the tie no longer makes up the tie, it comes undone, sometimes by fusion, sometimes by atomization. All of our politics," he concludes, "are politics of undoing [*dénouement*] into self-sufficiency" (*SM*, 173/*SW*, 111). Thinking through the political necessities of today thus demands that we practice a politics of "non-self-sufficiency," a politics whose resistance to closure and refusal of teleology simultaneously opens toward a politics of finitude. This is a politics whose rhythm or gesture is composed less by the tie that binds than the tie that "reties," less the tie that encloses than the tie that "makes up a network" (*SM*, 177/*SW*, 114).[16]

Two initial implications follow from this argument, returning us to this motif of tying, knotting, and weaving that has recurred with some frequency across the previous chapters. First, if Nancy's references to tying and knotting constitute a rewriting of the *symploke* that binds the art of politics to the weaver in the *Statesman*, the networks to which Nancy appeals cannot be collapsed back into, or reduced to, networks of global communication systems and information technology. Second, Nancy's appeal to a politics of the tie also opens toward the genealogy of politics discussed in the previous chapter, for it is precisely this politics of the tie that has "sought itself obscurely, from Rousseau to Marx, and from the barricades to the counsels, in the diverse figures of the 'left.'" Even though this politics has also been mixed up with different schemas of self-sufficiency (because never sufficiently disengaged from the "expectations and demands of the theologicopolitical"), we recall that Nancy nevertheless claims that the politics of the tie has also always distinguished itself from this scheme insofar as the "'leftist' exigency" has been that exigency that arises "neither out of a foundation (or archi-subjectivity) nor out of a legitimacy (archi-citizenship) but, rather, without foundation and without right, incommensurable, unassignable, as the exigency to grant its 'rightful place' [*de faire 'droit' et 'place'*] in the in-common, to every singular tying, to the singularity of all ties" (*SM*, 177/*SW*, 113–14). No doubt we can now question whether Nancy's reference to "figures" of the "left" suggests how it is precisely through an appeal to *figures* that the "left" finds disengagement from the theologicopolitical and different "figures of self-sufficiency" all the more difficult to sustain, a question that Nancy's exchange with Lacoue-Labarthe concerning the figure has explored at length, and a question that Nancy has also explored in his writings on Marx and communism.[17] Nancy's argument here also suggests how this emphasis on the singularity of ties is not reducible to common assumptions concerning the fragmentation of the left, for which a will to figuration (including its new found digital mediations) might begin to constitute a compensatory mechanism or imaginary resolution. Or rather, if Nancy's placement of "left" in scare quotes foregrounds the difficulty of thinking the politics of the tie detached from a will to figuration, and not just another appeal to the ways in which "left" and "right" have become increasingly impertinent as political categories, it also corresponds to his further claim that it is the "lateral displacement" implied by the terms "left" and "right" that ought to be substituted for "theological verticality," for it is the latter that prevents the former from "opening itself up" (*SM*, 176/*SW*, 112). In short, recalling this geometrical configuring of spatial vectors in Hardt and Negri's *Empire*, it is precisely in this opening toward a "lateral displacement" that we might begin to reconceive a politics of the tie in and as a network.

If Nancy's exposition of the politics of the tie pertains to both the political necessities of today as well as a more circumscribed genealogy of the "left," then his articulation of this tie in and as a network finds its *fils conducteur* in a reading of Heidegger. As we have seen, Nancy's rewriting of "fundamental ontology" or "first philosophy" in *Being Singular Plural* rethinks Heidegger's marginal references to *Mitsein* and *Mitdasein* both raised and closed off in *Being and Time*. It is this reading of Heidegger's writings that begins to re-elaborate for Nancy the stakes of their political rewriting while opening toward a thought of the "singular plural essence of being" or "being singular plural." In this sense, Nancy's demand that we touch that limit or "extremity" (where "all ontology, as such, gets tied up with something else") is also a demand to rewrite the grammar that binds or ties the ontological to itself, at least insofar as this binding does not secure a form of self-sufficiency or simple identity but constitutes a knot. It is this knot that then creates the enabling condition for thinking the singular "exposure" or "disposition" of Being, understood, as their prefixes suggest, as constituted from out of their own exteriority. Returning to the text of *Being and Time*, Heidegger argues in §50 that *Dasein's* "ownmost [*eigensten*] potentiality-of-being" finds its measure defined not just in terms of its finitude but in and at an "extremity [*äußerste*]," an extremity where "all relations to other *Dasein* are untied [*gelöst*]," and so the point—the knot, node, or nexus—where this separation or detachment is constitutive of *Dasein's* "nonrelational [*unbezügliche*] ownmost possibility."[18] One could argue that Nancy's reading of Heidegger is not just a way of reengaging the relatively marginal references to *Mitsein* in *Being and Time* but demands rethinking the ways in which this "extremity" can be read as the condition of *Dasein's* "nonrelational" possibility (a question also posed by Derrida in his reading of Marx when he asks whether "the extremity of the extreme" can ever be comprehended).[19] For Nancy reads *Dasein's* extremity not in terms of a concentrated gathering of *Dasein's* "ownmost" possibility (a possibility whose political stakes we now recognize for Heidegger) but as a limit, and a limit that continually remarks *Dasein's* separation and dissociation from itself and thus its exposure to its own exteriority or disposition or an alterity. Or rather, Nancy picks up on one of the strands of Heidegger's language here and argues that this limit and extremity is not a rigorous demarcation between an inside and outside but now conceived as the tying of a knot. More pertinently, the relations to other *Dasein* are not "dissolved" (as Stambaugh translates *gelöst*), but always implicated less dialectically in *Dasein's* (un)raveling into and out of itself, a slackening, loosening, or unfastening—a stitching or suturing—in which *Dasein's* ontological constitution presents itself as a knot in which "all ontology, as such gets tied up with something else."[20] In this sense, *Dasein* is never "*completely* [*völlig*] thrown back upon its ownmost potentiality-of-being," as Heidegger italicizes, for there always remains a residual trace of an alterity constitutive of this completion of *Dasein's* solipsistic "intimacy" and individuating potential. Remarking this extremity as a limit also reinscribes the (non)relation to an alterity as a relation without relation, an articulation or "jointing" (in Derrida's terms) conceived in Heidegger's text as a lacing or knotting. Closer to the language weaving these various texts, we might call this a reticulation or network (and indeed, in his later book on Schelling, Heidegger will use precisely this word for articulating the system in which to think the essence of human freedom).

Rather than opening toward a regional ontology such as a political ontology, Nancy rewrites Heidegger's existential analytic as constitutively coexistential and so parses out the logic of this relation or reticulation opened up at this extremity by presenting the ontological as the "singular plural essence of being" or "being singular plural." And the singularity is "agrammatical" and without measure, since nothing or no one is given in advance of a given limit's outside, no one is given in advance of *Dasein's* potential (un)raveling *with*. In short, what marks Nancy's texts here is the way in which the ontological constitution of the singularities that compose or dispose the singular plurality of Being is not a politics based on exclusion, nor a form of articulation based on negation, but an attempt to approach another concept of the political given in and *as* a politics of the tie, that is, given in and *as* a network.

In light of the limits inscribed in this extremity, and a limit itself delimited in and as a knot, the question of space reimposes itself. For what kind of space does this extremity presuppose, and what space is opened up in Nancy's rearticulation of these limits? In short, how would the rearticulation of these limits relate to Nancy's earlier discussion of "lateral displacements" as well as the larger ambition in *The Sense of the World* to open up an exploration of "the space that is common to us all, that makes up our community"—in short, how do these limits reopen the political as "the place of the in-common as such" (*SM*, 139/*SW*, 88)?

If the logic informing Nancy's affirmation of a politics of the tie is inseparable from networks, then the spatial composition of this tie is also described as one having "neither interiority nor exteriority but which, in being tied, ceaselessly makes the inside pass outside, each into (or by way of) the other, the outside inside, turning back on itself without returning *to* itself" (*SM*,

174/*SW*, 111). Proposed here in terms of a chiasmatic structuring or spacing, Nancy's description of the network of political ties invites a number of preliminary observations and questions.

First, Nancy's presentation of political ties echoes his refusal of a politics of self-sufficiency while bringing his description close to questions of topology informing much of the literature on networks. Thus, Nancy's description simultaneously extends and displaces the widespread references to "autopoietic systems" that organize some of the most sustained and ambitious discussion of networks today, including Manuel de Landa's concept of "meshworks," as well as the reworking of Maturana and Varela's concept of autopoietic systems in the writings of Niklas Luhmann and "systems theory" (references that Hardt and Negri acknowledge in their discussion of distributed and swarm intelligence). The chiasmatic topology of networks described by Nancy also suggests an attempt to rewrite the appeals to topology constituting the subject within psychoanalytic discourse (i.e., through Borromean knots and Möbius strips), while reopening a reading of Bruno Latour's more recent argument (subsequent to the widely cited discussion of networks in *We Have Never Been Modern* and the project of "retying the Gordian knot") that the concept of networks should be replaced by "attachments." Nancy's description of networks here also invites a rereading of Deleuze and Guattari's writings, including their concepts of the rhizome or, more pertinent in this context, smooth and striated space. Given Nancy's insistence on the tying and knotting of political ties, one might recall in particular that Deleuze and Guattari's elaboration of smooth and striated space in *A Thousand Plateaus* also makes references to the material composition of fabrics (including quilts and felt) and thus constitutes a further way of rethinking the reference to weaving or the *symploke* in Plato's *Statesman*, notably the ambivalent place given to felt in Plato's text.[21]

Second, two textual references might help rethink Nancy's description of networks and the opening of a chiasmatic space it implies. The first is from the preface of Claude Lévi-Strauss's *The View from Afar*. Returning to his earlier work on kinship and social exchange, Lévi-Strauss writes, "If one wishes to understand the nature of social ties, one should not first take a few objects and try immediately to establish connections between them. Reversing the traditional approach, one should first perceive the relations as terms and, then, the terms themselves as relations. In other words, in the network of social bonds, the knots have logical priority over the lines, even though, empirically, the lines form knots by crisscrossing one another."[22]

Taking up his earlier description of networks in *The Sense of the World* in terms of a chiasmatic structuring or spacing, Nancy's thought of the politics of the tie rewrites Lévi-Strauss's own appeal to the "network of social bonds," transforming its structuralist and anthropological assumptions by rearticulating the very space that Lévi-Strauss begins to explore here in terms of its "logical" priorities. In *Being Singular Plural*, Nancy rewrites the ontological scansion of networks in terms that respond precisely to this change in logical priority:

> Everything, then, passes *between us*. This "between," as its name implies, has neither a consistency nor continuity of its own. It does not lead from one to the other; it constitutes no connective tissue, no cement, no bridge. Perhaps it is not even fair to speak of a "connection [*lien*]" to the subject; it is neither connected nor unconnected (*ni lié, ni delié*); it falls short of both; even better, it is that which is at the heart of a connection, the *inter*lacing of strands (*l'entrecroisment des brins*), whose extremities remain separate even at the very center of the knotting (*nouage*). The "between" is the stretching out (*distension*) and distance opened by the singular as such, its spacing of sense. That which does not maintain its distance from the "between" is only immanence collapsed in on itself (*en soi*) and deprived of meaning.[23]

The reference to "extremities" obviously marks Nancy's further rearticulation—one might suggest, spatial rechoreographing—of Heidegger's argument in *Being and Time* concerning *Dasein*'s spatial possibilities. At the same time, Nancy's rewriting of the relation "between" in terms of its topological implications also responds to Blanchot's *The Infinite Conversation*, notably the section where Blanchot returns to Lévinas's proposal in *Totality and Infinity* to rethink the relation with the other—the relation *as* relation, or the relation without relation—in terms of a "curvature of space." In response to Lévinas, Blanchot argues that such a relation to the other, the relation without relation, is "doubly dissymmetrical": "We know—at least we sense—that the absence between the one and the other is such that the relations, if they could be unfolded, would be those of a non-isomorphic field in which point A would be distant from point B by a distance other than point B's distance from point A; a distance excluding reciprocity and presenting a curvature whose irregularity extends to the point of discontinuity."[24] It is in this sense, Blanchot affirms, that "the terms between which a relationship could take place" become displaced to an "Other" that is no longer contained by the terms of the relationship; as

he concludes his analysis, in the "space-time of interrelation," it becomes necessary to think under a double contradiction—"to think the Other first as the
distortion of a field that is nevertheless continuous, as the dislocation and the
rupture of discontinuity—and then as the infinite of a relation that is without
terms and as the infinite termination of a term without relation."[25] One might
argue that Nancy's *Being Singular Plural* unfolds in large part as a commentary
not just on the spatial articulation of Heidegger's existential analytic but on the
topological implications of Blanchot's reading of Lévinas, at least insofar as the
appeal here to an "Other" is transposed to the "between" as such. Or rather,
Nancy's emphasis on this "between" reopens the grammar of the relation without relation by thinking this "without" not as an empty relation or a relation
with emptiness but as the enabling condition for thinking being-in-relation or
being-with, in the sense of a spacing whose distension and distance is opened
by the singularity of the singular as such.

The sense of displacement registered across all these references and citations still leaves us with a question concerning how to rethink the political
in terms of its spatial or topological implications. For as Nancy argues, the
fundamental political question still remains: "how to induce the *ensemble*
comprised of indeterminate *ties*—ties that have come untied or are not yet
tied—to configure itself as a space of sense that would not be reabsorbed into
its own truth." He continues, "This sort of *configuration* of space would not
be the equivalent of a political figuration (fiction, myth). It would trace the
form of being-toward in being-together without identifying the traits of the
toward-*what* or toward-*whom*, without identifying or verifying the 'to what
end' of the sense of being-in-common—or else, by identifying these traits as
those of *each one* [*tout un chacun*]: a different 'totality,' a different unicity of
truth. Of being-in-common, it would operate a transitivity, not a substantiality. But still, there would remain something of the figure, something traced
out" (*SM*, 142/*SW*, 90).

Nancy's language and references to the "configuration of space" in terms
of political figurations and truth draws from and simultaneously transforms
Heidegger's argument in his essay on "The Origin of the Work of Art," notably Heidegger's preoccupation concerning the truth of the work of art as
it relates to the spatial problematic of the "rift-design," a problematic that
includes questions of framing or the "bounding" and "blurring" of outlines
that repeatedly punctuate Heidegger's text.[26] The fundamental question nevertheless imposes itself how there would remain "something of the 'figure'"
or "something traced out" in the configuration of space defining the "form"

of our being-toward or being-in-common. Or again, how are we to think of all figuration as inscribed and simultaneously fractured by its con-figuration, its figuring-with. In *La comparution*, Nancy writes, "Politics will not come to gather, order, and melt into its hypostasis all extremes where existence yields to meaning. To say it again: among the multiple shards of these 'accesses,' each of which implies community and communication, politics would propagate that of the *in* as such. Without hypostasis, that is without a substantial presentation: and still, not without a recognizable figure. But what would be the figure of the *in-* and the *between*? A figure between *us* which would neither dominate nor tear us apart?"[27]

Nancy goes on to situate this rethinking of the figure in terms of the "communist exigency" to designate the "distorted figure" of a class that is the dissolution of all classes. This exigency suggests the ways in which Marxism hinges on a revolutionary transformation in which the "radical disfiguration" of class passes to an "absolute transfiguration," and so opens itself to a transfiguration that refuses the hypostasis, self-sufficiency, or enclosure of any limit or extremity defined by a single figure.[28]

Nancy's proposal here is to think an inaugural or originary opening, and to do so in light of a traced out contour that makes possible such an opening. Indeed, it is precisely this reference to a figure, contour, or outline that itself "forms of the contour, if not the aporia, at least of the paradox of political sense today": "Without figuration or configuration, is there still any sense? But as soon as it takes on a figure, is it not 'totalitarian' truth? What outline would retain the unexpectedness of sense, its way of continuing to come and to be on its way [*sa venue*], without confounding them with an indeterminacy that lacks all consistency? What name could trace open [*frayer*] an access for the anonymity of being-in-common?" (*SM*, 142–43/*SW*, 90).

The marked ambivalence informing Nancy's argument at once extends and displaces the aporia that closed our reading in the first chapter of Lacoue-Labarthe and Nancy's texts for the Center in Paris, as well as Nancy's exchange with Lacoue-Labarthe concerning the figure. It also recalls the effacement of alterity imposed by totalitarianism, such that the reference to the figure here refocuses the earlier analysis of the reincorporation, resubstantialization, or hypostasis of the body politic. But the question of how to discern the outline or traced out space that might "retain the unexpectedness of sense" still remains. For in one sense, Nancy refers to this space as deserted, abandoned, left free, without horizon—a space that thus resists all appropriation. But such a space is not merely an endless and infinite opening of space, as the references to a desert seem to imply and as Lévinas and Blanchot's appeal to an infinity in terms of a curvature of space also seems to imply. For Nancy also proposes that the topological features of this space are characterized by a seemingly paradoxical and finally aporetic "nonfigurable contour," acknowledging that "we will certainly have to learn how to trace its edges," even if we have "no model, no matrices for this tracing or for this writing."[29]

The "spacing" to which Nancy consistently appeals in his writings suggests that tracing out the outline, limit, or extremities of this "nonfigurable contour" also implies more of a "cutting movement," a "cutting out" whose topology is never closed or self-contained but "traces another space [*lieu*] of enunciation," or a "space of emission." In his exchange with Lacoue-Labarthe concerning the figure, Nancy suggests that Lacoue-Labarthe's own preoccupation with the figure stems from his work on "onto-typology," which he paraphrases as "a figural and fictional assignation of the presentation of being and/or truth." In terms of his own writings, Nancy suggests that his related thinking concerning myth, notably as explored in *The Inoperative Community*, leads him "to the exigency of a certain figuration," going on to argue that the "'interruption' of myth does not appear to me a simple cessation, but rather a cutting movement which, in cutting, traces out another place of articulation."[30] In the conclusion to the sections on politics in *The Sense of the World*, Nancy refers to this other space of articulation or enunciation in terms of the "concatenation of acts of speech" and the "seizure of speech" (*prise de parole*), paraphrasing the "seizure of speech" as "the emergence or passage of some*one* and every *one* into the linking of sense effects" and arguing that "every *one* as such subverts in fact the virtual closure or totalization of the network" (*SM*, 178/*SW*, 114).[31] The phrase "some*one*" refers to the "unicity of the singular" and not an identity, substantiality, or form of self-sufficiency, for this unicity consists in its very multiplicity, an essential or existential determination that reopens all attempts to posit any single individuality or autonomy. If this unicity of the "some*one*" opens toward a network whose closure or totalization is always effectively subverted, it does not stem from adding to a "postulation of individuality or autonomy a certain number of relations and interdependencies" and so from positing an infinite extension of individuals that comprise the network. It is not a question here of someone entering into a relation with or connecting to other someones. Nor does a community exist that precedes interrelated individuals, any more than a communication network exists in which individuals then communicate with one another in order to create a community, group identity, or specific bond, or as if the subject were inserted "into" a web of relations and *then* communicates or collaborates with others. As Nancy insists, "the singular is not the particular, not *part* of a group (species, gender, class, order)," for the relationship is strictly contemporaneous with the singularities.

If Nancy is able to articulate this "someone" or unicity in terms of networks, then the "enchainment of sense effects" in this same context is defined as a "statement and offering in phrase or outline," including, as examples, "the cry, the call, and the complaint as much as discourse, the poem, and the song, along with the gesture and silence" (*SM*, 180/*SW*, 115)—a list that reinforces the necessary "tracing out" and singularity of every cry, complaint, and so on, while clearly moving us far beyond the exclusive domain of information technology for thinking the linking of sense effects and the role of networks today. If these "seizures of speech" are thus both "idiosyncratic and common," as Nancy argues, they are also inscribed by all of the "singular decipherings" that comprise the "wandering labor of sense" today, which Nancy locates at once "within language and beyond (or just short of) language, but always responding to something inherent in language, in that language itself is the insubstantial tie" (*SM*, 180/*SW*, 115).[32]

In this sense, it is the concatenation of acts of speech—literally, this linking or binding together of the acts of speech that compose the *res gestae*—that subverts the closure of networks in which they are simultaneously articulated, further suggesting that the tie that binds these acts of speech is not completeable, "is infinitely reticulated, infinitely interrupted and retied" (*SM*, 182/*SW*, 117). The (in)finity proposed here is not for Nancy a "wandering of sense" that disperses into a "generalized drift" but a necessary dimension of what Claude Lefort terms the invention of democracy and so its permanent reinvention. The reticulated network created by the seizure of speech is also the incessant rearticulation of a dialogue. Dialogue is not understood as the communication of a message, a conversation, or a will to consensus. For dia-logue is the rhythmic interruption of the logos and its simultaneous spacing, a spacing that is at once interrupted—delimited, configured, traced out—and infinitely reticulated (with "neither interiority nor exteriority but which, in being tied, ceaselessly..."). Dialogue is also the sharing of voices, *la partage des voix*, a *partage* or sharing out that remains at once a separation and an attachment, a parting of ways (*voies*) that opens the space or spacing of the political as the place of the in-common as such. Indeed, if Nancy's name for the "anonymity of being-in-common" at stake here is *communism* (and it is one of Nancy's decisive arguments that it is as much Blanchot as Marx who gives us the terms for thinking this), then it is this spacing of the political as the place of the in-common that defines our exposure to a politics or communism to come, to a communism that refuses all forms of self-production or self-sufficiency and so exists "in coming itself" and the knotting—and network—of political ties.

Alain Badiou once suggested that Nancy was the "last communist."[33] The claim probably only makes sense if situated within a historicist schema of great communist figures. Perhaps more interestingly, though certainly less glamorously, Nancy's writings point toward an anonymity, toward those someones, those singular pluralities and plural singularities whose "being disposed" begin to communicate our "being-with." When Nancy calls this communism, it is not to the historical forms of communism to which he refers. For the communism in question has never existed. Communism is the "archaic name," Nancy argues, "for a thought which is all still to come," a phrase that deliberately echoes Blanchot's earlier claim that communism is "that which excludes (and is itself excluded from) any already consti-tuted community."[34] Or again, if communism for Nancy is an "ontological proposition, not a political option," the question remains how to parse out the grammar of such a proposition, the grammar that opens toward the "positioning and disposition of existence" or the singular plurality of being communist.[35]

If Nancy's appeal to communism is elaborated most fully in *La comparu-tion* and his writings on community, it also turns us back to the writings of Blanchot, less to those writings in which Blanchot directly engages Nancy concerning the question of community than the brief note written just after May '68 that opens *The Infinite Conversation*. Foregrounding here what he terms the "exigency of writing," Blanchot goes on to specify the conditions in which we are to think this exigency:

No longer the writing that has always (through a necessity in no way avoidable) been in the service of the speech or thought that is called idealist (that is to say, moralizing), but rather the writing that through its own slowly liberated force (the aleatory force of absence) seems to devote itself solely to itself as something that remains with-out identity and little by little brings forth possibilities that are en-tirely other: an anonymous, distracted, deferred, and dispersed way of being in relation [*d'être en rapport*] by which everything is brought into question—first of all the idea of God, of the Self, of the Subject, and then of Truth and the One, then finally the idea of the Book and the Work—so that this writing (understood in its enigmatic rigor), far from having the Book as its goal rather signals its end: a writing that could be said to be outside discourse, outside language.[36]

As Blanchot goes on to insist, the so-called end of the book has nothing to do in this sense with developments in contemporary technology, notably those "audio-visual means of communication with which so many experts are concerned": "If one ceased publishing books in favor of communication by voice, image, or machine, this would in no way change the reality of what is called the 'book': on the contrary, language, like speech, would thereby affirm all the more its predominance and its certitude of a possible truth. In other words, the Book always indicates an order that submits to *unity*, a system of notions in which are affirmed the primacy of speech over writing, of thought over language, and the promise of communication that would one day be immediate and transparent."

If writing opens toward "being in relation," as Blanchot affirms, and thus exposes us to the dislocation of everything that presupposes an identity, or if Blanchot's appeal to an absence is less a dialectical negation than the condition of any affirmation of writing and its force, then it is precisely writing that "passes through the advent of communism, recognized as the ultimate affirmation—communism being still always beyond communism." Or as Nancy has rephrased Blanchot's affirmation, writing is now considered political "in its essence," or political to the extent that, in thinking and spanning all being-in-relation, writing is the "tracing out [*frayage*] of the essenceless of relation."[37]

If writing gestures toward a being-in-relation that precludes any unity, identity, or common substance, or if writing exposes us to possibilities that are entirely other—"an anonymous, distracted, deferred, and dispersed way of being in relation by which everything is brought into question," whether God, Self, or Subject—then writing for Blanchot shares Marx's guiding premise that "the end of alienation can only begin if man agrees to go out from himself (from everything that constitutes him as interiority): out from religion, the family and the State."[38] Indeed, this "call to go out" (*l'appel au-dehors*)—this opening to an "outside that is neither another world nor what lies behind the world"—constitutes for Blanchot a gesture that must be opposed to all forms of patriotism or identification with the State, notably those forms of identification that work to "integrate" or "reconcile" everything, "be they deeds, men or classes." This "outside" remains irreducible to those forms of integration or reconciliation that Blanchot sees as working to "prevent all class struggle, to establish unity in the name of particularizing values (national particularism raised to the level of the universal) and to ward off necessary division, which is that of infinite destruction." To be sure, Blanchot also thinks this division and destruction as the constitutive and enabling condition of all construction, creation, and organization against the State, as well as against other forms of identification that efface being-in-relation. Indeed, "between the liberal-capitalist world, our world, and the present of the exigency of Communism (a present without presence)," there remains for Blanchot only the "hyphenation of a disaster," but it is precisely this *trait d'union* that creates the conditions for posing the question of a "we" or "us" in the first place, precisely this disaster that gives rise to thinking the exigency of being-in-relation and the configuration of a collectivity in terms of a communist exigency.[39] Without this originary thought of the outside and the constitutive exteriority implied by writing, there exists no being-in-relation of the in-common, no disposition of being and its reticulated spacing, no reticulated multiplicity that we call the world (as Deleuze and Guattari once noted, it is not a question here of "a world to reproduce" but of finding "an adequate outside with which to assemble in heterogeneity").[40] In short, without this thought of an outside, without thinking this assemblage in terms of its finite exposure, there is no abolishing the present order of things, and so no thought of a communism to come.

5

Seattle and the Space of Exposure

For Keir Milburn, Gaia Guiliani, and Nate Holdren

Desert in the desert (the one signaling toward the other), desert of a
messianicity without messianism and therefore without doctrine and religious
dogma, this arid and horizon-deprived expectation retains nothing of the great
messianisms of the Book except the relation to the arrivant who may come—or
never come—but of whom, by definition, I must know nothing in advance.
Nothing, except that justice, in the most enigmatic sense of the word, is at
stake. And, for the same reason, revolution, in that the event and justice are
tied to this absolute rip in the foreseeable concatenation of historical time. The
rip of eschatology in teleology, from which it must be dissociated here, which is
always difficult. It is possible to renounce a certain revolutionary imagery or all
revolutionary rhetoric, even to renounce a certain politics of revolution, so to
speak, perhaps even renounce every politics of revolution, but it is not possible
to renounce revolution without also renouncing the event and justice.

—Jacques Derrida

A demonstration is political not because it takes place in a specific locale and
bears upon a particular object but rather because its form is that of a clash
between two partitions of the sensible.

—Jacques Rancière

In a short essay commissioned for *Retreating the Political*—the volume of
translations of Lacoue-Labarthe and Nancy's writings on the relation between the political and philosophical that was the focus of the first chapter—
Nancy rethinks the presuppositions informing one of the most potent political questions, the question taken up and reposed by Lenin: "What is to be
done?" And Nancy assumes this question from the outset by asking a supplementary question that already displaces the *tense* in which the "to be done"

is posed—"how to make a world for which all is not already done (played out, finished, enshrined in a destiny), nor still entirely to do (in the future for always future tomorrows [*à venir pour des lendemains toujours à venir*])."[1]

In order to get some initial measure of Nancy's subtle but decisive displacement of Lenin's question, the appeal to Lenin recalls Althusser's commentary on the early years of Mitterand's government, also cited in the first chapter, the commentary that was written, as it were, in the wings of Lacoue-Labarthe and Nancy's Center in Paris for Philosophical Research on the Political, whose lectures and discussions Althusser had himself facilitated. Responding to a number of progressive reforms announced in the early 1980s by Mitterand and Mauroy's newly elected socialist government, Althusser had warned (citing Bergson), "One has 'to wait until the sugar dissolves'":

> Everything takes time to mature, and nothing is worse than the
> kind of premature development that opens the doors to all sorts of
> misadventures. The France of 1792 and 1871 is well aware of this, in
> its wisdom and the popular memory which knows, precisely, how to
> bide its time until the moment comes [*les temps soient enfin venus*],
> how to wait until things come to term. It waits, certain that the game
> is worth the candle, that everything can go awry, but that it must at
> least attempt this unhoped-for experiment, meditated and prepared
> long in advance; it is an experiment that can, the effort once made,
> open the way to a world of prosperity, security, equality and peace
> established on surer foundations.[2]

Written in 1982, Althusser's commentary and warning concerning the potential outcome of the government's progressive reforms was uncannily prescient, for the collapse of the socialists' progressive policies and economic measures and their turnabout embrace of neoliberalism a year later suggested that it had been more than a little precipitous to scent the pages of the left-wing newspaper *Libération* with rose petals after Mitterand's election two years earlier, especially given the newly elected voices of the *Front National* that were also beginning to emerge on the political scene as Althusser was writing his text and reflecting on his moment. In one way, Althusser's appeal to historical models and his desire to deal out historical lessons recalls his earlier argument in *For Marx* that Lenin's pamphlet "What is to be Done?" was written precisely at a time when Lenin was responding to an overdetermined conflict, "struggling against an opportunist policy that tagged along behind the 'spontaneity' of the masses."[3] Indeed, commensurate with Althusser's commitment throughout *For Marx* to rethinking the role of Marxist *theory* in revolutionary class struggle, he claims that Lenin's pamphlet attempts to define the theoretical and historical bases for Russian Communist practice and so prepares a way for a "programme of action," even if ultimately the pamphlet does not constitute a "theoretical reflection on political practice as such."[4] Given that the reference to Lenin's "What is to be Done?" mirrors Althusser's later recognition that his own essays collected in *For Marx* did not elaborate on the "fusion" of Marxist theory with the workers' movement, or the "union" of theoretical practice within political practice and "concrete forms of existence," then what Althusser shares with Lenin (or what Althusser presumes to share) is the sense that spontaneous action too easily lends itself to bourgeois ideology and its recuperation by counterrevolutionary power.[5]

If Althusser's commentary on the socialist reforms of the 1980s can be traced back to his earlier references to Lenin, as we are suggesting, it can also be read as a barely veiled critique of the events of May '68 and their aftermath, those events that Althusser had already characterized in years past as a misadventure or a premature development (that "Paris was not Pertrograd," as the saying went, and "May did not reach October"). Indeed, Althusser's lessons might have also reminded the editors of *Libé* and their rose petals that within weeks of the May barricades, de Gaulle was already back in power. Refusing any claim that revolutionary transformation will stem from spontaneous confrontation with the existing social order, as all these various references to historical models and lessons intimate, Althusser's commentary and cautionary tale on the socialists' progressive measures in the 1980s thus appears to recapitulate his own deeply ambivalent, even reactionary position on the events of '68.[6] As a number of occasional texts, public reflections, and personal correspondence suggest, Althusser was clearly caught between an affirmation of revolutionary transformation and his own compromised position in relation to the French Communist Party (it was not for nothing that his references to Lenin in *For Marx* were originally published in journals associated with the Party), a compromise, as Gregory Elliott argues, that had fairly disastrous consequences, both short- and long-term, for Althusser's credibility as a Marxist philosopher. "When the time of politics intersected with—indeed outstripped—the time of theory," Althusser's ambivalence regarding the events was punctuated by a seemingly insurmountable contradiction between his very writing, his commitment to Marxist theory, and the political situation at hand, even as Althusser did not seek a new philosophy but a new *practice* of philosophy in his engagement with the Marxist tradition. Elliott arrives at that fatal question Althusser seemed never to confront in his reflections on the events of '68: "What is the *raison d'être* of a revolutionary party armed with theory but to know when an objectively favourable situation obtains—and act accordingly?"[7]

On the one hand, Althusser's various texts and reflections on the events suggest that he was open to both the hope and possibilities of effective revolutionary transformation. Sustained by a belief that the masses "make history," Althusser was prepared to accept that the events were part of a process that would take time to unfold and play out, and the events would therefore have consequential political repercussions. At the same time, the protests had an important international dimension in their voicing of anti-imperialist struggles (Algeria, Cuba, and Vietnam) and their confrontation with bourgeois ideology on a global and not simply local scale. But that was precisely the problem. It was an ideological revolt, at best "objectively progressive" in its confrontation with both global and local power but eventually devolving into an ideological opposition to the educational system and the role of education in France, understood now as an ideological state apparatus. Althusser's studied reserve concerning the events thus turned on his claim that the student movement was nothing more in reality than a "heterogeneous social phenomenon" composed of diverse "middle strata" and dominated by "petty-bourgeois ideology" or "petty-bourgeois leftism." Its very heterogeneity and fluidity—Althusser cites the dominance of libertarian anarchism, but also Trotskyism, anarcho-syndicalism, Guevarism, and the ideology of the Chinese Cultural Revolution—suggests that the students needed to acknowledge not just the leading role but very leadership of the Workers' Movement in revolutionary struggle, for which, as Althusser takes care to note, the historical example of Lenin might offer some rectitude. At best, the events still left open the possibility, if also the problem, of the conditions and time scale in which this amorphous and heterogeneous diversity of political voices could be merged with the Worker's Movement, thus reconciling the utopian dreams of the former with the concrete demands of the latter. The contingency of the "encounter" that characterizes the events of '68 would then give way to realizing the "fusion" between an all too spontaneous uprising and sustained working-class revolt, and revolt that is less a sudden insurrection than part of a longer, premeditated process—of stages, we might say, rather than tendencies and potentialities—a process that is constrained to acknowledge its historical precedents and models as its very condition of possibility. As Elliott phrases the tension, citing Althusser, "for the requisite fusion to transpire in the future, the students would have 'to come a very long way from where they presently are, and the Workers' Movement (yes, it too) will also have to move a certain distance.'"[8] Through an awareness that the action of the masses was therefore possible, as the events of '68 at least made clear, it is this action that nevertheless remains prescribed by historical models and past references seemingly ignored by the students, actions that "one day," Althusser concludes, "could lead to something that the working class has heard spoken of—since the Paris Commune, since 1917 in Russia and 1949 in China: the *Proletarian Revolution*."[9]

Althusser's ambivalence concerning the events of '68 appears to inform, even overdetermine, his later characterization of the socialists' progressive reforms in the early 1980s, even if the two moments can also be characterized as specific and irreducible conjunctures. In both cases, historical references and models are called upon to deflect the naiveté of spontaneous and un-meditated enthusiasm, as if indefinitely deferring to the future the archeo-teleological presuppositions of revolutionary transformation. It is these same presuppositions that will eventually work to efface the contingent encounter in favor of a longer-lasting and deeper fusion of shared political interests. And yet, before assimilating the earlier analyses of the events of '68 with the later commentary, we might note that Althusser's commentary on the social-ists' reforms in the early 1980s serves to open an essay in which he rethinks the very foundation of the Western philosophical tradition by foregrounding what he terms "the underground current of the materialism of the encounter," as if all the previous writings that focus on the differences between historical and dialectical materialism were now reconfigured according to a related yet radically different trajectory, as well as a quite different set of philosophical references.[10] If Althusser's late essay may be read in terms of a displacement from the prior, even *a priori*, emphasis on a fusion between students and workers to an affirmation of the encounter, or a displacement from the ma-terialist telos of proletarian revolution to the nonteleological contingency of the chance encounter, such a displacement will have decisive consequences for any assumption that Althusser's later commentary simply recapitulates his earlier ambivalence concerning the events of '68. Or again, the displace-ment in question here suggests at the very least that it remains somewhat reductive to assume that such ambivalence might be translated into a projec-tion of Althusser's own mental fragility at the time, or into Althusser's naïve or opportunistic acceptance of a set of philosophical references that had themselves refused to take the Marxist legacy seriously and compromised its revolutionary traditions beyond redemption, or into a more general malaise characterizing the widespread disillusion in the 1980s with contemporary politics and the seemingly insurmountable and inexorable expansion of neo-liberalism, on a scale that was not just local but now global.

Turning back to Althusser's description of the socialists' reforms and his admonishing that one has to wait until the sugar dissolves, we might note that the reference to *waiting* also becomes pivotal to the larger argument. It is precisely this reference to waiting that itself reconfigures any reading of the commentary hasty to assume that Althusser's appeal to historical models and precedents, coupled with his desire to deal out historical lessons, merely reproduces a closed and all too linear narrative that is reactionary, histor-icist, or restrictedly dialectical, a narrative that then finds its resources in evolutionary, developmental, or preformationist metaphors (reinforced by the translation in English of *les temps soient enfin venus* as "the moment is ripe"), something like the revolutionary natural order of things as ordained from on high by the French Communist Party (PCF). The reference to wait-ing in the argument is divided, even dispersed, across a series of irreducible conflicts and tensions animating Althusser's argument, oscillating between biding time "until the moment comes," thus leaving that interrupted mo-ment suspended in time, and the ways things "come to term," and so resolve themselves in the future. In other words, the text is marked by a permanent and irresolvable tension between an absolute openness to the future, to what comes in its absolute imminence—*kairós*—and a future that finds its (re)assurance in the past in order to think the future in the first place, to that future that is prescribed in advance and determines from its own effaced, dialectical origins how the future will realize itself. An absolute imminence and anticipation that opens a world *as* world is set against a series of implied oppositions between hope and prediction, contingency and precedence, op-portunity and constraint, chance and maturation. In this sense, once we ac-knowledge that things could go awry, that misadventures and misfortunes could happen, either we think of the past as a set of precedents and stable models that help close off these possible diversions and aberrations, warning us in advance, or the way things go awry is a condition of thinking the future *as* future, that misadventures are constitutive of the very moment that comes. Failure here is not the truth of the situation but one of the ways of thinking how things come to take place, devoid of stable guarantees or legitimation. The emphasis on waiting is thus not constrained by any fixed distinction between spontaneity and premeditation, promise and delay, improvisation and certainty, radical contingency and the constraint of models and historical precedents, history or utopia. No more is it a complacent acceptance of apathy or political paralysis. For the waiting in question here is not prescribed by any established opposition between passivity and action, theory and practice. Waiting becomes the immeasurable measure of the moment that comes—suspended—a radical passivity that exposes itself to that very moment in its absolute potentiality or overdetermination, to this attempt at an "unhoped-for experiment." It holds open the distance that separates the time when the moment comes and that point when things come to term, or it refuses to close off that moment by translating *les temps soient enfin venus* either as a ripeness, or by some other metaphor, or as the time that *finally* comes ("*enfin!*") when things come to an end and achieve completion, perfection, and closure (as Kieslowski once demonstrated, there are several ways to film that *durée* in which a piece of sugar dissolves). It is this waiting that exposes and holds open the irreducible, irrecuperable, and unconditional disjunction between an experiment and a foundation, an invention and an absolute demand. Or rather, it is this waiting—this waiting without waiting—that makes experimentation the enabling condition of all desire to seek a surer foundation, this waiting that makes invention constitutive of all absolute demands for a world of prosperity, security, equality, and peace. In short, there remains no essential or dialectical contradiction between waiting and the question "what is to be done?"

If we recall Althusser's understanding of the terms in which to think political transformation, or if we have suggested another reading of Althusser's commentary on the socialists' reforms of the 1980s that works to displace any assumption that Althusser merely closes off and recuperates the real possibilities and potentialities of effective political transformation, it is not simply to recall Nancy Fraser's own critique that Lacoue-Labarthe and Nancy's Center in Paris in the early 1980s remained fundamentally complicitous with, or at least compromised by, the very forces of economic neoliberalism and political neoconformism, terms already acknowledged by the Center's own organizers in their letter on the Center's closure. For Althusser's commentary also throws into relief again the ways in which the temporal presuppositions informing the question "what is to be done?" open toward the supplementary question that Nancy also asks—"how to make a world for which all is not already done nor still entirely to do?" But in what ways does Althusser's commentary and its emphasis on waiting open onto these supplementary questions, to that sense of waiting that at once punctuates and simultaneously reopens the irreducible difference between the moment that comes and the point where things come to term, or between an unhoped-for experiment and the desire for a secure foundation? Or in what sense does it displace the passage that is said to lead from *interpreting* the world to *changing* the world?

Reading Nancy's supplementary question back across Althusser's commentary reconfigures any given priority of practice over theory, action over thought, or reconfigures any assumption that the question "what is to be done?" presupposes that one already knows what it is to think, or what it is right to think, and that the only issue now is how one might then proceed to act: "Behind us theory, and before us practice—the key thing is knowing what it is opportune to decide in order to embark on specific action. But this is what is presupposed most ordinarily by the question. And 'what is to be done?' means, in that case, 'how to act' in order to achieve an already given goal. 'Transforming the world' then means: realizing an already given interpretation of the world, and realizing a hope" (*RP*, 157).[11]

Nancy's supplementary question is already punctuated by a displacement in which any temporal unfolding, passage, or linear sequence is rewritten according to a more disconcerting movement in which it is precisely these temporal presuppositions that are challenged, a movement in which the past, present, and future are no longer stable or linear, temporal markers from which some measure of political calculation finds its orientation and eventual realization. It is this temporal displacement of any linear succession of temporal markers that does not merely devolve into an endlessly recursive situation but places us before "a doubly imperative response," a double imperative or exigency toward which the question "what is to be done?" also gestures:

> It is necessary to measure up to what nothing in the world can measure, no established law, no inevitable process, no prediction, no calculable horizon—absolute justice, limitless quality, perfect dignity—and it is necessary to invent and create the world itself, immediately, here and now, at every moment, without reference to yesterday or tomorrow. Which is the same as saying that it is necessary at one and the same time to affirm and denounce the world as it is—not to weigh out as best one can equal amounts of submission and revolt, and always end up halfway between reform and accommodation,

but to *make* the world into the place, never still, always perpetually reopened and stirred up [*agité*], of its own contradiction, which is what prevents us from ever knowing in advance *what* is to be done, but imposes upon us the task of never making anything that is not a world. *(RP*, 158)

As we have suggested with some frequency in preceding chapters, the world to which Nancy appeals here is not reducible to the global, in the sense of some set of nameable conditions (economic, communicational, techno-logical) that constitute the potentially integrated and enclosed totality that we subsume under the term globalization. For the world that exists here only exists in its permanent invention and creation, as if the world only exists, in its very origins, as open to its own alterity and multiplicity, to a *becoming-worldwide* that thus exposes the world, once and again, to its own incessant reinvention and re-creation. The "place" that is to be created or invented is still of *this* world, or *in* and *of* this world, rather than deferred either to the future or to some other world existing beyond and transcending this world in its becoming-world. Indeed, it is precisely in this sense that the slogan "another world is possible" finds an initial measure of its force.

Any sense that Nancy's argument is merely rhetorical in its philosophical phrasing is immediately offset by his acknowledgment that these same lines were written in January 1996, just after a series of strikes the previous month (against Juppé's proposed and eventually withdrawn reforms of social security) had dominated the political scene in France:

France's December strikes show clearly the whole difficulty, not to say aporia, that exists in "what is to be done?" once all guarantees are suspended and all models become obsolete. Resignation in the face of the brutalities of economic *Realpolitik* clashed with feverish or eager words that hardly took the risk of saying what was to be done. But between the two, something was perceptible: that it is ineluctable to invent a world, instead of being subjected to one, or dreaming of another. Invention is always without model and without warranty. But indeed that implies facing up to turmoil, anxiety, even disarray. Where certainties come apart and undo themselves [*se défont*], there too gathers the strength [*se rassemble la force*] that no certainty can match. *(RP*, 158)

Nancy's closing sentence turns us back to a number of arguments presented in earlier chapters, notably as they stem from the Center's lectures and discussions, from the necessity of rethinking the identity, destination, and sovereignty of the collectivity in the wake of Marx to Lefort's essay on totalitarianism, in which he argues that the permanent reinvention of democracy is instituted and sustained by the "dissolution of the markers [repères] of certainty."[12] In this sense, the "undoing" of certainties—the "collapse of certainties" that characterized the moment when Lacoue-Labarthe and Nancy opened the Center in Paris—is the enabling condition for thinking "what is to be done?" Less explicitly though no less decisively, Nancy's phrasing appears Heideggerian in its tone, as if the prophetic phrase "there too gathers the strength" at once echoes and simultaneously distorts the "only a God can save us" prophecy that becomes the title of Heidegger's last interview with Der Spiegel. The reference to Heidegger here is not fortuitous. For Nancy's reference to a gathering in his closing phrase appears to be a deliberate gesture toward one of the most essential motifs of Heidegger's thought, the very Versammlung or gathering that constitutes Heidegger's own most resonant appeal to the destiny of the German people, what one might term Heidegger's own (decisively anti-Marxist) "what is to be done?" But Nancy also enacts a decisive displacement of this motif by inflecting this appeal to a gathering with a more studied transformation. For what gathers here is not a people organized according to their destiny, nor a gathering of individuals, but a strength or force, and a force that finds its force, as it were, in the "ineluctable" imperative of inventing a world. Or rather, such a gathering is neither an identifiable group nor a figure, neither a form of power nor a representative entity, but something more modest and more aporetic—a subjectivity or agency without subject, or an emergence or an "act" in which "something" becomes "perceptible," even if it's constituent potentiality or historicity cannot be named or articulated in advance of its acts and the ineluctability of its emergence. The Heideggerian inflection of Nancy's conclusion also suggests that Nancy's framing of the general strike in terms of Lenin's question not only opens onto Althusser's commentary and its emphasis on waiting, as we have suggested. It cannot be dissociated from Heidegger's "Letter on Humanism." For it is this same letter that seeks to respond both to Sartre's celebrated concept of "engagement" as well as to Marx's appeal to "collectivities" by claiming, as its opening line argues, that "we are still far from thinking the essence of action decisively enough."[13]

Nancy's conclusion concerning this strength or force that gathers also returns us one last time to *Les fins de l'homme* conference at Cérisy, notably the Political Seminar, which constitutes the initial basis for the Center's subsequent lectures and discussions. During the discussion following Jacob Rogozinski's paper, "Déconstruire—La Révolution," Derrida argues why he refuses to hold a position against revolution and so why he refuses to hold any position considered "anti-Marxist," even when Marxism offers a defense of revolution that might be considered "theoretically naïve."[14] No doubt Derrida's refusal to hold a position against Marx or Marxism was made in the face of the widespread resistance to Marxism in France in the 1970s and early 1980s. This resistance was represented most vociferously by the *nouveaux philosophes* but also evident in the equally widespread claim that the questioning of humanism (for which Althusser's writings but also Derrida's own "Ends of Man" essay might be considered exemplary) was fundamentally complicitous with the barbarism of Stalin's gulags, now considered the truth of Marxism. As the transcription of the discussion at Cérisy states, Derrida's primary interest in the writings of Marx and Marxism—the "principle" defining his "taking of a position"—"was (and remains) of not weakening, either theoretically or politically, what Marxism or the proletariat might constitute as a force in France." Indeed, if we might remain skeptical about the idea of revolution, especially given the metaphysical nature of the concept, Derrida claims that this should not lead us to devalue what the idea of revolution itself might have "in certain situations," notably, he insists, as a "force of gathering [*force de rassemblement*]."

Derrida's appeal here to a gathering is perhaps curious given the multiple ways in which his writings seek to delimit and reassess the implications, at once philosophical and political, of Heidegger's own privileged motif of a gathering, to such a degree, we might argue, that Derrida's insistence on rethinking this motif led him on occasion to conflate the organization that constitutes a political party with all forms of political organization and collectivity. Or again, Derrida's reticence concerning the concept of fraternity, whatever its justice, suggests a larger ambivalence concerning any affirmation of political organization and gathering, or at least intimates that Derrida was uneasy about the distinction between a force that gathers and other ways of conceptualizing this problematic (it is in this sense that his appeal to a "New International" names a problem rather than offers a solution). It is this unease that further spans Derrida's resistance to community as a viable, critical concept, to his later affirmation, more or less unacknowledged, of Nancy's elaboration of "being-with." And it is this same unease that recalls Nancy and Lacoue-Labarthe's own insistence on rethinking forms of political organization in terms of their *self*-organization, as if the question at stake here were now how to distinguish, between Derrida's defense of Marxism at Cérisy and Nancy's retrospective appraisal of the Center's work in "What is to be Done?" a force that gathers from any form of *self*-organization, or as if what remains at stake in these references were precisely this appeal to a force that works to displace such a gathering from its ontological and founding presuppositions in the Subject.

In his preface to *Rogues*, Derrida returns to the question of *force* by situating it in light of a distinction that remains central to the book's larger argument: between sovereignty ("which is always in principle indivisible") and unconditionality.[15] Derrida continues by arguing that this distinction, distribution, or "sharing out (*partage*)" between sovereignty and the unconditional presupposes that we think at once "the unforeseeability of an event that is necessarily without horizon, the singular coming of the other, and, as a result, a *weak force*." It is this "vulnerable" force or this force "without power" whose distribution or *partage* not only severs and disarticulates the indivisibility of sovereignty; it exposes us, unconditionally, to what or who "*comes*." Derrida then articulates this weak force and this exposure to what or who comes as an "act of messianic faith—irreligious without messianism" (13/xiv).

Resonating with the question of space that has preoccupied us in previous chapters, Derrida's appeal to this weak force is also framed within a quite specific spatial problematic, notably as it relates to his previous writings on the concept of the *khôra* in Plato's *Timaeus*.[16] In this context, he argues that the proximity of this affirmation of a weak force with the *khôra* opens toward thinking "*locality* in general, spacing, interval," or again as "another *place* without age, another 'taking place' [*avoir lieu*], the irreplaceable place or placement of a 'desert in the desert,' a spacing from 'before' the world, the cosmos, or the globe" (14/xiv). It is the *khôra* that would create the conditions for this weak force to "take place," and to take place without any ground or foundation. Or again, the *khôra* would "make or give *place*; it would give rise—without ever *giving* anything—to what is called the coming of the event": "Without belonging to that to which it gives way or for which it makes place [*fait place*], without *being a part* [*faire partie*] of it, without *being of it*, and without being something else or someone other, giving nothing other, it would give rise or allow to take place" (14/xiv).[17]

Derrida warns that there is no politics, ethics, or law that can be *deduced* from this weak force and its "taking place." In this sense, "nothing can be *done* with it [*on ne peut rien en faire*]." And yet, Derrida insists, if nothing can be *done* with this weak force, should we then conclude that this thought "leaves no trace on what is to be done [*ce qu'il y a à faire*]." In other words, although he makes no explicit reference to Lenin here, it is the question "what is to be done?" that leaves its trace in what Derrida terms the politics, the ethics, or law *to come*. Or again, it is precisely Lenin's question that leaves its trace in what Derrida further terms the event *to come* or a democracy *to come*—in short, "what is to be done?" inscribes itself in Derrida's larger ambition in *Rogues* to think a "reason *to come*."

If the inscription of Lenin's question in Derrida's argument remains largely implicit, or if this inscription leaves its own trace in Derrida's argument concerning the relation between sovereignty and the unconditional, as we are claiming, the force of Lenin's question also remains decisive in thinking the "to come" in terms of what Derrida also phrases as a "call," and a call that suggests hope, even if it remains without hope and so presents itself as something like a "prayer": "Not hopeless, in despair, but foreign to the teleology, the hopefulness, and the *salut* of salvation. Not foreign to the *salut* as the greeting or salutation of the other, not foreign to the *adieu* ('come' or 'go' in peace), not foreign to justice, but nonetheless heterogeneous and rebellious, irreducible, to law, to power, and to the economy of redemption" (15/xv).[18]

Recalling the reference in *Rogues* to a "weak force" or "messianicity without religion" at the conclusion of his interview with Derrida in 2004, and acknowledging that it reads somewhat like a prayer, Lieven De Cauter asks Derrida to elaborate on its wider implications, notably in the context of the BRussels Tribunal and its inquiry into the "New Imperial Order."[19] In response to these questions, Derrida closes the interview by noting that this "weak force" refers to his earlier texts on Walter Benjamin, so that he claims no particular originality in using the term. More provocatively, he then suggests that one of the implementations or "incarnations" of this weak force or messianicity without religion may be found in the alter-globalization movement:

> Movements that are still heterogeneous, still somewhat unformed,
> full of contradictions, but that gather together [*rassemblent*] the weak
> of the earth, all those who feel themselves crushed by the economic

hegemonies, by the liberal market, by sovereignism, etc. I believe it
is these weak who will prove to be the strongest in the end and who
represent the future. Even though I am not a militant involved in
these movements, I place my bet on the weak force of these
alter-globalization movements, who will have to explain themselves, to unravel their contradictions, but who march against all the
hegemonic organizations of the world. Not just the United States,
also the International Monetary Fund, the G8, all those organized
hegemonies of the rich countries, the strong and powerful countries,
of which Europe is a part. It is these alter-globalization movements
that offer one of the best figures of what I would call messianicity
without messianism, that is to say a messianicity that does not belong
to any determined religion....What I call messianicity without messianism is a call, a promise of an independent future for what is to
come, and which comes like every messiah in the shape of peace and
justice, a promise independent of religion, that is to say universal....
My intent here is not anti-religious, it is not a matter of waging war
on the religious messianisms properly speaking, that is to say Judaic,
Christian, Islamic. But it is a matter of marking a place [*lieu*] where
these messianisms are exceeded by messianicity, that is to say by that
waiting without waiting [*cette attente sans attente*], without horizon
for the event to come, the democracy to come with all its contradictions. And I believe we must seek today, very cautiously, to give force
and form to this messianicity, without giving in to the old concepts
of politics (sovereignism, territorialized nation-state), without giving
in to the Churches or to the religious powers, theologico-political or
theocratic of all orders.

Given our reading in the previous chapter of the role of the figure in Hardt
and Negri's proposal for the multitude, no doubt we are now prepared to suggest that it is precisely Derrida's appeal to alter-globalization movements as
a *figure* or *form* that tends to efface and close off the very force and heterogeneity of the movement (or movement of movements) he seeks to address,
just as the way they are said to "represent the future" comes into tension with
this "promise of an independent future for what is to come." Or rather, as
Derrida suggests elsewhere, if we are to insist on the question of a form or
formation here, it should be thought as a "movement that engenders by giving form" or as "the figure that gathers up [*rassemble*] a mobile multiplicity,"

which Derrida rephrases as a "configuration in displacement."[20] The barely veiled biblical reference to the meek inheriting the earth in Derrida's interview response also recalls Nancy's own prophetic phrasing of the strength that gathers, which we can now read as another act of messianic faith without religion. In his last published interview, given a few months before the end of his life, Derrida argues that this later affirmation of the alter-globalization movement was already anticipated in *Specters of Marx* and his appeal to a New International and so participates in thinking beyond cosmopolitanism, beyond the notion of a world citizen, beyond a new world nation-state, beyond the logic of political parties. In this sense, the affirmation of the alter-globalization movement in light of a messianism without religion coincides for Derrida with mutations in international law and in all the organizations that establish world order (IMF, WTO, G8, UN and its Security Council). The proposal for a New International in *Specters of Marx* "anticipates all the 'alter-globalist' imperatives in which I believe and which appear more clearly today (though still insufficiently, in a chaotic and unthought way)."[21] No doubt the alter-globalist movement, even in its heterogeneity and contradictions, is a little less confused and chaotic than Derrida somewhat condescendingly suggests. Or rather, it knows with a certain lucidity how to acknowledge its contradictions and turn those contradictions into its force. Derrida's privileging of Europe in thinking this process, however nuanced, also remains open to any number of forceful critiques, notably in light of the geopolitical constitution of the alter-globalization movement. Nevertheless, what remains at stake here is the way in which the alter-globalization movement opens toward this "waiting without waiting," this waiting for the event or democracy to come.

Shortly after Derrida's death in 2004, Nancy recalls Derrida's affirmation of the alter-globalization movement in the BRussels interview earlier that year, his belief that the alter-globalization movement represented "a real political opportunity or chance."[22] Recalling Derrida's own emphasis on chance in our discussion of teletechnologies in the second chapter, Nancy suggests that, even when Derrida "was forced to admit the weaknesses or contradictions in the political discourses of alter-globalization, he would speak in terms of strategy and wanted to be able to count on a vector of hope." But Nancy immediately cautions that such hope must be dissociated from a romantic vision of the future or some utopia:

> In Derrida the to come, the *à venir*, is always strictly opposed to
> the future, to *l'avenir*, that is, to the present-future that is projected,

represented, given in advance as an aim and as a possible occurrence. The to come that he loved to speak of designates the proper nature of what is essentially and always in the coming, of what has never come or come about, come down and made itself available. If democracy is given, if it is there, made, confected [*faite*], established, then one will no longer be able to say that democracy is to be improved; but if one says that it has not been perfect [*parfaite*], then it must be understood that its essence perhaps eludes all representable, antici- patable, and realizable perfection—not because it would be a utopia but because its essence is the very tension of an exigency that is not related to a realization.[23]

If Nancy's argument recalls his own insistence in his earlier writings with Lacoue-Labarthe on thinking the *essence* of the political, he stipulates that it is not a question here of "renouncing real struggles or actual transforma- tion." "Far from it!" he adds. Rather, the refusal to think democracy as finite and perfected, *faite* and *parfaite*, is not only the precondition of thinking a democracy to come; it now becomes the enabling condition for thinking the intricate rapport between "what is to be done?" a "democracy to come," and the "force of gathering."

As we move forward and backward through the different scenes, three groups are immediately discernible within the sequence of photographs—the dem- onstrators, the police, and the governmental representatives with their aides and secretaries—even as we begin to sense that it is the relation *within and between* these three groups, the relation *as such* and not their identification or distinction, that constitutes the very "subject" of the photographs. But the question immediately arises: in what sense can a relation or rapport *within and between* individuals or groups, whether of indifference, mutual accord, or violent confrontation, become the subject of a single photograph, or the subject, in this case, of a sequence of photographs? In what sense can this question of photographic articulation, without fixed or discernible identity, constitute a relation between subjects in the process of their mutual engage- ments, their oppositional or antagonistic self-transformation, their continual becoming-other to themselves, for which the concept of social change or even revolutionary conflict begins to create at once the terms in which the problem is posed for us and the stakes of a potential outcome? More gener- ally, in what sense does photography as a medium not only index the visual

relation between subjects, revealing and remarking their identities and differences, including the space of their antagonisms, divisions, or inequalities, their subjugation or subjectification? The question also remains how photography exposes the different ways in which the relation *between* subjects is potentially a relation *with*, of ones *with* the others, of being-with-one-another, as if the material conditions informing photographic reproducibility also transform the very grammar in which we are to think the displacement from a politics of the subject to shared or collective existence, to the existence of plural singularities and singular pluralities explored in the previous chapters. Finally, what is at stake when the subject positions informing the question of political agency become displaced to the concept of *nomadism*, one of the privileged terms when considering the so-called movement of movements, specifically (in Deleuze and Guattari's terms) a "nomadism of true nomads, or of those who no longer even move or imitate anything"—"a nomadism of those who only assemble [*agencent*]"?[24] If the reference to nomadism here challenges the more common assumptions and rhetoric concerning nomadic thinking and presupposes both a critique of the rhythms of global displacement as well as a question of *mimesis*, in what sense is this assemblage and the singularly ontopolitical constitution of its *agencement* informed less by an underlying question of position, self-organization, and representation than by its disposition, exteriority, and exposure?

Turning back across the sequence of photographs, we begin to remark that the governmental representatives, accompanied by their aides or secretaries, wear dark suits. They carry black briefcases or suitcases for short hotel stays. Their presence in the sequence of photographs seems easily recognizable from these different attributes and traits. Sometimes faceless in the photographs, they pass in and out of buildings whose entrances are protected by armed police.

Standing in rows or columns, the uniformed police appear behind protective shields and face guards. They wear padded legging. Some wield sticks. Others hold guns with tear gas canisters, rubber bullets, or concussion grenades. Others again encircle or arrest protestors, or ride on the back of armored vehicles. If there are no scenes of actual violence in the sequence of photographs, the presence of the police is also evident in those photographs in which they are absent—through the effects of violence, in the traces of blood, the effects of tear gas, and the scars caused by physical confrontation in the streets. The police also appear faceless in many of the photographs, hidden by protective masks, even as they see themselves (as in one photograph) reflected in mirrors held up to them by a line of demonstrators, as if this reflection becomes the visual emblem of the frequently chanted phrase that "the world is watching," or as if the mirrors demonstrated in what they come to expose that the world at stake here is precisely a partitioning of perception and the perceptible.

The largest number of photographs in the sequence is of the demonstrators themselves, dispersed across a wide display of urban contexts. Whether taken at night or day, in sun or rain, the photographs include individual portraits as well as group scenes. In several photographs, the demonstrators are seen marching behind banners, arms embraced. In others, different gestures of political enunciation are conspicuous, including peace signs, arms raised in militant defiance, or holding ground in the face of a cohort of armed police approaching in the near distance. In some photographs, the demonstrators are seen laughing. In others, they seem bemused, wary, pensive. There is a general sense of comraderie and complicity, of wry smiles of mutual understanding and respect, of human dignity and desire, as well as moments of fear and solemnity. A woman prays as blood flows from her mouth. Other protestors are illuminated under the street lights, caught in the sulphuric yellow of drifting tear-gas. An older woman sits in a blanket holding a wet towel, her eyes stinging from tear gas or pepper spray. In several scenes, the protestors mingle, waiting, a sense of calm before the demonstration moves on, or before a storm of assault, a rhythm of waiting and expectation, of hope and anxiety, that is more clearly marked when the series of photographs unfolds not just from page to page but as a timed slide sequence. And then there are scenes of carnival, in which figures are dressed up or performing roles—a masked devil with a cardboard chainsaw, a guitar-playing troubadour—as well as the photographs of others taking photographs or filming, as if the demonstrations were also the occasion of different kinds of performance or staging. These are all scenes of spontaneous action, in which no one seems posed, or in which the photographs are not composed, even if numerous protestors acknowledge the presence of the camera (it is this acknowledgment that reinforces the sense of spontaneity across the sequence of images).

This abbreviated description begins to recreate the various scenes that compose *Waiting for Tear Gas,* a sequence of photographs taken in 1999 by Allan Sekula during the demonstrations in Seattle against the World Trade Organization (WTO), whose delegates were then meeting in the city. A selection of the original eighty-one photographs was included in *Five Days That Shook the World* (a title that clearly echoes John Reed's celebrated book on the Russian Revolution), a modest text published by Verso and coauthored by Sekula with Alexander Cockburn and Jeffrey St. Clair.[25] The sequence concludes the Verso volume, constituting a photo essay after Cockburn and St. Clair's text, in which the authors, best known as editors of the political newsletter *Counterpunch* and a series of widely circulated books on political corruption and U.S. foreign policy, offer a journal narrative of the preparations leading up to the 1999 demonstrations and a critical response to the events that now constitute "Seattle."

In his introduction to the photographs, a short text titled "[white globe to black]," Sekula outlines the conditions in which the photographs were taken and the critical ambitions shaping the overall project:

> In photographing the Seattle demonstrations my working idea was to move with the flow of protest, from dawn to 3 a.m. if need be, taking in the lulls, the waiting and the margin of events. The rule of thumb for this sort of anti-journalism: no flash, no telephoto lens, no gas mask, no auto-focus, no press pass and no pressure to grab at all costs the one defining image of dramatic violence.
>
> Later, working at the light-table, and reading the increasingly stereotypical descriptions of the new face of protest, I realized all the more that a simple descriptive physiognomy was warranted. The alliance on the streets was indeed stranger, more varied and inspired than could be conveyed by the cute alliterative play with "teamsters" and "turtles."
>
> I hoped to describe the attitudes of people waiting, unarmed, sometimes deliberately naked in the winter chill, for the gas and the rubber bullets and the concussion grenades. There were moments of civic solemnity, of urban anxiety, and of carnival.
>
> Again, something very simple is missed by descriptions of this as a movement founded in cyberspace: the human body asserts itself in the city streets against the abstraction of global capital. There was a strong feminist dimension to this testimony, and there was also a dimension grounded in the experience of work. It was the men and women who work on the docks, after all, who shut down the flow of metal boxes from Asia, relying on individual knowledge that there is always another body on the other side of the sea doing the same work, that all this global trade is more than a matter of a mouse-click.
>
> One fleeting hallucination could not be photographed. As the blast of stun grenades reverberated amidst the downtown skyscrapers, someone with a boom box thoughtfully provided a musical

accompaniment: Jimi Hendrix's mock-hysterical rendition of the American national anthem. At that moment, Hendrix returned to the streets of Seattle, slyly caricaturing the pumped-up sovereignty of the world's only superpower.[26]

Prefacing the sequence of photographs that follow, Sekula's text invites a number of preliminary observations.

First, if journalistic reportage and cyberpolitics are cast aside for their stereotyping, political opportunism, or studied detachment from the events themselves, Sekula moves along with the "flow of the protest," physically participating within the protest and at its margins, and so effacing himself as a photographer before the event to be photographed. There is thus nothing in Sekula's text that situates the photographs in light of the numerous other documentary projects, both written and photographic, for which he is widely known, or in which he might stand out.[27]

Second, Sekula provides a critical context for situating the photographs, but he offers no single meta-narrative in which they should be read, no rationale for their sequence, no individual titles or captions through which the photographs find some measure of legibility or meaning, or no meta-narrative that is not internal to the photographs as they unfold from page to page or in the slide sequence. Everything extraneous to the mere taking of the photographs is excluded, whether technical (flash, telephoto lens, autofocus) or contextual and professional (gas mask, press pass). Indeed, everything that we might expect of a photographer in terms of photographic skills and techniques (chemical manipulation in the darkroom, Photoshop on the computer) is absent from consideration, evident in the photographs themselves through the occasional absence of focus, harsh reflection of lights, compositional distortions, arbitrary cropping, and so on. If there is anything technical informing these photographs, it is nothing more or less than the technical fact of their being photographs, taken with a camera, the production of an image through the relatively simple mechanisms of photographic reproduction. This is not an appeal to a technological determinism. It is the sheer fact of the photograph as reproducible document, irreducible, as the photographer later leans over the light-table to edit the sequence, to any concern with the essential or "pregnant" moment, the one essential shot that "captures" Seattle reduced to a spectacle, "the one defining image of dramatic violence" in which the event *as* event is effaced, reduced to a reproducible cultural icon (Marines erecting the flag at Iwo Jima, Tiananmen Square, the 9/11 Twin Towers, and so on).

Third, rather than interspersed throughout Cockburn and St. Clair's text, the placement of the photographs at the end of the Verso volume also suggests a refusal that the photographs should be read as mere illustration of the text, a refusal that they simply accompany and illuminate the narrative. This refusal of illustration is reinforced by the brackets framing the title Sekula gives to his own text—"[white globe to black]"—a reference to the two photographs of globes that frame the sequence in its relative autonomy. As published in the Verso volume (the effect is different when shown as a slide sequence), the photographs are printed over the entire surface of the paper, edge to edge, as well as back to back in their sequence and so appear without any emphasis on design or page layout. This refusal of illustration is also confirmed by the lack of accompanying titles or captions that might give any one photograph individual significance or legibility. All emphasis in Sekula's text is thus placed on the ways in which these photographs are to be seen as visual records of an event, in which the photographer and his camera were once present, and in which it is as much the camera itself as the photographer who is witness to this event at the moment of its taking-place, or at the moment when it comes into visibility. The camera as witness displaces emphasis on the photograph as mere spectacle. In this sense, the photographs, whether as published in the Verso volume or presented as a slide sequence, work metonymically, not metaphorically, but a metonymy without an implied totality or possible completion (if there is no one photograph that captures the events of Seattle, there is no larger sequence of photographs that could capture the events either, even if filmed).[28] In short, the photographs are marked by a sense of their radical contingency within the flow of events that constitute "Seattle," a contingency that continually punctuates the visual narrative that is internal to the edited sequence and which is as much the fact of photography itself as the way in which the photographs unfold in both the center of the action and at its margins.

If emphasis is thus placed in Sekula's text on what the photographs reveal visually or expose to view, the photographs also appear to lack all symbolism or self-reflexivity. Even the photographs of the globes at the beginning and end of the sequence lack the visual symbolism common to globes. Both photographs of two globes on a file cabinet in a library, the first in which the oceans are white, and the second in which the oceans are now colored black, these photographs suggest less the globes of the Renaissance and post-Renaissance world of cosmic theories, scientific discoveries, and Copernican revolutions—discourses framed by humanism, travel narratives, and territorial discoveries—than the globe that recodes these references in light of a complex survey of colonialist and postcolonialist histories, of imperialist practices, and contemporary neoimperialist interventions. If this history is repeatedly associated with the role of nation-states within the history of modernity, then the globes pictured here index the globalized economies and exchanges that mark the decline of the nation-state itself as a legislative and governing institution, including the associated transformations in the concept of sovereignty (the "pumped up sovereignty of the world's only superpower"), for which the events of Seattle and the protests against world trade become the very site of global conflict—in short, the space in which these histories and transformations are now given visibility. As Iain Boal recalls, if globes were originally emblems of sovereignty, they also became playthings of merchant princes and navigators, as seen in the props in Renaissance portraiture; "it was the task of cartography to project the globe into two dimensions; without the resulting maps and charts the business of empire and planetary capitalist hegemony would be literally unthinkable."[29] In terms of the two photographs that frame the sequence in *Waiting for Tear Gas,* the colors usually associated with individual states on a globe are now transposed to an emphasis on the color of the oceans, where it is now the oceans themselves that become the site of global exchange. This emphasis on the color of the oceans would then coincide with the importance of global trade across oceans and between ports in Sekula's documentary project, *Fish Story* (which was exhibited in the Henry Art Gallery in Seattle around the time of the WTO protests), an emphasis on global trade movements already suggested in the reference to the exchange of containers between Seattle and Asian docks in Sekula's prefatory text. If Sekula registers the importance of making the globe *visible* in the sequence of photographs, if he appropriates and recodes the globe as emblem of state sovereignty and the expansion of global capitalism, then this gesture suggests less a form of symbolism or iconography that demands decoding than ways in which Seattle constitutes an event to be seen on a global scale, an event, as Sekula's photographs *demonstrate,* given over to different conditions of visibility, perception, or exposure—in short, "a clash between two partitions of the sensible."[30]

The sequence of photographs that compose *Waiting for Tear Gas* also appears to preclude gestures of photographic self-reflexivity, at least beyond the more evident scenes in which other photographers and protestors are seen photographing and filming the protests. But there is one photograph included in the sequence that appears to contradict this more general assertion. The photograph in question shows two women in a sex shop or "peep show," standing behind the glass door of the entrance. Acknowledging the presence of the photographer/viewer situated in the street outside, one of the women faces toward the street, laughing. The other woman poses within the frame of the door, her back to the viewer, dressed in stilettos and a bright red and provocatively short skirt. Her legs spread open as she leans forward against a wall, she appears to taunt the photographer/viewer, waiting to be "frisked" or "taken in." With a sign reading "Best Deal in Town" posted to the wall behind the two women, the image provokes an obvious, if perversely coy echo of the numerous scenes occurring outside in the streets of Seattle itself, in which protestors were being thrown against walls, frisked, beaten, or arrested. However, if the photograph doubles back on the photographer/viewer by situating the photographer/viewer not just in the position of the law but as the voyeur of an event, and if the eroticism of the peep show recalls the eroticism that Roland Barthes once described as the very condition of urban life—a meeting-space and gathering with the *other*, and so a privileged space for the production and reproduction of desire—then the sudden moment of self-consciousness acknowledged in the photograph is arguably less a form of photographic self-reflexivity (hardly a discovery when attempting to photograph the "living flux of acting" that constitutes a mass protest) than an echo of Kaufman, the cameraman in Vertov's *Man with Movie Camera*. For it is Kaufman who continually reframes the modernity of urban life in terms of its specific visibility, notably in those early scenes of the film in which the camera and the technologies for making the world visible, combined with various metonymies of looking itself, are reframed in terms of windows, door frames, and the face, eyes, and body of a woman.[31]

And yet, even this analogy to *Man with a Movie Camera* appears out of place, its stylized avant-gardism and radical montage too self-evident for the different scenes composing the more modest sequence of photographs in *Waiting for Tear Gas*. Indeed, the terms of Sekula's argument in his introductory text appear disarmingly simple, especially since the critical exigencies accompanying his photographs also work to efface, at best ignore, the long and complex history of photographic genres, criticism, and interpretation that shapes the discourse on photography, notably in the wake of the now extensive literature, texts, and anthologies that inform photographic discourse and theory. There remains no reference, whether semiotic, discursive,

theoretical, or historical, to theories of representation or the sign, no reference
to a discourse of the subject, no contest of meaning, no reference to the endless
debates about photography's place in relation to modernism and aesthetics,
no debate about the different genres of photography in relation to art history
and visual culture, no referral to established traditions of socialist realism or
documentary street photography, no strategies of Brechtian "distancing"—all
discussions and debates in which, for several decades, Sekula has been actively
engaged and intervened. Even as such references are presupposed here, none
of this critical background is acknowledged in Sekula's text (including Sekula's
exemplary reading of Peircian semiotics across Lukács's writings on realism in
his early writings), as if the visual effects or affects created by the photographs
were now sufficient *alone* to convey a sense of the "varied and inspired" alliance between the different demonstrators. We are left in Sekula's text with
the mere fact of the photographs themselves—their realism, their transparent
referentiality, or their evidence—terms that one might have imagined both
historically and theoretically circumscribed, critiqued, and deconstructed in
the discourse of photographic criticism over the last several decades. What
you see in Sekula's photographs is what you see—which we might begin to rephrase as the space of the real rather than realism. The terms of this argument
are established in part by Sekula himself when, turning from the increasingly
stereotypical descriptions of the protests characterizing journalistic accounts,
he claims that the "new face" of protest warrants nothing more or less than a
"simple descriptive physiognomy."

Sekula's appeal to a physiognomy that is "simple and descriptive" is
no doubt curious given his widely influential readings of physiognomy in
photographic discourse, notably in relation to police archives, disciplinary society, and forms of surveillance and governmentality as elaborated
in the writings of Foucault.[32] Commonly applied to large and usually stereotypical photographic surveys of a given population, as suggested in the work
of August Sander or Richard Avedon, or as in Lincoln Kirstein's description
of Walker Evans's book, *American Photographs*, in which "the physiognomy
of the nation is laid on your table," Sekula's affirmation of a physiognomy that
is "simple" nevertheless opens the question whether there is a physiognomy that is not a form of subjectification or governmentality.[33] Or to redeploy a distinction specific to Hardt and Negri, the question remains whether
there exists a constituent physiognomy that is irreducible to the constituted
physiognomy of sovereign power or the law. Situated in light of these in-
terpretive possibilities, and unfolding according to Sekula's affirmation of

a simple descriptive physiognomy, the sequence of photographs in *Waiting for Tear Gas* appears to constitute less an intervention into the politics of representation and the discourse of photography, less a documentary of merely historical interest—a *historia rerum gestarum*—than the *res gestae* or visual chronicles of the Seattle protests, the *res gestae* that recodes the real as the expression, lived experience, and struggles defining collective opposition to the WTO, the *res gestae* that accompanies Hendrix's "mock-hysterical" rendition of the American national anthem as it is heard across the blasts of the stun grenades.[34]

If Sekula's text appears to presuppose much of the established critical discourse on photography, it also mentions nothing of the exponential growth of interest in social movements, notably the sociological literature, readers, and anthologies, in which mass protests and the conditions for creating mass social movements are analyzed from the perspective of statistical analysis, group dynamics, case studies, social network theory, and so on. Nor is there any affirmation in Sekula's text concerning the discourse of cyberpolitics, in which the "movement of movements" now finds its rationale and *modus operandi* in the Internet (the "network of networks"), "swarm intelligence," or "smart mobs," all of which find one of their earliest manifestations in 1999 in the Seattle protests themselves. Nor again does Sekula elaborate on the range of critical responses to media coverage of mass protests beyond the question of stereotype, nor the effects of photo-journalism on perceptions of global justice movements.[35] If all this literature and critical background is both presupposed and conspicuously absent in Sekula's brief text, this absence only works to reinforce the ways in which these photographs constitute a "simple descriptive physiognomy" of the protests, one in which the "alliance" on the streets and the "new face" of protest are given visibility in ways that do not merely lend themselves to a *narrative* unfolding (from whatever political, sociological, or personal perspective), whether such narratives are framed in terms that are historical, revisionist or whether they unfold as critiques, a memoir, a diary, a blog, or something else.[36] Or the visibility of this "new face" of protest remains irreducible to a narrative unfolding that is not internal to the edited sequence of photographs themselves (page to page, slide to slide, internal color sequences, transitions between individual and group formation) and the rhythm of their unfolding (the passage from days to nights, from hope and expectation to violence and assault). In other words, there is no story to recount here, as in Cockburn and St. Clair's preceding text in the Verso volume, or as in Naomi Klein's evocative "dispatches" from the front lines of the global justice movement.[37] There is no politics of representation either, in the sense that there is no attempt to represent the protestors and derive or deduce a politics *from* that representation. There is only an exposure, in which the demonstrators are presented in terms of their appearance and visibility—their "new face"—or in which the relation *within and between* the demonstrators, police, and WTO representatives comes into view.

The photographs thus show both what happened in Seattle and what still remains present. But as this event comes into appearance and exposure in the photographs—an exposure that is subject to both repetition and displacement as the photographs pass through their reproduction in books and catalogues, slide shows, Web sites, and exhibition spaces—the temporal constitution of the "event" of Seattle is declined across different tenses. At once past, present, and future, the photographs are framed by Sekula himself in terms of an anticipation and threat (*Waiting for Tear Gas*) even as the same event becomes the basis of both the past (this is what happened in Seattle) and future (these photos will constitute a permanent memory of the event), a future anterior in which "Seattle" is subject to continual revision or reinvention and endlessly punctuated by this act of waiting.[38] The photographs thus become less historical documents, archives, or visual records illustrating the events of Seattle, part of a larger narrative in which Seattle becomes historical reference or reproducible model. Even less does Seattle become here mere myth or folklore. For the photographs are a measure in which the literature and critical response to the events of Seattle remain open to this demand for reinvention and rethinking, a revisioning now seen to be constitutive of the medium of photography itself. Or rather, the photographs are not merely an invitation toward "revisionist" histories, any more than they recreate the events of Seattle as a model to be reproduced and imitated. For the question remains how the photographs ask us to rethink the relation between this revisioning and reinvention opened by photography as a medium and the continual redefinition of the very content of political action and reflection in its incessant transformation and invention, a turn in which the global justice movement reinvents itself in ways that refuse to locate Seattle as an imitable model.[39] It is in and as photography and the spectrality of its aftereffects that *Waiting for Tear Gas* demonstrates how the global justice movement reinvents itself as it reinvents the world, as if it is precisely through the photographic that the world is reopened into "the place, never still, always perpetually reopened, of its own contradiction." In this sense, the displacement of Seattle as event to photographic image-event resists all appropriation in and as an identifiable *image* of Seattle, as if the rhythm of waiting and the lulls that Sekula sequences in the photographs become an index of this very resistance. In terms of the visibility and exposure of this "new face" of protest, Seattle as image-event resists its very legibility, including those writings, narratives, and knowledges that attempt to sum up and explain the situation, assume its representation, or take it fully into account (those forms of narrative and explanation that can be left to the police, journalists, and historians).

If three groups are immediately discernible in the sequence of photographs, the question of how each of the groups becomes legible or identifiable in relation to the two others becomes more difficult to discern. On the one hand, the police and the WTO delegates appear clearly representative—of "the law" and "world trade" respectively—even if the terms in which these figures are said to be "representative" or what constitutes or exceeds "the law" also remain open to question and contestation. Not that there existed a cohesive image within the WTO delegates when they met in Seattle, evident in the discord within the actual meetings between the "Third World" delegates and the trade policies of the United States, its allies, and the World Bank. But the relation between the WTO delegates and the police is clearly recognizable in the photographs themselves, the former physically and symbolically protecting the latter as they attempt to gather in Seattle. Of the three groups, however, it is the demonstrators who are arguably the least legible or identifiable, not so much from an uncertainty about their relation to the WTO delegates and the police—that is clearly legible in the photographs, and was no doubt audible too. Rather, the difficulty is registered in Sekula's own accompanying text and stems from the very claim that the demonstrators at Seattle constituted a "new face" of protest in the first place. The question, in other words, remains how it is precisely this "face" that remains unrecognizable in the photographs in terms of its identity and legibility, at least in the same way as the police or the delegates are recognizable and so constitute relatively stable forms of political and legal representation (even when they refuse to show their faces).

To phrase the photographs of the demonstrators in terms of a larger question of legibility, identification, and recognition is clearly problematic in that much of the literature on the protests in Seattle turns on narratives of exactly who or which group did what, where, and when in the sequence of events. Whether this information is given in the mainstream media, in the increasingly expansive secondary literature on "Seattle," or in the more informal records of demonstrators on Web sites and through indymedia channels, a sense of almost propriety pride is made in establishing the specific details of the protests and the timelines, even if these details are made from specific viewpoints or interests or, more predictably, contested for their partisanship and veracity. Phrasing the photographs of the protests in terms of legibility, identification, and recognition also displaces emphasis on documenting police violence and its increasingly widespread use in mass demonstrations.[40] Not that many of the photographs in *Waiting for Tear Gas* are devoid of legible signs and indications of police violence, nor of specific and identifiable group affiliation, including the "teamsters" and "turtles" mentioned in Sekula's text (the latter in reference to the environmental politics of fishing practices); such indications are also evident in banners, signs, and various symbols related to specific causes (chainsaws as reference to the environmental politics of logging in the Pacific Northwest, and so on). But these signs and identifications always take place in the implied association *between* the demonstrators and not simply as the signs of an individual cause, part of a shared "alliance" of contestation against the terms of world trade as the demonstrators move in a continuous process of formation and transformation across the streets of Seattle. And even if the individuals or groups in the photographs can be described as individual figures of protest and their faces recognizable, we are also still left with a number of difficulties concerning the ways in which they are identifiable, as if the usual labels (age, gender, class, nationality, race, ethnicity, sexuality, and so on), while perhaps specific to individual photographs, and while discernible when compared to the masked faces of the police, appear wholly inadequate—indeed, they lack both the direct pertinence and justice—in light of a sequence of photographs of collective protest against the WTO and its policies. In this sense, the photographs also become an enabling measure for rethinking a larger set of critical initiatives, in which the very constitution of contemporary political movements is debated and proposed, including the creation of new terms for defining this "new face" of protest itself (the new left, identity politics, equivalence building, global assemblages, the movement of movements, the multitude, and so on).

To compound the problem of legibility, the photographs of Seattle do not correspond in any immediate way to an established history or iconography of protest and demonstration. Unlike previous representations of protest, there remains no clear correspondence to a historically established set of images in which police violence is recorded. The photographs in *Waiting for Tear Gas* do not correspond easily to the quite specific histories of American labor, union organization, and class protest in terms of exclusively economic issues, however pertinent such references also remain. There is no clear correspondence to the visual documentation of civil rights protests, race riots, or violent clashes related to urban areas or neighborhoods already characterized by their class or ethnic associations. There is little here that might simply correspond to the quite specific images associated with, say, '68, or the Los Angeles riots that took place farther down the Pacific coast earlier in the 1990s, or marches for reproductive rights, and so on, even if the photographs may be said to also presuppose such references. There is no one group of people defined by their national origins or citizenship, no one section of the population or minority group that has been excluded, no special interest group with which the demonstrators are usually identified (and identified, as usually happens, only in order to be at once targeted or dismissed by the media, governmental spokespeople, or police). Or if Sekula's photographs register the effects of violence, there is no clear analogy to ways in which, say, images of Rodney King beaten by the Los Angeles Police Department could feed into a longer and more recognizable iconography, including past images of slavery, lynchings, or police assaults on civil rights protestors. There is thus nothing in the sequence of photographs from Seattle that can be identified *exclusively* in terms of labor, class, race, ethnicity, gender, or sexuality alone, and thus no claims for specific rights that are evident here either (civil rights, reproductive rights, gay rights, workers' rights, immigration rights, and so on). In this sense, the "new face" of protest remains irreducible to these established or preexisting forms of political legibility, even in their modern nomenclatures (the "movement of movements," "equivalence building," the "multitude," and so on) and even as the photographs of the protestors as well as the protestors themselves draw from long traditions of mass political conflict, traditions repeatedly effaced and ignored in the secondary literature, and especially by the media. Indeed, it could be argued that it is precisely the lack of recognition and legibility in the "new face of protest" that necessitates the very turn to stereotyping by the mainstream media.

Not that the protests at Seattle were not framed by the quite legible and explicit demand for global justice in the face of the conditions informing world trade and global capitalism, demands that could also pertain to quite local contexts. Nor, as Sekula's text also points out, does the question of global justice take place outside of the specificities of those individual men and women who work on the docks, whether on the West Coast or on the other side of the

Pacific. But even here there exist no established forms of legibility beyond the ways in which a coalition of voices and action comes into appearance in the photographs, no attempt to represent a group of people that could be recognized and identified in advance of the "varied and inspired" contingency of their alliance. There remains no given identity that is not shared out in and across the sequence of photographs, no identity that does not become radically transformed, effaced, and simultaneously reopened across the photographs as they unfold from slide to slide, as if the next slide presented the possibility that any given identity or recognizable face in the previous slide could find itself exposed to a radically different set of allegiances and associations, another configuration (or disfiguration). Or rather, there is something in-common *between* the demonstrators that refuses to be pinned down and identified, or which nowhere identifies itself prior to or beyond the radical alliance of this collectivity, as if the specificity of the photographs *as* photographs opened and exposed the possibility of asserting not the particularity or universality of the demonstrators and their existence on the streets but their singularity, their constitutive plurality, and their inherent multiplicity—in short, not an opposition between the one and the many but what we have come to term, after Nancy, a plural singularity and singular plurality.[41] Or it is as if the photographs were the *expression* of the "new face" of protest and its *exposure* and not the *representation* of different, if identifiable bodies, subsumable and locatable within a body politic or movement. In short, what the "new face" of protest attests to is not an identity or essence that exists behind the face that is then represented but the face that offers and exposes itself as the very site of the political, the very site of being-in-common.[42]

In his introductory text to *Waiting for Tear Gas,* Sekula remarks that "the human body asserts itself in the city streets against the abstraction of global capital," an assertion he associates in the protests with a strong feminist dimension. In making this assertion, the human body is marked by its refusal to accept those decisions and acts in which the body is subject to the arbitrary and abstracting measure of capitalist calculation and exchange, a refusal of the history in which the body is reduced to a codified form of labor power, the creation of surplus values, and thus the (mostly invisible and effaced) condition of profit. No doubt Sekula's assertion of the body in the face of its appropriation and exploitation remains ambiguous in the context of the history of photography's own appropriation and exploitation of the body, the commerce and visual transactions of the reproducible body that are also subject to quite specific rules of calculation, investment, and exchange (a question, of course, that Sekula's own writings have also explored at considerable length). But Sekula's argument suggests less a form of nostalgic humanism, a fetishizing and reappropriation of the uncontaminated, pure body against its capitalist exploitation, than a studied reserve about the discourse of the body in visual representation. In other words, we might argue that this reserve is set against a more pervasive discourse of the body in photography that finds its measure in avant-gardist provocations, those discourses that invariably reinscribe a form of incarnationist discourse, even when framing the body as site of resistance and conflict in the most explicitly political and not theological terms. The body to which Sekula appeals is not a transgressive body in this sense. More contentiously, Sekula's text suggests a way in which the assertion of the body in the protests in Seattle does not constitute a form of physical *sacrifice*, a concept that tends to reproduce an incarnationist or ineffable discourse of the body even as it reinforces the rationale and justification for state-sanctioned bodily mutilation and death. Or rather, what the photographs demonstrate is less the transgressive or sacrificial body than its immanent or shared resistance.

The terms in which this argument plays out find resonance in Hardt and Negri's *Empire*, specifically the point at which the authors refuse any nostalgia for an essential humanism and so affirm the "new barbarians" within Empire's imperial constitution.[43] In the demand to escape from "the local and particular constraints of their human condition," it is these barbarian figures composing the "multitude" who must continually attempt to construct a "new body" and a "new life." Hardt and Negri further suggest that the construction of the multitude's new body is not just evident in human relations in general but recognized first and foremost in "corporeal relations" and reconfigurations of gender and sexuality, specifically reconfigurations in which the distinctions between human and animal and human and machine are displaced into the "posthuman body" (218). It is this displacement into the posthuman body that is vividly evoked in the writings of Donna Harraway (cited by Hardt and Negri) and clearly evident in piercings, tattoos, punk fashion, as well as those various aesthetic "mutations" of the body recognizable from many of the demonstrators in *Waiting for Tear Gas*.

If this emphasis on the posthuman body is the mark of an "anthropological exodus" and an "ontological mutation" constitutive of the multitude's constituent power and resistance to Empire's imperial constitution, as Hardt and Negri argue, then any affirmation of this body must also acknowledge a fundamental ambiguity at the basis of this affirmation. For as Hardt and Negri also argue, it is precisely such mutations and celebrations of "hybridity" that also constitute the very methods of imperial sovereignty against which the multitude defines its exodus (including, no doubt, the "posthuman" bodies of the armored and faceless police in Seattle). Faced with this ambivalence, Hardt and Negri nevertheless argue that it is through these "anthropological mutations" of the body that the multitude finds a measure of its resistance within Empire. Indeed, it is precisely through such mutations of the body that the multitude remains "incapable of adapting to family life, to factory discipline, to the regulations of traditional sex life, and so forth" (216). In this sense, the body as expressed in the multitude is defined not just by its refusal of any discourse of normalization but by a "coherent political artifice, an *artificial becoming*," an artifice that is inspired less by the "form and order" of a new aesthetics than determined by a radical mobility and transformation in the very regimes and practices of production characterizing late twentieth century and early twenty-first century capitalism. It is then only in terms of this transformation in the conditions of production that it becomes possible to recognize that this mobility and artificiality do not merely represent the "exceptional experiences of small privileged groups" (217) but indicate instead the "common productive experience" of the multitude, part of its ability to invent and create new spaces for its existence.[44]

Sekula's introductory text is clearly characterized by its reticence toward the terms characterzing Hardt and Negri's larger argument. *Waiting for Tear Gas* as a project is itself framed by a deep suspicion that social or revolutionary transformation will stem from what Hardt and Negri term the "plastic and fluid terrain" of the new communicative, biological, and mechanical technologies, technologies that inform the post-Fordist conditions of the multitude's anthropological exodus and post-*operaismo* Marxism's privileged terrain of contestation and conflict. Containers might be shipped across the Pacific at a mouse-click, but there are still men and women moving these containers, still bodies defined by the experience of work. Whatever the division of focus and strategies such arguments suggest, including the need to take into account Hardt and Negri's repeated observation that post-Fordist production is not the *exclusive* site of the multitude's existence but marks the *hegemony* of immaterial labor, what we want to hold onto here is the appeal to the body as an "artificial becoming." For what the photographs in *Waiting for Tear Gas* attest to is an artifice—a performance of the body shaped by feminism, as Sekula acknowledges, and an exposure of the body—that does not merely represent the exceptional experiences of small privileged groups but indicates something in-common, a bodily resistance that is not so much individualized as shared out among the demonstrators. No doubt within this shared resistance there are those prepared (in every sense) to throw their bodies on the line, as well as those unprepared for the potentially (in later WTO protests, very real) lethal brutality of the police assaults. But nowhere does Sekula appeal in the photographs or his text to the ways in which the discourse of the body is subject to the "exceptional experiences" that one might associate with the more performative presentations of the (neo-)avant-garde artist (yet another Deleuze-inspired reading of Stelarc and the posthuman body, yet another privileged space in which the appeal to a pseudoemancipatory political rhetoric of "the body" is all the more circumscribed by its theological and incarnationist affirmation of sacrifice). No doubt Sekula's photographs also offer a sober response to the neo-avant-gardist rhetoric that tends to inform much of Hardt and Negri's own appeal to the multitude's posthuman body and anthropological exodus. But what both arguments share here is not the body that reacts to imperial force through sacrifice or transgression but an exposure and affirmation of the human body in the experience of life and death, a body defined by action and speech, the experience of work, and the potentialities inherent in shared resistance, a body defined not just by its biopolitical constitution but by material contiguities and tangential contacts with other bodies as the demonstrators acompany Hendrix, bodies in separation and simultaneous attachment—in short, the body that was being negotiated away in the WTO talks, the body individualized and abstracted by global capital—even as those same bodies were outside in the streets of Seattle resisting violence, arrest, stun grenades, tear gas, pepper spray, rubber bullets, arrest, incarceration, and death.

The distinction Sekula offers between the stereotypical photographs of the "mainstream" media and the photographs included in *Waiting for Tear Gas* is difficult to make outside of the contexts in which they are published or exhibited, or at least outside of the conditions in which a sequence of photographs is edited and then displayed, for it is also clear that many of Sekula's photographs could have been used by the mass media or in established journalistic contexts. Certainly the lack of explicitly violent scenes in Sekula's sequence distinguishes his meticulous editing from the impulse to encapsulate the events of Seattle in a dramatic and violent clash between the protestors and the police, and the titles, partisan rhetoric, and often inflammatory captions accompanying the publication of photographs in newspaper layout and television presentations are also absent (police as "peacekeepers" and so on). But there is nothing intrinsic to the photographs themselves that permits the distinction Sekula makes in his text. Indeed, one could argue that the photographs composing *Waiting for Tear Gas* find their critical force less in terms of their opposition to stereotypical photojournalist clichés than in light of the same types of photograph now seen endlessly on personal and indymedia Web sites created during and after antisummit protests and political conventions.[45] No doubt these sites were in part created by the cyberpolitics Sekula cautions us against in his argument, a political cyberspace that found one of its earliest opportunities in the protests in Seattle in 1999, notably in the newer technological possibilities available to circulate images and communicate narratives about the events outside of the more established institutional contexts of official journalism and the mass media. Since Seattle, these images have obviously continued to flourish and have increased exponentially in volume. But it is not the distinction between the documentary photographs of street protests and cyberpolitics that is important here either. For what all these photographs attest to is the untechnical matter-of-factness of their visual description, their banal, almost dumb facticity (in spite of the exceptional nature of the event itself), their lack of any other pretension than a recognition of the photograph as an image-event offered to be seen and reproduced. In short, what these photographs lay claim to is an event that passes into its own exposure and visibility, an event that exists in its becoming-visible, or an event in which the photographs begin to constitute less the documentary representation of the protestors than the very space of their appearance.

In these terms, the distinction Sekula makes between the sequence of photographs in *Waiting for Tear Gas* and stereotypical photojournalism can also be rethought in light of a distinction proposed by Jacques Rancière between a concept of democracy that rethinks the ontological and political conditions informing democracy in a nihilistic age and the consensus system characteristic of what he terms "postdemocracy."[46] It is this distinction that turns precisely around different ways in which to rethink questions of visibility, perception, and appearance as they inform our rethinking of contemporary democracies.

Refusing to situate democracy in terms of the usual appeals to a parliamentary system of elected officials, public institutions, or the legitimate State, Rancière proposes three theses. First, he argues, democracy is "the kind of community that is defined by the existence of a specific sphere of appearance of the people" (139/99). Appearance in this sense is not an illusion that is opposed to the real or a simulacrum that subsumes the real; "it is the introduction of a visible into the field of experience, which then modifies the regime of the visible." Recalling Nancy's insistence on distinguishing the real from realism,[47] appearance for Rancière is not opposed to reality; "it splits reality and reconfigures it as double" (139–40/99). Second,

> the people occupying this sphere of appearance is a "people" of a particular kind, one not definable in terms of ethnic properties, one that does not identify with a sociologically determinable part of a population or with the sum of the groups that go to make up this population. The people through which democracy occurs is a unity that does not consist of any social group but that superimposes the effectiveness of a part of those who have no part on the reckoning [décompte] of society's parties. Democracy is the designation of subjects that do not coincide with the parties of the state or of society, floating subjects that deregulate all representation of places and portions. (140/99–100)

It is this reference to "a part of those who have no part (le compte des incomptés)" that constitutes the basis of Rancière's argument throughout Disagreement.[48] From the aporetic origins of political philosophy, what counts here is not the sum total of a community (the identities of its members, the classes, the population, and so on) but a "supplementary part" to any count of the population, the part of those who have no part, the "supplement that disconnects the population from itself." It is this supplement that creates the enabling conditions in which to think the "sphere of appearance" of the people, or the nemeïn—the dealing out and distribution—that founds the nomos. Third, Rancière argues that this sphere or space of appearance, the place where the people appear, is the place where a "dispute" (litige) unfolds: "The political dispute is distinct from all conflicts of interest between constituted parties of the population, for it is a conflict over the very count of those parties. It is not a discussion between partners but an interlocution that undermines the very situation of interlocution. Democracy thus sets up communities of a specific kind, polemical communities that undermine the very opposition of the two logics—the police logic of the distribution of places and the political logic of the egalitarian act" (140–41/100).

Rancière concludes his proposal for rethinking democracy by remarking the intersection of three factors. The first turns on a question of mimesis (or aesthesis in Rancière's terms)—there is democracy if there is a specific sphere where the people *appear*. The second turns on a refusal to situate "the people" either as a coherent body or in terms of a sociological allocation of different parts (including the calculable intersections between different social identities), identifiable parts that, once reassembled, constitute or presuppose a social totality, notably a totality that remains determinable or accountable within a state formation. In other words, "there is democracy where there are specific political performers who are neither agents of the state apparatus nor parts of society, if there are groups that displace identities as far as parts of the state or society go" (141/100). And the third is the opening of a space of conflict, "a dispute conducted by a nonidentary subject on the stage where people emerge." In the reciprocal determination of these three factors, Rancière then argues that a quite specific sense of the political becomes possible, one in which the question of perception and appearance remains central and decisive, notably in the confrontation with what Rancière terms "policing." For Rancière reserves the term *politics* for an "extremely determined activity" that is antagonistic to policing. It is this activity or situation that opens toward a politics understood in terms of "whatever breaks with the perceptible [*sensible*] configuration whereby parties and parts or lack of them are defined by a presupposition that, by definition, has no place in that configuration—that of the part of those who have no part."

Given the argument raised in previous chapters concerning Agamben's own references to community, we could argue that it is precisely through Rancière's own appeal to community or a "people" that the ontological presuppositions of the "the supplementary part of those who have no part" are once again exposed, at least insofar as it is the concept of community or people that risks reducing or effacing the radicality alterity opened by this very supplement.[49] But what remains decisive in the context of our reading of Sekula's *Waiting for Tear Gas* is the significance of Rancière's larger argument in relation to mass demonstrations and protests. As Rancière argues,

> Police intervention in public spaces does not consist primarily in the interpellation of demonstrators, but in the breaking up of demonstrations. The police is not the law interpellating individuals (as in Althusser's "Hey, you there!") unless one confuses it with religious subjectification. It is, first of all, a reminder of the obviousness of what there is, or rather, of what there isn't: "Move along! There is nothing to see here!" The police says that there is nothing to see on the road, that there is nothing to do but move along. It asserts that

the space of circulating is nothing other than the space of circulation. Politics, in contrast, consists in transforming this space of "moving-along" into a space for the appearance of the subject: i.e., the people, the workers, the citizens. It consists in reconfiguring the space, of what there is to do there, what is to be seen or named therein. It is the established litigation of the perceptible, of the *nemeïn* that founds any communal *nomos*.[50]

It is in this context of mass demonstrations that the break or rupture with the "perceptible configuration" becomes acute. Mass demonstrations and protests are constituted precisely around a clash between "two partitions of the sensible." Exploring the potentialities inherent in such demonstrations, Rancière goes on to argue that

this break is manifest in a series of actions that reconfigure the space where parties, parts, or lack of parts have been defined. Political activity is whatever shifts a body from the place assigned to it or changes a place's destination. It makes visible what had no business being seen, and makes heard a discourse where once there was only place for noise; it makes understood as discourse what was once only heard as noise. It might be the activity of Ballanche's plebeians who make use of a faculty of speech they do not "possess." It might be the activity of those nineteenth-century workers who established a collective basis for work relations that were solely the product of an infinite number of relationships between private individuals. Or again, the activity of demonstrators and those manning the barricades that literally turned urban communication paths into "public space." Spectacular or otherwise, political activity is always a mode of expression [*manifestation*] that undoes the perceptible divisions [*partages sensibles*] of the police order by implementing a basically heterogeneous assumption, that of a part that have no part, an assumption that, at the end of the day, itself demonstrates the sheer contingency of the order, the equality of any speaking being with any other speaking being. (53/30)

Reconfiguring the Aristotelian definition of the "political animal" as characterized by its capacity for speech, it is precisely this undoing of the "perceptible divisions" defining the police order that turns us back to Sekula's distinction between the sequence of photographs that compose *Waiting for Tear Gas* and the media's representations of the events in Seattle. Echoing Rancière's refusal to reduce democracy and politics to the postdemocratic system of consensus characteristic of our nihilistic age and contemporary societies, it is the media's representations of the events of Seattle that are not merely stereotypical but now seen to participate within a larger set of consensual procedures that remain at once sociological, scientific, and juridical. It is these procedures that constitute specific regimes, mechanisms, or *dispositifs* of perception and visibility that Rancière defines by "policing" in the larger sense of the term:

> The so-called consensus system is the conjunction of a determined
> regime of *opinion* and a determined regime of *right*, both posited
> as regimes of the community's identification with itself, with noth-
> ing left over [*sans reste*]. As a regime of opinion, the principle of
> postdemocracy is to make the troubled and troubling appearance of
> the people and its always false count disappear behind procedures
> exhaustively presenting the people and its parts and bringing the
> count of those parts in line with the image of the whole. The utopia
> of postdemocracy is that of an uninterrupted count that presents the
> total of "public opinion" as identical to the body of the people. What
> in actual fact is this identification of democratic opinion with the sys-
> tem of polls and simulations? It is the absolute removal of the sphere
> of appearance of the people. In it the community is continually pre-
> sented to itself. In it the people are never again uneven, uncountable,
> or unpresentable. They are always both totally present and totally
> absent at once. They are entirely caught in the structure of the visible
> where everything is on show and where there is thus no longer any
> place for appearance. (143–44/102–3) [51]

If *Waiting for Tear Gas* finds a measure of its force in light of Rancière's larger claims, as we are arguing, it does so not only by privileging those paradigmatic points of rupture to which Rancière appeals in his references to mass demonstrations. The sequence of photographs also insists on remarking that there is indeed *something to see*. The demonstrations become a clash between two "partitions of the sensible," in which the creation of a space of appearance through the photographs resists the police demands to circulate and "move on!" At the same time, the sequence of the photographs as they unfold as a timed slide sequence, coupled with the sense of waiting and expectation that marks their own internal sequence, together open a partitioning of the visual that cannot be closed off either by the one dramatic image that encapsulates the event, nor by the sense that there is nothing to see here. In this sense, the photographs not only refuse to subordinate the demonstrations to those policing procedures that serve to structure what becomes visible (and thus invisible); through the force of their very exposure, the photographs are inscribed in and as a supplement to any community's identification with itself (including that of the so-called movement of movements). Or again, the photographs do not simply expose the part of those who have no part and give that part an identity, thus reinscribing the very system of consensus and representation the protests seek to challenge in the first place. Instead, they gesture toward the *appearance* of a people, in the sense that they expose a new face or in the sense in which this space of appearance is simultaneously transformed into the space of exposure. Or again (and here we register a shift in phrasing closer to Nancy than Rancière), the photographs expose the sense of a multiplicity or *mêlée* that excludes (and is excluded from) any already constituted community.[52] It is this *mêlée* (proposed here as action, not substance) that exists beyond—or prior to—Rancière's delimitation of the people, worker, or citizen as the excluded part of a political community, a *mêlée* whose very appearance remains open to its own alterity or exteriority and thus permanently exposed to the other, to the first comer who may or may not come and join forces.

In "Eulogy for the *Mêlée*," Nancy recalls our reading in previous chapters of Heidegger's description of the *polis* by arguing, "A city does not have to be identified by anything other than a name, which indicates a place, the place of a *mêlée*, a crossing and a stop, a knot and an exchange, a gathering [*concours*], a disjunction [*déliaison*], a circulation, a radiating [*un étoilement*]. The name of a city, like that of a country, like that of a people and a person, must always be the name of no one; it must never be the name of anyone who might be presented in person or in their own right [*en propre*]."[53]

As we move forward and backward through the sequence of photographs in *Waiting for Tear Gas*, the most usual way in which to conceive of the place of appearance is as a public sphere, or simply a public space. In the sequence of photographs themselves, the physical context in which the events of Seattle unfold is curiously present and absent. On the one hand, Seattle becomes a stage set for both the WTO and the protestors, even if the police are called in to decide who will occupy this space, both physically and symbolically. In this sense, the photographs register the different ways in which public space or the public sphere is negotiated as a conflict of power, of inclusion and exclusion. The photographs also suggest the multiple ways in which the city of Seattle is constituted as a space that is physically occupied and traversed, with all the bite in which the city is experienced as a contested space and not merely an object of studied detachment, for which the discourse of urbanism and city planning remain our most powerful emblems. It is this space that cannot be contained by or simply identified with the more official and familiar associations with Boeing, Microsoft, and Starbucks, and thus Seattle's associations with the "new economy" as it was championed in the years leading up to the 1999 protests. If the scenes take place downtown, the space also has no fixed or prior image in the photographs, at least beyond the ways in which the inhabitants who occupy the city at that moment come into appearance in that space, such that Seattle does not exist prior to the contingent alliances of those who come into appearance there. The photographs reveal no constructed, publicized, or idealized image that is suddenly broken by scenes of violence destroying the calm of the average workday, the space of commodified urban spectacle, or tourism (the favorite tropes of mass media coverage of such events). Nor is the inner city here a stage set for advertising, carefully choreographed scenarios, in which rival gangs or basketball games or kids standing at street corners become the backdrop for Nike ads, rap videos, or clothing commercials. What is at stake here is neither just the definition of a public space or the public sphere, nor the role of Seattle as the physical site of conflict over world trade, nor the creation of the "movement of movements" across sovereign borders. For what remains at stake here is the very possibility of defining the *polis* itself, notably its continued, critical pertinence as a concept within the tendencies defining contemporary globalization. As Daniel Hoffman-Schwartz has argued, what *Waiting for Tear Gas* throws into relief is whether the "occupation of space and the taking of time as forms of negativity" are still capable of "activating the *polis*."[54]

This description of the events of Seattle can be rethought in light of Rancière's references to the "place of appearance" in *Disagreement*. We should recall that this expression is a revision of Hannah Arendt's argument in *The Human Condition*, in which the "space of appearance" is a critical dimension in which to think the effaced place of "speech and action" in the constitution of our modernity.[55] As Arendt insists, action and speech constitute the "modes" in which human beings appear to one another, "where I appear to others as others appear to me, where men exist not merely like other living or inanimate things but make their appearance." It is precisely in these terms that Arendt reconfigures the distinctions and relations between work, labor, and action, arguing that these concepts now constitute a decisive index for rethinking the political as a concept, including the related affirmation of human plurality. Situated in relation to the events of Seattle, it is a pivotal dimension of her larger argument that Arendt also claims that this emphasis on action and speech will have decisive implications for the constitution of the *polis*, the very space in which to think the "sharing of acts and deeds." The *polis* to which she appeals in *The Human Condition* is not the city-state in its *physical* location, any more than Arendt mourns for the lost *polis* of the Greeks. Indeed, the space of appearance that defines the *polis* for Arendt exists *prior* to "all formal constitution of the public realm and the various forms of government," that is, prior to "the various forms in which the public realm can be organized" (199). For the *polis* is the "organization of the people as it arises out of acting and speaking together," and its "true space" for Arendt "lies between people living together for this purpose, no matter where they happen to be" (198). Action and speech thus create an absolutely contingent and precarious space *between* people, a space that cannot be reduced to an individual's occupation of a space or "ways of being" but finds its proper location "almost any time and anywhere." In this sense, the *polis* for Arendt is constituted through a permanent displacement of itself, not in the sense of a displacement in which individuals move *from* one place *to* another (the global as the space of nomadic travel and summit-hopping) but a displacement that marks an interval, a fissure, or an interruption, a scansion *in-between* that is neither simply "here" nor "there."[56] More decisively, Arendt claims that this space does not always exist, few people live in it, and no one can live in it all the time (as the events of Seattle demonstrate, and as Rancière also insists, politics is rare). Moreover, this space of appearance "does not survive the actuality of the moment which brought it into being," disappearing not only with the dispersal of those who occupy the space but with the "disappearance or arrest of the activities themselves" (199). The difficulty in which to characterize the topological and mimetic instability of the *polis* continually punctuates Arendt's argument, as when she attempts to define the *polis* by evoking the proto-Deleuzian image of the soldiers returning from the Trojan War who might have wished to "make permanent the space of action which had arisen from their deeds and sufferings" or when she has to resort to the metaphor of a séance. Rethinking what constitutes the public realm as a "common world," Arendt argues that the difficulty in accounting for "mass society" is not simply the number of people (the ways they can be counted) but the fact that "the world between them has lost its power to gather them together, to relate and to separate them," going on to suggest that "the weirdness of the situation resembles a spiritualistic séance where a number of people gathered around a table might suddenly, through some magic trick, see the table vanish from their midst, so that two persons sitting opposite each other were no longer separated but also would be entirely unrelated to each other by anything tangible" (53).

Arendt's turn to the image of a spiritualistic séance and the acknowledged weirdness of this situation suggests the real difficulty of how to think the relation-*between* as a simultaneous attachment and detachment, a gathering and separation or proximity and distance that defines for Arendt the singular space or spacing that we call the *polis*. Rancière rewrites Arendt's argument at precisely this point by proposing a related, if less spiritual, conclusion. For if politics is not the "consensual community of interests that combine," then nor is it for Rancière "the community of some kind of being-between [*inter-être*]," in the sense of an "*interesse* that would impose its originarity on it, the originarity of a being-in-common based on the *esse* (being) of the *inter* (between) or the *inter* proper to the *esse*." Rather, Rancière proposes that "the *inter* of a political *interesse* is that of an interruption or an interval. The political community is a community of interruptions, fractures, irregular and local, through which egalitarian logic comes and divides the police community from itself. It is a community of worlds in community that are intervals of subjectification: intervals constructed between identities, between spaces and places. Political being-together is a being-between: between identities, between worlds" (185–86/137).[57]

Framed in terms of a space of appearance as well as a gathering, the fundamental aporia that both Arendt and Rancière confront, the aporia that Arendt simultaneous evades and nevertheless discloses in her appeal to the image of a séance, is how to define the *polis* when it constitutes a world that, like every in-between, not only foregrounds the part of those who have no part but "relates and separates men at the same time" (52). In other words, the different topological descriptions both Arendt and Rancière turn to throughout their respective texts are inscribed by this simultaneous relation *and* separation, a proximity and distance that constitutes the permanently interrupted or suspended grammar of the "in-between"—in short, a simultaneous attachment and detachment that comes to determine Arendt's references in her text to a "gathering," as well as to the more well-known affirmation of human plurality. If Arendt's argument clearly informs Rancière's writings, or if thinking through the force of this in-between transforms the space of appearance into the space of an exposure, as we are arguing, it is perhaps significant that this aporia leads Arendt to rearticulate the *polis* not in terms of a negativity but of an uncontrollable resistance. For "while the various limitations and boundaries we find in every body politic may offer some protection against the inherent boundlessness of action," as Arendt observes, such limitations and boundaries are "altogether helpless to offset its second outstanding character: its inherent unpredictability" (191).

Derrida's argument and specification cited at the beginning of the chapter that the concept of revolution should be retained as a way of thinking the "force of gathering" *in certain situations* recalls Giorgio Agamben's "Marginal Notes" on Guy Debord's *Commentaries on the Society of the Spectacle,* an essay in which he turns to the Situationist's concept of a "constructed situation" in order to rethink its political implications and potential force.[58] Referring back to the conceptual language of an essay published in the first issue of the *Internationale Situationniste,* Agamben defines the constructed situation as a "moment in life, concretely and deliberately constructed through the collective organization of a unified milieu and through a play of events." Irreducible to either the becoming-art of life or the becoming-life of art, and so irreducible to any form of aestheticism, the constructed situation constitutes a politics that is "finally adequate to its tasks," one in which the Situationists begin to counteract capitalism, which "concretely and deliberately" organizes environments and events "in order to depotentiate life," with an equally concrete, confrontational project. Arguing that this utopia is perfectly topical because it "locates itself in the taking-place [*aver luogo*] of what it wants to overthrow,"[59] Agamben then turns to Nietzsche in order to elaborate on the seemingly aporetic nature of the argument. For it is in a "bare scenography" from Nietzsche's *The Gay Science* that Agamben is able to give us a better example of what exactly constitutes a constructed situation, as well as a sense of the topological characteristics of its "taking-place": "A constructed situation is the room with the spider and the moonlight between the branches exactly in the moment when—in answer to the demon's question: 'Do you desire this once more and innumerable more times?'—it is said: 'Yes, I do'" (65/79).

If this section from *The Gay Science* is usually considered paradigmatic for understanding Nietzsche's concept of the eternal return, what remains decisive for Agamben in this scenography or séance is the "messianic shift" or transition that "*integrally* changes the world, leaving it, at the same time, *almost* intact" (65/79), such that everything stays the same yet loses its identity. Agamben draws the terms of this argument from the writings of Walter Benjamin, specifically a parable about the Kingdom of the Messiah that Benjamin heard from Gershom Scholem. According to Ernst Bloch's transcription that Agamben recalls in *The Coming Community*, "A rabbi, a real cabalist, once said that in order to establish the reign of peace it is not necessary to destroy everything nor to begin a completely new world. It is sufficient to displace this cup or this bush or this stone just a little, and thus everything. But this small displacement is so difficult to achieve, and its measure is so difficult to find that, with regard to the world, humans are incapable of it and it is necessary that the Messiah come." Benjamin's version of the story goes like this: "The *Hassidim* tell a story about the world to come that says everything there will be just as it is here. Just as our room is now, so it will be in the world to come; where our baby sleeps now, there too it will sleep in the other world. And the clothes we wear in this world, those too we will wear there. Everything will be as it is now, just a little different" (*CC*, 36/53).

Thinking through the displacement that the story introduces in the messianic world and the difficulty of explaining it, Agamben argues that this displacement does not refer to the "real circumstances" or the "actual state of things" but to their "sense and limits." This displacement does not take place *in* things but "at their periphery" (*CC*, 37/54), at the edges or through an indetermination of limits. Turning us back to the concept of "reciprocal extraterritoriality" raised in the second chapter, and thus to the related appeals to topology that defined Agamben's rethinking of the figure of the refugee within contemporary geopolitics, his interest in rethinking this parable in terms of a topology of things is to argue that it "introduces a possibility there where everything is perfect, an 'otherwise' where everything is finished forever." In other words, he seeks a supplement to whatever is closed off in itself (perfected), a supplement to what remains bound by its finite limits. If the fundamental question thus remains—"How is it possible that things be 'otherwise' once everything is definitively finished?"—then it is precisely this supplementary and spatial displacement that constitutes at once an "irreducible aporia" and a simultaneous force or potentiality (*CC*, 37/54). In short, it is not a question of moving on to another place or creating a new space but of intensifying the very "taking-place" of the event, an intensification or constitutive excess that seeks to open the taking-place of the constructed situation to its potentiality or force.

The events of Tiananmen Square offer a forceful rearticulation of this scenography and its "taking-place," notably as the Situationist's appeal to a constructed situation now confronts a world politics characterized in Debord's terms by the "integrated spectacle," which Agamben paraphrases as the final stage in the evolution of the state-form or, more succinctly, as the "spectacular-democratic-state." Articulated as a globalizing tendency, and encompassing at once monarchies and republics, tyrannies and democracies, racist regimes and progressive regimes, this tendency throws into relief not only the resurgence of national identities but a tendency toward the constitution of a supranational police state, in which "the norms of international law are abrogated one after the other":

> All appearances notwithstanding, the spectacular-democratic world
> organization that is thus emerging actually runs the risk of being
> the worst tyranny that ever materialized in the history of human
> ity, against which resistance and dissent will be practically more and
> more difficult—and all the more so in that it is increasingly clear that
> such an organization will have the task of managing *the survival of
> humanity in an uninhabitable world.* One cannot be sure, however,
> that the spectacle's attempt to maintain control over the process it
> contributed to putting in motion in the first place will actually suc
> ceed. The state of the spectacle, after all, is still a state that bases itself
> (as Badiou has shown every state to base itself) not on social ties [*le
> game*], of which it is purportedly the expression, but rather on their
> dissolution [*scioglimento*], which it forbids. (71/86–87)

Given this conflict over what constitutes the social bond—the "unbinding" that the State prohibits—Agamben argues that the State can now recognize any claim for identity. But what the State cannot tolerate in any manner is that singularities "form a community without claiming an identity," or that human beings "co-belong without a representable condition of belonging (being Italian, working-class, catholic, terrorist, etc.)" (71/87).[60] In other words, if a being that is "radically devoid of any representable identity" becomes absolutely irrelevant to the State, then this attests for Agamben to the "hypocritical dogma" of the sacredness of life or the "vacuous declaration" of human rights in our contemporary cultures (CC, 59/86). But the conflict over the social bond also points to the one of the enabling conditions in which the State produces the means of its own dissolution: "The state of the spectacle—inasmuch as it empties and nullifies every real identity, and substitutes the *public* and *public opinion* for the *people* and the *general will*—is precisely what produces massively from within itself singularities that are no longer characterized either by any social identity or by any real condition of belonging: singularities that are truly *whatever* singularities" (71–72/87).[61]

Recalling Rancière's distinction between policing and appearance, as well as their shared debt to Badiou's argument in *Being and Event* concerning the State's relation to the tying or untying of social ties, Agamben views the society of the spectacle as a society in which social identities are dissolved. Or rather, as he concludes, the different identities that have marked the so-called tragicomedy of universal history are now exposed and gathered with a "phantasmagorical vacuity" in the global petite bourgeoisie, something like a parody of Marx's project for a classless society but the very basis on which fascism and Nazism understood themselves as the mark of modernity (which is why they continue to mark our modernity). As Agamben then argues (and it is an argument, as we noted in our introduction, proposed by Nancy in his reading of Hegel), "the coming politics" will not turn on a struggle between society and the State, as Pierre Clastres as well as the history of protest movements have repeatedly claimed, but between the State and the non-State, creating an "irresolvable disjunction" between "whatever singularities" and the State organization.

Pursuing further this definition of "whatever singularities"—where the "whatever" is the "matheme of singularity, without which it would be impossible to conceive either of being or the individuation of singularity" (*CC*, 13/17) and where singularities do not constitute a *societas* within a society of the spectacle because they "do not possess any identity or any social bond whereby to seek recognition" ("a part of those who have no part" in Rancière's terms)—Agamben turns to the events of Tiananmen Square, noting that the most striking aspect of the demonstrations was the relative absence of specific or determinate contents of the demonstrator's demands. Indeed, given this lack of visible demands, the disproportionate violence unleashed against the demonstrators seems all the more inexplicable. And yet, Agamben argues, while the West was preoccupied with relatively facile distinctions between democracy and communism, it is more probable that the Chinese authorities acted with "perfect lucidity":

> In Tiananmen the state found itself facing something that could not and did not want to be represented, but that presented itself nonetheless as a community and as a common life (and this regardless

of whether those who were in that square were actually aware of it). The threat the state is not willing to come to terms with is precisely the fact that the unrepresentable should exist and form a community without either presuppositions or conditions of belonging (just like Cantor's inconsistent multiplicity).[62] The whatever singularity—this singularity that wants to take possession of belonging itself as well as of its own being-into-language, and that thus declines any identity and any condition of belonging—is the new, nonsubjective, and socially inconsistent protagonist of the coming politics. (73/89)

As Agamben warns, closing his essay, whenever these singularities gather—or whenever they "peacefully manifest their being-in-common" and expose themselves—"there will be another Tiananmen and, sooner or later, the tanks will appear again."

The conclusion toward which Agamben draws us is characterized less by its resignation and pessimism (as if mirroring, in reverse, the historical or spiritual destiny of a people) than an acknowledgment that the tanks will always only ever constitute a belated response to the demonstrator's constituent resistance to the State and their simultaneous affirmation of a coming politics. What defines the demonstrators in this instance is not a form of political representation that responds to a prescribed theory or model of politics—it is not a politics of representation in this sense—but their very presentation and appearance, not figures who are representative or identities that belong to a given "set" (Chinese, working class, communist, even in their intersections) but those whatever singularities, as it were, who no longer even move or imitate anything, those singularities that only assemble (it is in this sense that the journalists intent on tracking down the identity of the anonymous figure who stood in front of the tanks remain fundamentally complicitous with the Chinese authorities). Or rather, it is not that such singularities no longer even move, in the sense of something that remains static, for the "taking-place" of a constructed situation is inscribed by repetition, movement, and spacing as well as by its inherent imperfection and reproducibility.[63] The "taking-place" at stake in Agamben's appeal to the Situationist's concept of a constructed situation is not something that takes place once and for all—it does not constitute a "place of its own"—but a taking-place that we are now obliged to think in terms that are at once spatial—a spacing or tracing out of a limit— and photographic ("to grasp a whateverness," Agamben argues in *The Coming Community*, "one needs a photographic lens"). Constituted from their "innermost exteriority," Agamben argues that the "communication of singu-larities in the attribute of extension" does not unite, fuse, or gather them into a common substance, identity, or essence but "scatters [*sparpaglia*] them in existence" (*CC*, 14/19), a scattering in the sense that this dispersion or dissem-ination of existence is at once random and anarchic, but only insofar as such a scattering, dissemination, or excess occurs in relation to what takes-place in, at, and *as* this spacing or tracing out of a limit.[64] Such a scattering is arguably not so much unrepresentable, as Agamben claims. For the inconsistence of the multiplicity that forms a community without either presuppositions or conditions of belonging is less unrepresentable; it is the immeasurable mea-sure of a politics that refuses any form of self-sufficiency, and it is through this very refusal that such a politics or "politics to come" remains open to its own alterity and exposure, open to what appears.[65] Drawing from a number of Kantian distinctions, the spacing or place inscribed in the taking-place of a situation creates a "bordering" that is not a *Schranke* or "limit that knows no exteriority" but a *Grenze* or threshold, a "point of contact with an external space that must remain empty" (*CC*, 45/67)—a phrase whose logic, we might argue, defines not just a constitutive exteriority but the singular framing that we call *photographic*. The outside is not another space that exists beyond a given or determinate space; it is the opening of the "passage" itself, "the ex-teriority that gives it access" (*CC*, 46/68). In short, as Agamben insists, the threshold that defines the taking-place of the event must be thought in terms of a "face" or an "exposure."

It is this very exposure that then determines the ways in which the "what-ever singularity" evoked by Agamben is not just a "whatever being" but a "coming being"—the "socially inconsistent protagonist of the coming politics." And this politics is articulated precisely in and as a coming, as a politics to come, as a politics that does not found itself on a self-presence or form of self-sufficiency but an infinity of presentation, an *e-venire* or coming into presence that is never fully present, finished, self-sufficient, or closed off but remarked by its permanent imperfection, movement, and exposure. Refusing the nihil-ism of the event that has never taken place because the event only appears as its simulacrum, this is precisely what *Waiting for Tear Gas* will have taught us: why this coming—the movement of movements—is always already taking place, opening toward the subtlest and most unpredictable of displacements in which what is exposed is not the real circumstances but the sense and limits of an event.

In a short tract written shortly after the events of May '68, Blanchot seeks to understand "the movement of those forces" that tends toward a rupture or break in time: "As soon as, through the movement of those forces tending toward a break, revolution appears [*se manifeste*] as something *possible*, with a possibility that is not abstract but historically and concretely determined, then in those moments revolution has *taken place*. The only mode in which revolution is present is that of its real possibility. At that moment, there is a stop, a suspension. In this stop, society falls apart [*de part en part se défait*]. The law collapses. Transgression is accomplished: for an instant, there is innocence; history is interrupted."[66]

Blanchot goes on to recall Benjamin's "Theses on History," to that anecdotal moment in the July revolution in which, in several places, people fired on the clock towers of Paris, as if what was achieved in this gesture was precisely a suspension or temporal interruption (an "absolute rip in the foreseeable concatenation of historical time," to recall Derrida's phrase). In other writings related to the events of '68, Blanchot notes that this was a moment in which an "*explosive communication* could affirm itself" and "affirm itself beyond the usual forms of affirmation," in the sense that this moment "gave permission to everyone, without distinction of class, age, sex or culture, to mix [*frayer*] with the first comer [*le premier venu*] as if with an already loved being, precisely because he was the unknown-familiar."[67] One might say that it is this anonymous first comer appearing here that is the part of those who have no part, in the sense that it is this first comer who is a supplement to a society that comes apart, part by part. If the events of '68 were a moment "without project, without conjuration," then the terms in which we are asked to think this event also remain without established horizon, or without projection into the foreseeable future, to that future, as it were, in which things come to term and resolve themselves:

"Without project": that was the characteristic, all at once distressing and fortunate, of an incomparable form of society that remained elusive, that was not meant to survive, to set itself up, not even via the multiple "committees" simulating a disordered-order, an imprecise specialization. Contrary to "traditional revolutions," it was not a question of simply taking power to replace it with some other power, nor of taking the Bastille or the Winter Palace, or the Elysée or the National Assembly, all objectives of no importance. It was not even a question of overthrowing an old world; what mattered was to let a possibility manifest itself, the possibility—beyond any utilitarian gain—of *being-together* [*d'être ensemble*] that gave back all the right to equality in fraternity through a *freedom of speech* that elated everyone. Everybody had something to say, and, at times, to write (on the walls); what exactly, mattered little. Saying it [*Le Dire*] was more important than what was said. Poetry was an everyday affair. "Spontaneous" communication, in the sense that it seemed to hold nothing back, was nothing else than communication communicating with its transparent, immanent self, in spite of the fights, the debates, the controversies, where calculating intelligence expressed itself less than a nearly pure effervescence (at any rate an effervescence without contempt, neither highbrow nor lowbrow). Because of that one could have the presentiment that with authority overthrown or, rather, neglected, a sort of *communism* declared itself, a communism of a kind never experienced before and which no ideology was able to recapture or claim as its own. No serious attempts at reforms, but an innocent presence (supremely uncanny because of that) which, in the eyes of the men of power and eluding their analysis, could only be put down with typical sociological phrases such a *chienlit* [ragtag, mess, etc. from *chie-en-lit*, shits-in-the-bed—de Gaulle's phrase for the demonstrators], that is to say the carnavalesque redoubling of their own disarray, the disarray of a command that no longer commanded anything, not even itself, contemplating, without seeing it, its own inexplicable ruin.

An innocent presence, a "common presence" (René Char), ignoring its limits, political because of its refusal to exclude anything and its awareness that it was, as such, the immediate-universal, with the impossible as its only challenge, but without determined political wills and therefore at the mercy of any sudden push by the formal institutions against which it refused to react. It is that absence of reaction (Nietzsche could be said to be its inspiration) that permitted the adverse manifestation to develop and that it would have been easy to prevent or to fight. Everything was accepted. The impossibility of recognizing an enemy, of taking into account a particular form of adversity, all that was vivifying while hastening the resolution [*dénouement*], though there was nothing to be resolved [*dénouer*], given that the event had taken place. The event? And had it taken place?[68]

In one sense, the pages leading up to this passage have been an attempt to create the conditions in which we might begin to read, and so reread, Blanchot's rethinking of the events of '68—so that in repeating Blanchot's commentary, we find some measure of its displacement. Such a claim is meant to evoke no nostalgia, nor a privileging of '68 over other moments of extreme conflict, nor a model to emulate or imitate. As Blanchot insists, we have no way of fully knowing what takes place in the taking-place of the event, at least insofar as any recollection of the event and its unforeseeable potentiality must of necessity hold open thinking the event as event, and so hold open its endless rewriting, its way of surviving—beyond pathos, beyond mourning. No doubt the reference to Bakhtin offers a sober warning to those on the "left" who find their sole political investments in carnavalesque antagonism to established power and authority, at least insofar as such carnavelesque gestures for Blanchot do not suggest an alternative to those forms of power they end up reinscribing but only ever reveal and demonstrate power's own carnavalesque disarray and ruin. If Blanchot also evokes Schmitt in order more deeply to refuse a politics premised on the friend–enemy distinction, the possibility left open here is of a potentiality defined in terms of a withdrawal, a refusal to take power, a neglect of authority, a radical passivity that finds its force prior to any distinction between active and passive, an exodus toward a fraternity or communism that has never existed—in short, a "common presence" that has no identity or no presence because it only exists in its being shared out, *partagé*, exposed.

In situating itself in and as the taking-place of what it wants to overthrow, in and as a snapshot of the real, the photographs in *Waiting for Tear Gas* offer us a related gesture to Benjamin's anecdotal moment in which people fired on the clock towers of Paris, or to Blanchot's recollection of May '68 that "whatever the detractors of May might say, it was a splendid moment, when anyone could speak to anyone else, anonymously, impersonally, welcomed with no other justification than that of being another person."[69] In doing so, the photographs begin to offer some justice to the movement of movements in its suspension of history—its opening to a politics, democracy, or communism to come—some justice not to its identity or its future but its inherent unpredictability, the ways in which the movement of movements moves on, waits, scatters, and so takes place, even if its constituent potentiality or historicity—the force of its gathering—cannot be named or articulated in advance of its acts and the ineluctable force of its emergence.

Notes

Introduction

1. See Rodolphe Gasché, *Minimal Things: Studies on the Notion of Relation* (Stanford, Calif.: Stanford University Press, 1999), 1–13.

2. The phrasing does not disqualify the continued relevance of Fred Dallmayr's critical reelaboration of the relation between *polis* and *praxis* in *Polis and Praxis: Exercises in Contemporary Political Theory* (Cambridge, Mass.: MIT Press, 1984).

3. Jacques Rancière, *La Mésentente: Politique et philosophie* (Paris: Galilée, 1995), trans. Julie Rose as *Disagreement: Politics and Philosophy* (Minneapolis: University of Minnesota Press, 1999).

4. Michel Foucault, *La volonté de savoir: Histoire de la sexualité, Vol. 1* (Paris: Gallimard, 1976), 188, trans. Robert Hurley as *The History of Sexuality, Volume 1: An Introduction* (New York: Vintage, 1990), 143.

5. Giorgio Agamben, *Homo sacer: Il potere sovrano e la nuda vita* (Turin: Giulio Einaudi, 1995), trans. Daniel Heller-Roazen as *Homo Sacer: Sovereign Power and Bare Life* (Stanford, Calif.: Stanford University Press, 1998).

6. See Alain Badiou, *L'être et l'événement* (Paris: Seuil, 1988), trans. Oliver Feltham as *Being and Event* (London: Continuum, 2005).

7. See Jacques Derrida, *Politiques de l'amitié* (Paris: Galilée, 1994), trans. George Collins as *Politics of Friendship* (London: Verso, 1997).

8. See Manual DeLanda, *A New Philosophy of Society: Assemblage Theory and Social Complexity* (London: Continuum, 2006); John Protevi, *Political Physics: Deleuze, Derrida and the Body Politic* (London: Athlone, 2001).

9. Judith Butler, *Antigone's Claim: Kinship between Life and Death* (New York: Columbia University Press, 2000), 24.

10. Jean-Luc Nancy, "La comparution," in *La comparution: Politiques à venir*, ed. Jean-Christophe Bailly and Jean-Luc Nancy, (Paris: Christian Bourgeois, 1991), 98, trans. Tracy B. Strong as "La Comparution/The Compearance: From the Existence of 'Communism' to the Community of 'Existence,'" *Political Theory* 20, no. 3 (August 1992): 392 (translation modified). Nancy's text was written in 1990 in part as a response to the facile declarations characteristic of the time concerning the "end of communism."

11. Jean-Luc Nancy, "La comparution," 98/"La Comparution/The Compearance," 392. In *Being Singular Plural*, Nancy writes, "There are two different measures of the incommensurable to be found within the very depths of our tradition, two measures that are superimposed, intertwined, and contrasted: one according to the Other and the other according to the with. Because the intimate and the proximate, the same and the other, refer to one another, they designate a 'not being with' and, in this way, a 'not being in society.' They designate an Other of the social where the social itself—*the* common as *Being* or as a common *subject*—would be in itself, by itself, and for itself: it would be the very sameness of the other and sameness as Other. In contrast, being-with designates the other that never comes back to the same, the plurality of origins. The just measure of the with or, more exactly, the *with* or being-with as just measure, as justness and justice, is the measure of the dis-position [of Being] as such." See Jean-Luc Nancy, *Être singulier pluriel* (Paris: Galilée, 1996), 105, trans. Robert D. Richardson and Anne E. O'Bryne as *Being Singular Plural* (Stanford, Calif.: Stanford University Press, 2000), 81.

12. Jean-Luc Nancy, "La comparution," 98/ "La Comparution/The Compearance," 392.

13. Here we should acknowledge the proximity of Nancy's rethinking of the political *arche* in terms of an essential an-archy to the writings of Emmanuel Lévinas as well as Reiner Schürmann. More recently, Simon Critchley has reworked this reference to Lévinas in his chapter on "Anarchic Metapolitics" in *Infinitely Demanding: Ethics of Commitment, Politics of Resistance* (London: Verso, 2007), 88–132.

14. See Jean-Luc Nancy, "La juridiction du monarque hégélian" in *Rejouer le politique*, ed. Luc Ferry, Jean-Luc Nancy, et al., (Paris: Galilée, 1981), 90; trans. Mary Ann and Peter Caws as "The Jurisdiction of the Hegelian Monarch" in *The Birth to Presence* (Stanford, Calif.: Stanford University Press, 1993), 142, an argument concerning the State that has been taken up in the writings of Alain Badiou, and then rearticulated through Badiou by both Agamben and Rancière. Given the ways in which Nancy's reading of Hegel, both here and elsewhere, opens up another point of departure in rethinking the question of the political, we might note that Nancy also refers in this essay to the proximity and distance between Hegel and Aristotle, notably in terms of rethinking "the individuation of the *zoon politikon*." As Nancy notes, what remains at stake here is "less a political problematic than the problematic of the existence of the political as such."

15. Christopher Fynsk also points to the necessity of understanding "the essence of the human as entailing a structure of exposure *where a relation to alterity is immanent*," and it is precisely this exposure that opens toward "the anarchic grounds of the ethicopolitical relation and materiality of existence." The difficulty nevertheless remains in what sense "the question of relationality" in play here "*exceeds the political*," as Fynsk argues. See Christopher Fynsk, *The Claim of Language: A Case for the Humanities* (Minneapolis: University of Minnesota Press, 2004), 68–69, 99 (my italics).

16. As Rancière argues, "at a time when the political was contested in the name of the social, of social movements and social science, it was still manifest in the multiplicity of modalities and spaces, from the street to the factory to the university. The resurrection of the political is today revealed in the discretion of such modalities or the absence of such places." See Rancière, *La Mésentente*, 10; *Disagreement*, viii.

17. Carl Schmitt, *Politische Theologie: Vier Kapitel zur Lehre von der Souveränitat* (1922; Berlin: Duncker & Humblot, 1934), 59–60, trans. George Schwab as *Political Theology: Four Chapters on the Concept of Sovereignty* (Chicago: University of Chicago Press, 1985), 46 (translation modified). Schwab refers in his translation to "what the world immediately understands to be appropriate as a form of its political organization," while the French translation taken up by Nancy (by Jean-Louis Schlegel) reads, "ce qui lui paraît l'évidence même en matière d'organisation politique."

18. Jean-Luc Nancy, *Le sens du monde* (Paris: Galilée, 1993), 145, trans. Jeffrey S. Librett as *The Sense of the World* (Minneapolis: University of Minnesota Press, 1997), 92.

1. The Deposition of the Political

1. Philippe Lacoue-Labarthe and Jean-Luc Nancy, "Avertissement," in *Le retrait du politique*, ed. Philippe Lacoue-Labarthe and Jean-Luc Nancy (Paris: Galilée, 1983), 9 (hereafter cited as *RT*), trans. Simon Sparks in *Retreating the Political* (London: Routledge, 1997), 180n1 (hereafter cited as *RP*). The Center was opened in November 1980 at the École Normale Supérieure on the rue d'Ulm. In addition to Lacoue-Labarthe and Nancy's opening "Avertissement" and concluding essay, "Le 'retrait' du politique" (also translated with an "Annexe" and transcriptions of the discussions in *RP*, 122–42), *Le retrait du politique* includes essays by Jacob Rogozinski, Claude Lefort, Jacques Rancière, Denis Kambouchner, and Philippe Soulez. An earlier volume of essays from the Center's lectures was published as *Rejouer le politique*, ed. Philippe Lacoue-Labarthe and Jean-Luc Nancy. (Paris: Galilée, 1981) (hereafter cited as *RJ*), which includes Lacoue-Labarthe and Nancy's "Avertissement" and "Ouverture" (both translated in *RP*, 105–21) and individual essays by the two authors, in addition to further essays by Luc Ferry, Jean-François Lyotard, and Étienne Balibar. A projected third volume of essays was never published. *Retreating the Political* also translates two essays by Lacoue-Labarthe and Nancy commissioned for the volume, as well as a previously unpublished letter, "Chers Amis," on the closing of the Center in late 1984 (*RP*, 143–47). Given the precision of Lacoue-Labarthe and Nancy's language and the difficulty of rendering certain concepts into English, I have occasionally modified existing translations.

2. Nancy's frequent use of words derived from the French verb *frayer* not only suggest a clearing, marking out, or tracing but might also be read here as drawing from the more figurative connotations of the verb including "having relations with."

3. Since the term *retrait* punctuates the pages that follow with some frequency and is translated in various ways according to its context, it is important to acknowledge in what ways Lacoue-Labarthe and Nancy rethink this *retrait* in light of Derrida's various writings on Heidegger, notably Derrida's early essay from 1978, "Le retrait de la métaphor," in *Psyché: Inventions de l'autre* (Paris: Galilée, 1987), 63–93, trans. Peggy Kamuf as "The *Retrait* of Metaphor," in *Pysche: Inventions of the Other*, vol. 1 (Stanford, Calif.: Stanford University Press, 2007), 48–80. In a coauthored text on the relation between the political and psychoanalysis published the same year in which the Center opened, Lacoue-Labarthe and Nancy propose a further definition: "A *retrait* or withdrawal does not mean an absence, a presence simply taken away. No prior identity can here be taken away. To withdraw or draw back [*se retirer*] is not to disappear; it *is* not, strictly speaking, any mode of being. Let us say, without entering in other analyses, that the *retrait* is the act of appearing disappearing. Not only to appear *while* disappearing, but to appear *as* disappearance, in disappearance itself. The larger idea at stake here, as is well known, is that of an inscription, which traces itself only in drawing back [*retirant*] (into the unfigurable density of matter) the very incision which inscribes it. The incision—or the excision—of the surface of an Ego withdraws into an unfigurable matter—which, however, will have to be called the social matter. There is no prior inscription (thus an inscription is never *a priori*). There is no prior pact, neither symbolic nor social—for there is no subject and no Other to conclude such a pact. Rather, it is a question of a primordial withdrawal, which, however, does not precede anything, because the *retrait* or withdrawal *is* nothing, does not appear, is not figured." See Philippe Lacoue-Labarthe and Jean-Luc Nancy, "Le peuple juif ne rêve pas," in *La psychanalyse, est-elle une histoire juive?* (Paris: Seuil, 1981), 66, trans. Brian Holmes as "The Unconscious Is Destructured like an Affect (Part 1 of 'The Jewish People Do Not Dream')," *Stanford Literature Review* 6, no. 2 (Fall 1989): 201 (translation slightly modified). Lacoue-Labarthe and Nancy's definition of the *retrait* extends beyond its more immediate implications for psychoanalysis and comes closest to presenting the *deconstruction* of the idealist–materialist divide also at stake in their references to the *retrait* of the political. The best introductions to Derrida's rethinking of Heidegger in this context remain Rodolphe Gasché's "On the Nonadequate Trait" and "Joining the Text," in *Of Minimal Things: Studies on the Notion of Relation* (Stanford, Calif.: Stanford University Press, 1999), 195–241, and the section on Heidegger in Christopher Fynsk, *Language and Relation:...that there is language* (Stanford, Calif.: Stanford University Press, 1996), 17–131.

4. In *La Communauté affrontée* (Paris: Galilée, 2001), 31, Nancy recalls that space for the Center's lectures at the École Normale Supérieure was made available by both Derrida and Althusser, even though he was unable to participate (Althusser had strangled his wife the same month in which the Center was opened and had been placed in psychiatric care). While Althusser does not figure largely in the

Center's discussions or Lacoue-Labarthe and Nancy's writings in general, we recall that Nancy had published an early review of Althusser's *For Marx* and *Reading Capital* in "Marx et la philosophie," *Esprit* 34 (May 1966): 1074–87.

5. My thanks to Leslie Hill for making available a copy of the original letter in French.

6. Louis Althusser, "Le courant souterrain du matérialisme de la rencontre," in *Écrits philosophiques et politiques*, vol. 1 (Paris: Stock IMEC, 1994), 549, trans. G. M. Goshgarian as "The Underground Current of the Materialism of the Encounter," in *Philosophy of the Encounter: Later Writings, 1978–87* (London: Verso, 2006), 165.

7. In her review of the Center's work, Nancy Fraser concludes her argument by claiming that the "neo-liberal position represents one—if not the—legitimate working out of at least some of Nancy and Lacoue-Labarthe's own views" and that the "demise of the Center recapitulates its constitutive dilemma." See Nancy Fraser, "The French Derrideans: Politicizing Deconstruction or Deconstructing the Political?" *New German Critique* 33 (Autumn 1984): 127–54. For a critical response to Fraser's essay and her misreading of Lacoue-Labarthe and Nancy's proposals for the Center, see Bill Readings, "The Deconstruction of Politics," in *Reading de Man Reading*, ed. Lindsay Waters and Wlad Godzich (Minneapolis: University of Minnesota Press, 1989), 242–43.

8. Fraser is not alone in this regard. One of the arguments that unfolds in the pages that follow is that the reception of the Center and Lacoue-Labarthe and Nancy's texts in particular has invariably marginalized, and indeed mostly effaced, the question of *relation*, the very question that Lacoue-Labarthe and Nancy repeatedly foreground in their presentations of the Center's work. This is not to say that the argument has not benefited greatly from the various texts devoted to the Center's work and reception, including Simon Sparks, "Editor's Preface" and "Editor's Introduction: Politica Ficta," in *RP*, ix–xxviii; Simon Critchley, "Lacoue-Labarthe and Nancy: Retracing the Political," in *The Ethics of Deconstruction: Derrida and Lévinas* (Oxford: Blackwell, 1992), 200–219; Simon Critchley, "Re-tracing the Political: Politics and Community in the Work of Philippe Lacoue-Labarthe and Jean-Luc Nancy," in *The Political Subject of Violence*, ed. David Campbell and Michael Dillon (Manchester: Manchester University Press, 1993), 73–93; David Ingram, "The Retreat of the Political in the Modern Age: Jean-Luc Nancy on Totalitarianism and Community," *Research in Phenomenology* 18 (1988): 93–124; Ian James, *The Fragmentary Demand: An Introduction to the Philosophy of Jean-Luc Nancy* (Stanford, Calif.: Stanford University Press, 2006), 155–73; and Oliver Marchart, "Retracing the Political Difference," in *Post-Foundational Political Thought: Political Difference in Nancy, Lefort, Badiou and Laclau* (Edinburgh: Edinburgh University Press, 2007), 61–84. One might note that the French reception of the Center's work is defined less by essays *on* the Center than inscribed, for the most part without reference or acknowledgment, in later texts

published by the Center's participants (including Balibar and Rancière, to whom we will return), or in more recent arguments concerning the political (I'm thinking here in particular of the writings of Alain Badiou).

9. Jacques Derrida, *L'écriture et différence* (Paris: Seuil, 1967), 367, trans. Alan Bass as *Writing and Difference* (Chicago: University of Chicago Press, 1978), 250.

10. Jacques Derrida, *L'écriture et différence*, 367; *Writing and Difference*, 250. In fact, as Derrida notes, it is "the movement of the world as play" that is inaugurated here, a phrasing that will get taken up more extensively by Nancy in his more recent writings.

11. See Jacques Derrida, "Les fins de l'homme," in *Marges—de la philosophie* (Paris: Minuit, 1972), 131, trans. Alan Bass as "The Ends of Man," in *Margins of Philosophy* (Chicago: University of Chicago Press, 1982), 111.

12. The full proceedings of the colloquium are published in *Les fins de l'homme: À partir du travail de Jacques Derrida*, ed. Philippe Lacoue-Labarthe and Jean-Luc Nancy (Paris: Galilée, 1981) (hereafter cited as *FH*). Organized by Lacoue-Labarthe and Nancy just prior to the opening of the Center later that same year, the colloquium outlines many of the problematics pursued in the Center's lectures and discussions, notably as they were presented in Christopher Fynsk and Philippe Lacoue-Labarthe's "Séminare 'politique'" and the ensuing discussion (*FH* 487–500, trans. Simon Sparks as "'Political' Seminar," in *RP*, 87–104). Gasché's essay "On the Nonadequate Trait" (see note 3 above) was first presented at the same colloquium.

13. Lacoue-Labarthe and Nancy implicitly refer here to the section on "total domination" in Arendt's *The Origins of Totalitarianism*, the section that opens by defining total domination as that which "strives to organize the infinite plurality and differentiation of human beings as if all humanity were just one individual." In other words, the effacement of human plurality, differentiation, and alterity in the name of "humanity" is the simultaneous effacement of *relation* at stake in Lacoue-Labarthe and Nancy's reading of Arendt. See Hannah Arendt, *The Origins of Totalitarianism* (New York: Schocken, 2004), 565. Acknowledging the central role of Arendt's writings on totalitarianism for retreating the political, Lacoue-Labarthe and Nancy note, "Work on totalitarianism has obviously come a long way since then, but Arendt's analyses remain the first major study of the phenomenon. Doubtless there has, until now, been no thematic use of this author in the Center; the implicit reference has, however, been constant, and if, today, we are once more adopting certain motifs from her descriptions, this is no way signifies a pure and simple support on our part to the whole of her thinking" (*RT*, 187–88/*RP*, 181).

14. See Jean-François Lyotard, *La Condition postmoderne: Rapport sur le savoir* (Paris: Minuit, 1979), 102–3, trans. Geoff Bennington and Brian Massumi as *The Postmodern Condition: A Report on Knowledge* (Minneapolis: University of Minnesota Press, 1984), 63–64.

15. The reference to phraseology also turns back to Lyotard's demand to rethink the political beyond accepted "ideological phraseology," an argument that was proposed in his own lecture at the Cérisy colloquium, "Discussions, or phraser 'après Auschwitz'" (*FH*, 283–315), as well as at the Center, "Introduction à une étude du politique selon Kant" (*RJ*, 91–134). See also Lyotard's *The Differend: Phrases in Dispute*, trans. Georges Van Den Abbeele (Minneapolis: University of Minnesota Press, 1988). Lyotard's discussion of the Center itself in terms of phrases and performatives is discussed by Lacoue-Labarthe and Nancy in *RT*, 195–96/*RP*, 132.

16. See Lefort's own presentation to the Center, "La question de la démocratie" (*RT*, 71–88, notably the passage on page 85), to which Lacoue-Labarthe and Nancy are in part responding. In "Lacoue-Labarthe and Nancy: Re-tracing the Political" (see note 8 above), Critchley returns to Lefort's text in order to rethink Lacoue-Labarthe and Nancy's own writings for the Center.

17. The argument follows closely from Lacoue-Labarthe's earlier essay, "*La transcendance finie/t dans la politique*" (included in *RJ*, 171–214), trans. Peter Caws as "Transcendence Ends in Politics" in Philippe Lacoue-Labarthe, *Typography: Mimesis, Philosophy, Politics*, ed. Christopher Fynsk (Cambridge, Mass: Harvard University Press, 1989), 267–300. The question of alterity is raised quite specifically in the discussion following Lefort's paper, notably in terms of a distinction drawn by Derrida in which the proximity between totalitarianism and democracy comes into further relief. For if totalitarianism is said to be the "without-other," as Derrida points out (or without "remainder" or "sharing out" in Lacoue-Labarthe and Nancy's terms), then this argument rests upon an "exterior viewpoint." "*Within* the totalitarian operation [*fonctionnement*] itself," Derrida continues, "there is a place-holder of the other [*tenant-lieu de l'autre*]" (as in a "classless society" or the "cult of personality"). "Is this so different from democracies?" Derrida asks Lefort. Or rather, "what is thus the suspension of alterity in totalitarianism? Is it a real or phantasmagoric suspension?" (*RT*, 87).

18. Lacoue-Labarthe and Nancy's references to transcendence in their texts for the Center are difficult to circumscribe on a number of levels, and not only because the commentary is rarely developed in any sustained way. Nevertheless, a few preliminary and parenthetical remarks can be made.

First, beyond rethinking the central place of *Dasein*'s finite transcendence in Heidegger, and notably the ways in which Heidegger's writings open toward an alterity that is repeatedly closed off, the terms of Lacoue-Labarthe and Nancy's argument in their writings for the Center are drawn in significant measure from the writings of Emmanuel Lévinas, even if his name rarely appears in the lectures and discussions. No doubt Lévinas will only title a series of published interviews *Alterity and Transcendence* some years after Center's closure, but the terms of the argument are well established by the early 1960s in *Totality and Infinity*. It is this text in which Lacoue-Labarthe and Nancy (and Derrida as well) appear to find their most resonant resource in rethinking the relation between transcendence and alterity, at least insofar as the question of *relation* and *exteriority* opened up in *Totality and Infinity* is simultaneously thought out of an originary separation (of the "relation without relation" in Lévinas's terms). Equally pertinent to the ways in which Lacoue-Labarthe and Nancy rethink the question of relation informing the larger argument of *Totality and Infinity*, Lévinas's text can be read here as rearticulating the specific relation between transcendence, alterity, and immanence in light of the section from *The Basic Problems of Phenomenology* in which Heidegger proposes to think *Dasein*'s transcendence as that which "oversteps" a limit (a reading that Nancy will also explore some years later in *The Experience of Freedom*). Thus, if Lacoue-Labarthe and Nancy's writings for the Center gesture, if only implicitly, toward a rereading of *Totality and Infinity*, it is a reading that takes into account not only Lévinas's own reading of Heidegger but also the ways in which the question of *limits* becomes decisive for rearticulating the relation between transcendence, immanence, and alterity in the first place. Or again, it is in light of rethinking this same limit that Lacoue-Labarthe and Nancy work to rethink the problematic distinction between religion and the political in Lévinas's writings.

Part of the further difficulty in circumscribing Lacoue-Labarthe and Nancy's reading of Lévinas and his influence on the writings for the Center is the way in which the question of ethics that is so central to Lévinas's writings (ethics as "first philosophy") becomes transformed, or addressed in a manner that is considerably more oblique, even reticent, than suggested in the reception of Lévinas's own work. This reticence was already apparent in the discussion following Lacoue-Labarthe's paper at Cérisy (see *FH*, 440–42/*RP*, 81–83), although Nancy had already devoted a longer discussion to the "ethical pre-inscription of relation" in a reading of Kant (later included in *L'impératif catégorique*). However oblique or reticent Lacoue-Labarthe and Nancy's references to ethics remain in their various texts for the Center, the importance of Lévinas's writings for their larger argument, notably concerning the relation between transcendence and alterity, nevertheless suggests a potentially different reading of their texts than proposed by Simon Critchley in his reviews of the Center's work (see note 8 above), which tend to play Lévinas off against Lacoue-Labarthe and Nancy (and Derrida), arguing that it is in Lévinas's writings that we discern a more fully articulated passage from ethics to politics. No doubt Critchley notes the proximity of Nancy's later writings on community to Lévinas's proposal to think all relation in terms of what remains unbound—the relation without relation—while also acknowledging the pivotal consequences of this argument for rethinking the question of space, notably his proposal to think "political space" as an "open, plural, opaque network of ethical relations which are non-totalizable" ("Lacoue-Labarthe and Nancy: Re-tracing the Political," 225). But what remains to be articulated and explored more fully is the way in which the writings of Lévinas *already* inform Lacoue-Labarthe and Nancy's earlier texts for the Center, even if they remain largely unacknowledged, notably in regard to the question of *relation*, thus suggesting in what ways Critchley's critique finds an initial measure of its own displacement.

The reference here to Nancy's writings on community further complicates the references to transcendence and alterity in the earlier texts for the Center. Looking back from Nancy's later book, *The Inoperative Community*, we now know the different ways in which the concept of "immanentism" had become central to Nancy's re-thinking of community, while the references to transcendence (also defined in terms of an excess or "initial spacing") became transposed to what Nancy then locates as an "immanence in transcendence." Indeed, while Nancy will propose various ways of rethinking the relation between immanence and transcendence in his later writings, by *The Sense of the World* he writes that it is not a question of "immanentizing transcendence, but in inscribing the latter—or sense—*along the edge of* immanence (which signifies, ultimately, the insufficiency of these concepts themselves" (see Jean-Luc Nancy, *Le sens du monde* [Paris: Galilée, 1993], 90, trans. Jeffrey S. Librett as *The Sense of the World* [Minneapolis: University of Minnesota Press, 1997], 183n48). Nancy then reworks the distinction again in later writings, notably in "Imm/Trans," trans. Laura Balladur, *Polygraph* 15/16 (2004); 11–12.

Further clouding Lacoue-Labarthe and Nancy's various appeals to transcendence and immanence in their earlier writings for the Center, we might also note the widespread acceptance at the time in which the Center was open of treating Derrida's writings in terms of an appeal to "quasi-transcendentals," while Nancy's increasing circumspection regarding transcendence and immanence as ways to think alterity is contemporaneous with Deleuze's turn to the "plane of immanence" as the very site for thinking the creation of alterity and difference. Indeed, the real difficulty in interpreting the terms in which Lacoue-Labarthe and Nancy explore the question of alterity in the writings for the Center stems from the subsequent ways in which the very terms of the argument are subject to continual displacement. Thus, in an incisive commentary on Nancy's writings written some years after the Center's closure, Alexander García Düttmann argues, "To think immanence as such and to think the possibility of that which separates immanence from itself amounts to going beyond all immanence *within immanence itself*. One thus comes upon the decisive question for a finite thought: How is one to think the strange transcendence that seems to be essential to this thought and that describes the movement of its grasp without in the least opposing any kind of immanence? If the concept of transcendence remains, at this point, as insufficient as that of immanence, it will still be retained insofar as it designates that difference by means of which finite thought exceeds its own inscription in [what Nancy terms] the 'absoluity of the finite.' Because it is situated on the limit of a closure, because it marks the 'closure of an immanence,' which is not a loss or a lack of transcendence, finite thought, free in its own finitude, radicalizes immanence to the point of attaining the limit where the closure is affected by an opening that it can no longer close. Immanence is not always the same: grasped as such, it separates from itself at the moment in which it fully becomes what it 'is.'"

As García Düttmann goes on to argue—and here we begin to join up again with the question of totalitarianism that frames Lacoue-Labarthe and Nancy's references to transcendence and immanence in the first place—the finite thought of the *partage* or sharing out of community does not constitute a new social or political philosophy, for the political and the ontological must be joined in their shared-out origins. Immanentism, on the other hand, is a logic of presupposition, "the accomplishment of an essence through the economic link, the technological operation, and political fusion." In other words, "existence becomes work [*oeuvre*] and the onto-political is transformed into 'totalitarianism' when the community erects itself on a presupposition which is to be realized in the actuality of 'pure immanence.'" If totalitarianism, in the sense of the creation of a pure immanence, is the "general horizon of our time," or if the West continues to extend "its own delimitation" and thus to form the horizon of its closure, García Düttmann concludes that "finite thought first thinks this closure as that which never closes or as that which closes only by means of the suppression of finitude." See Alexander García Düttmann, "Immanences, transcendences," trans. Peggy Kamuf, *Paragraph* 16, no. 2 (1993): 187–88.

Although he does not cite the earlier writings for the Center, or Lacoue-Labarthe and Nancy's debts to Lévinas, François Raffoul offers a useful commentary on questions of immanence and transcendence in Nancy's writings in his preface to Jean-Luc Nancy, *The Gravity of Thought* (Atlantic Highlands, N.J.: Humanities Press, 1997), xv–xvii.

19. The question of revolution was raised at key points in the various texts and discussions comprising the Political Seminar in the *Les fins de l'homme* colloquium, notably Jacob Rogozinski's presentation, "Déconstruire—La Révolution" and the ensuing discussion (*FH*, 516–29), and then taken up by Nancy in many later texts. See Jean-Luc Nancy, "L'histoire finie," in *La Communauté désœuvrée*, rev. ed. (Paris: Christian Bourgeois, 1990), 235–78, trans. Brian Holmes as "Finite History," in *The Birth to Presence* (Stanford, Calif.: Stanford University Press, 1993), 143–66.

20. In his introduction to *Retreating the Political* (*RP*, xx–xxv), Simon Sparks situates Lacoue-Labarthe and Nancy's writings for the Center in quite specific rapport with this question of the figure, a question to which we will return in later chapters.

21. This reading is taken up at further length by John Martis in *Philippe Lacoue-Labarthe: Representation and the Loss of the Subject* (New York: Fordham University Press, 2005).

22. The reference to the Greek *envoi* and the related question of mimesis recalls Derrida's more extensive rethinking of the concept of representation in "*Envoi*," *Psyché: Inventions de l'autre*, 109–43; "*Envoi*," in *Pysche: Inventions of the Other*, 94–128.

23. Nancy's writings have consistently refused to assimilate any form of closure to a return. See Jean-Luc Nancy, *L'Oubli de la philosophie* (Paris: Galilée, 1986), trans.

François Raffoul and Gregory Recco as "The Forgetting of Philosophy," in *The Gravity of Thought*, 7–71. François Raffoul offers an extensive commentary on Nancy's rethinking of the motif of return in his preface to the volume.

24. Philippe Lacoue-Labarthe, "Poétique et politique," in *L'imitation des modernes: Typographies II* (Paris: Galilée, 1986), 188 (quoted in *RP*, xi).

25. It is in Lacoue-Labarthe's writings in particular that Heidegger's politics are given their most decisive re-elaboration in light of the more general terms outlined in the Center's work and the retreat of the political in particular. In an essay commissioned for the *Retreating the Political* volume of translations, Lacoue-Labarthe offers a useful synthesis of his reading of Heidegger and the terms in which such a reading may be considered contentious. See Philippe Lacoue-Labarthe, "The Spirit of National Socialism and its Destiny" (*RP*, 148–56). The essay resumes Lacoue-Labarthe's more extensive analysis of Heidegger's encoding of the unthought of National Socialism in "national aestheticism" in "La transcendance finie/t dans la politique," as well as in *La Fiction du politique* (Paris: Christian Bourgeois, 1987), trans. Chris Turner as *Heidegger, Art and Politics* (Oxford: Basil Blackwell, 1990). See also Philippe Lacoue-Labarthe and Jean-Luc Nancy, *Le mythe nazi* (La Tour d'Aigues: Éditions de l'Aube, 1991), trans. Brian Holmes as "The Nazi Myth," *Critical Inquiry* 16, no. 2 (1990): 291–312; Christopher Fynsk, "Postface: The Legibility of the Political," in *Heidegger: Thought and Historicity*, exp. ed. (Ithaca: Cornell University Press, 1993), 230–49; and John Martis, *Philippe Lacoue-Labarthe*, 128–55.

26. As Lacoue-Labarthe and Nancy ask in referring to their use of the phrase "the philosophical," "What is this sort of element or milieu which we appear to be substituting for the thing itself? And why, for example, are we not content to stick with 'metaphysics' in Heidegger's sense of the term, which no more signifies some mode or region of what, since Aristotle, has generally been called philosophising than our 'philosophical' refers to the discipline, to the literature, to the tradition, to the scholastic category, even, of so-called philosophy?" Responding to their own question, Lacoue-Labarthe and Nancy note two reasons. First: "the way in which Heidegger, on the basis of a certain epoch, usually uses the word and concept of metaphysics—even if we subscribe to this, and even if our 'philosophical' is not foreign to this metaphysics—silently but obstinately preserves a sort of 'positive value' attached to philosophy and to philosophizing. Despite such and such a declaration from the 'Letter on Humanism,' despite the lecture 'What is Philosophy?'—despite, even, the opposition of 'thinking' and philosophy—metaphysics too often remains that which, through philosophy, shields philosophy from thinking....An entire code is constructed and an entire metaphysical language is elaborated on the word 'metaphysics,' a language and a code which we feel it necessary to try to escape." And yet, as they also acknowledge, the appeal to the "philosophical" is in many regards the same as the "metaphysical" in Heidegger's sense, insofar as both designate "a general historico-systematic structure—which, up until recently, one could have called the

West—of which philosophy is each time the thematisation, the prefiguration or the anticipation, the reflection (critical or not), the contestation, etc., but which largely overflows the basically restricted field of operations of actual philosophizing" (*RT*, 186/*RP*, 124). One might note how this phrasing already displaces the widespread assumptions concerning the ontologico-historical schema of the West as a single narrative, a "unicity-singularity of the History of Being" that gets (re)produced not only by Heidegger but in Derrida, Lacoue-Labarthe, and Nancy's purported "Heideggerianism." It is tempting to say that what distinguishes their writings from any single narrative, or what continually displaces this narrative as a narrative, is an attention to not only the specificity of what "overflows the basically restricted field of operations of actual philosophizing"—including the "political" effects of this specificity—but *reading*. On this same question, see Nancy's discussion in *Le sens du monde*, 44; *The Sense of the World*, 24–25, and for further elaboration of the phrase "each time" in the above quotation, see Nancy's *L'Experience de la liberté* (Paris: Galilée, 1988), trans. Bridget McDonald as *The Experience of Freedom* (Stanford, Calif.: Stanford University Press, 1993).

27. As Nancy argues in *The Sense of the World*, "The words with which one designates that which is coming to an end (history, philosophy, politics, art, world...) are not the names of subsistent realities in themselves, but the names of concepts or ideas, entirely determined within a regime of *sense* that is coming full circle and completing itself before our (thereby blinded) eyes....If there is an illusion from which one must protect oneself today more than ever, it is the illusion that consists in getting hung up on *words* (history, philosophy, politics, art...) as if they were immediately to be equated with *things*. Those who insist obstinately on this illusion—that is, basically on the realism of the idea—reveal by this type of somnambulistic Platonism that they have not yet joined our time or its ends." See Jean-Luc Nancy, *Le sens du monde*, 14; *The Sense of the World*. 4.

28. The reference we are making to thinking this nonlocalizable "place" in terms of a "topology" is prompted by Heidegger's own references to topology in his later writings and taken up by a number of more recent commentators, including Reiner Schürmann and Jeff Malpas. See also Derrida's commentary in "De l'esprit: Heidegger et la question," in *Heidegger et la question: De l'esprit et autres essais* (Paris: Flammarion, 1987), 118, trans. Geoffrey Bennington and Rachel Bowlby as *Of Spirit: Heidegger and the Question* (Chicago: University of Chicago Press, 1989), 132; and Howard Caygill's reference to a "topology of the political" in his critique of Nancy in "Philosophy, Violence, Freedom," in *On Jean-Luc Nancy: The Sense of Philosophy*, ed. Darren Sheppard, Simon Sparks, and Colin Thomas (London: Routledge, 1997), 22.

29. One does well here to recall the opening lines of Derrida's "The Ends of Man" essay: "Every philosophical colloquium necessarily has a political significance. And not only due to that which has always linked the essence of the philosophical to the

essence of the political. Essential and general, this political import nevertheless burdens the *a priori* link between philosophy and politics, aggravates it in a way, and also determines it when the philosophical colloquium is announced as an international colloquium." See Jacques Derrida, "Les fins de l'homme," in *Marges—de la philosophie*, 131; "The Ends of Man," in *Margins of Philosophy*, 111. If the opening address is cited frequently, and the date marking Derrida's text (May 12, 1968) also widely discussed in the reception of the essay, less conspicuous though no less pertinent to the following argument is Derrida's closing question, posed in the wake of "the ends of man": "But who, we?" In other words, in what sense is Derrida's question imposed by the question of the co-belonging of the philosophical and the political as that co-belonging simultaneously reopens the grammar of relation informing this "we"?

30. While the distinction between the political and politics is widely defined and argued, the definitions proposed here are taken from Christopher Fynsk, foreword to Jean-Luc Nancy, *The Inoperative Community*, ed. Peter Connor (Minneapolis: University of Minnesota Press, 1991), x. As the following pages will further insist, the question still remains how to think the spatial or topological conditions of this "site" of being in common, what Lacoue-Labarthe and Nancy also term the "circumscription of a domain."

31. In his contribution to the Political Seminar at the *Les fins de l'homme* colloquium, Lacoue-Labarthe insists on recognizing that Derrida's writings from early on were engaged in a continual dialogue with Marxism, notably in terms of their reception, acknowledging that Marxism "still represents…the most powerful of political theories or ideologies—at least in France, and that is to say in Europe as well" (*FH*, 496/*RP*, 97). As Lacoue-Labarthe continues, "I am not persuaded that one does deconstruction (including the undoubtedly deconstructive element that Marxism *also* conceals) any service in keeping Marxism sheltered from it: if there is in Marxism an onto-teleology of the proper and of appropriation or of reappropriation (of the appropriation or reappropriation of man), of self-production and of effectuation, if there is a 'metaphysics of Marx' (as there is a metaphysics of Nietzsche), why should it be untouchable? And if certain political presuppositions, for example those which are at work in the theory (of the 'withering') of the State, derive from a (far too) simple critique and reversal of Hegel or from the acceptance of contestable models (the Jacobin model, among others), in the name of what do we pass silently over this?" As Lacoue-Labarthe concludes, "There existed, and there still exists, a *revolutionary* critique of Marxism and its 'realisations'—and that is to say, for what is of most immediate concern here, a critique of all that follows from the Leninist reorientation [*infléchissement*]" (*FH*, 496; *RP*, 98). The reference to Lenin here will be discussed in the final chapter. Nancy Fraser's claim that Lacoue-Labarthe and Nancy's project, "like deconstruction itself, is only a temporary waystation on the exodus from Marxism now being traveled by the French intelligentsia" ("The French Derrideans," 143)

can only be read as an expression of bad faith. In this context, we also recall that Michael Ryan's *Marxism and Deconstruction: A Critical Articulation* (Baltimore: The Johns Hopkins University Press, 1984) was published at the same time the Center in Paris was closing.

32. For further discussion of Nancy's writings in relation to the State, see Jason Smith, "Introduction: Nancy's Hegel, the State, and Us," in Jean-Luc Nancy, *Hegel: The Restlessness of the Negative*, trans. Jason Smith and Steven Miller (Minneapolis: University of Minnesota Press, 2002), ix–xxix. For a recent reading of Marx, democracy, and the State that turns on this same problematic, see Alain Badiou, "A Speculative Disquisition on the Concept of Democracy," in *Metapolitics*, trans. Jason Barker (London: Verso, 2005), 78–95.

33. If Lacoue-Labarthe and Nancy were already writing this several years before the fall of the Berlin Wall and the collapse of the Soviet bloc countries, and so prior to the more widespread celebrations concerning the "end of Marxism," such "repression" (what Derrida has elsewhere characterized as "manic disavowal") is still widespread and continues to this day in the writings of such figures as Francis Fukuyama or Thomas Friedman.

34. See Martin Heidegger, "Brief über den Humanismus," in *Wegmarken* (Frankfurt am Main: Vittorio Klosterman, 1967), 172, trans. Frank A. Capuzzi and J. Glenn Gray as "Letter on Humanism," in *Basic Writings*, ed. David Farrell Krell (San Francisco: Harper & Row, 1977), 221. The reference to collectivism in Heidegger's "Letter on Humanism" is discussed by Christopher Fynsk in his presentation at the Political Seminar at Cérisy (*FH*, 492; *RP*, 93).

35. See Étienne Balibar, *La philosophie de Marx* (Paris: La Découverte, 1993), 6, trans. Chris Turner as *The Philosophy of Marx* (London: Verso, 1995), 5 (translation slightly modified). Further page references to the French and English editions will be cited in the text. We recall that Balibar was one of the participants in the Center's lectures and discussions. The importance of his text on Marx is acknowledged by Nancy in *Être singulier pluriel* (Paris: Galilée, 1996), 95, trans. Robert D. Richardson and Anne E. O'Bryne as *Being Singular Plural* (Stanford, Calif.: Stanford University Press, 2000), 202n62.

36. We recall in this context that the same term figures decisively for Lacoue-Labarthe in his rethinking of the "caesura" of the speculative in the writings of Hölderlin, a reading mentioned briefly in his presentation at Cérisy (*FH*, 432–33/*RP*, 72–73) and taken up more extensively in later writings, including his reading of Heidegger in *La Fiction du politique*.

37. To be sure, it could be contested whether Foucault's own writings end up "subjugating these struggles, in their finality, to this domination," notably in his later writings and the turn to biopolitics (which Foucault terms a "historical ontology of ourselves"), but this still leaves open whether the discourse of power effaces the

arch-political constitution of social relations that organizes Lacoue-Labarthe and Nancy's argument. At the time of the Center's discussions in the early 1980s, Foucault was presenting a series of lectures at the Collège de France around the "hermeneutics of the subject," gesturing at the end of his life toward the possibility of an "ethics" of relation that would remain irreducible to the work on self-relation, "the care of the self," subjectification, and governmentality, for which his writings are more widely known. But the possibilities for thinking the question of relation appear schematic, at best suggestive in the "Society Must Be Defended" lectures, cut short by Foucault's death in 1984.

If Lacoue-Labarthe and Nancy's argument opens toward and simultaneously displaces Heidegger's destruction of the metaphysical subject, the relation between Heidegger and Foucault demands a longer, parenthetical aside. Taking up the question of the subject in his introduction to *Typography* (a volume of translations of several texts by Lacoue-Labarthe), Derrida remarks that Lacoue-Labarthe's refusal to engage with any discourse concerning the "return of the subject" separates him from those discourses of the subject that had been animating Parisian conversations at the time "and which (and this is in *the best of cases*, no doubt the least dogmatic and the most refined) certain authors believe they find in Foucault's very last works." "Nevertheless," Derrida continues, "*in every case*, a rigorous reading of Heidegger, an effective working-across his text on the subject of subjectivity, has been carefully omitted." Against any "return of the subject" Lacoue-Labarthe thus does something entirely different: "He does not propose to restore, rehabilitate, or reinstall 'the subject'; rather, he proposes to think [what Derrida locates as its] desistance by taking into account *both* a deconstruction of the Heideggerian type *and* that about which he thinks Heidegger maintained a silence." Since Derrida locates Lacoue-Labarthe's "desistance" of the subject in light of his reading of Heidegger, and since, as we have seen, Heidegger plays such a prominent role in Lacoue-Labarthe and Nancy's "retreating" of the political, Derrida's accompanying footnote merits further citation: "Heidegger was almost never named by Foucault, who in any case never confronted him and, if one may say so, never explained himself on his relation to him. This is also true of Deleuze. This did not prevent Foucault from declaring in his very last interview: 'My entire philosophical development [*devenir*] was determined by my reading of Heidegger.' Nor did it prevent Deleuze, in the very last pages of his book on Foucault, from speaking of a 'necessary confrontation of Foucault with Heidegger.' How, then, is one to interpret, retrospectively, this twenty-five year silence? I must be brief. If, in attending to this silence, one thinks at the same time of those who like Lacoue-Labarthe have constantly taken into account, in the most difficult, hazardous, indeed 'necessary' dimensions, the said 'confrontation' [i.e., *Auseinandersetzung*] with Heidegger, one obtains—allow me to say nothing on the subject here—a kind of film of the French philosophical scene in this quarter-century"

(Jacques Derrida, "Introduction: Desistance," trans. Christopher Fynsk, in Philippe Lacoue-Labarthe, *Typography*, 17). Timothy Raynor's *Foucault's Heidegger* (New York: Continuum, 2007) would no doubt play a prominent role in this film.

In order to renew the stakes of Derrida's undeveloped aside, we might turn to Deleuze and Guattari's own references to Heidegger in *What Is Philosophy?* Rearticulating how philosophical concepts become "territorialized" and "reterritorialized," Deleuze and Guattari remark that the "Heidegger affair has complicated matters: a great philosopher actually had to be reterritorialized on Nazism for the strangest commentaries to meet up, sometimes calling his philosophy into question and sometimes absolving it through such complicated and convoluted arguments that we are still in the dark" (see Gilles Deleuze and Félix Guattari, *Qu'est-ce que la philosophie?* [Paris: Minuit, 1991], 104, trans. Graham Burchell and Hugh Tomlinson as *What Is Philosophy?* [London: Verso, 1994], 108). Given the stakes involved—nothing less than thinking the question of fascism and totalitarianism, including "the tracking down of all varieties of fascism" that Foucault famously champions in Deleuze and Guattari's own writings—and given the various texts presumably implied here—not just Victor Farias's *Heidegger et le nazisme* (1987) that in many ways prompted or at least reopened the "Heidegger affair" but the books written in its wake, including Lacoue-Labarthe's *La Fiction du politique* (published in 1990, the year prior to *What Is Philosophy?*), Lyotard's *Heidegger et les juifs* (1988), Derrida's *De l'esprit* (1987), and a number of essays by Granel, to name only some of the most well known—Deleuze and Guattari's reference to "convoluted arguments" seems at once evasive and pitifully inadequate, while the implied assumption that any such texts *absolve* Heidegger disingenuous. The ensuing discussion of "shame" in *What Is Philosophy?* also tends to reintroduce a pious moralizing to the argument by two writers whose body of writings and whose critical engagements characteristically and quite resolutely otherwise refuse any such morality. Less polemically, however, it seems more than significant in their discussion of Heidegger in *What Is Philosophy?* that Deleuze and Guattari's various meditations on the concept of friendship throughout the text (drawn from Blanchot and Mascolo) meet up not only with their references to Heidegger but also with their claims concerning "the becoming of subjected peoples," a claim to be distinguished from the *demos* of democracies, and voiced most eloquently in the work of art and the most "aristocratic" of writers. No doubt Deleuze and Guattari attempt to withdraw that "becoming" from the rhetoric of "destiny" proposed by Heidegger—"the people no longer exists, or not yet…*the people are missing*" they write—but the argument in all its political *and* philosophical ambivalence (at least in *What Is Philosophy?* for the earlier collaborative texts would demand an entirely different reading) remains not entirely unrelated to the very terms in which Heidegger himself worked to rethink National Socialism, at least as Lacoue-Labarthe has argued. The least that might be said here is that these various asides demand extensive re-elaboration beyond the more predictable rhetorical exchanges or studied lack of dialogue between "Deleuzians" and "deconstruction," and certainly beyond the widely discussed and reductive assumptions voiced by Ferry and Renault that all these writers can be labeled by their "anti-humanism."

Conversely, it seems curious and significant that the Center's lectures and discussions on the retreat of the political unfold without any direct reference to Deleuze and Guattari's two-volume *Capitalism and Schizophrenia*, notably the attention given to Marxism in the first volume and to questions of totalitarianism or "molar thinking" in the second (published in the same year in which the Center was opened). At the same time, *A Thousand Plateaus* and, notably, the "Treatise on Nomadology," turns with some insistence on the question of relation that also animates Lacoue-Labarthe and Nancy's writings for the Center. Again, such omissions might provide further footage in Derrida's proposed film on the French philosophical scene in this quarter-century.

38. See Jean-Luc Nancy, *L'"il y a" du rapport sexuel* (Paris: Galilée, 2001), which rearticulates many of the arguments first explored in the texts for the Center in Paris.

39. The reference is to the volume edited by Nancy with Eduardo Cadava and Peter Connor, *Who Comes after the Subject?* (London: Routledge, 1991). The French title of the volume, published in *Cahiers Confrontations* 20 (Winter 1989), is "Après le sujet qui vient?" which suggests at once a "who" that "comes after the subject"—in which case, the subject is finite or finished and the "who" comes in its wake—but also points to a "who" that comes after the subject who is (still) coming and has not, as it were, arrived (yet). The implications of this double reading will get taken up in later chapters.

40. The turn to psychoanalysis continues a series of readings that started with Lacoue-Labarthe and Nancy's early text on Lacan, *Le titre de la letter: Une lecture de Lacan* (Paris: Galilée, 1973), trans. François Raffoul and David Pettigrew as *The Title of the Letter: A Reading of Lacan* (Albany: State University of New York Press, 1992). Other related texts by Lacoue-Labarthe and Nancy include "La panique politique," *Cahiers Confrontations* 2 (1979): 33–57 (translated in *RP*, 1–31); and "Le peuple juif ne rêve pas," in *La psychanalyse, est-elle une histoire juive?* (Paris: Seuil, 1981), trans. Brian Holmes as "The Unconscious Is Destructured like an Affect (Part 1 of 'The Jewish People Do Not Dream')," *Stanford Literature Review* 6, no. 2 (Fall 1989): 191–209; and "'From Where Is Psychoanalysis Possible?' (Part 2 of 'The Jewish People Do Not Dream')," *Stanford Literature Review* 8, nos. 1–2 (Spring–Fall 1991): 39–55.

41. The lecture by Philippe Soulez for the Center had taken up the question of the "mother" as its primary theme. See "La mère est-elle hors-jeu de l'essence du politique?" in *RT*, 159–82.

42. Other possible connotations of this *Schwärmerei* suggest military movements, in the sense of roving migrants and nomadic displacements, in other words, terms that are rearticulated by Deleuze and Guattari and Hardt and Negri in their respective writings.

43. See the longer discussion taken up by Lacoue-Labarthe and Nancy in a footnote in "La panique politique" (*RP*, 167–68n15). The same question is also taken up

by Alain Badiou in his essay "A Speculative Disquisition on the Concept of Democracy," 88–90.

44. See Jean-Luc Nancy, "Le juridiction du monarque hégélien" in *RJ*, 51–90, trans. Mary Ann and Peter Caws as "The Jurisdiction of the Hegelian Monarch," in *The Birth to Presence* (Stanford, Calif.: Stanford University Press, 1993), 110–42.

45. Lacoue-Labarthe and Nancy refer here to Lyotard's questions to Lefort concerning "the presupposition of the us" (*RT*, 87), Rancière's assumption that the only common predicate of class is "being in the place of the other" (*RT*, 89–111), and Soulez's reading of the concept of the "mother" (*RT*, 59–181).

46. See Lorenzo Fabbri, "Philosophy as Chance: An Interview with Jean-Luc Nancy," trans. Pascale-Anne Brault and Michael Naas, *Critical Inquiry* 33 (Winter 2007): 434–45. Nancy notes here the importance of Reiner Schürmann's *Heidegger on Being and Acting: From Principles to Anarchy*, trans. Christine-Marie Gros (Bloomington: Indiana University Press, 1987).

47. Martin Heidegger, *Sein und Zeit* (Tübingen: Max Niemeyer, 1986), 390, trans. Joan Stambaugh as *Being and Time* (Albany: State University of New York Press, 1996), 356. Further page references are cited in the text. Unless otherwise noted, all italics are Heidegger's.

48. See also Christopher Fynsk, *Heidegger: Thought and Historicity* and François Raffoul, *Heidegger and the Subject*, trans. David Pettigrew and Gregory Recco (New Jersey: Humanities Press, 1988).

49. The reference here is to Nancy's *Le partage des voix* (Paris: Galilée, 1982), trans. Gayle L. Ormiston as "Sharing Voices," in *Transforming the Hermeneutic Context: From Nietzsche to Nancy*, ed. Gayle L. Ormiston and Alan D. Schrift (Albany: State University of New York Press, 1990), 211–59. Published at the time of the Center, the closing section may be read as hinging the lectures and discussions unfolding at the Center itself and Nancy's later work, notably the argument that community remains to be thought according to the "*partage du* logos."

50. See Martin Heidegger, *Einführung in die Metaphysik* (Tübingen: Max Niemeyer, 1987), 117, trans. Gregory Fried and Richard Polt as *Introduction to Metaphysics* (New Haven, Conn.: Yale University Press, 2000), 162 (translation modified). Lacoue-Labarthe translates the "place of history" as "*le site historial*" and the way in which "history happens" as "*l'histoire advient*," while Gilbert Kahn translates the "place of history" as "*le site de pro-venance*" and "history happens" as "*la pro-venance pro-vient*" (see *Introduction à la métaphysique* [Paris: Gallimard, 1967], 159), thus emphasizing with Lacoue-Labarthe the ways in which history originates and proceeds in and as a modification of what comes, or what comes to pass. The passage from *Introduction to Metaphysics* is cited in Lacoue-Labarthe's presentation at Cérisy (*FH*, 431/*RP*, 71) and taken up again in his re-elaboration of Heidegger's politics in *La Fiction du politique*, 33; *Heidegger, Art and Politics*, 17.

51. Hannah Arendt, *The Human Condition* (Chicago: University of Chicago Press, 1958), 124.

52. While we are reading this question of space through Arendt—a reading taken up again in later chapters—other points of departure are no doubt possible here, including Lefort's concept of the "empty space" of power discussed in the Center's lectures and discussions.

53. Lacoue-Labarthe and Nancy are referring to Pierre Clastres's *La Société contre l'état* (Paris: Minuit, 1974), trans. Robert Hurley and Abe Stein as *Society Against the State* (New York: Zone, 1987). Lacoue-Labarthe and Nancy's reservations concerning Clastres's text might be usefully compared to the brief discussion of Clastres by Deleuze and Guattari in *Mille Plateaux: Capitalisme et schizophrénie* (Paris: Minuit, 1980), 441–46, trans. Brian Massumi as *A Thousand Plateaus: Capitalism and Schizophrenia* (Minneapolis: University of Minnesota Press, 1987), 357–61, although all of the "Treatise on Nomadology" is at stake here.

54. We return here to Gasché's *Of Minimal Things: Studies on the Notion of Relation* and Fynsk's *Language and Relation* cited earlier. The effacement of the question of relation also turns us to the much more influential reception of Lyotard's *The Postmodern Condition*, where the emphasis on "grand narratives" and the debates concerning the relative merits of postmodernity as a concept have largely effaced the pivotal if problematic discussion of the "nature of the social bond" in Lyotard's text, notably the ways in which "social bonds" are transformed by capitalism, changes in the nation-state, and contemporary communication technologies.

55. The positing of this "passage" punctuates Critchley's critique of the Center's work in "Lacoue-Labarthe and Nancy: Re-tracing the Political," although the assumption is also resonant in other texts on the Center.

56. Looking ahead, we could also suggest that these two ways of conceiving the political find resonance in Lacoue-Labarthe and Nancy's later exchange concerning the "figure" in "Scène," *Nouvelle Revue de Psychanalyse* 46 (Autumn 1992): 73–98, trans. Maiko Behr as "Scene: An Exchange of Letters," in *Beyond Representation: Philosophy and Poetic Imagination*, ed. Richard Eldridge (Cambridge: Cambridge University Press, 1996), 273–302.

57. On (re)invention, see Sparks in *RP*, xxvii. While we are not pursuing the analogy further here, Lacoue-Labarthe and Nancy's rearticulation of the space of the political finds one of its most resonant resources in rethinking Heidegger's references to space in his writings on "the origin of the work of art," a reading we will take up on another occasion.

58. See "The Question of the Common and the Responsibility of the Universal," an interview with Jean-Luc Nancy, Artem Magun, and Oxana Timofeeva, in "What do we have in common?" special issue, *Chto delat? / What Is to Be Done?* 9 (May 2005), http://www.chtodelat.org.

59. The scare quotes around "civility" are repeated in Nancy's later argument in *Being Singular Plural* that "philosophy begins with and in 'civil [*concitoyenne*]' coexistence as such." As we will see, the argument thus reconfigures the emphasis on relation in the earlier writings for the Center by now claiming that "the 'city' is not primarily a form of political institution; it is primarily being-with *as such*" (*Être singulier pluriel*, 51; *Being Singular Plural*, 31).

2. From Paradox to *Partage*

1. See "Paradoxes of Citizenship: Environments, Exclusions, Equity," opening statement to the *Canadian Federation for the Humanities and Social Sciences* 2005 Congress, University of Western Ontario, http://www.fedcan.ca/congress2005/theme.htm.

2. See T. H. Marshall, *Citizenship and Social Class and Other Essays* (Cambridge: Cambridge University Press, 1950).

3. While our argument foregrounds the specific references to paradox within the literature on citizenship, it should be noted that references to paradox figure prominently in recent political theory (I'm thinking here especially of the writings of William Connolly, Chantal Mouffe, and Wendy Brown). Pending a more sustained discussion of this wider appeal to paradox in political philosophy and recent political theory, a useful start might be to determine its force between the closing lines of Kant's "What is Enlightenment?" and Foucault's references to paradox and "modes of problematization" in his reading of Kant's text.

4. Seyla Benhabib's writings are situated decisively around this same post-Kantian tension. See Seyla Benhabib, *The Rights of Others: Aliens, Residents, and Citizens* (Cambridge: Cambridge University Press, 2004). See also the conclusion to Dominique Leydet's entry on "Citizenship" in the *Stanford Encyclopedia of Philosophy* (http://plato.stanford.edu/entries/citizenship/), which outlines the tensions at stake in thinking citizenship today with some precision.

5. Derek Heater, *A Brief History of Citizenship* (New York: New York University Press, 2004), 143.

6. See Herman R. van Gunsteren, *A Theory of Citizenship: Organizing Plurality in Contemporary Democracies* (Boulder, Colo.: Westview Press, 1998).

7. See Étienne Balibar, *We, the People of Europe? Reflections on Transnational Citizenship*, trans. James Swenson (Princeton, N.J.: Princeton University Press, 2004), 10. More recently, Balibar has rethought the concept of citizenship in light of aporias in "Strangers as Enemies: Further Reflections on the Aporias of Transnational Citizenship," *Globalization Working Papers Series* (Institute on Globalization and the Human Condition, McMaster University), http://globalization.mcmaster.ca/wps/balibar.pdf. The writings of Étienne Balibar have offered one of the most incisive

genealogical rearticulations of citizenship in recent years. In writing the chapter, I'm also grateful to my colleagues Gene Holland, whose forthcoming book on nomadic citizenship has offered a compelling counterpoint to the argument that follows, and Nina Berman, who offered a compelling commentary on an earlier draft.

8. The term constitutes the basis of Isin and Wood's genealogical investigations into citizenship. See Engin F. Isin and Patricia K. Wood, *Citizenship and Identity* (London: Sage, 1999); and Engin F. Isin, *Being Political: Genealogies of Citizenship* (Minneapolis: University of Minnesota Press, 2002). Other related proposals include Will Kymlicka, *Multicultural Citizenship: A Liberal Theory of Minority Rights* (Oxford: Oxford University Press, 1995), Aihwa Ong, *Flexible Citizenship: The Cultural Logic of Transnationality* (Durham, N.C.: Duke University Press, 1999), the essays included in *Dimensions of Radical Democracy: Pluralism, Citizenship, Community*, ed. Chantal Mouffe (London: Verso, 1992), and Saskia Sassen, *Territory, Authority, Rights: From Medieval to Global Assemblages* (Princeton: Princeton University Press, 2006).

9. Aihwa Ong, "Latitudes of Citizenship: Membership, Meaning, Multiculturism," in *People Out of Place: Globalization, Human Rights, and the Citizenship Gap*, ed. Alison Brysk and Gershon Shafir (New York: Routledge, 2004), 53.

10. Heater, *A Brief History of Citizenship, 143.*

11. See Michael Walzer, *Spheres of Justice: A Defense of Pluralism and Equality* (New York: Basic Books, 1983), and "The Civil Society Argument," in Mouffe, *Dimensions of Radical Democracy*, 89–107.

12. No doubt the assumption remains on much of the "left" that citizenship and the discourse of rights prolongs its originary association with progressive politics and emancipatory, revolutionary discourses, at least when it refuses to decline into moral exhortations to be a good "private citizen" and an upright member of the community. This reception of citizenship should be situated in light of the role citizenship plays in more reactionary, conservative, antiglobal, anti-immigrant, protectionist, nationalist, and fundamentalist political discourses. At the same time, the coincidence of citizenship and consumerism is increasingly dominant (evident in numerous government reports), and capitalism has been forced into an unusually defensive position in its increasingly widespread appeal to "corporate citizenship" in their corporate newsletters and publicity relations rhetoric. The degree to which such an "appropriation" of the revolutionary and emancipatory discourses of citizenship is already inscribed in liberal, communitarian, and republican traditions of citizenship clearly remains open to question.

13. A number of statistical references and empirical data can be found in the essays collected in Brysk and Shafir, *Peoples Out of Place.* The volume offers a useful overview of the primary debates concerning citizenship in the contexts of contemporary globalization.

14. Balibar, *We, the People of Europe?* 132. The argument is proposed in light of van Gunsteren's transformation of citizenship in terms of "communities of fate."

15. See Giorgio Agamben, "Beyond Human Rights," in *Means without End: Notes on Politics*, trans. Vincenzo Binetti and Cesare Casarino (Minneapolis: University of Minnesota Press, 2000), 16. Agamben is referring to Arendt's early writings on refugees, notably the closing chapter in the "Imperialism" section of *The Origins of Totalitarianism* (New York: Schocken Books, 2004), 341–84.

16. The phrase is central to the more general argument proposed in Isin's *Being Political: Genealogies of Citizenship*.

17. Jacques Derrida and Bernard Stiegler, *Échographies de la télévision: Entretiens filmés* (Paris: Galilée-INA, 1996), trans. Jennifer Bajorek as *Echographies of Television: Filmed Interviews* (Cambridge, UK: Polity Press, 2002). The text is a transcription of the interview, filmed in 1993 by Jean-Christophe Rosé under the auspices of the Institut National de l'Audiovisuel (INA) in France. Further page references (to the French and English versions respectively) are cited in the text.

18. The reference to "spacing" goes back at least to Derrida's reading of Husserl in *Speech and Phenomena* and touches on his early elaboration of the "trace" as "archi-writing." Given that the logic of this spacing will appear with some frequency in the pages that follow, we recall here Derrida's commentary: "Since the trace is the intimate relation of the living present with its outside, the openness upon exteriority in general, upon the sphere of what is not 'one's own' [*non-propre*] etc., *the temporalization of sense is, from the outset, a 'spacing'.* As soon as we admit spacing both as 'interval' or difference and as openness upon the outside, there can no longer be any absolute inside, for the 'outside' has insinuated itself into the movement by which the inside of the nonspatial, which is called 'time,' appears, is constituted, is 'presented.' Space is 'in' time; it is time's pure leaving-itself [*la pure sortie hors de soi du temps*]; it is the 'outside-itself' as the self-relation of time. The externality of space, externality as space, does not overtake time; rather, it opens as pure 'outside' 'within' the movement of temporalization." See Jacques Derrida, *La voix et le phénomène* (Paris: Presses Universitaires de France, 1967), 96, trans. David B. Allison as *Speech and Phenomena and Other Essays on Husserl's Theory of Signs* (Evanston, Ill.: Northwestern University Press, 1973), 86.

19. In "Force of Law," Derrida takes up again the question of politicization in the context of law, arguing that politicization is "interminable even if it cannot and should not ever be total. To keep this from being a truism or a triviality, we must recognize in it the following consequence: each advance in politicization obliges one to reconsider, and so to reinterpret the very foundations of law such as they had previously been calculated or delimited." See Jacques Derrida, "Force of Law: The 'Mystical Foundation of Authority,'" trans. Mary Quaintance, in *Deconstruction and the*

Possibility of Justice, ed. Drucilla Cornell, Michel Rosenfeld, and David Gray Carlson (New York: Routledge, 1992), 28.

20. The rapport between teletechnologies and the concept of the political is not reducible to contemporary technology, including computers or information technology. As Derrida and Stiegler discuss further in the interview, the technology implied by writing and the alphabet, for example, were also the enabling conditions for the constitution of citizenship in classical Greece. If any genealogy of citizenship cannot be dissociated from the technologies that inform it, what remains in question is whether the exponential growth in contemporary teletechnologies constitutes not just a quantitative change but a qualitative change in the rapport between technology, politics, and citizenship. On this question, Derrida and Stiegler appear to part company in the interview. For a fuller account and critical engagement with this aspect of *Echographies*, see Richard Beardsworth, "Towards a Critical Culture of the Image," *Tekhnema: A Journal of Philosophy and Technology* 4 (1998): 114–41.

21. Derrida explores this question further in "Foi et savoir: Les deux sources de la 'religion' aux limites de la simple raison," in *La religion*, ed. Jacques Derrida and Gianni Vattimo (Paris: Seuil, 1996), 9–86, trans. Samuel Weber as "Faith and Knowledge: The Two Sources of 'Religion' at the Limits of Mere Reason," in *Religion*, ed. Jacques Derrida and Gianni Vattimo (Stanford, Calif.: Stanford University Press, 1998), 1–78.

22. The reference to *chance* in French implies a wider set of semantic possibilities than suggested in English. Later in *Echographies* (and prolonging the reference to Marx throughout the interview), Derrida refers to the necessity of rethinking the relation between use and exchange value in Marx's writings as a way of thinking what "constitutes the market's *chance*—in the best sense of the word." Jennifer Bajorek (the English translator of *Echographies*) offers a useful gloss on Derrida's reference to *chance* in this context: "The French *chance* is much richer than its English counterpart. To say that something constitutes the market's 'chance' may be to say that it constitutes its chance and hope in the sense of its condition of possibility. In this sense, it is indissociable both from the risk and from promise. It may also be to say that it constitutes the happy or fortunate thing *of the market* (double genitive)—either that this thing *is* what is happy or fortunate *about the market,* or that the market is *itself* an opportunity, and thus a happy or fortunate thing" (169–70). The chance and hope opened by teletechnologies offers an analogous situation.

23. See Louis Althusser, "Le courant souterrain du matérialisme de la rencontre," in *Écrits philosophiques et politiques*, vol. 1 (Paris: Stock IMEC, 1994), 551–94, trans. G. M. Goshgarian as "The Underground Current of the Materialism of the Encounter," in *Philosophy of the Encounter: Later Writings, 1978–87* (London: Verso, 2006), 163–207. This reference to Althusser will be discussed in later chapters.

24. A conference was organized in 2002 around Derrida's thinking of a "democracy to come." The proceedings have been published as *La démocratie à venir: Autour de Jacques Derrida*, ed. Marie-Louise Mallet (Paris: Galilée, 2004).

25. Stiegler's own references to networks are further explored in "Hypostases, phantasms, désincarnations," in *Penser les réseaux*, Daniel Parrochia (Seyssel: Éditions Champ Vallon, 2001), 136–48.

26. Nancy's frequent use of the French verb *partager* and its derivatives is usually translated as "to share," with the proviso that the French also implies a division and so a "sharing out." As Nancy notes in *La comparution*, synonyms also include "partition, repartition, part, participation, separation, communication, discord, split, devolution, destination." See Jean-Luc Nancy, "La comparution," in Jean-Christophe Bailly and Jean-Luc Nancy, *La comparution: Politiques à venir* (Paris: Christian Bourgeois, 1991), 54–55, trans. Tracy B. Strong as "La Comparution/The Compearance: from the Existence of 'Communism' to the Community of 'Existence,'" *Political Theory* 20, no. 3 (August 1992): 374. If Derrida acknowledges Nancy's use of the term in this context, it is not without repeated reservations concerning the concept of community in Nancy's other writings.

27. Derrida explores the implications of this commentary in "Fidélité à plus d'un," in *Idiomes, nationalités, déconstructions: Rencontre de Rabat avec Jacques Derrida* (Casablanca: Editions Toubkal, 1998), 221–65. The text includes both references to networks as well as various unacknowledged gestures toward Nancy's *Being Singular Plural* (published the same year as the conference).

28. The phrase is taken from André Green and figures as the epigraph to Étienne Balibar's essay "What is a Border?" trans. Chris Turner, in *Politics and the Other Scene* (London: Verso, 2002), 75.

29. Giorgio Agamben, "Beyond Human Rights," 24. Further references are cited in the text.

30. See Gilles Deleuze and Félix Guattari, *Mille Plateaux: Capitalisme et schizophrénie* (Paris: Minuit, 1980), 35, trans. Brian Massumi as *A Thousand Plateaus: Capitalism and Schizophrenia* (Minneapolis: University of Minnesota Press, 1987), 24.

31. No doubt it still remains uncertain what remains of "Europe" in this argument, a question that Derrida and Nancy (among others) have also addressed.

32. See Jacques Derrida, *Politiques de l'amitié* (Paris: Galilée, 1994), 258, trans. George Collins as *Politics of Friendship* (London: Verso, 1997), 231. As we will see, the phrasing originally emerges in a dialogue between Lévinas and Blanchot.

33. See Eduardo Cadava and Aaron Levy, *Cities without Citizens* (Philadelphia: Slought Foundation, 2003), xv–xvi. All further quotations are from Cadava and Levy's brief introduction. *Cities without Citizens* is a catalogue of essays and documentation for an exhibition and installation on cities, citizenship, refugees, and

human rights, held in 2003 at The Rosenbach Museum and Library in Philadelphia. Agamben's essay "Beyond Human Rights" is reprinted in the volume.

34. Engin F. Isin, *Being Political*, 3–4. Since it is not acknowledged in Cadava and Levy's catalogue, one might also note that Isin has used the phrase "cities without citizens" as the title of an earlier book.

35. Pending a more sustained reading, the question of the political broached here would need to be taken up in Isin's own extensive writings on citizenship, starting with the ontological assumptions that inform the title framing his genealogical investigation, *Being Political*. *Being Political*, as Isin insists, "is not about politics. It is about citizenship and otherness as conditions of politics. It assumes an ontological difference between politics and the political. Being political, among all other ways of being, means to constitute oneself simultaneously with and against others as an agent capable of judgment about what is just and unjust. Citizenship and otherness are then really not two different conditions, but two aspects of the ontological condition that makes politics possible. *Being Political* aims to make it more difficult to refer to historical forms of citizenship as though there were an unbroken continuity between us and them by questioning the narratives given to us by citizens and recovering some moments of strangers, outsiders, and aliens becoming political; in a sense, it aims to make us strangers to ourselves" (*Being Political*, x). A reading of Isin's text might start from the ways in which this closing phrase, an echo from Sophocles's *Antigone*, gets taken up by Heidegger in *What Is Metaphysics?*, itself the basis of numerous commentaries on Heidegger's text. On rethinking the relation between citizenship and related concept of hospitality in this context, see Jacques Derrida, *De l'hospitalité* (Paris: Calmann-Levy, 1997), trans. Rachel Bowlby as *Of Hospitality* (Stanford, Calif.: Stanford University Press, 2000), and Gregg Lambert, "Universal Hospitality," in Cadava and Levy, *Cities Without Citizens*, 13–31.

36. Again, the argument would need to be extended in a much longer reading of Isin's *Being Political*, especially given that the book centers its argument precisely around the question of space.

37. The same questions are worked through in Ian Balfour and Eduardo Cadava's compelling introduction to their edited volume on human rights (*South Atlantic Quarterly* 103, nos. 2–3 [Spring–Summer 2004]), which significantly concludes by referring to the paradox of human rights today. Unfortunately, I came across this extraordinary volume of essays too late to take into account in the following argument.

38. The same argument could be made concerning the widespread explorations into post-Kantian theories of cosmopolitanism.

39. Jacques Derrida, "The Villanova Roundtable: A Conversation with Jacques Derrida," in *Deconstruction in a Nutshell: A Conversation with Jacques Derrida*, ed. John D. Caputo (New York: Fordham University Press, 1997), 12.

40. Richard Beardsworth offers an incisive reading of Derrida's rethinking of the political in terms of questions of temporality in *Derrida & the Political* (London: Routledge, 1996).

41. See Jean-Paul Martinon's excellent commentary in *On Futurity: Malabou, Nancy and Derrida* (Basingstoke: Palgrave Macmillan, 2007).

42. As Derrida writes in *Rogues*, "the thinking of the political has always been a thinking of différance and the thinking of différance always a thinking *of* the political, of the contour and limits of the political, especially around the enigma or autoimmune *double bind* of the democratic." Since it responds to the discourse of rights commonly associated with citizenship, the larger context in which Derrida makes this general claim merits recalling: "Democracy is what it is only in the *différance* by which it defers itself and differs from itself. It is what it is only by spacing itself beyond being and even beyond ontological difference; it is (without being) equal and proper to itself only insofar as it is inadequate and improper, at the same time behind and ahead of itself, behind and ahead of the Sameness and Oneness of itself; it is thus interminable in its incompletion beyond all determinate forms of incompletion, beyond all the limitations in areas as different as the right to vote (for example in its extension to women—but starting when?—to minors—but starting at what age?—or to foreigners—but which ones and on what lands?—to cite at random just a few exemplary problems from among so many other similar ones), the freedom of the press, the end of social inequalities throughout the world, the right to work, or any other number of other rights. Such limitations thus involve the entire history of a right or a law (whether national or international) that is always unequal to justice, democracy seeking its place only at the unstable and unlocatable border between law and justice, that is, between the political and the ultrapolitical. That is why, once again, it is never certain that 'democracy' is a political concept through and through." See Jacques Derrida, *Voyous: Deux essais sur la raison* (Paris: Galilée, 2003), 63, trans. Pascale-Anne Brault and Michael Naas as *Rogues: Two Essays on Reason* (Stanford, Calif.: Stanford University Press, 2005), 38–39.

43. Jean-Luc Nancy, *Le sens du monde* (Paris: Galilée, 1993), 144–45 (hereafter cited as *SM*), trans. Jeffrey S. Librett as *The Sense of the World* (Minneapolis: University of Minnesota Press, 1997), 91–92 (hereafter cited as *SW*).

44. As Nancy notes, "the very idea of the *Republic* represents this point of reciprocity, in its more than infinitely delicate equilibrium" (*SM*, 167–68/*SW*, 106). The argument might be read across the references to the specific *spatial* problematic (if not aporia) of "postmodern republicanism" in the writings of Hardt and Negri (to whom we will turn in chapter 4), notably their argument concerning the possible "*place* from which we can launch our critique and launch an alternative" to Empire. As they argue (and here we recall Lacoue-Labarthe's affirmation of ek-sistence, following Heidegger, as "the place without a space of its own, non-localisable as such (and which nevertheless

remains a place)," "as if we are consigned to the non-place of Empire, can we construct a powerful non-place and realize it concretely, as the terrain of a postmodern republicanism?" See Michael Hardt and Antonio Negri, *Empire* (Cambridge, Mass.: Harvard University Press, 2000), 208.

45. Jean-Luc Nancy, *Être singulier pluriel* (Paris: Galilée, 1996), 50 (hereafter cited as *ESP*), trans. Robert D. Richardson and Anne E. O'Bryne as *Being Singular Plural* (Stanford, Calif.: Stanford University Press, 2000), 30 (hereafter cited as *BSP*). Nancy translates Hegel's *Gemeinschaftlichkeit* as "community." Dominique Leydet's entry on "Citizenship" in the *Stanford Encyclopedia of Philosophy* (http://plato.stanford.edu/entries/citizenship/) also concludes by turning on this distinction between citizenship and the subject and its implications for thinking the future of citizenship.

46. See Carl Schmitt, *Politische Theologie: Vier Kapitel zur Lehre von der Souveränität* (1922; Berlin: Duncker & Humblot, 1934), trans. George Schwab as *Political Theology: Four Chapters on the Concept of Sovereignty* (Chicago: University of Chicago Press, 1985). The reference to Schmitt's seminal concept of the theologicopolitical again points to a paradoxical situation. As Nancy writes, "if it is exact that 'all significant concepts of the modern theory of the state are secularized theological concepts' [as Schmitt states], it is not less exact that it is *also*, at the same time, in order to exit from the State, and in any case from the State according to its merely secularized theory, that, in principle, the exit from the theologicopolitical has been employed" (*SM*, 145/*SW*, 92). As Nancy goes on to suggest, the argument points less to a paradox than to the terms in which to rethink the "end of philosophy." Or again, the question might be reformulated by arguing that the "retreat" of the political inaugurated by the end of philosophy is not defined in terms of a paradox.

47. Or as Nancy writes in *Being Singular Plural*, "sovereignty is nothing but the *com-*; as such, it is always and indefinitely 'to be completed,' as in *com-*munism or *com-*passion" (*ESP*, 56/*BSP*, 36). Nancy's rethinking of sovereignty suggests several proximities to Derrida's reading of the concept in *Rogues*, notably given the relation between Nancy's foregrounding of questions of political self-sufficiency in *The Sense of the World* and Derrida's concept "auto-immunity." In an argument that turns us again to the language in which Nancy articulates his own rethinking of forms of political self-sufficiency, Derrida writes, "To confer sense or meaning on sovereignty, to justify it, to find a reason for it, is already to compromise its deciding exceptionality, to subject it to rules, to a code of law, to some general law, to concepts. It is thus to divide it, to subject it to partitioning, to participation, to being shared. It is to take into account the part played by sovereignty. And to take that part or share into account is to turn sovereignty against itself to compromise its immunity. This happens as soon as one speaks of it in order to give it or find in it some sense or meaning. But since this happens all the time, pure sovereignty does not exist; it is always in the process of positing itself by refuting itself, by denying or disavowing itself; it

is always in the process of autoimmunizing itself, of betraying itself by betraying the democracy that nonetheless can never do without it" (*Voyous*, 144/*Rogues*, 101). Significantly, this rethinking of the place of sovereignty in democracy for Derrida is not only a question of "paradox" but takes us "beyond citizenship," a pronouncement reiterated throughout the text and shared by Rodolphe Gasché in his review of *Rogues*. See Rodolphe Gasché, "'In the Name of Reason': The Deconstruction of Sovereignty" *Research in Phenomenology* 34 (2004): 289–303, which also offers a useful set of comparisons between a deconstructive reading of sovereignty and the writings of both Habermas and Agamben.

48. See Jean-Luc Nancy, *Être singulier pluriel*, 50; *Being Singular Plural*, 30, which may be read as an extension of Nancy's longer reading of Hegel in "La juridiction du monarque hégélian" in *Rejouer le politique*, ed. Luc Ferry, Jean-Luc Nancy, et al., (Paris: Galilée, 1981), trans. Mary Ann and Peter Caws as "The Jurisdiction of the Hegelian Monarch," in *The Birth to Presence* (Stanford, Calif.: Stanford University Press, 1993), 110–42. In his introduction to Nancy's book on Hegel, Jason Smith offers a compelling argument concerning the implications of Nancy's reading of Hegel for theories of the State. See Jason Smith, "Introduction: Nancy's Hegel, the State, and Us," in Jean-Luc Nancy, *Hegel: The Restlessness of the Negative*, trans. Jason Smith and Steven Miller (Minneapolis: University of Minnesota Press, 2002), ix–xxix.

49. Jean-Luc Nancy, *La communauté désoeuvrée* (Paris: Christian Bourgeois, 1986), 75, trans. Peter Connor as *The Inoperative Community* (Minneapolis: University of Minnesota Press, 1991), 29–30. The term *comparution* or "compearance"—a legal term that refers to an act of appearing before a court—is explored by Nancy in "La comparution," 47–100; "La Comparution/The Compearance," 371–98. For a reading of the aporetic structure of Rousseau's "contract" that turns on the same problematic raised in Nancy's argument, notably as this reading turns us back to Paul de Man's writings on Rousseau, see Samuel Weber, "In the Name of the Law," in *Deconstruction and the Possibility of Justice*, ed. Drucilla Cornell, Michel Rosenfeld, and David Gray Carlson, 232–57.

50. As noted in the first chapter (see note 39, p. 26), the reference is to the volume edited by Nancy with Eduardo Cadava and Peter Connor, *Who Comes after the Subject?* (London: Routledge, 1991). One might note that Étienne Balibar's essay in this same volume is titled "Citizen Subject," an essay that might usefully be read in light of Nancy's larger argument in *The Sense of the World*.

51. Thus Raffoul notes that Nancy's references to *partage* refer to a "paradoxical indissociability; in sharing something, we necessarily also divide it," thus suggesting "the paradoxical concept of a sharing that cannot be shared" or "the indissociability of singularity and plurality." See François Raffoul, "The Logic of the With: On Nancy's *Être Singulier Pluriel*," *Studies in Practical Philosophy* 1, no. 1 (Spring 1999): 42–43.

As noted in our introduction, we recall that, in *Being Singular Plural*, Nancy terms an "extreme paradox" the logic in which to think the other as "the other of the with." The question remains whether an insistence on thinking this extremity allows us to prolong the logic of paradox to which it is tied here. At the same time, the question of paradox opens up the relation of Nancy's writings to those of Lacoue-Labarthe, for whom the appeal to paradox is quite frequent. As Lacoue-Labarthe writes in his presentation at Cérisy, "every relation—*and there is* relation—is, as Blanchot would say, 'relation without relation,'" and this would constitute for Lacoue-Labarthe "the pure form of the paradoxical" (*FH*, 432–33/*RP*, 72).

52. See David Held, *Democracy and the Global Order: From the Modern State to Cosmopolitan Governance* (Stanford, Calif.: Stanford University Press, 1995).

53. See Derrida, "Force of Law," 21.

3. The Disposition of Being

1. See Jean-Luc Nancy, *Être singulier pluriel* (Paris: Galilée, 1996), 47–48 (hereafter cited as *ESP*), trans. Robert D. Richardson and Anne E. O'Bryne as *Being Singular Plural* (Stanford, Calif.: Stanford University Press, 2000), 28 (hereafter cited as *BSP*).

2. Lévinas refers to "la trame de l'être" in *Totalité et Infini: Essai sur l'extériorité* (The Hague: Martinus Nijhoff, 1961), 79, trans. Alphonso Lingis as *Totality and Infinity, An Essay on Exteriority* (Pittsburg: Duquesne University Press, 1969), 81.

3. Jean-Luc Nancy, *Le sens du monde* (Paris: Galilée, 1993), 80 (hereafter cited as *SM*), trans. Jeffrey S. Librett as *The Sense of the World* (Minneapolis: University of Minnesota Press, 1997), 40 (hereafter cited as *SW*).

4. For a representative introduction to the "new science" of networks, see Albert-László Barabási, *Linked: How Everything Is Connected to Everything Else and What It Means for Business, Science, and Everyday Life* (London: Plume, 2003). On global assemblages, see Aihwa Ong and Stephen J. Collier, *Global Assemblages: Technology, Politics, and Ethics as Anthropological Problems* (Malden, MA: Blackwell, 2005). See also Niklas Luhmann, *Social Systems*, trans. John Bednarz, Jr. (Stanford, Calif.: Stanford University Press, 1995); Gilles Deleuze and Félix Guattari, *A Thousand Plateaus: Capitalism and Schizophrenia*, trans. Brian Massumi (Minneapolis: University of Minnesota Press, 1987); Annelise Riles, *The Network Inside Out* (Ann Arbor: University of Michigan Press, 2000); Manuel Castells, *The Internet Galaxy: Reflections on the Internet, Business, and Society* (Oxford: Oxford University Press, 2001); Mark Taylor, *The Moment of Complexity: Emerging Network Culture* (Chicago: University of Chicago Press, 2001); and Manuel de Landa, *A Thousand Years of Nonlinear History* (New York: Zone, 2000).

5. In addition to *Being Singular Plural* and *The Sense of the World*, see *The Creation of the World or Globalization*, trans. François Raffoul and David Pettigrew (Albany:

State University of New York Press, 2007), which includes essays on globalization, biopolitics, and ecotechnics.

6. We encounter here the well-known problem of translating the German *Sein* into English (in distinction from *Seiendes* in Heidegger's lexicon), where the usual compromise of capitalizing Being tends to efface precisely what is at stake in its disposition or "being-with" (where the capitalization is removed). It should be recalled, even when Being is capitalized in the pages that follow, that being-with for Nancy is not a *subsequent* displacement of Being but co-originary and co-essential.

7. This is not to say that there are not vestiges of "being-with" or the "disposition of Being" in the vast literature on networks. One could argue that even the "six degrees of separation" thesis that so mesmerizes the gurus of the "new science" of networks attests to the question of relation or disposition that concerns us in the pages that follow. No doubt Nancy's insistence on rethinking networks in terms of ontology also serves to reopen the question of ontology within the vast literature on networks. Whether in the numerous appeals to redefine the identity of the networked subject in terms derived from anthropology or theories of complexity, or in the wide diversity of writings on cyberculture, virtual communities, and the posthuman body, ontological assumptions and presuppositions are pervasive in the literature, however radical the proposed critique of the subject. While this is not the task pursued in the pages that follow, one could also find the same ontological presuppositions informing the seminal writings of Bruno Latour, Michel de Certeau, or Niklas Luhmann, however contentious or innovative their respective proposals to rethink the place of networks in our modernity. But it is not just the metaphysical and ontological presuppositions of the subject that is at stake here. The question remains how the discourse of networks in general avoids Augustine's ontotheological definition of God, of a Being that is everywhere and whose center is nowhere.

8. A motif taken up by Carl Schmitt, as well as in the writings of Arendt, Sartre, and Derrida, among others, Nancy shares the Nietzschean motif of the desert with Deleuze, specifically acknowledging Deleuze and Guattari's references to the desert and "nomadic" space in *A Thousand Plateaus*. See *L'expérience de la liberté* (Paris: Galilée, 1988), 187–88, trans. Bridget McDonald as *The Experience of Freedom* (Stanford, Calif.: Stanford University Press, 1993), 145–46.

9. For a comprehensive introduction to Nancy's writings on the subject, see Ian James, *The Fragmentary Demand: An Introduction to the Philosophy of Jean-Luc Nancy* (Stanford, Calif.: Stanford University Press, 2006), 11–64. References to Nancy's writings on the subject also figure prominently in John Martis, *Philippe Lacoue-Labarthe: Representation and the Loss of the Subject* (New York: Fordham University Press, 2005).

10. In addition to *Being Singular Plural*, Nancy offers an extensive reflection on singularities in "Limits, Borders, and Shores of Singularity," trans. Michael Sanders, in *Encounters with Alphonso Lingis*, ed. Alexander E. Hooke and Wolfgang W. Fuchs (Lanham, Md.: Lexington, 2003), 101–8.

11. If Nancy refers to a syntax of being throughout both *The Sense of the World* and *Being Singular Plural*, the reference to grammar is raised in his introduction to Eduardo Cadava, Peter Connor, and Jean-Luc Nancy, eds., *Who Comes after the Subject?* (New York: Routledge, 1991), 1–8. François Warin inflects this grammar by proposing that "between the 'us all' of abstract universalism and the 'me, I' of miserable individualism, there is the 'we others' of Nietzsche, a thinking of the singular case that thwarts the opposition of the particular and the universal" (cited in *ESP*, 23/*BSP*, 194–95). The question of grammar at stake here is also taken up in relation to ontology in Judith Butler, *The Psychic Life of Power: Theories in Subjection* (Stanford, Calif.: Stanford University Press), 1997, notably in her reading of Althusser.

12. Jean-Luc Nancy, *L'Oubli de la philosophie* (Paris: Galilée, 1986), 95, trans. Francois Raffoul and Gregory Recco in *The Gravity of Thought* (Atlantic Highlands, N.J.: Humanities Press, 1997), 62.

13. See Peggy Kamuf's incisive discussion of hyphenation in Nancy's *Being Singular Plural* in "Singular Sense, Second-Hand," in *Book of Addresses* (Stanford, Calif.: Stanford University Press, 2005), 268–81. The question of writing foregrounded here cannot be detached from Nancy's long-standing concern (which he shares with Lacoue-Labarthe) with philosophy's own style of presentation or *Darstellung*.

14. As the reference to "touching" in the previous quotation suggests, other paths through Nancy's writings are also possible. See notably Jacques Derrida's *Le toucher* (Paris: Galilée, 2000), trans. Christine Irizarry as *On Touching—Jean-Luc Nancy* (Stanford, Calif.: Stanford University Press, 2005).

15. In addition to Nancy's own writings on Heidegger's references to *Mitsein* and *Mitdasein*, see Christopher Fynsk, *Heidegger: Thought and Historicity* (Ithaca, N.Y.: Cornell University Press, 1986); and François Raffoul, *Heidegger and the Subject*, trans. David Pettigrew and Gregory Recco (New Jersey: Humanities Press, 1988).

16. In an accompanying footnote to *Being Singular Plural*, Nancy situates his appeal to the disposition of Being in light of a number of other contemporary thinkers in which the question of the relation of the "One" and the "Many" is rethought. As Nancy proposes, "one should look at those texts where this preoccupation comes to us in the first place: the texts of Gilles Deleuze along with those of Jacques Derrida (and this *with* will demand its own commentary some day). Basically, this preoccupation travels in the same direction as that undertaken by Giorgio Agamben, on one side, and Alain Badiou, on the other (even if Badiou wants to put the question in the form of an opposition by playing multiplicity against the One). All of this is to make the point that we are only thinking about the ones *with* the others [*les uns* avec *les autres*] (by, against, in spite of, close to, far from, in touch with, in avoiding it, in digging through it)" (*ESP*, 48–49/*BSP*, 198).

17. As Julian Wolfreys suggests, the *between* "names, even as it traces, an unmappable space, a spacing whose crossing implicates a temporality without measure.... Preceding in principle any subject or object, it nonetheless is constituted through an

uncanny motion, uncanny precisely because not only is this *between*, every *between* without a proper home, but also its interval and traversal is comprehended or recognized after the fact, as the *retrait* of some *après-coup.*" See Julian Wolfreys, "Between: Speculations," in *Occasional Deconstructions* (Albany: State University of New York Press, 2004), 88. The force of thinking this "between" also emerges throughout the writings of Homi Bhabba.

18. Nancy's insistence on thinking this interval "between" ties into a number of feminist writings. To cite only two prominent references close to Nancy, the writings of Hélène Cixous refer to this motif with some frequency, while Luce Irigaray writes, "The problem of *we* is that of a meeting which occurs through good fortune, as it were (a *kairos*?), or partly that of a coincidence whose necessity escapes us, but it is also or especially that of constituting a temporality: together, with, between. All too often, sacramental or juridical commitment and the obligation to reproduce have compensated for this problem: how to construct a temporality between us?" See Luce Irigaray, *I Love to You*, trans. Alison Martin (London: Routledge, 1996), 110–11. We recall that, for Irigaray, democracy "begins between two."

19. Citing Nancy's *Being Singular Plural* as part of his argument, the aporetic condition of Being in its disposition is prompted by Samuel Weber's reading of Heidegger in *Theatricality as Medium*, where he proposes "the aporetical juncture of being (as *Sein*) with to-be (as *Seienden*): that is, what might be described as the *aporetical singularity of being.*" We are suggesting, in turn, that Nancy's rewrites this "aporetical singularity" by articulating the dis-position of being in terms of its reticulated spacing. See Samuel Weber, *Theatricality as Medium* (New York: Fordham University Press, 2004), 62.

20. Nancy's engagement with Husserl in *Being Singular Plural*, including Husserl's consideration of a "transcendental intersubjectivity," is briefly explored by Jason Smith in his "Introduction: Nancy's Hegel, the State, and Us," in Jean-Luc Nancy, *Hegel: The Restlessness of the Negative*, trans Jason Smith and Steven Miller (Minneapolis: University of Minnesota Press, 2002), ix–xxix. Ian James also takes up Nancy's references to Husserl in *The Fragmentary Demand*. Nancy's engagement with Husserl throughout his writings awaits extensive commentary.

21. Nancy specifically refers to the role Marx and Marxism plays in the writings, among others, of Jacques Rancière, Étienne Balibar, Antonio Negri, Gilles Deleuze, Alain Badiou, Jacques Derrida, and Michel Henry.

22. Nancy's review of Althusser's *For Marx* and *Reading Capital*, "Marx et la philosophie," appeared in *Esprit* (May 1966): 1074–87.

23. See Jean-Christophe Bailly and Jean-Luc Nancy, *La comparution: Politiques à venir* (Paris: Christian Bourgeois, 1991), 66, trans. Tracy B. Strong as "La Comparution/The Compearance: From the Existence of 'Communism' to the Community of 'Existence,'" *Political Theory* 20, no. 3 (August 1992): 378.

24. See Lorenzo Fabbri, "Philosophy as Chance: An Interview with Jean-Luc Nancy," trans. Pascale-Anne Brault and Michael Naas, *Critical Inquiry* 33 (Winter 2007): 436.

25. Of course, *Specters of Marx* is not a belated engagement with Marx and Marxism but part of a longer dialogue concerning the political that Derrida shared with Nancy and others over several decades. More recently, Derrida echoes the tenor of Nancy's argument by suggesting that "this same insurrection in the name of justice to give rise to critiques that are Marxist in *inspiration*, Marxist in *spirit*—this cannot fail to happen again. There are signs of it. It is like a new International without party, without organization, without association.…This insurrectional restlessness will recover from Marxist inspiration forces for which we have no names." See the interview with Derrida in "La déconstruction de l'actualité," *Passages* 57 (1993): 74, trans. Jennifer Bajorek as "Artifactualities," in Jacques Derrida and Bernard Stiegler, *Echographies of Television: Filmed Interviews* (Cambridge, UK: Polity Press, 2002), 27. We will take up Derrida's reference to force in the last chapter, simply commenting for the moment that it will be necessary to rethink Derrida's insistence on equating the political institution of the "party" with questions of organization and association.

26. See Jean-Christophe Bailly and Jean-Luc Nancy, *La comparution: Politiques à venir*, 61; "La Comparution/The Compearance," 376.

27. Nancy explores this question further in the section on "labor" in *The Sense of the World* (see *SM*, 149–62/*SW*, 95–102), in several essays published between 1979 and 2004 in the journals *Diagraphe* and *Futur Antérieur* under the general title "Monogrammes," as well as in *The Creation of the World or Globalization*. See also Christopher Fynsk's discussion in the political seminar at Cérisy (included in *RP*, 93). A similar argument is explored in recent debates between Giorgio Agamben and Antonio Negri.

28. Nancy refers to the *découplage* of politics from being-in-common in *La Communauté affrontée* (Paris: Galilée, 2001), 34. The same argument is pursued in a number of recent interviews, including "Rien que le monde," *Vacarme* 11 (April 2000), trans. Jason Smith as "Nothing but the World: An Interview with *Vacarme*," *Rethinking Marxism* 19, no. 4 (October 2007): 521–35; "Is Everything Political?" trans. Philip M. Adamek, *New Centennial Review* 2, no. 3 (2002): 15–22; "The Question of the Common and the Responsibility of the Universal," an interview with Jean-Luc Nancy, Artem Magun, and Oxana Timofeeva, in "What do we have in common?" special issue, *Chto delat? / What Is to Be Done?* 9 (May 2005), http://www.chtodelat .org; and the recent book *Vérité de la democratie* (Paris: Galilée, 2008).

29. See Michel Foucault, "What is Enlightenment?" in *The Essential Foucault*, ed. Paul Rabinow and Nikolas Rose (New York: The New Press, 2003), 54; Ernesto Laclau and Chantal Mouffe, preface to the second edition of *Hegemony and Socialist Strategy: Towards a Radical Democratic Politics* (London: Verso, 2001), xiv; Giorgio

Agamben, preface to *Means without End: Notes on Politics*, trans. Vincenzo Binetti and Cesare Casarino (Minneapolis: University of Minnesota Press, 2000), ix; Judith Butler, "Competing Universalities," in *Contingency, Hegemony, Universality: Contemporary Dialogues on the Left*, ed. Judith Butler, Ernesto Laclau, and Slavoj Žižek (London: Verso, 2000), 178.

30. See John Arquilla and David Ronfeldt, *Networks and Netwars: The Future of Terror, Crime, and Militancy* (Santa Monica, Calif.: RAND, 2001), v (my emphasis). Given that the book appears under the auspices of the RAND National Defense Research Institute, it is perhaps hardly surprising that the authors tend to make such conflations appear self-evident. Since the writing of their book, definitions of terrorism have expanded to such a degree as to make such a conflation legally binding.

31. See Alexander R. Galloway, *Protocol: How Control Exists after Decentralization* (Cambridge, Mass: MIT Press, 2004), and Alexander R. Galloway and Eugene Thacker, *The Exploit: A Theory of Networks* (Minneapolis: University of Minnesota Press, 2007), which offer an important and engaged response to this task.

32. While genealogies of networks are conspicuously lacking in English, it might be suggested that the language of tying and knotting that Nancy inherits from Plato exists in numerous other traditions, an observation whose implications we will take up on another occasion.

33. It is difficult to know exactly what Nancy has in mind when he refers here to a gesture. Agamben offers us a provisional response in his "Notes on Gesture" in *Means without End*, 49–60, though Nancy appears to be drawing from Lévinas, who refers to *"la geste de l'être"* in the opening lines of *Humanisme de l'autre homme* (Paris: Fata Morgana, 1972), 8, trans. Nidra Poller as *Humanism of the Other* (Urbana: University of Illinois Press, 2006), 3.

34. The argument proposed here opens onto a rereading of numerous texts in which the constitutive possibility of dissociation and disconnection is closed off or excluded in the positing of social relations and political ties. To take one prominent example, Bruno Latour's seminal writings on networks, attachments, and actor-network theory are continually marked by their refusal to engage in the problematic of dissociation and disconnection that concerns us here, a refusal that comes to shape Latour's often ambivalent rapport with questions of the political. For two thinkers close to Nancy who engage the question of dissociation and "unbinding" as constitutive of rethinking the political, see Alain Badiou, "Politics Unbound," in *Metapolitics* (London: Verso, 2005), 68–77; and Jacques Rancière, "Ten Theses on Politics," *Theory and Event* 5, no. 3 (2001), a text that continues a number of proposals outlined in his lecture for the Center in Paris (see *RT*, 89–111). Nancy's own re-elaboration of this motif informs his brief essay on Deleuze, in which he reads their proximity and simultaneous distance from one another precisely in terms of the tying and folding of knots. See Jean-Luc Nancy, "The Deleuzian Fold of Thought," in *Deleuze: A Critical*

Reader, ed. Paul Patton (Oxford: Blackwell, 1996), 107–13. Nancy frequently refers to the same language of tying and untying when thinking the relation between Deleuze and Derrida (see, for example, *SM*, 73/*SW*, 180). Lastly, the reference to networks in terms of the tying and untying of knots invites a rereading of Foucault's concept of genealogy. In his discussion of Nietzsche, for example, Foucault argues that the analysis of *Herkunft*—which Foucault defines as "the ancient affiliation [*appartenance*] to a group, tied together by the bonds of blood, tradition, or social class [*celui qui se noue entre ceux de même hauteur ou de même bassesse*]"—"often puts into play or displays [*met en jeu*] a consideration of race or social type. But the traits it attempts to identify are not the exclusive generic characteristics of an individual, a sentiment, or an idea, which permit us to qualify them as 'Greek' or 'English'; rather, it seeks the subtle, singular, and subindividual traits that might possibly intersect [*s'entrecroiser*] in them to form a network [*réseau*] that is difficult to unravel. Far from being a category of resemblance, this origin allows the different traits to be unraveled [*débrouiller*] in order to set them apart." See Michel Foucault, "Nietzsche, la généalogie, l'histoire," in *Dits et écrits*, vol. 2 (Paris: Gallimard, 1994), 140–41, trans. Donald F. Bouchard and Sherry Simon as "Nietzsche, Genealogy, History," in *Language, Counter-Memory, Practice: Selected Essays and Interviews* (Ithaca: Cornell University Press, 1977), 145 (translation modified). The question remains to what extent Foucault's more widely known analysis of "subjectification" or "technologies of the self" effaces the "subtle, singular, and subindividual" network of traits that remain in play here.

35. For a compelling exploration of this question, see Steven Shaviro, *Connected, or What It Means to Live in the Network Society* (Minneapolis: University of Minnesota Press, 2003).

36. It is not just reference to German that is illuminating here. As we explored in the first chapter, according to the *OED*, the prefix *dis-* in English is defined as something being "in twain," implying a movement in different directions, apart, or asunder, and so further implies a movement abroad or away, a "between," in the sense of "to separate or distinguish," and a separation in the sense of "singly" or "one by one." When prefixing verbs having already a sense of "division, solution, separation, or undoing," the *dis-* is intensive.

37. Nancy is referring to Giorgio Agamben's essay "From-of-Life" in *Means without End*, 10 (first published in French in *Futur antérieur*). Agamben's writings are taken up more extensively in the last chapter.

38. See Christopher Fynsk, *Language and Relation:...that there is language* (Stanford, Calif.: Stanford University Press, 1996). If the title draws from Lacoue-Labarthe's presentation at Cérisy, Fynsk extends this question of language and relation to close readings of Heidegger, Celan, Irigaray, Benjamin, and Blanchot. He frames these readings by remarking that he is "drawn constantly by the question of relation as such (as given in language), a question, once again, of ontological, political, and ethical

import. I am drawn to a thought of the an-archic relationality of Being, and the possibility of an affirmative assumption of that relationality—both for the extremity of play it involves and for what it promises of engagement" (11). If Fynsk finds Hölderlin and Francis Bacon exemplary in this regard, the argument that follows turns to more collective affiliations of such relationality, closer, perhaps, to Agamben's "whatever singularities" or Nancy's anonymous "someones." As we will argue, the "an-archic relationality of Being" also finds its force of engagement and affirmation in the (im)possibilities of these collective affiliations, and so touch on the limits of Nancy's thinking in different ways than suggested by Fynsk's remarkable book.

39. Ian James has offered a useful and comprehensive overview of Nancy's writings on space in *The Fragmentary Demand*, 65–113.

40. See Jacques Derrida, *Specters of Marx: The State of the Debt, the Work of Mourning, and the New International*, trans. Peggy Kamuf (New York: Routledge, 1994), 82.

41. See Emmanuel Lévinas, *Totalité et Infini: Essai sur l'extériorité*, 323; *Totality and Infinity, An Essay on Exteriority*, 291; and Maurice Blanchot, *L'Entretien infini* (Paris: Gallimard, 1969), trans. Susan Hanson as *The Infinite Conversation* (Minneapolis: University of Minnesota Press, 1993), 66–79, where Blanchot rephrases this curvature of space in terms of a "Riemann surface."

42. Jason Smith, "Introduction," xi. While questioning Smith's assertion that these questions come into focus in the wake of Nancy's *The Inoperative Community* and not earlier, the argument that follows is clearly indebted to Smith's brief, if suggestive, introduction.

43. Claude Lefort's influential writings on political typologies are presented in *The Political Forms of Modern Society: Bureaucracy, Democracy, Totalitarianism*, ed. John B. Thompson (Cambridge, Mass.: MIT Press, 1986). If Lefort's writings had figured prominently in Lacoue-Labarthe and Nancy's Center in Paris, it should be noted that both Nancy and Derrida's respective rethinking of the political contains a number of largely implicit references to Lefort's seminal work. As regard Agamben's concept of "form-of-life," a concept that is central to his own articulation of "bare" or "naked" life in *Homo Sacer*, it can be suggested that Nancy's articulation of the "disposition of Being" is offered as an exact counterpoint to Agamben's "form-of-life," just as his gesture to seek the "merest opening of space" creates a counterpoint to Agamben's paradigmatic site of the biopolitical (the camps). If this argument invites a more extensive reading of Nancy and Agamben's sustained dialogue with each others' work, one that will get taken up in the last chapter, suffice it to remark that Agamben continually reduces the "form-of-life" or "whatever singularities" to identifiable *figures*. As we will argue in the next chapter, it is precisely this turn to the figure that the metaphysics of the Subject remains presupposed.

44. In *The Sense of the World*, Nancy notes that, "to avoid all ambiguity, it is necessary to point out that religion has nothing to do with the tie, contrary to what a

counterfeit etymology pretends. *Religio* is scrupulous observation, and consequently, it implies that the knot is already tied or given" (*SM*, 173–74/*SW*, 192n119). Nancy's assertion here gestures toward a rereading of Lévinas.

45. Jean-Luc Nancy, *The Inoperative Community*, xxxvii. On the question of collectivity, see also Jean-Luc Nancy, *L'Oubli de la philosophie*, 94; *The Gravity of Thought*, 62.

46. Jean-Luc Nancy, *L'Oubli de la philosophie*, 100–101; *The Gravity of Thought*, 65–66.

47. Nancy elaborates on the Lacanian implications of this reading in a long footnote in *SM*, 179/*SW*, 123–24n123. Nancy's most extensive discussion of fraternity (and rejoinder to Derrida's criticisms) is his essay in *La démocratie à venir: Autour de Jacques Derrida* (Paris: Galilée, 2004), 341–59. If the essay significantly turns on a reading of the great revolutionary song, "Le Chant du Départ," Nancy's essay also addresses Hardt and Negri's concept of the multitude, to which we will turn in the next chapter. In *The Experience of Freedom*, Nancy argues that freedom has nothing to do with the autonomy of subject but the *"partage de la liberté."* As he writes, "the linking or interlacing of relations [*l'enchaînement ou l'entrelacement des rapports*] doubtless does not precede freedom, but is contemporaneous and coextensive with it, in the same way that being-in-common is contemporaneous with singular existence and coextensive with its own spatiality." See *L'expérience de la liberté*, 91; *The Experience of Freedom*, 66.

48. Having listed a number of these "bloody conflicts" occurring in the world as he was writing the preface to *Being Singular Plural* in the summer of 1995, Nancy writes, "This earth is anything but a sharing out [*partage*] of humanity. It is a world that does not even manage to constitute a world; it is a world lacking in world, and lacking in the meaning of world. It is an enumeration that brings to light the sheer number and proliferation of these various poles of attraction and repulsion. It is an endless list, and everything happens in such a way that one is reduced to keeping accounts but never taking the final toll. It is a litany, a prayer of pure sorrow and pure loss, the pleas that falls from the lips of millions of refugees every day: whether they be deportees, people besieged, those who are mutilated, people who starve, who are raped, ostracized, excluded, exiled, expelled." Nancy concludes with the suggestion that what he is talking about here is "compassion, but not compassion as a pity that feels sorry for itself and feeds on itself. Com-passion is the contagion, the contact of being with one another [*d'être les uns avec les autres*] in this turmoil. Compassion is not altruism, nor is it identification; it is the disturbance of violent relatedness [*l'ébranlement de la contiguïté brutale*]" (*ESP*, 12/*BSP*, xiii).

49. Nancy's argument invites a rereading of Laclau and Mouffe's influential notion of "equivalence building" in *Hegemony and Socialist Strategy: Towards a Radical Democratic Politics*. The ontological presuppositions of Laclau and Mouffe's concept are briefly addressed in Alex Thompson, *Deconstruction and Democracy: Derrida's*

Politics of Friendship (London: Continuum, 2005) and in several essays in *Laclau: A Critical Reader*, ed. Simon Critchley and Oliver Marchart (London: Routledge, 2004).

50. Without speaking," Lacoue-Labarthe continues, "of the colonization of Eastern Europe, of the repression of all acts of open revolt (Poznan, Budapest, etc.) or, more generally, of Soviet imperialism—which is every bit equal to that of America" (*FH*, 496; *RP*, 98). The question of councils and their relation to the writings of both Arendt and Nancy was taken up by Artem Magun in a wonderful paper presented at the Annual Meeting of the International Association for Philosophy and Literature (IAPL), University of Helsinki, in June 2005.

51. See Nancy's own commentary on this question of community in *La Communauté affrontée* (Paris: Galilée, 2001); and "Conloquium," in Roberto Esposito, *Communitas: Origin et destin de la communauté* (Paris: Presses Universitaires de France, 2000), 3–10. See also the essays included in the volume "Community," ed. Dorota Glowacka, *Culture Machine* 8 (2006), http://www.culturemachine.net/index.php/cm/issue/view/4. Even though Nancy has published widely since its publication, the essays included in the Miami Theory Collective's *Community at Loose Ends* (Minneapolis: University of Minnesota Press, 1991) have also lost little of their critical resonance.

52. Maurice Blanchot, "Le communisme sans héritage," in *Écrits Politiques: 1958–1993* (Paris: Editions Leo Scheer, 2003), 115, trans. Michael Holland as "Communism without a Heritage," in *The Blanchot Reader* (Oxford: Blackwell, 1995), 203. The text was first published anonymously in *Comité*, a single-issue journal published in relation to the events of May '68.

4. Being Communist

1. Michael Hardt and Antonio Negri, *Empire* (Cambridge, Mass.: Harvard University Press, 2000), 413 (hereafter cited as *E*).

2. See Negri's discussion of these references in his interview with Cesare Casarino, "It's a Powerful Life: A Conversation on Contemporary Philosophy," *Cultural Critique* 57 (Spring 2004): 151–83.

3. Antonio Negri, "The Specter's Smile" in *Ghostly Demarcations: A Symposium on Jacques Derrida's Specters of Marx*, ed. Michael Sprinker (London: Verso, 1999), 5–16. See also Negri's "Pour une définition ontologique de la multitude," *Multitudes* 9 (May 2002), http://multitudes.samizdat.net/spip.php?article29, trans. Arianna Bove as "Approximations: Towards an Ontological Definition of the Multitude," http://www.generation-online.org/t/approximations.htm.

4. See Paolo Virno, *A Grammar of the Multitude*, trans. Isabella Bertoletti, James Cascaito, and Andrea Casson (New York: Semiotexte, 2004).

5. Cesare Casarino raises several related problematics in his interview with Negri in "It's a Powerful Life: A Conversation on Contemporary Philosophy." Our reading of *Empire* in terms of figures would also need to take into account Hardt and Negri's references to the writings of Deleuze and Guattari, less the more overt debt to *A Thousand Plateaus* acknowledged at the opening of *Empire* than *What Is Philosophy?*, in which Deleuze and Guattari propose a definition of the "plane of immanence" by distinguishing between "figures" and "conceptual personae." See Gilles Deleuze and Félix Guattari, *Qu'est-ce que la philosophie?* (Paris: Minuit, 1991), 60–81, trans. Graham Burchell and Hugh Tomlinson as *What Is Philosophy?* (London: Verso, 1994), 61–83.

6. The question of disfiguring is a persistent aspect of Gayatri Spivak's writings and suggests a close debt to the writings of Paul de Man. One might also note here Derrida's argument concerning Marx that the "essence of the political will always have the inessential figure, the very anessence of a ghost." See Jacques Derrida, *Spectres de Marx* (Paris: Galilée, 1993), 167, trans. Peggy Kamuf as *Specters of Marx* (New York: Routledge, 1994), 102.

7. Nancy rethinks the concept of the biopolitical through the question of the figure in *La création du monde ou la mondialisation* (Paris: Galilée, 2002), 137–43, trans. François Raffoul and David Pettigrew as *The Creation of the World or Globalization* (Albany: State University of New York Press, 2007), 93–95.

8. See Ernst Jünger, *Der Arbeiter* (Hamburg: Hanseatische Verlagsanstalt, 1932) and Gilles Deleuze and Félix Guattari, *Mille Plateaux: Capitalisme et schizophrénie* (Paris: Minuit, 1980), 501, trans. Brian Massumi as *A Thousand Plateaus: Capitalism and Schizophrenia* (Minneapolis: University of Minnesota Press, 1987), 403. In a response to an earlier essay by Negri, Nancy also refers to Jünger's book in his essay on work ("Du travail") in *Futur Antérieur* 18, no. 4 (1993–94), an argument taken up again in Jean-Luc Nancy, *Le sens du monde* (Paris: Galilée, 1993), 155–62 (hereafter cited as *SM*), trans. Jeffrey S. Librett as *The Sense of the World* (Minneapolis: University of Minnesota Press, 1997), 98–102, 192n114 (hereafter cited as *SW*). Of related interest, see also Alain Badiou's discussion of the necessary distinction of different social figures, notably the relation between the "figure of the worker" and the "place of the factory," in "Politics as Thought," trans. Jason Barker in *Metapolitics* (London: Verso, 2005), 40–42.

9. See Martin Heidegger, "Zur Seinsfrage" (1955) in *Wegmarken* (Frankfurt am Main: Vittorio Klostermann, 1976), 385–426, trans. William McNeill as "On the Question of Being," in *Pathmarks* (Cambridge: Cambridge University Press, 1998), 291–322. An earlier version of Heidegger's text was titled "*Über die Linie*" or "Over the Line." As we will see, an important aspect of our reading is the way in which references to a *Gestalt* in Heidegger's writings are frequently translated into English as "configuration."

10. Gilles Deleuze and Félix Guattari, *Mille Plateaux*, 501; *A Thousand Plateaus*, 403. In an accompanying footnote, Deleuze and Guattari observe, "It is in the *Traité*

du rebelle that Jünger takes his clearest stand against national socialism and develops certain points contained in *der Arbeiter*: a conception of the 'line' as an active escape passing between the two figures of the old Soldier and the modern Worker, carrying both toward another destiny in another assembly (nothing of this remains in Heidegger's notion of the Line, although it is dedicated to Jünger)" (*Mille Plateaux*, 501–2; *A Thousand Plateaus*, 561), a reading I will take up on another occasion. As regards Deleuze and Guattari's references to lines and limits, I am indebted to Claudia Brodsky Lacour's paper on Deleuze, delivered at the American Comparative Literature Association meeting in Ann Arbor in 2004.

11. In this sense, Hardt and Negri's insistence on figures opens the text to what Philippe Lacoue-Labarthe has termed an "onto-typology." Suffice it to quote part of Lacoue-Labarthe's elucidation of Heidegger's reading of Nietzsche and the type of figure (*Gestalt*) that Zarathustra represents: "If Zarathustra is a *figure*, in the strongest sense (and we will see…that for Heidegger it is a historial necessity that commits metaphysics, in the process of completing itself, since Hegel, to (re)presenting itself (*sich darstellen*) in figures, as well as to representing (*vorstellen*) transcendence, from the perspective of the 'subjective' determination of Being, as the form, figure, imprint, type of a *humanity*: Nietzsche's Zarathustra, Jünger's Worker, even Rilke's Angel)—it is also true that such 'figuration' is programmed from the most distant sources of metaphysics." See Philippe Lacoue-Labarthe, "Typographie" in *Mimesis: Des articulations*, ed. Sylviane Agacinski et al. (Paris: Flammarion, 1975), 179, trans. Christopher Fynsk as "Typography" in *Typography: Mimesis, Philosophy, Politics* (Cambridge, Mass.: Harvard University Press, 1989), 52–53. As Lacoue-Labarthe asks rhetorically in an accompanying footnote, "Should we add Freud's Oedipus and Marx's Proletarian" to the list?

12. Michael Hardt and Antonio Negri, *Multitude: War and Democracy in the Age of Empire* (New York: Penguin, 2004), xv (hereafter cited as *M*).

13. In this sense, Hardt and Negri may be read as drawing from a longer utopian tradition in which the appeal to networks is instrumental, as in the role of networks in Saint-Simon's presentation of socialist utopias. See Pierre Musso, *Télécommunications et philosophie des réseaux: La postérité paradoxale de Saint-Simon* (Paris: Presses Universitaires de France, 1997).

14. This is the argument Ernesto Laclau takes to task in his reading of *Empire*, arguing that Hardt and Negri's insistence on the concept of immanence effaces the very forms of "articulation" presupposed by these struggles. See Ernesto Laclau, "Can Immanence Explain Social Struggles?" in *Empire's New Clothes: Reading Hardt and Negri*, ed. Paul A. Passavant and Jodi Dean (New York: Routledge, 2004), 21–30. What Laclau ignores in his reading of the passage from *Empire* cited above is Hardt and Negri's phrase "singular emergence."

15. Jean-Luc Nancy, *Le sens du monde* (Paris: Galilée, 1993), 173 (hereafter cited as *SM*), trans. Jeffrey S. Librett as *The Sense of the World* (Minneapolis: University of Minnesota Press, 1997), 111 (hereafter cited as *SW*).

16. If *réseau* in French derives from *rete-retis*, the word for net in Latin, then network in English is similarly inscribed by the material practice of tying and knotting suggested in Nancy's argument.

17. See Jean-Luc Nancy and Philippe Lacoue-Labarthe, "Scène," *Nouvelle Revue de Psychanalyse* 46 (Autumn 1992): 73–98, trans. Maiko Behr as "Scene: An Exchange of Letters," in *Beyond Representation: Philosophy and Poetic Imagination*, ed. Richard Eldridge (Cambridge: Cambridge University Press, 1996), 273–302. If this exchange turns around Nancy and Lacoue-Labarthe's divergent readings concerning the "figure," Nancy elaborates on the political implications of the figure in a number of essays published between 1992 and 1994 in *Futur Antérieur*, notably in "Monogrammes VI: De la figure politique à l'événement de l'art," *Futur Antérieur* 10 (February 1992), http://multitudes.samizdat.net/spip.php?article613. While Negri's exchange with Derrida is more widely read, less well known are Nancy's more extensive references to Negri's writings, references that extend back several decades. Our opening epigraph is from Jérôme-Alexandre Nielsberg's interview with Nancy, published as "Un peuple ou des multitudes?" in *l'Humanité* (December 26, 2003), reprinted on the Web site of *Multitudes*, http://multitudes.samizdat.net/article.php3?id_article=1617.

18. Martin Heidegger, *Sein und Zeit* (Tübingen: Max Niemeyer, 1986), 250, trans. Joan Stambaugh as *Being and Time* (Albany: State University of New York Press, 1996), 232. Translations for *die äußerste* suggest the farthest, furtherest, uttermost, utmost, extreme, hence the extreme limit.

19. In Jacques Derrida, *Spectres de Marx* 31; *Specters of Marx*, 10.

20. The passage is also taken up by Christopher Fynsk in his foreword to Jean-Luc Nancy, *The Inoperative Community*, ed. Peter Connor (Minneapolis: University of Minnesota Press, 1991), xvi–xvii. Nancy writes in *Being Singular Plural*, "the singular-plural constitutes the essence of Being, a constitution that undoes [*défait*] or dislocates every single, substantial essence of Being itself. This is not just a way of speaking, because there is no prior substance that would be dissolved [*dissoute*]" (*ESP*, 48/*BSP*, 28–29). The reference to knots here can be read across Heidegger's further references to an interlacing (*Geflecht*), a motif also often taken up in Derrida's writings on Heidegger, notably in "The *Retrait* of Metaphor" cited in the first chapter as well as by Nancy in *La partage des voix* (Paris: Galilée, 1982), 86–87n55, trans. Gayle L. Ormiston as "Sharing Voices," in *Transforming the Hermeneutic Context: From Nietzsche to Nancy*, ed. Gayle L. Ormiston and Alan D. Schrift (Albany: State University of New York Press, 1990), 258–59n57. Citing Derrida's essay on the *retrait* of metaphor, and demonstrating in what ways Heidegger closes off the question of relation he simultaneously opens up in his essay "The Way to Language," Nancy concludes his argument by suggesting, "Perhaps it will be necessary to say that the *Geflecht* is what provides the order or the nature of the *Ge* of *Gespräch*: that is to say, a 'collective' (that is the ordinary nature of the *Ge-*), but with the function of '*between*' [*entre-*] (interlacement, dialogue [*entrelacement, entretien*]), and finally of a *dia-* which is not dialectical, but which shares and divides

[*partage*]. What we interlace we share out; what we share out we interlace." It is Nancy who also places the reference to a "collective" in scare quotes.

21. We recall again that, in his brief essay on Deleuze, Nancy also frames his relation to Deleuze in terms of weaving. See Jean-Luc Nancy, "The Deleuzian Fold of Thought," in *Deleuze: A Critical Reader*, ed. Paul Patton (Oxford: Blackwell, 1996), 107–13. I am also grateful here to Chris Thompson's forthcoming writings on felt in the work of Deleuze and Guattari and Joseph Beuys.

22. Claude Lévi-Strauss, *Le regard éloigné* (Paris: Plon, 1983), 12, trans. Joachim Neugroschel and Phoebe Hess as *The View from Afar* (New York: Basic Books, 1985), xii (translation modified).

23. See Jean-Luc Nancy, *Être singulier pluriel* (Paris: Galilée, 1996), 23 (hereafter cited as *ESP*), trans. Robert D. Richardson and Anne E. O'Bryne as *Being Singular Plural* (Stanford, Calif.: Stanford University Press, 2000), 5 (hereafter cited as *BSP*).

24. Maurice Blanchot, *L'entretien infini* (Paris: Gallimard, 1969), 104, trans. Susan Hanson as *The Infinite Conversation* (Minneapolis: University of Minnesota Press), 73. Nancy will seek to transform any suggestion that the terms of this relation be understood as an "intersubjective space."

25. Maurice Blanchot, *L'entretien infini*, 104–5; *The Infinite Conversation*, 73–74. The closing section of Nancy's *Being Singular Plural* may also be read as a critical rethinking of this section from *The Infinite Conversation*.

26. Nancy insists on the place of contours in rethinking Heidegger's theme of the Open in his discussion with Derrida. See "Responsibilité—du sens à venir" in *Sens en tous sens: Autour des travaux de Jean-Luc Nancy*, eds. Francis Guibal and Jean-Clet Martin (Paris: Galilée, 2004), 191.

27. See Jean-Luc Nancy, "La comparution" in Jean-Christophe Bailly and Jean-Luc Nancy, *La comparution: Politiques à venir* (Paris: Christian Bourgeois, 1991), 96, trans. Tracy B. Strong as "La Comparution/The Compearance: from the Existence of 'Communism' to the Community of 'Existence,'" *Political Theory* 20, no. 3 (August 1992): 391 (translation modified).

28. In *The Sense of the World*, Nancy returns to the well-known motif of the "Theses on Feuerbach" by arguing, "Marx's concept of 'transformation' was still caught up—if not entirely, at least largely—in an interpretation, the interpretation of the world as self-production of a Subject of history and of History as subject. Henceforth, 'to transform' should mean 'to change the sense of sense,' that is, once again, to pass from having to being. Which means also that transformation is a *praxis*, not a *poiesis*, an action that effects the agent, not the work" (*SM*, 19/*SW*, 9).

29. Jean-Luc Nancy, "La comparution," 100; "La Comparution/The Compearance," 393.

30. Jean-Luc Nancy and Philippe Lacoue-Labarthe, "Scène," 74; "Scene: An Exchange of Letters," 274 (translation modified).

31. Significant for the next chapter, Nancy's phrase *la prise de parole* is the title of Michel de Certeau's book on the events of May '68. See Michel de Certeau, *La prise*

de parole et autres écrits politiques (Paris: Seuil, 1994), trans. Tom Conley as *The Capture of Speech and Other Political Writings* (Minneapolis: University of Minnesota Press, 1997).

32. If Nancy's argument here rearticulates the passage from Blanchot's *The Infinite Conversation* cited above, it also unfolds in light of Heidegger's essay "The Essence of Language." The rapport is discussed at length in Christopher Fynsk's "Foreword" to Jean-Luc Nancy, *The Inoperative Community*, xix–xxv. Nancy also appears to be gesturing here to Blanchot's description of the different tracts, posters, wall graffiti, slogans, etc., that circulated in May '68. See Maurice Blanchot, "Tracts, affiches, bulletin," in *Écrits politiques 1958–1993* (Paris: Léo Scheer, 2003), 118–20 (first published in *Comité* in October 1968), trans. Michael Holland as "Tracts, Posters, Bulletins," in *The Blanchot Reader* (Oxford: Blackwell, 1995), 204–5.

33. Alain Badiou makes the comment about Nancy in "L'offrande réservée," in *Sens en tous sens*, 15.

34. Jean-Luc Nancy, "La comparution," 62; "La Comparution/The Compearance," 377; and Maurice Blanchot, "Le communisme sans héritage," in *Écrits politiques*, 115; "Communism without a Heritage," in *The Blanchot Reader*, 203. Blanchot goes on to paraphrase this communism by referring to the "proletarian class: a community with no other common denominator than penury, lack of satisfaction, lack in every sense." If Nancy rethinks Blanchot's writings on communism, he also acknowledges in *La comparution* Étienne Balibar's discussion of communism in "Le non-contemporain," included in *Écrits pour Althusser* (Paris: La Découverte, 1991), 91–118, notably Balibar's discussion of Althusser's thought of communism as "untimely." The reference is missing in the English translation.

35. Jean-Luc Nancy, "La comparution," 65; "La Comparution/The Compearance," 378. In response to an interview with Artem Magun, Nancy remarks that a "(neo)communist" politics "could be a politics of spacing as well as of collecting, a politics of the singular as well as the common. But these formulas do not yet amount to 'politics'—far from it! A philosopher does not have a politics to propose: he has to explicate the conditions under which politics is possible today. And these conditions are perhaps now in the process of becoming very different from those we have known: that is, first of all, that 'politics' cannot aspire to the totality of social existence, common or not common. Marx wanted politics to disappear as a separate sphere, 'to impregnate all the spheres of social existence': but today it is the proper distinction of the political sphere that requires renewed attention (because it is this distinction that liberalism wants to undermine if not suppress)." See "The Question of the Common and the Responsibility of the Universal," an interview with Jean-Luc Nancy, Artem Magun, and Oxana Timofeeva, in "What do we have in common?" special issue, *Chto delat? / What Is to Be Done?* 9 (May 2005), http://www.chtodelat.org.

36. Maurice Blanchot, *L'Entretien infini*, vii–viii; *The Infinite Conversation*, xii. The following quotations are from the same "Note" prefacing the volume.

37. The quotation by Nancy is from the section on "Political Writing" in *SM*, 184/ *SW*, 119. Nancy continues: Writing is not political "as the effect of an 'engagement' in the service of a cause, and it is not political—qua 'literature'—according to either the principle of the 'aestheticization of politics' or its inversion into the 'politicization of aesthetics.' It is indeed necessary to ask in what way literature and, consequently, aesthetics and fiction become involved here, but only after one has affirmed the political nature of writing: *the in-finite resistance of sense in the configuration of the 'together.'*" In *The Inoperative Community*, Nancy had referred to a "literary communism," though he moves away from this term in later writings.

38. Maurice Blanchot, "Le communisme sans héritage," in *Écrits politiques*, 113; "Communism without a Heritage," in *The Blanchot Reader*, 202. We recall again Hegel's argument from the *Logic* cited in chapter 2, to which Nancy concludes that "what is left for us to hold onto is the moment of 'exteriority' as being of almost essential value, so essential that it would no longer be a matter of relating this exteriority to any individual or collective 'we' without also unfailingly [*indéfectiblement*] holding onto *exteriority itself and as such*" (*ESP*, 50/*BSP*, 30).

39. Maurice Blanchot, "Le communisme sans héritage," in *Écrits politiques*, 115; "Communism without a Heritage," in *The Blanchot Reader*, 204. The question of the "we" or "us" that Nancy poses to Negri in our opening epigraph turns us back to Blanchot's writings on the communist exigency but also forward to Alain Badiou's repetition of the same question in light of communism in the opening pages of *D'un désastre obscur: Sur la fin de la vérité d'État* (Paris: Éditions de l'Aube, 1998).

40. Gilles Deleuze and Félix Guattari, *Mille Plateaux*, 35; *A Thousand Plateaus*, 24.

5. Seattle and the Space of Exposure

1. Jean-Luc Nancy, "What is to be Done?" in *Retreating the Political*, ed. Simon Sparks (London: Routledge, 1997), 157 (hereafter cited as *RP*). My thanks to Leslie Hill for providing a copy of Nancy's text in its unpublished and original French version.

2. Louis Althusser, "Le courant souterrain du matérialisme de la rencontre," in *Écrits philosophiques et politiques*, vol. 1 (Paris: Stock IMEC, 1994), 549–50, trans. G. M. Goshgarian as "The Underground Current of the Materialism of the Encounter," in *Philosophy of the Encounter: Later Writings, 1978–87* (London: Verso, 2006), 165.

3. Louis Althusser, *Pour Marx* (Paris: François Maspero, 1965), 169, trans. Ben Brewster as *For Marx* (London: Verso, 1979), 168.

4. Louis Althusser, *Pour Marx*, 178; *For Marx*, 176.

5. Since Althusser's text, we have no doubt learned to read Lenin differently. For a representative overview of the debates, see Sebastian Budgen, Stathis Kouvelakis, and Slavoj Žižek, eds., *Lenin Reloaded: Towards a Politics of Truth* (Durham, N.C.: Duke University Press, 2007).

6. The following account of Althusser's response to the events of '68 is indebted to Gregory Elliott's commentary in "The Time of Theory, The Time of Politics," in *Althusser: The Detour of Theory* (London: Verso, 1987), 235–44.

7. Elliott, *Althusser: The Detour of Theory,* 241.

8. Ibid., 238.

9. Quoted in ibid., 239.

10. Beyond the reference to Epicurus and the originary "swerve" of atoms as they encounter one another, as well as Spinoza, Althusser cites the writings of Heidegger, Derrida, and Deleuze and Guattari.

11. If Nancy's writings address Marx's celebrated slogan from the "Theses on Feuerbach" with some frequency, he also addresses Lenin's slogan in *L'expérience de la liberté* (Paris: Galilée, 1988), 24, 38–39, trans. Bridget McDonald as *The Experience of Freedom* (Stanford, Calif.: Stanford University Press, 1993), 19, 31.

12. Claude Lefort, "La question de la démocratie," in *Le retrait du politique*, ed. Philippe Lacoue-Labarthe and Jean-Luc Nancy (Paris: Galilée, 1983), 84.

13. See Martin Heidegger, "Brief über den Humanismus," in *Wegmarken* (Frankfurt am Main: Vittorio Klosterman, 1967), 313, trans. Frank A. Capuzzi and J. Glenn Gray as "Letter on Humanism," in *Basic Writings*, ed. David Farrell Krell (San Francisco: Harper & Row, 1977), 193. In *Being Singular Plural*, Nancy suggests that the concept of engagement is a good translation of *conatus*, going on to argue that understanding both humanity and *mondialité* or "globalness" today implies an "engagement without measure," which also translates as a "measureless engagement." See Jean-Luc Nancy, *Être singulier pluriel* (Paris: Galilée, 1996), 210–11 (hereafter cited as *ESP*), trans. Robert D. Richardson and Anne E. O'Bryne as *Being Singular Plural* (Stanford, Calif.: Stanford University Press, 2000), 183 (hereafter cited as *BSP*).

14. *Les fins de l'homme: À partir du travail de Jacques Derrida*, ed. Philippe Lacoue-Labarthe and Jean-Luc Nancy (Paris: Galilée, 1981), 526–27.

15. Jacques Derrida, *Voyous: Deux essais sur la raison* (Paris: Galilée, 2003), 13, trans. Pascale-Anne Brault and Michael Naas as *Rogues: Two Essays on Reason* (Stanford, Calif.: Stanford University Press, 2005), xiv. Further page references to the French and English versions are cited in the text.

16. See Jacques Derrida, *Khôra* (Paris: Galilée, 2003), trans. Ian McLeod as "Khôra," in *On the Name* (Stanford, Calif.: Stanford University Press, 1995), 89–127.

17. Derrida notes in *Echographies*, "What I name and try to think under this word [deconstruction] is, at bottom, nothing other than this very process, its 'taking-place' in such a way that its happening affects the very experience of place, and the recording (symptomatic, scientific, or philosophical) of this 'thing,' the trace that traces (inscribes, preserves, carries, refers, or defers) the différance of this event which happens to take place [*qui arrive au lieu*]—which happens to take place, and to taking-place [*qui arrive à (l')avoir-lieu*]." See Jacques Derrida and Bernard

Stiegler, *Échographies de la télévision: Entretiens filmés* (Paris: Galilée-INA, 1996), 45, trans. Jennifer Bajorek as *Echographies of Television: Filmed Interviews* (Cambridge, UK: Polity Press, 2002), 36.

18. The reference to prayer relates to the "*Prière d'insérer*" section of *Rogues*, which usually translates as "please insert" (as in a section of the text that is added after the text has been printed) but also suggests, more literally, a prayer to insert.

19. See "For a Justice to Come: An Interview with Jacques Derrida," trans. Ortwin de Graef, in The BRussels Tribunal, "Questioning the New Imperial World Order: A Hearing on the 'Project for the New American Century,'" (April 14–17, 2004), 18–25, http://www.brusselstribunal.org/pdf/DossierBRussellsTribunal.pdf. Following the Russell Tribunal, established in 1966–7 to investigate U.S. war crimes in Vietnam, the BRussels Tribunal was established in 2004 to investigate the Project for the New American Century (PNAC) and its role in establishing the new imperial order, notably its role in promoting the war in Iraq. PNAC was a neoconservative think tank, whose most prominent members included Dick Cheney, Donald Rumsfeld, and Paul Wolfowitz. My thanks to Ortwin de Graef for sending me a copy of the original interview in French.

20. See Jacques Derrida, "Avant-propos," in *Psyché: Inventions de l'autre* (Paris: Galilée, 1987), 9, trans. Peggy Kamuf as "Author's Preface," in *Psyche: Inventions of the Other*, vol. 1 (Stanford, Calif.: Stanford University Press, 2007), xii. Derrida continues by suggesting that "a formation must move forward but also advance in a group. According to some explicit or tacit law, it is required to space itself out without getting too dispersed."

21. See Jacques Derrida, *Learning to Live Finally: The Last Interview*, trans. Pascale-Anne Brault and Michael Naas (Hoboken, N.J.: Melville House, 2007), 22–23.

22. See Lorenzo Fabbri, "Philosophy as Chance: An Interview with Jean-Luc Nancy," trans. Pascale-Anne Brault and Michael Naas, *Critical Inquiry* 33 (Winter 2007): 431.

23. Ibid., 431.

24. See Gilles Deleuze and Félix Guattari, *Mille Plateaux: Capitalisme et schizophrénie* (Paris: Minuit, 1980), 35, trans. Brian Massumi as *A Thousand Plateaus: Capitalism and Schizophrenia* (Minneapolis: University of Minnesota Press, 1987), 24.

25. In gallery and museum contexts, *Waiting for Tear Gas* includes eighty-one 35-mm slides in color and is projected as a 16-minute timed slide sequence. A selection from the series is included in Alexander Cockburn, Jeffrey St. Clair, and Allan Sekula, *Five Days that Shook the World; Seattle and Beyond* (London: Verso, 2000). A selection from the same series is also reproduced in *Allan Sekula: Performance under Working Conditions*, ed. Sabine Breitwieser (Vienna: Generali Foundation, 2003), 312–13, and in *Constantin Meunier: A Dialogue with Allan Sekula*, ed. Hilde Van Gelder (Leuven: Leuven University Press, 2005). A version of the project is

announced as forthcoming on the Web site of *Multitudes*, the journal associated with the writings of Michael Hardt and Antonio Negri. In my reading of *Waiting for Tear Gas* I am especially indebted to Barry Shank's pointed critique of an earlier draft, which I will also take up again on another occasion.

26. Allan Sekula, "[white globe to black]," in *Five Days that Shook the World*, 122. The text is reprinted in *Performance under Working Conditions*, 310–11.

27. In terms of not standing out from the protestors, it is instructive to compare *Waiting for Tear Gas* with "Untitled Slide Sequence" (1972; included in *Performance under Working Conditions*, 74–85), in which the camera engages a shift of workers leaving an aerospace factory in San Diego.

28. See *This Is What Democracy Looks Like*, the documentary film made of the same WTO protests, coproduced in 2000 by the Seattle Independent Media Center and Big Noise Films. If the title of the film frames democracy in terms of what it "looks like," the protests are presented in terms of a "collective vision."

29. See Ian Boal, "Glossary," in *Confronting Capitalism: Dispatches from a Global Movement*, ed. Eddie Yuen, Daniel Burton-Rose, and George Katsiaficas (Brooklyn: Soft Skull Press, 2004), 397.

30. On globes as sites in which to think the relation between globalization and questions of visibility, see Hannah Arendt, *The Human Condition* (Chicago: University of Chicago Press, 1958), 250, and Samuel Weber, "Stages and Plots: Theatricality after September 11, 2001," in *Theatricality as Medium* (New York: Fordham University Press, 2004), 342–43.

31. Often acknowledging the importance of Vertov's film for his work, Sekula more explicitly quotes *Man with a Movie Camera* in the opening photographs of *Geography Lessons: Canadian Notes* (Vancouver: Vancouver Art Gallery/MIT Press, 1987), 4–5.

32. See Allan Sekula, "The Body and the Archive," *October* 39 (Winter 1986): 3–64.

33. In other words, a physiognomy that perhaps gestures toward the "face" in Lévinas or Agamben's terms, or the concept of "faciality" in the writings of Deleuze and Guattari, references that we will touch on later in the chapter, if only obliquely. The comment by Lincoln Kirstein is cited in Allan Sekula, *Fish Story* (Düsseldorf: Richter, 2002), 127.

34. The distinction between the *historia rerum gestarum* and the *res gestae* is made by Michael Hardt and Antonio Negri in *Empire* (Cambridge, Mass.: Harvard University Press, 2000). As Hardt and Negri conclude, the multitude's struggles against Empire's imperial constitution are "demonstrations of the creativity of desire, utopias of lived experience, the workings of historicity as potentiality—in short, the struggles are the naked reality of the *res gestae*" (*Empire*, 52). In his essay on Sekula and the photographer Andreas Gursky, Zanny Begg situates Sekula's work more extensively

in light of Hardt and Negri's writings. See "Photography and the Multitude: Recasting Subjectivity in a Globalised World," in *borderlands* 4, no. 1 (2005), http://www.borderlandsejournal.adelaide.edu.au/vol4no1_2005/begg_art.htm.

35. For a critical overview of these arguments, see Andy Opel and Donnalyn Pompper, eds., *Representing Resistance: Media, Civil Disobedience, and the Global Justice Movement* (Westport, Conn.: Praeger, 2003).

36. For representative overviews, see Janet Thomas, *The Battle of Seattle: The Story Behind and Beyond the WTO Demonstrations* (Golden, Colo.: Fulcrum, 2000) and the University of Washington WTO History Project, http://depts.washington.edu/wtohist/index.htm. No doubt the question of revisionism will further implode in the forthcoming volume by Rebecca Solnit and David Solnit, *The Battle of the Story of the Battle of Seattle*.

37. Naomi Klein, *Fences and Windows: Dispatches from the Front Lines of the Globalization Debate* (New York: Picador, 2002).

38. Walter Benjamin and Roland Barthes's respective writings on photography still provide the initial terms for rethinking this question of tense and temporality. For Benjamin, see especially Eduardo Cadava, *Words of Light: Theses on the Photography of History* (Princeton, N.J.: Princeton University Press, 1997). In terms that are related to the spectrality of the event, including its revolutionary implications, Barthes's writings on photography are explored at some length in Derrida and Stiegler's *Echographies of Television*.

39. If the question here is how this temporal inscription of the photographic inscribes itself in reinterpreting or re-envisioning the events that have come to be known as "Seattle," then the argument finds one of its initial emblems in the updating of *The Battle of Seattle: The New Challenge to Capitalist Globalization*, ed. Eddie Yuen, Daniel Burton-Rose, and George Katsiaficas (Brooklyn: Soft Skull Press, 2002)—an influential anthology published after the 1999 WTO protests—to its revised edition in 2004, now titled *Confronting Capitalism: Dispatches from a Global Movement* (see note 29 above). Across the two anthologies, the initial and widespread privilege accorded to the 1999 protests in Seattle (a privilege that includes Hardt and Negri's own subsequent claim that "Seattle was the first global protest") becomes part of a larger reassessment of the history of protests for global justice, not only outside the United States (notably in the Global South), but also well prior to 1999. The forthcoming feature-length film on the 1999 events, *Battle in Seattle*, will no doubt revive the question of revisionism in play here.

40. See Jill Nelson, ed., *Police Brutality; An Anthology* (New York: W. W. Norton, 2000); and Donatella della Porta and Herbert Reiter, eds., *Policing Protest: The Control of Mass Demonstrations in Western Democracies* (Minneapolis: University of Minnesota Press, 1998).

41. It is in this sense that we might begin to question Kaja Silverman's incisive reading of Sekula's *Waiting for Tear Gas* photographs, which starts by stating that the force of Sekula's work turns on a confrontation between the "one" and "many." See Kaja Silverman, "Disassembled Movies," in *Synopsis 3—Testimonies: Between Fact and Fiction* (Athens, Greece: New Museum of Contemporary Art, 2003), 191–95.

42. "The face of politics is changing," Retort writes. "Its underlying bone structure may or may not be altering too. In either case, new descriptions are needed." See Retort, *Afflicted Powers: Capital and Spectacle in a New Age of War* (London: Verso, 2005), 15. If we cite Retort here, it is to invite a closer reading of their text, which opens with a description of a mass demonstration (the 2003 antiwar protests) and turns with insistence around the same concerns that preoccupy us here—questions of "visibility," "face-to-face" organization, "appearances," "the experience of seeing an image," "image moments," and "sight lines"—notably as they are rearticulated within the larger framework of Guy Debord and the Situationist's concept of "spectacle."

43. Hardt and Negri, *Empire*, 214. Further page references to *Empire* will be cited in the text. We might argue that the reference to barbarians here is not just to Cavafy or Deleuze and Guattari's characterizations of nomadism in terms of "barbaric assemblages." It also reappropriates Bernard-Henri Lévy's self-promotion of the "nouveaux philosophes," notably in *Barbarism with a Human Face* and its argument that all Marxism ended up in Stalin's gulags.

44. For further rethinking of the body in the context of the protests against the G8 summit in Evian in 2003, see Keir Milburn, "The Multitude in the Crowd," *the anomalist* 1 (2005), http://www.theanomalist.com/papers.html; and the collection of essays in *Shut Them Down! The G8, Gleneagles 2005 and the Movement of Movements*, ed. David Harvie, Keir Milburn, Ben Trott, and David Watts (Leeds: Dissent! and Brooklyn: Autonomedia, 2005).

45. It suffices to look through photographs posted on indymedia Web sites to remark the proximity between these photographs and Sekula's *Waiting for Tear Gas* sequence. A clear example is the hundreds of photographs posted on various sites from recent Republican and Democratic National Conventions.

46. Jacques Rancière, *La Mésentente: Politique et Philosophie* (Paris: Galilée, 1995), trans. Julie Rose as *Disagreement: Politics and Philosophy* (Minneapolis: University of Minnesota Press, 1999). Further page references to the French and English versions will be cited in the text.

47. The question of the "real" (as opposed to realism) is taken up by Nancy in relation to Marx in *La Comparution*, notably as Marx's rethinking of what constitutes the real pertains more generally to the nineteenth century. As Nancy writes, "That which occurs in and *as* Marx's period is this: the 'real' becomes expressly the 'subject,' not the object of thought. Or again, the 'real' makes itself explicit as the 'subject' of thought. That is, thought touches a point where in order to manifest that which

makes it thought (and not only that which makes it think) and which is not 'yet' 'thought,' it must turn back, twist around on itself. It displays and in the same gesture manifests the exteriority and excessive character of all that 'thought' can designate or represent." See Jean-Luc Nancy, "La comparution," in *La Comparution: Politique à venir* (Paris: Christian Bourgeois, 1991), 72, trans. Tracy B. Strong as "La Comparution/The Compearance: From the Existence of 'Communism' to the Community of 'Existence,'" *Political Theory* 20, no. 3 (August 1992): 381–82. If Nancy turns to this thought of the real in the writings of Nietzsche, Freud, Heidegger, as well as Marx, suggesting that it is their singular proximity to one another that must be thought here, it would be instructive to pursue how the very terms in which Nancy approaches this argument are reopened by insisting on the *photographic* articulation of the "real" that also begins to manifest itself in the nineteenth century (and for which Marx's references to the camera obscura would be a part). Such an argument might then be relayed across the essays on socialist realism collected in Hilde Van Gelder, ed., *Constantin Meunier: A Dialogue with Allan Sekula*. In *American Exposures: Photography and Community in the Twentieth Century* (Minneapolis: University of Minnesota Press, 2005), Louis Kaplan has offered a compelling argument concerning the implications of Nancy's writings for a broad range of photographic practices.

48. One might note without further development that Rancière's references to the politics of "parts," "counting," and the "miscount" prolong a longer discussion of the same problematic in the writings of (among others) Deleuze, Badiou, and Nancy. It is perhaps in this same sense of a part that has no part that Deleuze and Guattari can appeal in *What Is Philosophy?* to "the still-missing people" or a "people to come."

49. While turning us back to the writings of Lacoue-Labarthe and Nancy explored in the first chapter, the argument raised here would also need to be further explored through Ranciere's debts in *Disagreement* to the writings of Alain Badiou.

50. Jacques Rancière, "Ten Theses on Politics," *Theory and Event* 5, no. 3 (July 2001), which condenses the principle arguments from *Disagreement* and from which our opening epigraph is also taken.

51. The reference to policing in Rancière's text opens a rereading of Guy Debord's references in *The Society of the Spectacle* to "police methods to transform perception." Turning back to this phrase in the "Preface to the Third French Edition," Debord notes that between the first and third edition of the book, the police in question "are of a completely new variety," an argument that Rancière at once extends and transforms in his writings. See Guy Debord, *La Société du Spectacle* (Paris: Gallimard, 1992), 101–9, trans. Donald Nicholson-Smith as *The Society of the Spectacle* (New York: Zone Books, 1995), 74–78.

52. In a photo, Nancy asks, "When does someone resemble themself [*se ressemble-t-il*]? Only when the photo shows something of him, or her, something more than what is identical, more than the 'face,' the 'image,' the 'traits' or the 'portrait,' something more than a copy of the diacritical signs of an 'identity' ('black hair, blue

eyes, snub nose,' and so on). It is only when it evokes an unending mêlée of peoples, parents, works, pains, pleasures, refusals, forgettings, transgressions, expectations, dreams, stories, and all that trembles within and struggles against the confines of the image. This is not something that is imaginary; it is nothing but what is real: what is real has to do with the mêlée. A true identification photo would be an indeterminant mêlée of photos and marks [*de photos et de graphies*] that resemble nothing, under which one would inscribe a proper name" (*ESP*, 169–82/*BSP*, 145–58).

53. Nancy, "Éloge de la mêlée," *ESP*, 171; "Eulogy for the *Mêlée*," *BSP*, 145–46.

54. As Hoffman-Schwartz continues, "Sekula's opaque, asignifying work offers us suspended views of a suspended city, forcing us to linger over the diverse actuality and absent concept of the protests, forcing us to linger, in other words, in the temporally uncertain zone between an event and its interpretation. 'Waiting for Tear Gas,' in its patient and disciplined serial rendering of the intersection between the quotidian life of a city and the dueling abstractions known as global justice and globalization, reminds us that theories pass in and out of everyday sites in odd, halting rhythms." See Daniel Hoffman-Schwartz, review of "Empire/State: Artists Engaging Globalization" (exhibition at CUNY, The Graduate Center, May 24–July 14, 2002), in *Afterimage* 30, no. 2 (September–October 2002): 13. The reading of *Waiting for Tear Gas* proposed by Hoffman-Schwartz echoes Sekula's own understanding of globalization in the context of *Fish Story*. In the accompanying catalogue text, and echoing a number of claims in the prefatory text for *Waiting for Tear Gas* Sekula notes, "my argument [in *Fish Story*] runs against the commonly held view that the computer and telecommunications are the sole engines of the third industrial revolution. In effect, I am arguing for the continued importance of maritime space in order to counter the exaggerated importance attached to that largely metaphysical construct, 'cyberspace,' and the corollary myth of 'instantaneous' contact between distant spaces." As he further notes, "large-scale material flows remain intractable," and "a society of accelerated flows is also in certain key aspects a society of deliberatively slow movement" (*Fish Story*, 50). Sekula's argument is taken up by Homi Bhabha in "Democracy Derealized," in *Democracy Unrealized: Documenta 11, Platform 1*, ed. Okwui Enwezor et al. (Ostfildern-Ruit: Hatje Cantz, 2002), 354.

55. See Arendt, *The Human Condition*. Further page references are cited in the text.

56. Our reading of Arendt here responds to Lacoue-Labarthe and Nancy's hesitation regarding Arendt's discussion of the *polis*, a hesitation that asks "whether or not the *polis*…had actually taken place" (*RT*, 194/*RP*, 131).

57. Rancière acknowledges in this context that his argument is a response to Nancy's writings on community. Nancy's response to Rancière is explored in several sections of *Being Singular Plural*.

58. Giorgio Agamben, "Glosse in margine ai *Commentari sulla società dello spettacolo*," in *Mezzi senza fine* (Bollati Boringhieri, 1996), 64, trans. Vincenzo Binetti and Cesare Casarino as "Marginal Notes on *Commentaries on the Society of the Spectacle*,"

in *Means without End: Notes on Politics* (Minneapolis: University of Minnesota Press, 2000), 78. Further references to the Italian and English versions are cited in the text. The essay (from 1990) mostly repeats the closing fragments from Agamben's *The Coming Community* published the same year. See *La comunità che viene* (Turin: Einaudi, 1990), trans. Michael Hardt as *The Coming Community* (Minneapolis: University of Minneapolis Press, 1993). Further references will be cited in the text as *CC*, followed by Italian and English page numbers. Agamben is drawing from the essay "Preliminary Problems in Constructing a Situation," first published in *Internationale Situationniste* in 1958 and translated in *Situationist International Anthology*, ed. Ken Knabb (Berkeley, Calif.: Bureau of Public Secrets, 1981), 43–45. The definition refers back to an earlier report by Debord, also translated in *Situationist International Anthology*, 17–25.

The following section was first read as part of an exchange with Keir Milburn at the Anarchist Studies Network 2007 conference at the University of Manchester. See David Harvie and Keir Milburn, "Moments of Excess," http://www.nadir.org.uk./excess.html; and the collective pamphlet by The Free Association, "Worlds in Motion," http://www.nadir.org.uk./worldsinmotion.html.

59. Offering suitable contexts for defining this sense of "taking-place" in Italian, and implying the unfolding of an event that is not foreseen but considered of general interest, Devoto's *Dizionari Della Lingua Italiana* refers as examples to incidents that "took place" or "occurred" at a public political meeting (*Comizio*) intended to provide political education, as well as to a "demonstration" that will "take place" or "happen" at the Piazza della Republica. My thanks to David Horn for referring me to these examples and to various possible translations of Agamben's texts.

60. The present antiwar movement in the United States is instructive here. Once Cindy Sheehan was identified as its spokesperson and central figure by the media and the politicians, the movement became (belatedly) visible, but it was precisely through such visibility and figuration that the movement was simultaneously effaced as a movement.

61. In a note to the English translation of *The Coming Community*, Michael Hardt notes that the term "whatever" (*qualunque*), while unusual in English, has several uses in Italian, while corresponding in French (*quelconque*) to a number of texts by contemporary philosophers, including Deleuze and Badiou. As Hardt also insists, "whatever" here refers to that which is "neither particular nor general, neither individual nor generic" (*CC*, 107). In this same context, one might also note that the cover notes to the English version translate the demonstrators in Tiananmen Square into "the multitude."

62. The reference here is to Alain Badiou's *Being and Event* (London: Continuum, 2005), notably the opening section in which Cantor provides the terms for rethinking the *a priori* conditions of any possible ontology.

63. In some informal notes on the concept of movement (as in the "movement of movements"), Agamben offers a provisional definition of a political movement as

"the threshold of indeterminacy between an excess and a deficiency which marks the limit of every politics in its constitutive imperfection." See Giorgio Agamben, "Movement," from a seminar given in January 2005, translated by Arianna Bove, http://www.generation-online.org/p/fpagamben3.htm.

64. Agamben appears to be reworking Nancy's reference to thinking the *pollokōs legetai* in terms of an "irremediable scattering [*éparpillement sans recours*], a dissemination of ontological specks." See Jean-Luc Nancy, "*L'être abandonné*," in *L'Impératif catégorique* (Paris: Flammarion, 1983), 144, trans. Brian Holmes as "Abandoned Being," in *The Birth to Presence* (Stanford, Calif.: Stanford University Press, 1993), 39. If Nancy's essay constitutes a prominent reference in many of Agamben's writings, it remains to be seen in what ways his productive (mis)reading of the essay opens toward a displacement of Agamben's larger argument, a reading we will take up on another occasion.

65. In a phrase that invites a reading across the later writings of Derrida, Agamben also suggests that this communication of singularities creates an empty space "offered to the one, irrevocable hospitality" (*CC*, 18/24).

66. See Maurice Blanchot, "Rupture du temps: Révolution," in *Écrits politiques 1958–1993* (Paris: Léo Scheer, 2003), 127 (first published in *Comité* in October 1968), trans. Michael Holland as "A Break in Time: Revolution," in *The Blanchot Reader* (Oxford: Blackwell, 1995), 205.

67. Maurice Blanchot, *La Communauté inavouable* (Paris: Minuit, 1983), 52; trans. Pierre Joris as *The Unavowable Community* (Barrytown, N.Y.: Station Hill, 1988), 29–30. Blanchot's text was written during the time Lacoue-Labarthe and Nancy's Center in Paris was open. Leslie Hill notes the critical proximity of both Blanchot's *The Unavowable Community* as well as the writings from 1968 to Lacoue-Labarthe and Nancy's colloquium at Cérisy and the Center in Paris in *Blanchot: Extreme Contemporary* (London: Routledge, 1997), 195–221. In later writings, notably in *The Sense of the World*, Nancy will seek to distinguish a politics based on love, as suggested in Blanchot's commentary, from a politics of being-with.

68. Maurice Blanchot, *La Communauté inavouable*, 52–54; *The Unavowable Community*, 30–31. We have translated *être-ensemble* not as "a being-together" but as "being-together," and so have attempted to capture the transitive action at stake in Blanchot's phrase rather than a substantive. In this same context, we might also recall that Michel de Certeau's commentary on May '68 offers an analogous rethinking of the event in terms of its taking-place. "In Charlie Chaplin's *The Gold Rush*," de Certeau recalls, "the swirling winds of a blizzard push the cabin in which the tramp is spending the night to the edge of a cliff. After waking up, he walks across the room to go out the door. With his footsteps, the cabin starts dangerously to lean, with the doorway opening onto thin air. If he opens the door he will fall to an instant death. When he backs up, he brings to cabin back to rest, but he is enclosed in a desperate state of affairs. Now and again his feet go forward, then retreat, gingerly touching the floor that

pivots on its invisible axis." De Certeau goes on to argue that "the image of a space in which it is equally impossible to live and to leave is comparable to the situation that was endured last May. For the inhabitants of an entire society, is there nothing more than a doorway opening onto chaos and a security anchored in conformism? Many signs indicate that a displacement has taken place. Drawn from unexpected choices, a line hereafter demarcates [*partage*], between order and speech, our cultural 'floor.' Although still intact, its has vacillated from one to the other." However, he concludes, the apparent opposition in place here needs itself to be displaced. For the "stability" and "equilibrium" sought by some (those who increasingly want to ensure the stability of the cabin in the wake of '68) is illusory. As de Certeau concludes, this illusion "accepts the instability of the 'event' created by displacing the entire system; it is satisfied with compensating for it and camouflaging it. In reality, a *global* problem can be discerned in the contrary reactions—a problem of the infrastructure [*en dessous*]. A society is no longer sure of its grounding. The *event* engages the *structure*. The whole order is at stake and, first of all, it seems to me, a system of representation, what grounds both knowledge and politics." See Michel de Certeau, "Le pouvoir de parler," in *La prise de parole et autres écrits politiques* (Paris: Seuil, 1994), 59–60, trans. Tom Conley as "The Power of Speech," in *The Capture of Speech and Other Political Writings* (Minneapolis: University of Minnesota Press, 1997), 25–26. Although I came across it too late to take into account in this chapter, Benjamin Arditti has offered a decisive and compelling rethinking of the spatial implications of contemporary political conflict, notably in light of Rancière's writings. See *Politics on the Edges of Liberalism: Difference, Revolution, Agitation* (Edinburgh: University of Edinburgh Press, 2007).

69. Maurice Blanchot, "Michel Foucault as I Imagine Him," trans. Jeffrey Mehlman, in *Foucault / Blanchot* (New York: Zone, 1987), 63.

Index

PHILIP ARMSTRONG is an associate professor in the Department of Comparative Studies at The Ohio State University.

Electronic Mediations